TROWELING THROUGH TIME

**Frontispiece:** With trowels in hand, the
Lancaster brothers make a small discovery
on Alkali Ridge, Utah, 1931. Photo courtesy
of the Breternitz Collection.

# TROWELING
# THROUGH
# TIME

*The First Century Of Mesa Verdean Archaeology*

FLORENCE C. LISTER

UNIVERSITY OF NEW MEXICO PRESS ✻ ALBUQUERQUE

Library of Congress Cataloging-in-Publication Data

Lister, Florence Cline.

Troweling through time :

the first century of Mesa Verdean archaeology / Florence C. Lister.

p. cm.

Includes bibliographical references and index.

ISBN 0-8263-3502-0 (pbk. : alk. paper)

1. Indians of North America—Colorado—Mesa Verde National Park—Antiquities.

2. Excavations (Archaeology)—Colorado—Mesa Verde National Park—History.

3. Mesa Verde National Park (Colo.)—History.

4. Mesa Verde National Park (Colo.)—Antiquities. I. Title.

E78.C6L48 2004

978.8'27—dc22

2004013688

DESIGN AND COMPOSITION: Mina Yamashita

In Recognition of

Stuart Struever, Sandy Thompson, and Bill Lipe

whose insightfulness and steadfastness of

purpose created a new driving force in

Southwestern archaeology

�֎

*Proceeds from this publication go to the*

*Robert H. Lister Memorial Fellowship for*

*Graduate Students in Southwestern Archaeology,*

*administered by the*

*Crow Canyon Archaeological Center*

# Contents

# PREFACE

FOR A HOST OF ENVIRONMENTAL REASONS, much of the Colorado Plateau seems an unlikely cradle of civilization. In many places this part of the continent has been wrought by elemental forces into stunning grotesqueness. Over eons of geological time its flat strata were deposited under primeval seas, then heaved upward to more than a mile in elevation. Peaks along its northern rim tower to over 13,000 feet. Slowly, lower layers were sliced into ribbons by roaring waters and scoured by howling winds. Their sheer walls defy trespass. Other erosional forces left bald pinnacles, arches, and hoodoos. Here and there, variegated strata were coated by hot lava, hit by a hurtling meteor, baked by searing suns. Cinder cones, volcanic necks, laccolithic mountains, synclines, anticlines, and cross-bedded solidified dunes dot the terrain. A forest of huge trees fell and fossilized. This geological chaos created expanses of piercing beauty and enclaves of nothingness.

Vegetation varies from none at the Colorado River slickrock in the west to spongy tundra grass at timberline in the east. In between there are blankets of sagebrush and saltbush at lower elevations and a pinyon-juniper and Gambel oak cover up above. Higher still are deep forests of pines and aspens. Seasonal temperatures slide from minus 20°F to 120°F above zero. Average precipitation is just as erratic. In one year several inches may fall in a particular spot, none in another, and deluges in others. There are only one or two drainages with running water on the southern flanks of the plateau. The northern plateau boasts more active rivers but also has many dry channels that at times carry horrendous flash floods.

All those seemingly adverse conditions notwithstanding, this is a place where one of the oldest cultures to be found in the Northern Hemisphere was spawned and subsequently flourished. There is scarcely a tract on the Colorado Plateau and its borderlands that ancient men and women did not know. For many millennia they scrambled up craggy heights in pursuit of faunal foods. They combed broad basins and uplands for edible greens, seeds, and tubers. They learned to poke kernels of corn, squash or pumpkin seeds, or dried beans into warming soils in spring and to anticipate a harvest. They bedded down on the terraces. They dug shelters deep beneath rocky surfaces or piled up a few rooms on ground level. Like swallows, some nested high on fractured precipices. As centuries passed, bands came together in large, substantial masonry communities out in the open. Others returned to cliff-side alcoves. And ultimately most of them moved elsewhere, leaving scattered smudges and wreckage of their passage on the landscape.

To reconstruct this human drama, early investigators found it helpful to view the plateau as divided into three parts. They saw the native peoples in each, regarded as the antecedents of the modern Pueblo Indians, as sharing a common mode of life but developing differences in some kinds of material culture and perhaps social orientation. One natural dividing line of the Colorado Plateau is the Carrizo, Chuska, and Lukachukai mountain chain stretching south from the San Juan River to the vicinity of Gallup. In this concept, to the west is the sere Kayenta Province, now heart of the Navajo Reservation. To the east is the Chaco Province covering the vast treeless San Juan Basin of New Mexico. The San Juan River, flowing east to west to join the mighty Colorado River at Lake Powell, divides these two areas from the Mesa Verde Province north of the river. Greater in aerial extent than the two regions to the south and more hospitable to human life, it spreads across a fraction of northern New Mexico, all of southwestern Colorado, and much of southeastern Utah from the foot of the southern Rocky Mountains westward to the Colorado River.

The Amerindian peoples of the Mesa Verde Province did not bequeath the nation a "lost civilization," as some romantics would have it. They merely lived there for a long time and then moved away without leaving a forwarding address. Nor did they leave a written record to tell of their worldviews, their mode of life, or their tribal wisdom. All that survives from their prolonged stay in the province are the silent jumbles of their vacated homes, a few scraps of their worldly goods, and ultimately their own bones.

Those precious few things have been sufficiently fascinating to promote a new branch of social science—the archaeology of the northern Southwest—and give mental nourishment to generations of the curious. This is the story of their adventures of the body and of the mind.

Methods and perspectives in the gradual evolution of Southwestern archaeology have changed as the culture of the observers has changed. Pothunters gave way to academicians, and relic collecting became artifact analysis, and then consideration of behavioral patterns. A bewildering vocabulary of technical terms appeared as scientific approaches grew more stringent and discrete. Archaeologists began to talk only to other archaeologists. The working tools altered. Horses pulling scrapers were replaced by backhoes and pickup trucks; typewriters and plane tables grew obsolete. Remote sensing and radiocarbon accelerator dating are in, and computers and CD-ROMs are here to stay. But through it all, the trowel remains the symbol of the science. It is often given, gold plated and inscribed, as a commendation because, even in this electronic age, basic archaeology means digging in the dirt.

The overview of the Mesa Verde Indian past presented here relies in part on a comprehensive technical report *Colorado Prehistory: A Context for the Southern Colorado River Basin* prepared by the research staff of the Crow Canyon Archaeological Center on behalf of the Colorado Council of Professional Archaeologists, with the support of the Colorado Historical Society. A primary mission of Crow Canyon is to educate the general public about regional prehistory, as well as to conduct its own research in which nonprofessionals under supervision participate. This book, therefore, is aimed at such interested persons and others not specifically versed in archaeology. In a nontechnical way it deals with the contributions to the methods and concepts that evolved in the province in accord with the reconstruction of the past. Some of the plethora of details important to researchers have been condensed or omitted, hopefully without loss of accuracy. My personal role as transcriber of this material has been made far easier by the courteous cooperation of this knowledgeable corps of scientists, closeted in the laboratory, out digging in the summer heat, enthusing over an occasional specimen or provocative idea, and reveling in their choice of occupation. It is my sincere hope that I do them no injustice in oversimplifying an enormously complex topic to which they have devoted years of energy and thought.

This book could not have reached its final form without the professional assistance of many archivists and others. I am especially indebted to Lynn and Dan Avery, Cortez Camera; Susan Thomas, Anasazi Heritage Center; Paul Rogers, Mesa Verde National Park; and Tracy Bodnar, Aztec Ruins National Monument. Thanks also to Time Traveler Maps, Mancos, Colorado, for regional maps.

Words are inadequate to express my indebtedness to a wonderful group of friends, among them Karen Adams, Mark Varien, Bill Lipe, Dave Breternitz, Jim Judge, Don Fowler, Kristin Kuckelman, and Nancy and Larry Hammack, for sharing their time, experiences, and expertise with me in order to set the record straight. To bring it into the second millennium, Leslie Goodwill Cohen kindly put it into a computerized format.

Finally, not to be forgotten are many of another day whose names appear in these pages. In step with their times, they furthered the new discipline of regional archaeology, and for some sixty years they have enriched my personal life. I salute them all! ✻

# A Pictorial Panorama
## of the First Century
## of Mesa Verdean Archaeology

**Fig. 1:** Members of the government's Wheeler Survey visited Salmon Ruin in 1874. The barrenness of the San Juan Valley then is in sharp contrast to today's verdant environment. Photo by Timothy O'Sullivan. Courtesy of the National Archives, photo no. 106-WA-436

**Fig. 2:** The first public news that some then unknown, presumably ancient people had lived in a small stone house high on a cliff of the Mesa Verde Plateau came with the first photograph of a cliff dwelling taken in 1874. Two Story House in Mancos Canyon was relatively inconsequential when compared to the structures to be discovered in several ensuing decades but was a novelty for the time. Photo by William Henry Jackson. Courtesy of the Museum of New Mexico, neg. no. 49787.

**Fig. 3:** In December 1888 the Wetherills dug in trash deposits at Sandal House, Mancos Canyon, one week before their first sighting of Cliff Palace. They named the site because of the number of sandals they recovered. Photo courtesy of the Lister Collection.

**Fig. 4a and b:** Articles discarded in 1890 at a Johnson Canyon cliff dwelling by Clayton Wetherill were found by a University of Colorado survey crew in 1975.

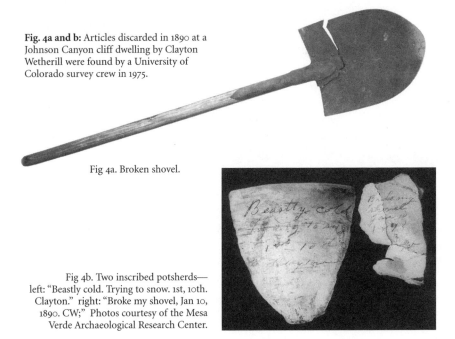

Fig 4a. Broken shovel.

Fig 4b. Two inscribed potsherds— left: "Beastly cold. Trying to snow. 1st, 10th. Clayton." right: "Broke my shovel, Jan 10, 1890. CW;" Photos courtesy of the Mesa Verde Archaeological Research Center.

**Fig. 5:** Cliff Palace at the head of Cliff Canyon as it may have first been seen by Richard Wetherill and Charlie Mason, December 18, 1888. Courtesy of the National Park Service, Mary Colter Collection, Mesa Verde National Park, box 1, folder 5, print 4.

**Fig. 6:** Wetherill camps on the Mesa Verde (1889–1891) were primitive, as shown in this photo presumably taken by Richard. Gustaf Nordenskiold described his quarters as a dirty piece of sailcloth stretched between trees and a bed frame of juniper trunks with a heap of horse gear beside it. The kitchen was little more than a pile of half-burned logs and a disarray of cooking pots. It must have been a shock to this Swedish aristocrat. The individuals in this photo are not identified. Photo courtesy of the Department of Library Services, American Museum of Natural History, neg. no. 337420.

**Fig. 7:** Wetherill Alamo Ranch, Mancos Valley. House in trees at right; small building (center) served as museum and sales room. Mesa Verde dominates the background. *Circa* mid-1890s. Photo courtesy of the Department of Library Services, American Museum of Natural History, neg. no. 411873.

**Fig. 8:** Charlie Mason at the Alamo Ranch, 1891. Together with Richard Wetherill, he participated in the first recorded sighting of Cliff Palace. Photo by Gustaf Nordenskiold; original at Ethnografiska Museet, Stockholm. Courtesy of the New Mexico State Records Center and Archives, Sallie R. Wagner Collection, image no. 7950.

**Fig. 9:** John Wetherill sitting in a storage cist in an unidentified alcove at Mesa Verde, 1891. Photo by Gustaf Nordenskiold; original at Ethnografiska Museet, Stockholm. Courtesy of the New Mexico State Records Center and Archives, Sallie R. Wagner Collection, image no. 7959.

**Fig. 10:** Long House, Wetherill Mesa, as it might have looked when Nordenskiold first saw it in 1891. The rubble covered rooms and kivas in the remainder of the alcove. The structure at upper left was called "the breastworks" by excavator George Cattanach because of small openings in the walls. Photo by Jesse L. Nusbaum, 1908. Courtesy of the Museum of New Mexico, neg. no. 60566.

**Fig. 11:** Cave 7, Whiskers Draw, as it was first seen by the Wetherill party. This was the place where the Basketmakers were first identified. Photo attributed to Charles Lang, 1893. Courtesy of the University of Pennsylvania Museum, neg. no. S4-140128.

**Fig. 12:** Hired in 1908 to photograph and note all the sites that should be included in Mesa Verde National Park, Jesse Nusbaum (right), Ted Kidder (center), and wrangler J. C. Frick (left) prepare to depart for Wetherill Mesa in front of the first tourist accommodations on Chapin Mesa, 1908. Courtesy of the Museum of New Mexico, Nusbaum Collection, neg. no. 139158.

**Fig. 13:** As the Nusbaum-Kidder team moved farther west, they came to the massive constructions of Twin Towers, Little Ruin Canyon, in modern Hovenweep National Monument. Photo by Jesse L. Nusbaum, 1908. Courtesy of the Museum of New Mexico, neg. no. 60705.

**Fig. 14:** Jesse Walter Fewkes (1850–1930), as a representative of the Smithsonian Institution (hence the U.S. Government), was responsible for preparing numerous major structures on Mesa Verde for public viewing. His yearly work at the park extended from 1907 to the mid-1920s. Photo courtesy of the National Park Service, Mesa Verde National Park.

**Fig. 15:** Earl Halstead Morris (1889–1956). Photo courtesy of the National Park Service, Aztec Ruins National Monument, neg. no. 1561.

**Fig. 16a and b:** During many projects in the La Plata Valley, Morris used abandoned houses such as these for headquarters. Photos courtesy of the Earl Morris Archives, University of Colorado Museum.

16a: The wagon at right carried camp gear in and recovered specimens out.

16b: . An abandoned houses used for headquarters

**Fig. 17:** In 1913 Earl Morris first entered Eagle Nest, perched on a nearly inaccessible ledge in Lion Canyon. The small house contains thirteen rooms and one kiva. Because artifacts were still present, it can be assumed to have escaped Wetherill explorations. Photo courtesy of the Lister Collection.

**Fig. 18:** Morris removed this upper part of a roof from the kiva in Eagle Nest in order to photograph the chamber's interior. Some of the logs dated to the early A.D. 1200s; others dated to A.D. 1140, apparently having been salvaged from some structure no longer present. Photo courtesy of the Earl Morris Archives, University of Colorado Museum.

**Fig. 19:** Earl Morris used the cribbed kiva roof in Square Tower House, Chapin Mesa, as a model for the plaza kiva at Aztec West in 1917. The flat top illustrates how the Eagle Nest kiva roof was constructed. Photo by Jesse L. Nusbaum, 1907. Courtesy of the Museum of New Mexico, neg. no. 43317.

**Fig. 20a and b:** Excavations at Aztec West.
Fig.20a. Workers loading spoil dirt dumped beside an exterior wall of Aztec West into mule-drawn farm wagons to be hauled either to the Animas River or to the road leading to the site. Photo courtesy of the National Park Service, Aztec Ruins National Monument, neg. no. 930.

Fig. 20b. Exterior walls were defined by teams of mules pulling scrapers. Rubble in the background came from collapsed walls. Photo courtesy of the Museum of New Mexico, neg. no. 46573.

**Fig. 21:** As a patron of the American Museum of Natural History, Talbot Hyde made a prolonged visit to Aztec West in 1918. After photographing two large ceramic bowls at the right, he turned his camera on an unexcavated part of the site. Photo courtesy of the Department of Library Services, American Museum of Natural History.

Fig. 22: This is a close-up of the same portion of Aztec West that Hyde photographed in 1918. The covering mound had been removed from the walls but excavation had not yet taken place. Chacoan core-and-veneer construction is evident. Photo courtesy of the Museum of New Mexico, neg. no. 45332.

Fig. 23: In 1934 extensive repairs were conducted at Aztec West, such as dismantling and relaying the exterior wall of the west wing, shown here. Most of the rooms behind remain unexcavated. Photo courtesy of the National Park Service, Aztec Ruins National Monument, neg. no. 97.

Fig. 24: Sylvanus Griswold Morley (1883–1948). Photo courtesy of the Museum of New Mexico, neg. no. 10316.

Fig. 25: Jesse L. Nusbaum (1887–1975), photo taken in 1912. Courtesy of the Museum of New Mexico, neg. no. 61798.

**Fig. 26:** Traveling west in 1908 through McElmo Canyon, Nusbaum and Kidder encountered what was left of Castle Rock Pueblo. Remnants of walls high on the crags were barely visible. Seven decades later, Crow Canyon scientists and participants uncovered evidence of a violent episode, possibly involving cannibalism, that ended the life of the settlement in the late A.D. 1200s. Photo by Jesse L. Nusbaum, 1908. Courtesy of the Museum of New Mexico, neg. no. 60721.

**Fig. 27:** As Nusbaum and Kidder passed by Sylvanus Morley's first archaeological field effort at Cannonball Ruin, Nusbaum gathered the crew of local workers and a few Harvard students for this "class photo." Morley was seated on the horse. Photo by Jesse L. Nusbaum, 1908. Courtesy of the Museum of New Mexico, neg. no. 60780.

**Fig. 28:** When Balcony House, Chapin Mesa, was first seen in the 1880s, it was in this dilapidated condition. Jesse Nusbaum, his father, and several others brought it back to the present state enjoyed annually by thousands of visitors. Photo by Jesse L. Nusbaum, 1907. Courtesy of the Museum of New Mexico, neg. no. 60501.

**Fig. 29:** Visitation to the new Mesa Verde National Park grew after its establishment, as illustrated in this photo of a 1910 group of visitors to Spruce Tree House. Alfred Kidder, who probably served as a guide, is seated at right in the front row. The woman in the second row, to the right, was wearing what appears to have been a divided skirt, appropriate for travel on horseback. Photo by Jesse L. Nusbaum. Courtesy of the Museum of New Mexico, neg. no. 60643.

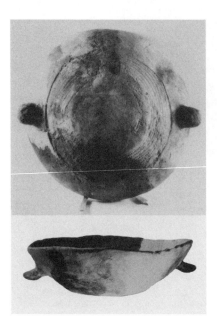

**Fig. 30:** In 1891 Gustaf Nordenskiold found pre-pottery basketry tray liners such as these in Step House. They date to the A.D. 600s. Impressions of the coils of the basket into which soft clay was pushed are clearly visible in this photo. Photo courtesy of the Earl Morris Archives, University of Colorado Museum.

**Fig. 31:** In anticipation of excavation and collection endeavors funded by John D. Rockefeller in 1925, Nusbaum used the trash deposits at the rear of Spruce Tree House as a training ground for a crew unfamiliar with scientific excavation methods. Floodlights lit the dark recess. Photo by Jesse L. Nusbaum, 1925. Courtesy of the Museum of New Mexico, neg. no. 139249.

**Fig. 32:** In the winter of 1926, this outfit headed for Step House, Wetherill Mesa, where Nusbaum hoped to find an occupation predating the cliff dwelling in one part of the overhang. The figure third from the left was his thirteen-year-old stepson, Deric, who returned to Mesa Verde in the 1950s to conduct excavations and tree ring sampling. Photo by Jesse L. Nusbaum, 1926. Courtesy of the Museum of New Mexico, neg. no. 139239.

**Fig. 33a and b:** Four Basketmaker III pithouses were found in Step House, Wetherill Mesa, in the portion of the alcove not obscured by a masonry houseblock. Three decades later others were noted below the house.

Fig. 33a. After excavation, 1926. Photo by Jesse L. Nusbaum. Courtesy of the Denver Public Library.

Fig. 33b. After stabilization, 1960. Ultimately one of these was reconstructed for the benefit of visitors. Photo by Fred Mang. Courtesy of the National Park Service, Wetherill Mesa Project Archives, Mesa Verde National Park, neg. no. 14656.

**Fig. 34:** Morris excavated Pueblo I Site 33 in the Ute Pasture in 1929; shortly thereafter the new tree ring calendar dated a log stump from the proto-kiva to A.D. 831. A 2002 wildfire is thought to have destroyed the surrounding vegetation. Photo courtesy of the Earl Morris Archives, University of Colorado Museum.

**Fig. 35 (above, left) :** Painted kiva, Lowry Ruin, in the early 1930s. Photo courtesy of the Field Museum of Natural History.

**Fig. 36: (above, right)** Right: Edgar Lee Hewett (1865–1946); left: John D. Rockefeller Jr. in front of the Laboratory of Anthropology, *circa* 1930. Rockefeller funded the establishment of the Laboratory of Anthropology, Santa Fe, now one of the Museum of New Mexico facilities. Photo courtesy of the Museum of New Mexico, neg. no. 7361.

**Fig. 37a and b:** In 1934 Earl Morris directed a stabilization project at Cliff Palace that involved dismantling some of Jesse Walter Fewkes's earlier repairs and rebuilding this four-story unit. Photos courtesy of the National Park Service, Mesa Verde National Park.

Fig 37a. Four-story unit under repair. Al Lancaster seated at base with other workers.

Fig 37b. Completed restoration, 1934.

**Fig. 38:** Civilian Conservation Corps recruits, under the direction of Al Lancaster, troweled the floor of an unknown ruin on Chapin Mesa in the 1930s. Photo courtesy of the National Park Service, Mesa Verde National Park.

**Fig. 39:** Cedar Tree Tower, connected to associated kiva, Chapin Mesa, *circa* 1940. Individuals not identified. The surrounding pinyon-juniper forest was consumed by the 2002 Long Mesa fire. Photo courtesy of the National Park Service, Mary Colter Collection, Mesa Verde National Park, box 1, folder 6.

**Fig. 40:** Archaeologist Alden Hayes mapping the Badger House Community, Wetherill Mesa, 1962. Photo courtesy of the National Park Service, Wetherill Mesa Project Archives, Mesa Verde National Park.

Fig. 41: The lower levels of the primary Pueblo II and Pueblo III structure of Badger House, Wetherill Mesa, 1963, prior to its stabilization and the erection of a modern protective roof. Photo courtesy of the National Park Service, Wetherill Mesa Project Archives, Mesa Verde National Park.

Fig. 42: Archaeologist Al Lancaster in 1963, working with the tools of his craft—trowel, whiskbroom, and field book. Photo courtesy of the National Park Service, Wetherill Mesa Project Archives, Mesa Verde National Park.

Fig. 43: Archaeologist George Cattanach views Long House, Wetherill Mesa, after the excavation that he directed, 1963. Photo courtesy of the National Park Service, Wetherill Mesa Project Archives, Mesa Verde National Park.

**Fig. 44:** Alfred Kidder smoking his customary pipe in front of Pecos Mission during a 1950 visit to the site where for nine seasons he had directed excavations of the large associated pueblo. Photo courtesy of the Lister Collection.

**Fig. 45:** University of Colorado field school students excavating what remained of an Early to mid-Pueblo II houseblock in the Far View group on Mesa Verde (Site 499), 1953. Photo courtesy of the Lister Collection.

**Fig. 46:** Alfred Vincent Kidder (1885–1963). The avowed dean of Southwestern archaeology, Kidder received the first ever Ph.D. in this region's archaeology from Harvard University in 1914, just seven years after he came west as an unenlightened interloper into the area's past. Photo courtesy of the Museum of New Mexico, neg. no. 7600.

**Fig. 47:** Harry Getty, at Gila Pueblo, Arizona, collecting a tree ring sample at Spruce Tree House by sawing off the end of a projecting beam, 1953. This method is no longer used. Photo courtesy of the National Park Service, Mesa Verde National Park, folder 3, print no. 268.

**Fig. 48a:** University of Utah crews moved along the Colorado River in boats such as these being landed at the mouth of Forgotten Canyon, 1959. Photo by Floyd Sharrock. Courtesy of the University of Utah Archaeological Center, photo no. 42SA183.

**Fig 48b:** Crew members excavated the Pueblo III Loper Ruin twelve miles down the Colorado River from Hite. Named for a long-time resident of Glen Canyon in the nineteenth century, the site was first recorded by the Powell expeditions of 1869 and 1871. Photo by William Lipe. Courtesy of the University of Utah Archaeological Center, photo no. 42SA364-114.

**Fig. 49:** Large-scale warlike painted figures, probably drawn in the A.D. 1200s, still hover over Defiance House, Forgotten Canyon. Photo by William Lipe. Courtesy of the University of Utah Archaeological Center, photo no. 42SA598-51.

**Fig. 50a and b:** Socializing at the Pecos Conference, Mesa Verde, 1974. Photos by Helga Teiwese. Courtesy of the Arizona State Museum.

Fig. 50a. Front, right to left: Florence Ellis and Robert Lister; rear, right to left: Walter Taylor, unidentified woman, and Richard Ambler.

Fig. 50b. Right to left: Charles DiPeso, David Breternitz, F. A. Calabrese, and Robert Lister.

**Fig. 51:** The Ute crew, including females, with National Park Service archaeologist Ed Sutterick (center) during development of the Ute Mountain Ute Tribal Park, 1975. Arthur Cuthair, seated at the left, remains active in tribal government. Photo courtesy of the Lister Collection.

**Fig. 52:** Navajo National Park Service stabilizers instructed Ute workers during excavation of Tree House, Lion Canyon, in 1972. The two structures comprising the site were built in the first two decades of the A.D. 1200s. Tree House is the first cliff dwelling visitors see on the standard tour of the Ute Mountain Ute Tribal Park. Photo courtesy of the Lister Collection.

**Fig. 53:** In the early to mid-1970s, Ute crews were primarily responsible for preparing trails for their tribal park. Government regulations required the wearing of protective hard hats. Photo courtesy of the Lister Collection.

**Fig. 54:** Ute workers excavated and repaired Fortified House located on the east escarpment of Lion Canyon. It is a four-unit structure of twenty-four rooms and one kiva that is dated between A.D. 1207 and 1230. Photo courtesy of the Lister Collection.

**Fig. 55:** In 1975 arsonists burned down the hogan of Ute chief Jack House in lower Mancos Canyon. A Ute pictograph panel is visible on the cliff face behind. Current park tours usually stop here to remind visitors that this canyon was not just the homeland of the ancestral Pueblos. Photo courtesy of the Lister Collection.

**Fig. 56:** A maze of forty seventh-century storage pits on a spit of land extending into the Navajo Reservoir on the San Juan River. First excavated by Frank Eddy, they were reexamined by Complete Archaeological Services Associates in 1987. The pontoon boat was used to survey reservoir shorelines. Photo courtesy of the Complete Archaeological Services Associates.

**Fig. 57:** Two University of Colorado students and Al Lancaster (right) working on a feature in a site in Mancos Canyon, 1974. Photo courtesy of the Mesa Verde Archaeological Research Center.

**Fig. 58:** Mesa Verde Archaeological Research Center crew stabilizing a Chaco-style kiva at Escalante Pueblo, 1975. Ute Mountain is in the background. Photo courtesy of the Mesa Verde Archaeological Research Center.

**Fig. 59:** Cynthia Irwin-Williams, Salmon Ruin, 1972. Photo courtesy of the Salmon Ruin Photographic Archives.

**Fig. 60a:** The Chimney Rock pinnacles at the head of the Piedra River Valley as seen from the south. They are believed to be the sacred Twin War Gods of the ancestral Pueblos. Photo courtesy of Bob Powell, Boulder, Colorado.

**Fig. 60b:** At the end of the A.D. 1000s a Chacoan houseblock was erected at the feet of the pinnacles. Pyramid Mountain is at center rear; Stollsteimer Mesa and the Piedra Valley are in the distance.

**Fig. 61a and b:** Field methods used during the Dolores Archaeological Program. Photos courtesy of the Bureau of Land Management, Anasazi Heritage Center.

Fig. 61a. Mechanical helpers doing the heavy work on a pit in the McPhee Village.

Fig. 61b. Precise work still required kneeling and troweling.

**Fig. 62:** An artist's conception of the Pueblo I McPhee Village on a slope above the right bank of the Dolores River. It is now under reservoir waters. Photo courtesy of the Bureau of Land Management, Anasazi Heritage Center.

**Fig. 63:** This houseblock in the Pueblo I Grass Mesa Village, in close proximity to the dam creating McPhee Reservoir, was excavated by the Dolores Archaeological Program from 1980 to 1983. Photo courtesy of the Bureau of Land Management, Anasazi Heritage Center.

**Fig. 64:** A new kind of archaeology was born when, with the help of heavy machinery, a Complete Archaeological Services Associates team stripped the surface of the Hovenweep Lateral Easement in preparation for the excavation of a Basketmaker III and Pueblo III site they named Knobby Knee, mid-1980s. Photo courtesy of the Bureau of Land Management, Anasazi Heritage Center.

**Fig. 65a, b, and c:** Complete Archaeological Services Associates crews uncovered a Knobby Knee Pueblo III kiva whose encircling banquette was decorated with a partially preserved mural of geometric elements. Photos courtesy of the Bureau of Land Management, Anasazi Heritage Center.

Fig. 65a. Crew at work.

Fig. 65b. Close-up of mural surrounding a niche opening.

Fig. 65c. Conservators applying preservatives.

**Fig. 66:** Stuart Streuver (center) conferring with Bill Lipe (right), Ricky Lightfoot (left), and an unidentified woman about the feasibility of establishing what became the Crow Canyon Archaeological Center. Grass Mesa Village, 1982. Photo courtesy of the Crow Canyon Archaeological Center.

**Fig. 67a, b, and c:** Crow Canyon Archaeological Center. Photos courtesy of the Lightfoot collection.

Fig.67a. Original lab trailer.

Fig. 67b. Early student housing, and modern lodge in the background.

Fig. 67c. Stage set where children talked about their archaeological experience, with their parents in the audience. Gates administrative building is now in this location.

**Fig. 68a and b:** High school students learning archaeological techniques at the Albert Porter Site, 2002. Photos courtesy of the Crow Canyon Archaeological Center.

Fig. 68a. Archaeologist Susan Ryan at right front.

Fig. 68b. Working a suspended screen.

**Fig. 69:** Crow Canyon intern working with adult participants at a local excavation. Photo courtesy of the Crow Canyon Archaeological Center.

**Fig. 70:** Crow Canyon staffers viewing rock art panel near Moab, Utah, with members of the Native American Advisory Council. Photo courtesy of the Crow Canyon Archaeological Center.

**Fig. 71:** Crow Canyon archaeologist Kristin Kuckelman taking notes at the Albert Porter Pueblo on the Great Sage Plain, 2002. Masonry of prehistoric walls is in the banded Chaco style. Photo courtesy of the Crow Canyon Archaeological Center.

**Fig. 72:** Robert and Florence Lister at Aztec Ruins National Monument, 1988. Photo courtesy of the Lister Collection.

# BEGINNINGS BEYOND COMPARE

IT ALL BEGAN WHEN A MILITARY MOUNTED PATROL rode up to Pueblo Pintado. What the soldiers saw was the weathered hulk of a large, ruined structure rising against the western horizon of a forlorn, windswept plain. There was no sign of life for miles around. On a blanket of fallen stone walls and splintered beams, the men tromped around a blocky maze of cubicles. Some were torn asunder; others recalled mine shafts with floors absent between several stories. All were drifted with a buildup of tumbleweeds and wind-blown dirt and enveloped with the unsettling gloom of abandoned places that testify to failure.

The year was 1849. The United States had just gained title to the Colorado Plateau and to an unsuspected segment of its past history. The revelation came about when a contingent of the Corps of Topographical Engineers bound westward from Santa Fe to the Navajo country happened upon Pueblo Pintado. Because the ruin had no resemblance to the low adobe buildings the soldiers knew along the Rio Grande Valley, they assumed it had been left by peoples other than the local Hispanics or Indians. Daringly and erroneously, First Lieutenant James H. Simpson attributed it to the Toltecs of Mexico.[1] A nebulous Mexican connection would continue to puzzle scientists from then until the present.

When the troops moved farther west and down the shallow valley by the Chaco Wash in northwestern New Mexico, they encountered a string of similar ruins. Simpson received permission to stay behind for a week to examine and document them. He assigned Richard and Edward Kern the task of making detailed maps of seven of the largest sites.[2] The report resulting from these combined efforts collected dust as did its subjects. However, it stands as the first bubble in a subsequent flood of literature, sometimes factual and other times frivolous, pertaining to the antiquities of the Southwest.

Quite by chance, the Topographical Engineers discovered the richest archaeological zone north of central Mexico. Not only that, but the Chaco structures now called Great Houses once had sheltered a population estimated into the thousands that attained a level of complexity unmatched elsewhere on the Colorado Plateau. It was a cultural efflorescence that had considerable effect on contemporary peoples of the Mesa Verde Province.

Ten years after the Chaco episode, the first American concern with the prehistory of the Mesa Verde Province was due to another Topographical Engineers survey, this one commanded by Captain John N. Macomb. His party entered a beautiful area at the northeastern periphery of the Colorado Plateau. It lay at the foot of the majestic San Juan Mountains, where tall timber, grassy meadows, and rushing waters invited Ute Indians to camp. It also once had invited more sedentary predecessors to settle. In 1859 Macomb's troops passed by the twin pinnacles of Chimney Rock, but they were unaware of the numerous, slumped individual dwellings and communal building of moderate size spread along the spine of a ridge sloping away from the feet of the spires.[3] Had the men climbed the heights a thousand feet above the valley below, they would have found another Chaco house now known as Chimney Rock Pueblo. This structure was one lost in the space of ninety airline miles from Chaco Canyon.

A more archaeologically informative event ensued when the Macomb survey swung south to the lower Animas River valley bordering the bleak San Juan Basin. There the geologist attached to the group, J. S. Newberry, inspected two huge artificial mounds covered with sage and chico brush through which poked spiky wall remnants, some standing twenty-five feet high, and rooms below banked with debris but still retaining bits of adobe plaster. Despite the sites' later designation as Aztec West and Aztec East, Newberry and his colleagues believed that there never had been appreciable connection with Mexican natives.[4]

Moving further northwestward, the Macomb expedition visited two sites on a rise above the Dolores River as it burst out of the La Plata Mountains. These places had been seen in 1776 by a Spanish outfit for whom the ruined houses of Dominguez and Escalante are named.[5] The ruins later proved also to have known Chaco colonists or influence. Thus, the first sites seriously examined by American teams represented Chaco intrusion into the Mesa Verde Province. Why and how this occurred would be a topic of much concern as regional archaeology matured.

Macomb's contingent traveled westward as the terrain flattened out into a seemingly level plateau. Newberry took note of the large ruin complex of Yellow Jacket in what is now southwestern Colorado and what he thought were prehistoric reservoirs and irrigation canals.[6] As it would turn out, for many centuries the locale was one of the most densely occupied by ancient peoples whose numbers far exceed modern census counts. After reaching the vicinity of what is now Moab, Utah, the men turned south to the San Juan River, thinking that the land to the west was too rugged for a route to the Colorado River.

While in the Montezuma Valley, and undoubtedly with great effort, Newberry climbed the north face of the precipice of Mesa Verde towering 2,000 feet above the valley in order to get an encompassing view from a high vantage point.[7] From a distance the block of plateau appears to be flat on top, hence the name that translates as "green table." Actually it is dissected by a confusion of sheer-walled canyons 800 to 1,000 feet deep that slice southward into the Mancos drainage along the east and south sides.

The capping of the plateau, at an average elevation in its midsection of 7,000 to 7,500 feet, is a thick stratum of porous, tawny-colored sandstone. Over past eons, moisture had percolated down through it until stopped by a bedding of impervious shale that forced the wetness laterally to the cliff face. Freezing and thawing that ensued caused enormous chunks of the sandstone to slough away, leaving vaulted openings and weeping waters at the juncture of sandstone and shale. Generally, smaller hollows appear above and below this layer. Virtually all these recesses were used as shelters and storehouses by some of the ancestral Puebloans, the cliff dwellings being the final manifestation of their presence.

Newberry did not explore the mesa beyond the northern Point Lookout promontory. Consequently, he missed out on the fame of being the first professional person to see the amazing structures in the canyons to the south and to tell the world about them. Exploration, like archaeology, is often a crapshoot.

Newberry's report was not published until after the Civil War. By then a parade of persons uprooted by the conflict and seeking new lives in the undeveloped West learned firsthand of the antiquities of the Mesa Verde Province.

One group of newcomers drifted south from the new, raw village of Durango to a broad valley where the Animas River turns west to join the San Juan a few miles downstream. At an elevation of 6,500 feet, with a temperate climate and loamy soil, the valley seemed a promising place for farming. As families settled in, it was immediately obvious that they were not the first to take advantage of the potential of such resources. Hand-dug irrigation canals cut off from both sides of the river onto valley bottom lands, where collapsed cobblestone rubble of former abodes was a common obstruction to modern development. Many such heaps of debris were plowed up. This disturbance revealed scatters of artifacts and occasional human bones. Sections of walls in two great mounds of Aztec Ruins near the bend of the river, explored originally by Newberry, were convenient sources of shaped sandstone for homes and outbuildings.[8]

On a Saturday morning in 1881, schoolchildren and their teacher broke into the northwest corner of the high, westernmost mound to find themselves in two connected rooms, by then buried beneath heavy overburden.[9] They were thrilled to see various discarded objects and scared at the sight of desiccated human bodies, which after death had been left on the dirt floors.

The finds inspired their fathers to follow them to the site; break through stone walls in a series of seven intact, ground-floor rooms; and gather varied pieces of pottery, basketry, stone tools, and other items that had been placed with the dead as offerings or tossed aside as trash. This brief exploit, the first penetration of the inner sanctum of a Mesa Verde Province site and the acquisition of its contents, must have caused a momentary stir among the neighbors but was soon forgotten in the exhausting work of creating homes in the wilderness.

The parcel of land surrounding the two main mounds passed into the hands of two successive owners. They stopped random looting but converted small, secondary structures into root cellars for their own use. Unknowingly, they contributed to site destruction by cultivating the ground around them and in the process eradicating possible earthworks and a prehistoric roadway.[10]

Scholars may have concluded that these ruins were places abandoned for unknown reasons by ancestral Pueblos, but the less-educated immigrants to the area had not. To them, these were homes left behind by the Aztecs. Their legend of having arrived in the Valley of Mexico from "the north," a mythical Aztatlan that some versions had extending into the Greater Southwest, had been published in a widely read account of the Spanish conquest of Aztecan Mexico. Consequently, with numerous ruins present, the uninformed considered the Colorado Plateau to be the fabled northland. Common reference to the ruins as Aztecan was soon an unquestioned fact. Shortly, the generic term "Aztec" became the proper name of both the most prominent piles of the past and the tiny 1880s village across the river. A few years later another white outpost became Cortez. It sat in the Montezuma Valley.

In the same post–Civil War era, the ambitious Geological and Geographical Survey of the Territories (also known as the Hayden Survey) sent three successive groups into the Mesa Verde Province. The two leaders of teams destined for the Mesa Verde vicinity proper were extraordinary individuals with the same given names and with complementary observational and artistic talents. They initiated scientific interest, albeit limited, in the cultural history of the region. Their missions were to inspect and record the many kinds of resources of this expansive frontier that still encompassed huge, unexplored tracts.

In 1874 a seven-man unit led by William Henry Jackson, a budding landscape photographer determined to be the first to capture on film some of the wonders of the West, came to the San Juan Mountains. They were accompanied by Ernest Ingersoll from the *New York Tribune*. While stopping at a mining camp in the upper La Plata Valley, Jackson was prompted to inspect what prospector John Moss assured him were photogenic ruins in the Mancos region to the west where a lone white settler had a hardscrabble ranch.

Jackson was hesitant about entering into this area that was part of traditional Ute territory. Earlier that season he had been warned that these natives did not take kindly to white men in general and to government agents in particular and that they were easily provoked. Moss assured Jackson that he was on friendly terms with any Indians they might encounter. Furthermore, over many years and with no trouble Jackson had taken numerous pictures of Plains Indians and so felt he could cope with unforeseen risks. Besides, this opportunity to examine a ruin in a cliff could not be missed.

The Mancos region is where the Rockies give way to lower foothills and stretches of sweeping, open lands grayed with sage and greened with patches of pinyon and juniper on uplands. A small, perennial stream lined with cottonwoods and willows runs diagonally through a valley to enter a craggy, deep canyon delimiting the eastern edge of Mesa Verde.

The Mancos Valley and Canyon were where Moss had seen rubble piles left from what he thought were old Indian houses. It is not known whether he had any knowledge of such places on the Mesa Verde itself. But from the 1860s on, prospectors, trappers, and assorted wanderers are believed to have viewed or climbed into some of them. Several left their initials or names on ruin walls or nearby rocky surfaces, a practice that continued for many years. Others are suspected to have churned through drifts of fill in random search for "relics." Hence, there was a general awareness abroad that antiquities were present.

As the Jackson crew warily rode their horses down into Mancos Canyon, they entered a narrow defile hemmed in between high escarpments where the river was deeply entrenched. To the south the valley spreads up to a mile in width. Many digitated canyons branch off to the northwest from the main stem like closely spaced fins of coral, but the explorers did not enter any of them. Had Jackson come a summer earlier, he might have wondered about plumes of smoke rising from Long Mesa, one of the arms of the Mesa Verde block, where a fire ignited by lightning blazed across the land leaving an eerie spectacle of black tree skeletons and seared ground.[11]

Here and there along the river, Jackson noticed heaps of walls fallen from long-deserted structures. None seemed interesting photographically. Then, as camp was being set up in late afternoon, one of the men spied a small masonry construction glued onto a sloping ledge at least 700 feet above the canyon floor. The next morning, loaded down with the cumbersome hardware of his profession—camera, tripod, glass plates, and chemicals—Jackson, followed by Ingersoll, laboriously climbed up to it. Jackson took the first photograph of a Mesa Verde cliff dwelling. With no great stretch of imagination, he named it Two Story House.[12] Over their morning coffee, readers of the *New York Tribune* later learned through the pen of Ingersoll of the unusual homes of the ancients embraced in the stony hold of Mancos Canyon. The romanticizing of the Southwest's past had begun.

Proceeding down canyon rather hastily, so as not to stretch their luck with the Indians, and out around the southern tip of Mesa Verde, Jackson's party passed the solitary pinnacle that guards the mouth of the canyon. It later bore his name. In more expansive country to the northwest, the men walked around the large group of rooms at Aztec Springs (today's Yucca House). Some scientists regard parts of that site as yet another incursion by Chacoans into the Mesa Verde Province which was situated around a spring now dried up. As he traveled further to the west down the red rock McElmo Canyon, out into the Great Sage Plain, and over to the foot of Cedar Mesa in Utah, Jackson photographed numerous archaeological sites of various ages. Predominately these were the most visible, latest remains. Worn down by scorching heat and little potable water, the small expedition turned back to the east. A few years later Jackson prepared a clay diorama of Mancos Canyon ruins for an exhibition in Philadelphia commemorating a century of American independence and for which he was given a bronze medal.[13]

William Henry Holmes, working in 1875 for the same Hayden Survey, entered Mancos Canyon from the south after having toured the lower La Plata Valley. What is now a very despoiled ruin there still is known as the Holmes Group. An artist by training, a geologist through chance contacts and opportunities, and at the height of his career a notable anthropologist, Holmes wrote about the physical and cultural features he saw on this far-flung trek. The latter included dwellings on open ground, such as multiroom compounds, tri-wall and D-shaped edifices, kivas, granaries, and courtyards. One tower in lower Mancos Canyon impressed him with its walls standing sixteen feet high. He named Sixteen Window House above the Mancos River and was the first to speculate about the defensive nature of all these cliff dwellings. Holmes also had the dubious distinction of taking part in the first recorded bit of pothunting. He dug out two large, corrugated earthenware jars from deposits in Sixteen Window House and carried them to civilization in a sling on his back and to final rest at the National Museum in Washington, D.C.[14]

As important as these two pioneering surveys were in recording the previously unrecorded, they scored another of the near misses inherent in exploration and archaeology. Jackson and Holmes failed to go up into any of the canyons located deep in the plateaus of Mesa Verde and Cedar Mesa. Like Newberry, by not doing so they missed the opportunity for their minutes of fame as "discoverers" of the cliff dwellings of both. In their defense, they had no inkling of the existence of such outstanding traces of the past, only the less impressive ones they did visit.

Jackson's uneasiness about encounters with the troublesome Utes and those of Holmes who followed him were justified in 1875 at different times. In one incident in Montezuma Canyon in the far west a band of exuberant Indians ran off pack and riding animals, leaving the Holmes party far from help. Fortunately, in the dead of night an alert packer was able to sneak up on the disturbed horses and mules milling about some distance away and lead them back to camp. In another affair the same noisy Indians stampeded Jackson's outfit into a wild ride down canyon. Nobody was hurt, but Jackson was in a helpless panic lest his delicate photographic paraphernalia and a season's worth of exposures be lost as they bounced out of control over the rough trail. In the end it was all treated as a joke when the chief of the Indian band invited the shaken surveyors to share his supper at his wickiup encampment.[15] Four years later a brief description of another Mancos Canyon cliff dwelling was published in the proceedings of the prestigious American Association for the Advancement of Science.[16] Little is known of its author or the specific ruin.

Meanwhile, at the same time that Holmes was in the field, geologist Frederick M. Endlich, also with the Hayden Survey, returned to the vicinity of the lower Animas. He and his men reconnoitered sites there for a second time and added some new observations to those made by Newberry sixteen years before.[17] He suggested that the two dominant mounds be named Acropolis, but that was too Grecian for those so focused on the Aztecs.

A newspaper account of Two Story House and other of the Mancos places of interest caught the attention of a young writer named Virginia (Donaghe) McClurg. She was so spellbound by them that in 1882 she had to go explore for herself as part of an assignment from the *New York Daily Graphic*. A major obstacle was that just a decade earlier, Mancos Canyon, the tributaries feeding into it, and the Mesa Verde had been officially designated as part of a reservation for the Weeminuche band of Ute Indians. Even with such sprawling range, the Indians considered all of western Colorado to be their traditional homeland. Not unexpectedly, they resented the mounting white invasion. Ugly hostilities occurred, as Jackson had been told. Therefore, McClurg appealed to the commander of Fort Lewis, a post established in the upper La Plata Valley to guard settlers moving into the area, for a military escort to accompany her on a horseback trip into the Mesa Verde country. He refused, no doubt thinking it a harebrained idea for a lone woman to risk an encounter with barbarians just to see something as unimportant as dirty wrecks of old houses. But McClurg persisted until the commander finally relented, probably in disgust.

McClurg's bizarre entourage traveling down Mancos Canyon examined the same sites others had described. This brief trek allowed McClurg to be the first white woman to view the ruins in the cliffs.

McClurg has been described as a person one would think unlikely to brave the hardships of the wilderness and the dangers of hostile natives.[18] She was obese, fond of large, feathered hats, and given to heavy use of cosmetics. But she was indomitable, thrilled by what she had seen on her earlier trip, and as a good journalist was going to get the story no matter the difficulties. In 1886, presumably with permission of the Indian agent, she organized her own expedition. In addition to the expected guide and photographer, with a nod to Victorian propriety she also hired someone listed as a "chaperonhousekeeper." This must have been a female cook who then became the second white woman in the Mesa Verde recesses.

Once a few miles down the Mancos Canyon and after being chased by some Utes, the group thrashed through dense underbrush that made access difficult to turn up one of the gorges ripped back into the Mesa Verde. They camped for three weeks in Soda Canyon, during which time they saw two or three cliff dwellings. One was Balcony House. McClurg was awed by this wreckage seemingly crunched one hundred feet below the rimrock and hundreds of feet up from the canyon floor. It was a sight she never forgot as the climax to what must have been an adventure of a lifetime.

Balcony House was named because of a shelf off the second-story rooms that allowed entrance into adjoining chambers. There is some evidence that this structure had been visited by a prospector several years earlier. Nevertheless, McClurg considered it her discovery. It made such an impression on her that she became an ardent leader in the movement to get all these monuments permanently protected. As a first step and in years after this initial sighting, she was instrumental in raising funds to get Balcony House repaired.[19]

Euroamerican families began arriving in the Mancos environs in the late 1870s and early 1880s, hoping to have come to a place where they could put down roots. Among the newcomers was the Wetherill family. Like the others, their days were consumed with grubbing out sagebrush, digging up a plenitude of rocks left from moraines of glaciers that flowed down from the mountains, and, as they planted pastures and gardens in cleared fields, hoping it would rain. And soon. Here and there they found the same sort of remains as those in the lower Animas because farmers, past and present, are drawn to similar environments. One particularly large ruin called Goodman Point Pueblo in the Montezuma Valley was reserved from homesteading as early as 1889. Perhaps incorrectly, John Wetherill is said to have been the first person to probe one of the mounds in the Mancos Valley.[20]

There were no high walls banked with centuries of wind- and water-borne earth in these sites. What was present was a smattering of crude, cobblestone foundations of a few rectangular rooms and perhaps a slump in the ground that those in the know called *estufas*, the Spanish word for "stove." Later, such depressions would be shown to have been subterranean chambers likely used for both rituals and lodging. These things aroused little interest beyond idle curiosity.

That attitude was to change for the five Wetherill brothers. The patriarch of the family, Benjamin Kite, whose gravestone still graces the Mancos Cedar Hill cemetery (died 1898), made a point over the years of befriending Utes who came by the ranch that he and his sons were carving out of the south Mancos Valley. In return for his friendliness and respect, the Utes gave him permission to winter his livestock in the protection of Mancos Canyon and its branches. These locales were part of the Southern Ute Indian Reservation where other outsiders were not welcome.[21] The sons took turns staying at primitive camps which were nothing more than wickiups comparable to those of their hosts or in a small cabin they put up in Johnson Canyon.[22] In their spare time they scouted around for Indian remains.

The first ruin in which the Wetherills did some cursory shoveling was one they later named Sandal House because of a large number of such items they took from the trash. Al Wetherill claimed to have dug there in 1882.[23] Sandal House was easily reached from the canyon trail and, consequently, was decorated through the years with numerous inscriptions left by passersby. Otherwise, a few grinding stones and stone axes, bone awls, and an occasional pot weathering out of an embankment were part of generally unexciting days on the range. That is, until December 18, 1888.[24]

The scene on that day had many of the ingredients of a Western epic. Two young frontiersmen, Richard Wetherill and his sidekick brother-in-law Charlie Mason, weary from searching for stray cows through the almost impenetrable growth on the Mesa Verde crest, rode out on a rimrock to an unbelievable sight across the canyon. It was something of which they had been told by Utes but, after three winters in the canyons, were not convinced that it really existed. In the murky atmosphere of an oncoming storm, they were astonished to make out a building larger than any these unsophisticated, country men had ever seen. It filled a huge, arched overhang high up on a cliff front at the head of a canyon. Although the structure was unintentionally camouflaged by having been built of the same stone as the background, Wetherill and Mason could see tall walls pierced with darkened openings, rooms apparently stacked on top of rooms, what appeared to be towers or multistoried skeletons of piled rooms, and a thick blanket of rocks spewed down in front as a result of crashed construction. The setting in a deep gash of a canyon laced with evergreens, the omnipresent silence of an uninhabited place, and the thought that this was a token of a past world of which they might be the first modern witnesses led them to regard it as the ultimate material achievement: a palace. So it became and has remained, Cliff Palace, once believed to be the largest such Pueblo edifice stuck in a cliff yet known.

What Richard Wetherill and Charlie Mason did not realize at the time was that younger brother Al Wetherill had seen this site a year or two before. Nor was he first. While engaged in the fruitless task of trying to find troublesome stock wandering deep in the canyon labyrinths, Al had looked up from the bottom of Cliff Canyon to glimpse the site through a curtain of trees. Being exhausted and in a hurry to meet comrades at camp, he rode on. Curiously, because of the demands of the ranch, he put it out of mind.[25] Thus, this was another of the missed chances that in this case gave his brother the undying credit for a fantastic find. Human nature being what it is, in the wake of public excitement over this discovery others also claimed to have seen the decaying house before the Wetherill-Mason sighting.[26]

If Richard and Charlie were in fact at the spot now usually pointed out as that from which Cliff Palace was first seen, they were next to a large, unusual structure, Sun Temple, on a mesa tongue between two canyons. To get to Cliff Palace, they had two choices. One was a circuitous ride around a canyon crevasse and down a strip of the mesa top to a spot above the ruin.[27] Descent into it would have meant sliding down a cleft in the rocks, using weathered hand and toe holds hacked into the sandstone by the original inhabitants, tying on to twisted trunks of trees with a long length of rope, and calling up a hefty dose of derring-do. The other choice was equally demanding. It would have meant scrambling hundreds of feet down a steep talus drift below them to the canyon floors and then climbing up an opposite slope. This is now recognized as the easiest access.

Once in the alcove, the men must have felt overwhelmed by its immensity up close and by the eeriness haunting wasted, lonesome places. Quite certainly, they were exhilarated to observe a sprinkling of specimens of the sort with which they were by then becoming familiar.

The events that followed that December 1888 day have been retold in altered versions so many times that it is now hard to be certain of the details. It is known that brother John Wetherill, Mason, and acquaintances Charles McLoyd, Howard Graham, and Levi Patrick, miners on the loose who also were caught up in the spirit of exploitation, were recruited to return to Cliff Palace. If it was a typical Mesa Verde winter day, it was logical that they camp in the protection of the alcove and its structure as well as in those sheltering Spruce Tree House and Square Tower House. These were other substantial cliff dwellings seen in the several days following the first sighting of Cliff Palace. The men spread their bedrolls on the dirt floors of interior rooms. They dumped camp gear, saddlebags, digging tools, and food in front. Old photos show that they hung a side of beef on Puebloan wall pegs, where it remained edible through natural refrigeration. Undoubtedly to ward off the cold, they kept a fire going. At Cliff Palace there was little fallen roof timber to be had, apparently having been stripped away sometime in the past. But there was an ample supply of fuel on the slopes below the house. According to one account, in coldest weather the men moved into a convenient subterranean kiva and possibly stretched a tarpaulin overhead.[28]

And then the explorers went to work. It was not easy, but the men were young with bodies toughened by the rigors of mining and ranching and with skills for coping with life in the raw. Gaining entrance to the cliff-side structures was hazardous regardless of whether they were reached from the canyon floors or from the mesa rim. In the latter case, it often meant going over the cliff edge on a taut rope anchored to a tree trunk or boulder and hanging out in space for a few adrenaline-flushed moments before swinging back into an alcove. Such daredevilry was necessary because notched pole ladders, earth ramps, and hand and toe holds used by the early inhabitants had disappeared or eroded. Another danger was clouds of noxious dust raised when trash deposits were disturbed. These clogged the lungs and made eyes water, not to mention caking faces and clothing. Al Wetherill called the clouds "mummy dust," the ancients' revenge for ignoring their universal desire to rest in peace.

Despite these drawbacks and the trials of camp and travel, there were many rewards. As the group set about gathering up objects that had been left where last used, or shoveling through discards thrown at the rear of rooms at the point where the cave overhang pinched down or out on the spill of rocks and earth in front of the dwellings, they were in a state of high excitement. For the first time it was possible to examine the full inventory of material things that the ancestral Pueblos, whom the Wetherills referred to as the Cliff Dwellers, had devised to keep their daily lives functioning.

The extraordinary wealth of specimens in the cliff dwellings came from the fact that the makers and users, without the benefit of beasts of burden, took only lightweight, portable possessions when they finally walked down the canyons and out of the Mesa Verde Province. The arid environment and protection from the elements afforded by the alcoves helped preserve perishable things made of feathers, hides, fibers, or wood that would not have survived in other, less kindly circumstances. Furthermore, these articles and assortments of nonperishables had lain untouched for centuries until white scavengers arrived.

The men could not help but be impressed with the variety, ingenuity, and skill the tenants of Cliff Palace and its neighboring cliff dwellings demonstrated in their handicrafts. All of them were fashioned from what nature provided. What was lacking were metal articles.

The most numerous and attractive specimens were those made of clay. They were also the most fragile. The sheer volume with which they had been turned out accounted for a high survival rate. Moreover, earthenwares were a customary grave furnishing. They were not made for such purpose but represented the typical output in daily use. Mesa Verde decorated wares made from a clay that fired to a dull gray or off-white color were slipped with an additional liquid coating of white kaolin clay over which decorations were painted. These were done in mineral or vegetal pigments, or a combination of both, that turned black under heat. The design vocabulary consisted of bold, balanced geometrics. Hemispherical bowls of various sizes, large water jars, pitchers, ladles, handled mugs, and squat, lidded jars were treated in this fashion. Found by cold ashes of dead hearths or lined up at the base of walls were commodious, round-bodied receptacles that were used for cooking or for storage. Their average size was about a twenty-five-quart capacity of dry foodstuffs or liquids. Typically, their interiors had been smoothed, but their exteriors retained the outlines of coils by which they had been formed, and potters had precisely pinched them into decorative patterns. Even though the purposes of these vessels were utilitarian, their makers gave vent to aesthetic urges that present-day artisans find hard to duplicate.

From stone the Cliff Dwellers ground axes and hammers, some of which retained wooden handles lashed in place by leather thongs. They shaped slabs on which the women pulverized dry corn kernels with a stone that fit snugly in their hands. In time scholars would know these implements by their Spanish names of *metate* and *mano*. From more finely grained stone of other kinds, the craftsmen flaked drills, knives, scrapers, and arrowheads.

Objects made from yucca fibers or leaves, apocynum, reeds, and willow withes included many round-toed sandals to fit young and old feet. Most were badly worn from rough travel over rocky terrain. Other finer things included hairbrushes, tumplines, belts, cordage, pot rests, netting, socks, panniers, and tightly coiled or plaited baskets. The explorers guessed that some articles consisting of an oval frame of willow interlaced with yucca leaves may have been handy snowshoes for tramping over the mesa tops in winter.

Among wooden artifacts the men collected were arrow shafts; long, pointed sticks with worked knobs on the other end that they thought might have been used in planting; sharply pointed drills that could be whirled in a secondary piece of wood to ignite fires; weaving tools; cradleboards for infants with padding of corn tassels; and pegs that were stuck into walls from which articles could be hung.

The Wetherills cut one amazing twelve-foot plank from a downed tree trunk in half in order to get it back to the Alamo Ranch. Their labors were minimal compared to those of the Cliff Dwellers, who probably toppled the old dead tree by burning it near its base and then using wedges of some sort to split off the plank. They then smoothed its rough surface with chunks of coarse sandstone. With the efforts expended on the plank, it surely was meant for some special purpose. Neither that nor where it was found is known.[29]

Leather items were not common, but pouches, sinew bowstrings, moccasins, tanned hides, and quivers verify hunting and processing skills.

Stone and bone beads; others of shell; tiny, stone fetishes; bone awls and needles essential in basket making; and corn husks tied at the ends to form containers for salt, beans, and squash seeds rounded out the repertory of Cliff Dweller goods.

A rare, fringed suit of mountain sheep- and buckskin appears on one list of artifacts.[30] Other than that and sandals, belts, and scraps of textiles and hides, clothing articles were few. The ancient people must have been scantily clad in fair weather and foul. Except for a few pieces of matting, there did not seem to have been household furniture—no tables, benches, stools, or beds. The occupants of the cliff dwellings ate, slept, gave birth, and died on the ground. All their tactile skills notwithstanding, they appear to have done little to further their own physical comfort. The fact that they laboriously made beads and other kinds of jewelry says much about human vanity.

During the 1889 winter, the Wetherill brothers and their associates unearthed a large collection of artifacts which, with difficulty, they carried back to the Alamo Ranch. Strings of up to ten animals were used to pack out most of the loot. Often they walked through deep snow along a rough trail up to forty-five miles in length that the men chopped out of the wall of growth of pinyon and juniper on the mesa top and down treacherous slopes of unstable rocks. Fragile objects, such as pottery, were carried on foot in what must have been exhausting ordeals.[31]

The diggers also recovered human skulls and desiccated bodies, many of children. Some were still shrouded in robes made of yucca fibers interlaced with the down of turkey feathers, sometimes enriched with bluebird feathers or strips of rabbit fur. The human remains were the first such discoveries of the former inhabitants of the cliff dwellings. At first, the Wetherills were inclined to think that they were not Indians because of the slight auburn coloration of some of the hair left on skulls or tied into hanks which probably was due to oxidation. They saw that the base of these skulls had been flattened. They assumed that this resulted from the "papoose" carriers used.

Benjamin, the elder Wetherill, put together a sales catalog. This was not a new idea; a network of relic hunters already had the same approach to profit. Wetherill sent one copy of his catalog to the Smithsonian Institution. He got no response. After a display of the objects in Denver, the Colorado Historical Society purchased the lot. Included were the human remains. This windfall was further augmented by publicity generated by the finds that brought more than fifty visitors to the ranch in the summer of 1890.[32] Some were from as far away as the East coast. For a fee Richard guided them to the mesa to view the old houses. It was obvious that antiquities and curiosity about them represented a lucrative, but not renewable, resource.

Any arrangement the Wetherills may have had with the Utes to glean the cultural riches from their reservation or to bring guests onto their private property is unknown. If the Utes protested what might be construed as a flagrant abuse of grazing rights, no one listened. The Wetherills felt they kept the Utes content by feeding them when they came to the ranch.

As soon as work slacked off in the fall, the men were back in the trenches. Their endeavors were beginning to have a different meaning for them. No longer was it just a hunting-gathering mode in overdrive but a growing intellectual inquisitiveness about the spectacle of the past played out virtually at their doorstep. Benjamin, in particular, recognized the potential scientific value of the sites. He wrote to the director of the Smithsonian Institution, umbrella organization for the National Museum founded just eight years earlier, and asked for professional help.

> I would like for the party to work under the auspices of your institution, as I expect them to make a thorough search, and get many interesting relics, particularly from a number of cliff houses discovered by my son, R. Wetherill, during the past summer, while guiding tourists over the mountains to view the dwellings.[33]

Benjamin's further comments were that the Mesa Verde was of no possible use other than as a preserve for "curiosities" and that it should be considered soon as a preserve because of the threat of mounting tourism.[34] He conveniently overlooked his family's almost exclusive role in removing cultural materials from the sites to sell and its escorting to the mesa those "threatening tourists."[35]

The secretary of the Smithsonian referred the Wetherill letter to Major J. W. Powell, head of the Bureau of Ethnology (later Bureau of American Ethnology). He turned it over to William H. Holmes, then in charge of the division of field exploration at the Bureau. Holmes responded that the Bureau was not able to purchase collections or to oversee the Wetherill work. This response is especially surprising since the new federal museum was actively trying to fill its shelves.[36] Holmes pointed out that records relating to place and manner of discovery were essential in order to give any collection scientific significance. He tactfully asked if it were possible for the Wetherills to map the sites where they worked and to keep notes on the work done.

Professionalism was rearing its head. Holmes recalled that he had been in the area in 1875 and hoped that his institution might be able to return someday. If so, he might desire Wetherill's services.[37]

Wetherill quickly responded that his sons did keep account of all things of interest, where they were found, and that they were careful not to harm the buildings in any way. He also included a long tabulation of the kinds of relics recovered, perhaps as further enticement.[38]

In March, B. K. Wetherill followed up with another letter to Holmes. With the 1890 season drawing to a close in three weeks, he wrote:

> Since writing you we have added a great deal to the collection of Cliff Dwellers relics: having visited and worked out 182 houses, containing one to one hundred and twenty four rooms, each on the ground floor and explored two hundred and fifty miles of cliffs, making full notes of all our work. From all the information we can gather, the collection is larger and contains a greater variety than the combined collections of that kind in the U.S. It consists of over 100 perfect pieces of pottery and a number broken. No two pieces painted the same. Cloth and three leggings of human hair, cotton and feather cloth, yucca bands, pieces of buckskin, wicker work panniers for carrying loads upon the back, baby boards, matting of rushes and willows, sandals, baskets, bunches of yucca fiber, bone implements consisting of awls, knives, needles, etc., eighteen stone axes with handles and a great many without, stone knives, seven smooth stones this shape [drawing of sandal last], arrow points, two pipes, sandstone used for sharpening tools, hammers or mauls, grinding stones, etc.—fire sticks and tinder made of bunches of cedar bark, sticks used for planting seeds, others used as weapons, or hatchets for beating out the yucca fiber, yucca rings for setting their pottery in, beads white and black, very small, others about two inches long made from the bones of turkeys' legs, also skeletons and dried bodies from the smallest child to the full grown man, and skulls, from a number of which the bodies have decayed.[39]

Wetherill went on to say that if desired, his sons would make a map of the entire area, pointing out that it would be an arduous task because of the tortured terrain. This was surely something of which Holmes was well aware. Wetherill also asked about how to compile the notes that Holmes might want. He enclosed a page from a daily log of work at Sandal House which Richard presumably kept (Appendix A). If he received an answer, there now is no available copy. This, too, can be interpreted as another of the missed opportunities because the Mancos novices were intent on doing a credible job. What they needed, and did not get, was academic guidance. This was the beginning of a schism between the lay and professional communities that would continue to plague Southwestern archaeology throughout its history. In this instance, as a sign of the attitude on both sides, the secretary of the Smithsonian Institution said it was hoped that the collection would be disposed of advantageously, meaning for profit.[40]

In 1890 during their second collecting enterprise, the Wetherills sought out sites in Mancos Canyon, Johnson Canyon, and then spent time on the finger of the plateau to the west of the Chapin tableland where they had been the previous year. A century later, researchers saw their signatures and an occasional date left on ruin walls or nearby rock falls. A find of special interest was made in 1975 by a survey crew in the Johnson Canyon area. It was a broken shovel in the dirt of a small cliff dwelling. In an interior room the crew picked up two potsherds with penciled messages. One read, "Broke my shovel, Jan 10, 1890, CW." The other read, "Beastly cold, trying to snow, 1st, 10th, Clayton."[41] Clayton Wetherill was having a bad day.

The diary page that Benjamin sent to Holmes confirms the efforts being made by the Wetherills to record necessary data about measurements and observations. Being pioneers in any field of endeavor where there are no established guidelines carries risks. Unfortunately, like the ancestral Pueblos themselves, in the early stages of their Mesa Verde work the Wetherills left no written documentation to explain their evolving broader interpretations of the ancient culture with which they were so engrossed. This is something for which they now are unfairly criticized.

In 1891, one year after the primary Wetherill activities at Mesa Verde, a young Swede named Gustaf Nordenskiold knocked at the door of the Alamo Ranch. He wished to be guided to the unusual houses in the cliffs of which he had heard and presented a letter of introduction. Of the same age as some of the Wetherill brothers, they soon became friends. He was welcomed as a paying guest whom they chose to call Gus. He planned to stay a week but remained for six months.

It was a strange relationship because these young men were products of totally different backgrounds. Gustaf was a college graduate traveling in America for his health. He came from an aristocratic, monied family housed on the grounds of the Royal Academy of Sciences in Stockholm, where his father was on the staff. The father was an internationally known Arctic explorer honored by the Swedish monarch with the title of Baron.[42] The family social circle was made up of the intelligentsia of the day.

Despite the trappings of comfort and wealth to which he was accustomed and the serious tuberculosis from which he was just recovering, Gustaf Nordenskiold was ready to adapt to the rough-and-ready camp life to which he was introduced by the young Wetherills.

The first day out the party rode for some twenty-five miles on an Indian trail into the defile of Mancos Canyon. It was a stony, dry, hot, sage-gray world unlike any Nordenskiold had known. To one used to lush, temperate Scandinavia, Mancos Canyon in July must have seemed like nothing short of the Sahara.

To complete his undoubted preconceptions of the Wild West, the men made camp in a clump of cottonwoods that the visitor was told were a favorite stop for the Utes. Cottonwoods in the Southwest are the trees of life, a sign of water, the providers of shade, and typical refuges for wanderers. To tease him a bit, Nordenskiold was assured that the once belligerent Indians who came to this spot were no longer as fierce as they had been just a few years earlier when Mancos residents were terrorized.

The next day the group entered Cliff Canyon, the longest of the lateral drainages cutting into the Mesa Verde to the west. Vegetation clogged the entrance to the canyon, making it difficult for animals and riders to get through. Over time, huge slabs of the sandstone embankments had cascaded down into the slot, blocking passage. Above this barrier towered talus slopes hundreds of feet high, deeply furrowed like the folds of a taffeta skirt. Above them were retreating terraces of sandstone reaching up to vertical cap rock.

After the tortuous miles up canyon, the riders came at last to its head. In a semicircular recess draped with shadows, there it was: mysterious, almost ghostly in its solitude, Cliff Palace. Nordenskiold's destiny was sealed.

During the following week, the Wetherill brothers led their visitor to the various places they knew. With wry humor, in his journal Nordenskiold wrote of his makeshift bed framed by juniper branches laid under a very dirty piece of sailcloth stretched between two trees. He complained of a monotonous diet of sowbelly, porridge, and unleavened bread cooked over campfires; of water that acted like castor oil; and of the many skunks that prowled camp at night. He told of his first uneasy meeting with men—the Utes—who were not of European extraction.[43] Through it all he was enthralled with visions of the deteriorating buildings stranded in breathtaking, rock-bound surroundings. Further, they had been unknown until just several years earlier. More importantly, he immediately recognized the need to document them in a worthwhile manner, not merely to strip them of their contents. He, too, was a geologist by training but almost instinctively knew how to go about documenting. Perhaps he and his younger brother Erland, who became an ethnographer of note in dealing with South American tribes, shared the same cultural perspectives.

Recognizing his lack of experience in archaeological methods, Nordenskiold was conscientious enough to decide to practice first on a small site before taking on one of the larger houses.[44] Richard Wetherill suggested such a ruin on a ledge in Soda Canyon. With the help of Richard and brother John, he spent two days exploring what he termed a house of nine rectangular and two circular rooms huddled along a narrow shelf of sandstone above which a shallow opening in the cliff had weathered.

Nordenskiold approached this trial run as a scientist. He took measurements and drew a rough map of the plan of the structure and its overhang. He noted details of construction. He made entries in his field book about how the various chambers may have been used for everyday routines, for ceremonies, for storage. Undoubtedly he discussed his interpretations with his guides and sought theirs. In the process, he was unknowingly introducing scientific methodology and thinking to the two Wetherills, Richard and John, who would spend the rest of their lives dealing with Colorado Plateau natives. Nordenskiold also introduced them and all later practitioners of Mesa Verde archaeology to the use of a trowel for precise excavation of archaeological features and artifacts.

With beginner's luck, the yield of specimens was considerable and did much to whet Nordenskiold's appetite. He later wrote that more perishables came from this site than from any others where he worked.

Nordenskiold was especially interested in the two circular rooms. He soon saw them as special chambers with some ritualistic purpose. This was because their features of six short columns set on an encircling, benchlike wall, a hearth in the center of the dirt floor, and an upright slab in front of an opening to a vertical shaft to the exterior were the same in both cases. The latter pair of features, the function of which he did not then understand, now are regarded as a deflector to keep drafts of air flowing down the vertical ventilator shaft from extinguishing fires in the hearth. Moreover, both chambers were at least somewhat subterranean. Entry probably was through an opening in the roof. Nordenskiold was to learn that all the circular rooms on the Mesa Verde were more or less of the same design except for variation in size and depth. They now are called *kivas* and are thought to have been used as Nordenskiold suggested, as well as for domestic needs.

With additional beginner's luck, Nordenskiold found that one of the circular rooms had another attribute that is not commonly found now because of destruction by the elements but likely was a rather frequent enrichment for both kivas and household rooms. This was a dado painted in dark red pigment enlivened with spaced clusters of three lanceolate elements that pointed upward onto a white wall. Probably there was a symbolic meaning to this design. It was a find that later researchers would relish, but Nordenskiold, into his first adventure and not realizing his good fortune, took it for granted as commonplace.[45] The ruin is now named the Painted Kiva Site.

Following this learning exercise, Nordenskiold hired John for more ambitious work and to oversee a varying number of laborers at what he considered an extravagant three dollars a day. He wrote that this was more than a professor in Sweden earned. Together the small crew explored many formerly occupied places along sheer bluffs and rocky shelves of a number of the canyons that fissured the Mesa Verde. He named two of the main arms of this landform. One he called Chapin's Mesa after Frederick Chapin, a druggist who visited there during two previous summers and wrote the first descriptive book about the plateau which, according to him, once had been inhabited by "wild tribes."[46] The other, a slice of the highland to the west, Nordenskiold named Wetherill's Mesa. Both names have been retained without the possessive implications.

As the group went from site to site, principally on Wetherill Mesa, in addition to the usual search for specimens Nordenskiold kept meticulous notes of careful observations, numbered or named sites for maps he painstakingly drew, and took 150 photographs.[47] The latter are invaluable today in showing the condition of the houses and their settings a century ago. Nordenskiold scratched some numbers on walls. Various members of the Wetherill clan left names or initials.

Although built in the same way with shaped sandstone blocks laid up in mud mortar, chinked with small stones, and in a few fortuitous circumstances still partially roofed with timbers topped with brush and earth, each cliff dwelling differed in configuration in order to conform to its particular haven. Most rooms had a single opening. Some apertures were rectangular. Others were wider at the top than bottom. Neither could be considered a window. Nordenskiold observed that the quality of workmanship varied from excellent to haphazard. The protection of the overhangs may have promoted carelessness on the part of masons, or, for unknown reasons, sloppiness may have come through haste. In some cases Nordenskiold saw that rooms had been raised over or around enormous chunks of the cave roof that had fallen before humans moved in. Other quarters at the rear of the houses often were so dark that they provided excellent places for his photographic work. He suggested that some cells built in openings away from obvious dwellings were too small for occupation and most likely were meant for storage.

In his notes Nordenskiold thoughtfully described the various kinds of artifacts he found, took their dimensions, and listed their exact placement when found. He tried to determine how they were made and their probable use. With admirable insight into the possibilities of greater understanding of the lifeways of the ancients, he saved materials such as animal bones, dried gourd rinds, and human feces. However, like others of the day, he did not keep or tabulate the volume of potsherds that in the future would be a fundamental resource for scientists.

It was whole pottery that interested Nordenskiold the most. After analyzing the sixty pieces he collected, he concluded that the design vocabulary was inspired by that on plaited basketry. In the case of those baskets, light and dark straws were used in such a way as to create angular patterns that highlighted both elements and the black-on-white palette. One infrequent type of pottery, most often recovered in fragmentary condition, bore polychromatic patterns in black, white, and red. Nordenskiold thought this must represent trade ware. He observed that this pottery was tempered with crushed potsherds, a fact that had gone unnoticed earlier. Nowadays researchers think such pottery was from areas to the south.

Explorations finally began at Long House on Wetherill Mesa. It was then considered to be the second largest of the Mesa Verde cliff dwellings. Not many specimens were recovered, and the great amount of work involved in removing a mass of rubble was too arduous for the small crew. Exploration then concentrated on Kodak House. This ruin was so named because Nordenskiold hid his camera there when it was not in use. Mug House to the north was examined after camp was moved for the third time. That place drew its name from a large number of such receptacles found in it.[48]

Eighty years later this final camp used by the Nordenskiold diggers was identified by a University of Colorado survey team working along what was to be a road right of way down Wetherill Mesa. Scattered under a tall evergreen were bits of glass, leather, and metal objects that dated to the 1890s period. Also present was a crude table made from four juniper stumps topped with split poles.[49]

From this locale the Nordenskiold crew gave considerable attention to Step House. A series of some sixty stone slabs laid by the ancients up the slope beside its alcove formed a stairway to the mesa top. The masonry structure in the opening occupied only part of the available floor space. This is the sole instance where, among the Swiss cheese holes in the Mesa Verde formations, such was the case. The vacant area was covered with a thick sheet of refuse consisting of turkey droppings, corn husks, castoffs, and wind-blown sand and dust.

After digging around in the very dilapidated house, Nordenskiold put his men to work shoveling in the refuse. It held little promise of producing anything of interest. However, here the diggers encountered eight graves. This is the only known instance where they discovered anything like a defined burial ground.[50] It doubtless had become so because of the ease of using a pointed stick to burrow out suitable depressions for bodies. Several graves were different because a pseudotomb had been formed by osiers laid across the top of the burial pit. Grave goods had been left with the dead. Nearby was an apparent cache, perhaps hidden long ago from attackers who seem never to have come or at least to have found the hoard.

Even with what Nordenskiold considered a profitable stint at Step House, Lady Luck forsook him in one regard. The men discovered several pots that appeared to be quite distinctive from the general run of Cliff Dweller pottery.[51] At least one of broad tray shape had not been fired. They were dull gray in color and thick. One piece showed ineptly executed punched designs on its interior.

In his autobiography written at least a half century after the find, Al Wetherill provides a further description of this pottery.

> At the building known as Step House, we had just about finished work when we came upon a little mud-and-stick [jacal] wall. In probing around in it, we came across some strange and unusual pieces of pottery. The largest was nearly fourteen inches in diameter and perhaps three inches deep and was all in fragments. It had been made in a basket, because the marks of the basket were pressed on the outside surface. It was uncolored and heavy, coarse in quality, and had been dried, or maybe burned a little, in the basket until hard enough to use. On the inside, there was a figure made by indentations with a

sharp implement while the clay was still soft. . . . One piece seemed to be just a chunk of mud beaten into shape on the inside of a basket. Three other pieces represented cups or drinking vessels. In shape, they were like a coconut with the top cut off. These were similar in quality to the bowls and none could have been baked.[52]

Nordenskiold failed to recognize that these tray-shaped objects were not true pottery since they had not been fired, but he speculated that they and the crude, baked examples were older than his usual run of earthenwares. This was the first inkling that cultural phases might be defined through pottery. Al attributed the vessels to the "wild fellows" who were on the Mesa Verde first. Nordenskiold had no proof of any culture older than that of the Cliff Dwellers.

Had the workers shoveled into one particular place in the refuse close to the foot of the steps, they would have had such proof in the presence of several pithouses.[53] Most of the roofing of these habitations had disappeared sometime in the past, leaving the walls of the houses completely hidden beneath the ground surface. When excavations were carried out in 1926, among the artifacts recovered at the spot were vessels like those puzzling ones in Nordenskiold's collection. Tree ring dates verified a few years later indicated that the pithouses were lived in some 600 years before the cliff dwelling was erected in the same alcove.[54] Researchers assigned them to a developmental phase in the history of the ancestral Pueblos now termed Basketmaker III.

Based upon these findings and others down talus slopes below many houses, scientists believe that most, if not all, the alcoves had been used at two intervals: one early in the Mesa Verde story and one at its prehistoric conclusion. Nordenskiold's contributions were many, but this was not one of them. He did, however, publish the first photograph of unfired Basketmaker tray liners although he was unaware of their age or significance.

Nordenskiold's schedule did not allow time for excavation of any surface remains on the Mesa Verde. He did note some of them, including what he concluded were small villages. He was unsure of how they related in terms of age to the houses in the cliffs, but both he and the Wetherills felt they had been homes to the same tribe. He observed towers, reservoirs, and many rows of rocks placed across numerous constricted drainages leading off the tableland. These latter features reminded him of terraced vineyards in southern Europe. From their presence, presumed to control runoff and build up soil, and the abundance of corn cobs and husks found at every ruin, he felt sure that the early residents had been farmers.

After spending four months studying these antiquities of Mesa Verde, Nordenskiold felt he had a good idea of what had transpired there, and he had a sizable collection of the paraphernalia that made life possible.

Gus and Al then took off on a horseback trip to the Hopi villages in northeastern Arizona. Seeing Hopi life in action, Nordenskiold was convinced that he had delved into their past and that of other Pueblo peoples along the Rio Grande in New Mexico. He correctly estimated that the early phase of this prehistory had ended as recently as several centuries before the Spaniards arrived in 1540.

The two travelers rode on to the Grand Canyon and then circled back to Mancos. At the end of 1891 Gus said goodbye to the Wetherills, who had given him an unforgettable experience. In return, he had given them food for thought.

As Nordenskiold sat in the train on his way back to New York, he surely must have been engulfed in memories. Some would have been of the many times he recklessly crawled on hands and knees along narrow fins of sandstone above precipitous drop-offs to peer into empty granary cells stuck on some sheer rampart. He must have smiled to recall John expertly tossing a lasso over a projecting beam in order to climb to a high room, while the others down below hoped the old timber would not split. Surely he also was glad that he had a photograph of the rickety scaffolding they made out of fallen branches and beams in order to risk their necks in attempting to reach places not entered for countless centuries.[55] It was all a far cry from his icy fieldwork among the glaciers of Spitsbergen, where the tuberculosis that sent him abroad had struck.

The negative side to the Swede's high-minded endeavor was that he had no qualms about keeping the recovered artifacts for himself. At the beginning of his explorations, he wrote his father asking if someone in Sweden might invest $600 in a specimen collection that he probably could obtain.[56] The answer was no. Therefore, since he paid for retrieval of such materials, he packed them up intending to send them to Stockholm. Then his troubles began.

The stationmaster in Durango refused to accept the shipment of seven boxes and two barrels containing an estimated 600 specimens. Nordenskiold was arrested. The agent for the Office of Indian Affairs with jurisdiction over the Southern Ute Indian Reservation notified the commissioner in New York that he had charged Nordenskiold with devastation of Aztec ruins near Mancos because some Indians complained that the remains of their dead were being disturbed.[57] Actually, the main protests were made by local white citizens with political clout because regional antiquities were about to be shipped abroad.[58] The agent asserted that he had issued Nordenskiold a passport allowing him to visit ruins on the reservation with the mutual understanding that no objects or human bones would be removed. For his part, Nordenskiold was untruthful in saying that he had not dug on Indian lands. He also chose not to mention the skulls and mummies of one adult and three children in his barrels.

Two weeks later, after Nordenskiold hired a lawyer and suffered considerable embarrassment and expense, the commissioner, in what today seems like shocking ignorance, dismissed this first recorded pothunting case, stating:

> As the relics taken seem to be of but little consequence and as there is an abundance of the same still to be had on the reservation, and noting the fact that the Baron did not deface any of the ruins, I have concluded to permit him to keep the relics with the exception of such skeletons or bones, if any, as may be in the lot, which are justly claimed by Indians as being the bones of their ancestors.[59]

Two months after Nordenskiold's exoneration, the Wetherills were arrested on the same charges. Richard wrote to his friend Gus about this incident. Because there were no witnesses, the Wetherill case also was dismissed. With a marked sense of self-righteousness, he commented, "We have applied to the proper authorities to do this kind of work regardless of the local croaking element."[60]

Even though the Utes may have had no interest in these things, they were wary about them because of their association with the dead, or were simply unaware of what was going on. The artifacts and the places from which they came were assets of the reservation given them by the United States Government. As the commissioner's letter demonstrates, in the 1890s it was a government not farsighted enough to regard them as part of the patrimony of the entire American public. Hence, the Utes were the losers in the artifact bonanza that Mesa Verde afforded.[61] However, in today's ethical climate, the real claimants to the dead and their belongings left behind are the modern Pueblo peoples whose forbears occupied the territory long before either Utes or Whites arrived to find a deserted land.

Back home in Sweden, Nordenskiold did not hold an official institutional position, but he presumably had use of the facilities of the National Academy. He set about getting notes and photographs in order for a technical report and for a small popular account of his western sojourn. Fifty examples from his collection and some photographs were exhibited, not in Stockholm but in Madrid as part of the observance of the four hundredth anniversary in 1892 of Columbus's first voyage. It was one of history's little ironies that descendants of those Spaniards forever changed the lives of descendants of the Mesa Verdean ancestral Pueblos.

Nordenskiold, the geologist, kept an exemplary archaeological field record for its time. Within two years it resulted in a detailed, profusely illustrated monograph entitled *The Cliff Dwellers of Mesa Verde*. This work demonstrated such a high level of scholarship in researching background literature, in technical analyses of materials, and in cautious deductions about prehistoric circumstances that a century later it remains a commendable resource.

As an appendix to the book, Professor G. Retzius described nine adult skulls and that of a child secreted by Nordenskiold from Long House, Step House, and Kodak House on Wetherill Mesa; from an isolated spot in Pool Canyon; and from Spruce Tree House on Chapin Mesa.[62] Retzius astutely noted cranial deformation that flattened the backs of skulls and provided line drawings to illustrate it. One other skull presumably found by a traveler in the Hovenweep region west of Mesa Verde had been published by craniologist Emil Bessets. Retzius's analysis was the first study of Cliff Dweller remains. For years skull deformation remained an attribute that distinguished Cliff Dwellers from earlier peoples and was thought to be evidence for two different populations.

With the novel turn of events that the entire Nordenskiold episode represented, the first technical publication on the prehistory of the Mesa Verde Province was in Swedish. Soon an English edition was published. The first book was the work of a twenty-four-year-old Swede, growing out of his first and last visit to America. With it, the discipline of Southwestern archaeology was inaugurated to which the work of the Wetherills was a prelude.

After Nordenskiold's untimely death two years later, a buyer donated his collection to the people of Finland. It remains in the National Museum in Helsinki halfway around the world from Mesa Verde. Until 1991, in commemoration of the one hundredth anniversary of Nordenskiold's exploits at Mesa Verde, it had never been exhibited.

By mail from Sweden, Nordenskiold continued to collect modern Indian handiworks through the auspices of traders Thomas Keam and O. E. Noland and aboriginal specimens through the Wetherills. Once Richard

Wetherill sent him seven pottery vessels, confirming active participation in the artifact market and the low returns received.

> Our prices on pottery at the present time in lots of 100, with some mended and some chipped more or less about 40 pieces to the pot, being entire and unbroken is $3.00 each, such as I have sent you averages about $8.00 a piece here and send you 7 as I would rather give you more than any one else.[63]

Benjamin shipped Nordenskiold twenty-seven additional pots a year later. Presumably these examples are part of the Helsinki holdings.[64]

At the outset of the 1890s, the scene of archaeological interest shifted to the Grand Gulch Plateau at the eastern periphery of the Mesa Verde Province. This highland and surroundings incorporate 1,000 square miles of the most broken terrain in North America. It is splintered by numerous deep, sheer-walled, tortuous canyons; jump-offs; stony arches; the earth's bare bones left as soaring shafts; and sheets of naked rock to reflect summer's rays or winter's sting. The plateau slopes upward from the Colorado River on the west, the San Juan River on the south, and the flat lands to the east to climax in Elk Ridge at some 8,000 feet in elevation. The heights are clothed in majestic stands of evergreens which are replaced downslope by a dense forest of dwarf pinyons and junipers. Scrub oak, cottonwoods, willows, and sage grow in the canyon bottoms some 4,000 feet below the mountain. Openings yawn along walls of stone that close in the canyons, some about two-thirds of the way up and others near the base. In contrast to the Mesa Verde landform, general access to these overhangs is from below, often requiring a vigorous scramble.

At the same time that settlers were taking over the lower Animas Valley and the area around Mancos, a Mormon colony was gaining a foothold on the north banks of the San Juan at the base of White Mesa. Optimistically, the migrants, who had spent six troubled months literally building and hacking their way from central Utah through the trackless wastes of southeastern Utah, named their tiny refuge of several dozen clapboards Bluff City. On a terrace above this village were the mounds of a prehistoric community that later researchers would see as another Chaco thrust into the Mesa Verde Province.

After the capricious San Juan washed away gardens that the industrious Mormons planted, many of the men turned to raising livestock. They found ranges in the canyons to the north and northwest to be useful. These introduced them to the old, wrecked houses crowded into the recesses. Their recovered trophies often ended up on the pantry shelves next to mothers' preserves.[65]

A gold rush to the San Juan in 1892 and another soon afterwards to the Glen Canyon of the Colorado River brought men into a wild country where they otherwise would not have ventured.[66] They, too, learned of the mud and stone buildings silently falling apart in the many crannies in the canyon walls. Their conversations and those of the cattlemen in the trading centers of Mancos and Durango spread the news. Few paid attention until it was also known that the Wetherill brothers had sold their first Mesa Verde collection for a staggering three thousand dollars.

With that in mind, Charles McLoyd, Charles Graham, and various associates decided that prospecting for relics would be more profitable than panning for the elusive flour gold washed along river banks. Included in one early crew was John Wetherill. From 1892 through 1893 the McLoyd-Graham outfit mounted at least four expeditions to the Grand Gulch Plateau.[67] Their primary goal was Grand Gulch itself, the major drainage gashing through the uplands for some seventy-five miles to end at the San Juan River west of the spot becoming known as Mexican Hat. The Mormons at Bluff City told them it was almost impossible to get down into Grand Gulch and, true enough, during their first explorations they scouted for days for a place of ready access for them and their pack animals. Finally they spent additional time cutting trees, sorting out rocks, and building a cribbed trail. The beasts remained so spooked that the men had to lead them down and then climb back up to the rim crest in order to carry tools and food down on their own backs. Apparently the thought of riches fueled their bodies.

Once down, the crew found itself in the mother lode of antiquities. Site after site never before rifled gave up its treasures. A handwritten catalog put together later lists stone, bone, fiber, wooden, and pottery objects as having been recovered.[68] Further, the catalog contains fifty-four entries of human remains. Some were complete, shrouded mummies, others were disarticulated body parts.

On this expedition and later ones in which McLoyd was a member, the party also reconnoitered White, Red, and Lake Canyons off the east side of the Colorado River. The pickings there were not as plentiful because inhospitable terrain had precluded extensive occupation.

Taken together, the ruins on the Grand Gulch Plateau were numerous but not as large as some on the Mesa Verde. Their contents, nevertheless, were comparable. The various McLoyd enterprises probably amassed several thousand articles. In 1893 they also inspired the first society in Durango dedicated to study of the province's historical and archaeological background.

This ragtag troop of adventurers unknowingly made a very significant discovery of a distinctive kind of site not previously encountered. When first viewed, some cave floors only exhibited the broken tops of stone slabs or circular depressions. McLoyd called them "underground rooms," but a later description is more explicit.

> Apparently at one time there was a smooth dirt floor in them [the caves] several feet in thickness. It is not likely that they were used as places of residence at all. In these floors egg-shaped holes were dug. In cases where the sand was soft, they were walled up and plastered, but the majority were merely finished with plaster smoothing the interior as it was dug. Many of these are found in the cave.[69]

The cists, or so-called underground rooms, actually were intended to be granaries. Baskets, leather pouches, and fiber bags left in some of them contained dry corn kernels, beans, seeds, or juniper nuts that somehow had escaped the ravages of rodents or insects.[70]

A secondary usage of the cists was as crypts for the dead. An eyewitness account reads,

> In these potholes or caches are found the bodies of all ages and sexes—sandals upon feet, human hair, gee strings, cedar bark, breechcloth. Beads around their necks. All wrapped in a blanket made of rabbit fur, of a weave similar to the feather cloth.
>
> Then they are in a mummy cloth or sack such as the Peruvians used. This is made from spruce fiber, and good cloth it is.
>
> Over the head is a small basket—flat, about twenty inches in diameter, usually found in good condition.
>
> Along the arms are scattered spear points; fine bone awl—all long ones. All have a hook on one end; a spatula about 8 inches long, 1/6 inch thick, 1 inch wide; (never a stone axe has been found); small basket containing corn and seeds, with ornaments is usually near the head. Wherever an atlatl has been found, it was broken and was on top. The atlatl points have been found in the quivers. The pipes are usually in small baskets near the head. Over all is the large basket. Nearly always two bodies have been found in one grave. No pottery has been found in one of these potholes. The skulls are all natural, long, and narrow.[71]

The baskets mentioned in the previous quote were of particular interest. They came in a variety of sizes and shapes. Some were flat bottomed and round; others were long and tapered and meant to be carried on the back. Others were very large, seamless bags. All were expertly fashioned, some so tight as to be waterproof. Most of the bags were as pliable as when new and their decorative colors of red and black as brilliant. No basketry as elegant was found at Mesa Verde.

McLoyd referred to the cist makers as the "cave people" to distinguish them from the builders of the masonry houses that by then were commonly known as the Cliff Dwellers. This was a confused terminology because both groups used the cliff-side openings, sometimes the same ones. These diggers regarded the two groups as neighbors, both of whom, almost perversely it seemed, chose to dwell in such an unforgiving land, where the air was motionless, storms came as downpours, and in which it was so hard for modern men to negotiate. They were unaware of the fact that they had happened upon the goods and corporeal evidence of the first farmers of the Colorado Plateau, who most likely were contemporaries of Jesus Christ. Had McLoyd and Graham known, they could have capitalized on their finds to gain dubious fame and fortune. As it was, they remained unheralded and penniless. Penniless, that is, until John Koontz, owner of Aztec Ruins, bought one assortment of specimens and Reverend C. H. Green of Durango bought another. The latter invested what appears to have been the going rate of three thousand dollars.[72]

Back at Mesa Verde, in 1892 the Wetherills were absorbed in their third and final sweep of the ruins. This was to gather specimens to be included in proposed displays of regional antiquities at another celebration of Columbus's first voyage of discovery. The fair was to be held in Chicago, just a year late (1893), with the venue of some of the genuine materials being a fake cliff dwelling in a fake bluff modeled after a landform in McElmo Canyon to the west of Mesa Verde. Warren K. Moorehead, a teacher at the Phillips Academy in Andover, Massachusetts, also was engaged in acquiring data, if not artifacts, across the northern San Juan district. Although Newberry had undertaken the same task thirty years earlier, Moorehead and his crew spent two weeks mapping Aztec Ruins for further information. No excavation was done.[73] A buyer of a McLoyd and Graham collection mounted the first public exhibition of what later would be identified as Basketmaker wares. Even though the visitors did not appreciate it, they were being shown things used at the very beginning of sedentary occupation of the Mesa Verde Province that were several thousand years old.

A stream of guests came to the Alamo Ranch during the 1892 planning stage for this groundbreaking affair. Among them was H. Jay Smith who, through his local agent, purchased the second Wetherill collection. It was said to contain some five thousand items from the seemingly inexhaustible Mesa Verde deposits. Other visitors that summer were Talbot and Frederick Hyde. They watched the Wetherills at work and the following summer toured their exhibit in Chicago, where Richard was the interpreter.

Out of this second meeting between the Hydes and Richard came an alliance that was to dictate the future of the oldest Wetherill son. The Hydes agreed to fund his proposed explorations in Grand Gulch. Undoubtedly, upon seeing the McLoyd-Graham materials and hearing John's tales of the distant utopia, Richard had to go there. His motivation was not just to get the goods. He made it clear in correspondence that he disapproved of his rivals' lack of documentation. The shadow of Nordenskiold loomed large. The Hydes agreed to buy all artifacts recovered but proposed to donate them to the American Museum of Natural History in New York, of which they were patrons. At the time and for years thereafter, such patronage was the financial and collecting underpinning of institutions of learning.[74] The financial arrangement was important to Richard, but his basic purpose was to ascertain whether or not there might have been a cultural phase in the region that preceded that of the Cliff Dwellers. Outside financial help might make that possible.

Exactly five years after the first sighting of Cliff Palace, the Wetherills were on the move into new territory. In December 1893, Richard, brothers Al and John, and five helpers loaded grub, gear, medicines, Dutch ovens, a coffeepot, and other necessities onto pack animals, saddled up, and headed for Bluff City.

To begin their investigations, the Hyde Exploring Expedition turned up Cottonwood Wash, a broad sandy arroyo along the eastern skirts of Cedar Mesa.[75] As the men progressed, Wetherill successively numbered the sites visited. Just a week into a planned months-long trek, he came to his Cave 7 in a tributary with the unusual name of Whiskers Draw. It was a wide, fifty-foot-deep recess at the base of a cliff just above an alluvial bench. At one end there sat a two-room masonry building. It already had been rummaged through, probably by the McLoyd group. The rest of the floor of the opening was a deep drift of barren earth and rocks. Richard must have immediately seen the similarity to the Step House setting. He put his diggers to work shoveling in the empty zone that had been ignored earlier. They hit pay dirt at three to six feet below the surface. Burial after burial lay in cists in the ground. The only goods with them were coverings, basketry, stone knives, and spear points. The fact that the remains were so far below the level of the surface building and its refuse convinced Richard that he had verified a cultural manifestation older than that of the dwelling. Surely Nordenskiold had pointed out to him the principle of geological stratigraphy wherein older strata underlay more recent deposition. He astutely applied that concept to the archaeological situation.

With obvious excitement, Wetherill wrote to the Hydes of his discovery.

> Our success has surpassed all expectations. . . . In the cave we are now working we have taken 28 skeletons and two more in sight and curious to tell and a thing that will surprise the archaeologists of the country is the fact of our finding them at a depth of 5 and 6 feet in a cave in which there are cliff dwellings and we find the bodies under the ruins, three feet below any cliff dweller sign. They are a different race from anything I have ever seen. They had feather cloth and baskets, no pottery.[76]

The letter to Hyde was followed several days later by a similar note to friend Gus. "We are making discoveries having found a people still older than the Cliff Dweller who occupied the same cave."[77]

The idea of a different "race" was due to lack of skull deformation on these remains. Another curious feature was that, according to John Wetherill, the mouths of most had been stuffed with beads.[78]

Talbot Hyde suggested calling these presumed earlier folks the Basket Makers. As unsuitable a designation as that was since many of the earth's peoples make baskets, the name stuck. Later it was written as one word.

Eager to share enthusiasm about these finds, three months later Richard shipped an assortment of Basketmaker skulls to Nordenskiold, thereby ignoring feeble protests against exhuming human remains or dispatching them out of the country. "I will be able to send you 12 or 13 skulls of the new race. I went back over the ground on purpose to get them. . . . I want you to have them, they will be the only ones outside of this collection."[79]

Richard must not have known that earlier his competitors had offered similar remains for sale. His was not the only collection. To underscore their admiration for and perhaps their intellectual indebtedness to the young Swede, Al and John took photographs and made drawings to accompany notes prepared by Richard for Nordenskiold on the burials and their associated goods. With this correspondence and package of skulls, the venerable

Basketmakers of the Mesa Verde Province were introduced to Europe. Nobody paid them heed.

Spurred on by the Cave 7 find, the Hyde Exploring Expedition spent another three months in the chasms cutting through Cedar Mesa, principally that of Grand Gulch. The men recovered large assortments of Cliff Dweller specimens, but they were particularly anxious to find objects associated with their newly identified horizon.

Richard Wetherill returned to Grand Gulch in the winter of 1897–1898 with a new wife and eleven workers. This time his sponsor was George Bowles, a wealthy Harvard student accompanied by his tutor C. E. Whitmore. For a month they excavated in a dozen sites. Precipitous trails and sheer exhaustion that caused the loss of nine pack animals, lack of browse for the remainder, and severe winter weather made work extremely unpleasant. Another lot of goods was acquired, but no significant new information was gained.

Richard Wetherill died without having the satisfaction of knowing that his determinations of the sequence of cultural phases would ultimately be praised by the emerging archaeological profession as a critical step forward in interpreting the region's human past. Prior to this time, it was generally believed that American prehistory lacked sufficient time depth for stratigraphic observations to be meaningful. Wetherill's observations of the differences in material culture between the two stages of development, such as the Basketmakers' use of the atlatl to the exclusion of the bow and arrow, their apparent ignorance of pottery-making technology, and their finely crafted basketry, were accepted as diagnostic attributes of the culture.[80]

Nor did Wetherill know that his Whiskers Draw Basketmakers would be found to predate the Cliff Dwellers by a thousand or more years and that they and the Cliff Dwellers were representatives of a single biological stock. The Basketmakers and the Cliff Dwellers were relatives separated only by time and not by blood. Furthermore, Wetherill did not recognize the pottery-producing early level at Step House as being a transitional stage between the two ends—early and late—of a long continuum.

The Whiskers Draw Basketmakers had a further distinction. Instead of being dehydrated, as was the usual case with humans left in the dry caves, they were skeletonized due to unusually moist conditions. And nearly all ninety-seven of them had been murdered.[81] Skulls were crushed; faces were smashed; jaws were cracked; limbs were broken. Many skeletons contained stone knives or spear points lodged in the bones. The condition of some skulls suggested blows with war clubs. No weapons of this sort were found in Cave 7, but they were recovered elsewhere in the region. Torture is implied. Knife blades meant death by stabbing, perhaps in an execution. Spear points would have been slung from a distance as in a raid. Mention of arrow points is puzzling because until recently, Basketmakers are not thought to have had use of the bow and arrow. Were strangers afoot?

Whatever the grisly event was, and Wetherills interpreted it as warfare, it must have taken place elsewhere. One possible scenario is that survivors of this carnage gathered their dead comrades and buried them in an unoccupied, sheltered place without the usual grave offerings. Two individuals were surrounded with arrangements of spear points and knives as if to suggest status. Otherwise the graves were little enriched with the things of life. As the centuries passed, water- and wind-borne sand and earth covered the surface of the cave to erase indications of former disturbance. Centuries later a Puebloan family unknowingly erected its home over the burial ground of their long-departed ancestors.

Jackson and Holmes were the first to suggest that warfare may have played a role in the choice by the ancestral Pueblos of cliff-hanger house locations and their eventual abandonment. These conclusions were shared by the Wetherills and by Nordenskiold. They encountered human remains in the structures on Mesa Verde that appeared not to have been formally interred and perhaps just left after a skirmish. The possibility of bloody strife was underscored by a farmer known to the Wetherills. While digging for a well in the vicinity of Aztec Springs (now Yucca House), he broke into a deeply buried kiva that had been filled with dumped bodies having crushed skulls. Unfortunately, this kiva, the first noted with many layers of colored plaster that likely had been part of symbolic murals, and its gruesome contents were only reported in a personal letter from Richard Wetherill to Moorehead.[82] The masonry kiva and its nearness to the large Aztec Springs complex suggest a late ancestral Pueblo date.

Thus, Cave 7 in Whiskers Draw produced the first demonstrable evidence obtained through somewhat careful excavation of mass violence. The perpetrators probably were other Basketmakers. Still, with little comparative data to go on, they and their adversaries might have been part of a preceding cultural horizon that some archaeologists now term the Late Archaic and others Basketmaker II. That was a lengthy period when tribes from many diverse backgrounds may have converged upon the Colorado Plateau. At any rate, the undeformed skulls of the victims confirm that they were not typical Cliff Dwellers for whom such artificial change was universal.

The reasons for the assault are unclear. Was it a matter of territoriality, of a drive for foodstuffs, of revenge for some affront, or of sheer blood-thirstiness? Whatever the cause, it was the first substantial hint to a thread of violent behavior by them or others that weaves through the history of the ancestral Pueblos. Wetherill was the first to demonstrate this.

These various expeditions inspired a flurry of popular writings, none of which contributed to scientific knowledge of this prehistory. A few other hardy souls took up shovels and tramped over the Grand Gulch Plateau looking for sources of salable curiosities. A host of more localized looters probed scores of small house sites profusely distributed over the Mancos and Montezuma Valleys. By the end of the nineteenth century, hundreds of mounds of varying ages had been robbed of their scientific integrity.

When settlers moved onto land where there were heaps of stones left from prehistoric structures, they regarded those building blocks as a useful resource for their own needs. The four homesteaders who moved into the northeastern canyons of the Mesa Verde in 1900–1903 were no exception. Two members of the Prater family, Mabyn Morefield, and Ellen Waters, who legally grazed cattle in the canyons now bearing their names and probably did so illegally earlier, helped themselves to these ready-made supplies. Remnants of their cabins bear witness to this practice.[83]

The reason prompting the efforts of some diggers was the acquisition of pots for profit. Hence the term *pothunting* was coined. For others, the attraction to digging was simply the lure of the search. The grubbers did not realize that their pursuits jeopardized the interpretation of the prehistoric record because regional archaeology was still something of the future. They themselves had no direct biological or cultural connection to the antiquities at hand that might have caused them to question the correctness of their activities. In their view, these old things were the castoffs of a vanished, inferior race which were theirs for the taking.

In just a decade, from the day when Wetherill and Mason stood in awe amidst the collapse of Cliff Palace to the end of the nineteenth century, a previously unsuspected substratum of Native American civilization had been exposed and exploited. Attention focused primarily on what would prove to be the climax of a very long occupation. With hundreds of places formerly used by an unknown people noted and thousands of their possessions recovered in such a brief time, it was an astounding episode never to be duplicated in promoting a recognition of the non-European past of North America.

In these remarkable beginnings were the seeds of a new branch of science to be devoted to study of an aboriginal people who had come and gone during an undetermined span of time—perhaps centuries, perhaps more—in a district that many of the men and women of 1900, if asked, would have discounted as an uninhabitable, sterile wasteland.

A few more perceptive individuals on the sidelines began to fear the loss of a precious legacy, one to which the bulk of the nation had no personal ties but to whose preservation it owed a moral responsibility. Their pleas for governmental help in protecting it slowly were being heard by distant legislators. Almost too late the era of freewheeling ransacking of some of America's most unique treasures was about to end. ✳

# The Formative Years

As the twentieth century dawned, men pillaged many of the antiquities of the northern San Juan mesa and canyon country. Women launched a campaign to stop them.

Spearheading the preservation movement was Virginia McClurg, then a resident of Colorado Springs, who took up the cause with the passion of a religious convert.[1]

Pressing the need for protection of what McClurg perceived as a threatened national heritage, she wrote articles describing her visits to the Mesa Verde ruins, thanks in part to the Wetherills whom she then condemned as desecrators. She delivered dozens of lectures across the country, buttonholed officials, sought support from like-minded women such as those in the Colorado Federation of Women's Clubs, and solicited donations. Later she backed a subsidiary organization calling itself the Colorado Cliff Dwellers Association, with chapters in several adjacent states.

McClurg returned to Mesa Verde several times after her escapade in 1886. On one trip in 1901 she was part of a group of fifteen academics, including Jesse Walter Fewkes. He would later be the first to legitimately excavate Mesa Verde ruins.[2] They came down the worn ruts in Mancos Canyon in four wagons accompanied by a chuck wagon and a string of saddle horses. After camping overnight in the canyon, they rode and hiked up to Cliff Palace, where they were impressed with its hushed grandeur.

On another occasion, McClurg saw to it that Vice President Theodore Roosevelt, in Colorado Springs for a civic celebration, was presented with an ancestral Pueblo pottery bowl from her husband's personal collection.[3] For McClurg, this was a bit of subtle lobbying but one which may have furthered Roosevelt's keenness for conservation of cultural, as well as natural, resources.

McClurg was helped in her well-meant endeavors by Lucy Peabody, another Coloradoan, with what it was hoped were influential Washington connections. She had been an assistant in the Bureau of Ethnology at the

Smithsonian Institution and had some familiarity with Indian matters. The earnest women started their relationship as collaborators by proposing to lease the portion of the Mesa Verde housing the largest of the ruins from the Ute tribe and operating it as a private park. All that was needed was the Indians' approval, native rangers to police the park, wagon roads, negotiable trails, and suitable lodgings. When that audacious plan failed because the Utes did not have the authority to enter into such an agreement, the ladies aggressively lobbied state and federal authorities to set aside a preserve, vacillating as to which entity would be the better watchdog. The state of Colorado was not interested, and successive bills put before the U.S. Congress mired in disinterest and then died in committee.

Dismayed but not defeated, the activists sensed that an abyss of public apathy might indeed be an insurmountable obstacle. The two leaders, who together had fought for many years to achieve their goal, slowly sank into an acrimonious squabble over differing solutions to the problem, with McClurg being discredited and Peabody being transformed into the heroine.

Then Edgar Hewett indirectly came to the rescue. From 1898 to 1903 he served as the first president of the New Mexico Normal School in Las Vegas. In that post he enthusiastically embraced the Pueblo people, their past history, and taught the first college course in American archaeology.[4] At the time excavations were underway at Chaco Canyon in the northwestern sector of his adopted territory. Hewett persuaded officials to call a halt to that project because Richard Wetherill, who was overseeing the work, did not have formal training in archaeology.[5] Neither did Hewett. So he resigned his position at the Normal School and went to the University of Geneva in Switzerland to obtain a Ph.D. in anthropology. His dissertation, written in French, dealt with the social organization of ancient peoples of the American desert.[6]

Upon his return to the United States, Hewett became a liaison between the Smithsonian Institution and members of Congress and others in various academic societies then being formed. He wrote several papers on the antiquities of the Southwest, listing sixteen clusters of sites in the Mesa Verde Province, which were published in Smithsonian reports.[7] Hewett stated the urgent need for their protection and offered suggestions as to how the federal government could do this without undue cost. He further recognized the responsibility of the scientific community, small as it was, to inform the public about these places and what they meant to an understanding of the past so that greater appreciation of their value would be forthcoming.

Hewett's advocacy for ruin protection came to the attention of

Representative John Lacey of Iowa, an ardent conservationist. Together he and Hewett drafted legislation that in 1906 became the Antiquities Act.[8]

This bill made it illegal to excavate on public lands nationwide without a permit from the controlling agency. Such permits were to be issued only to representatives of recognized educational or scientific institutions. Penalties were stipulated for violators.

In the Mesa Verde Province, with its abundance of archaeological materials spread over such expansive, craggy, and isolated tracts, custodial controls could never be sufficient to eliminate illicit digging. Nevertheless, the new law, combined with the fact that many sites had already been stripped and the waning interest in ownership of Indian things, did curb further destruction. Certain controversy was avoided by not applying the law to individual exploration of ruins on private property. Obviously, that meant continued abuse of some sites.

The rising sentiment favoring federal protection of places of prehistoric importance led to the establishment of Mesa Verde National Park in 1906 and Chaco Canyon National Monument in 1907. These had been preceded as federal archaeological preserves by Casa Grande, a single structure looming in the desert east of Phoenix, and Goodman Point Pueblo, a sprawling classic ancestral Pueblo community a few miles west of Cortez. The latter's designation in 1889 confirms local knowledge of aboriginal remains prior to the "discovery" of the cliff dwellings and some latent concern for their protection. But it also was just one place. In contrast, hundreds of unique edifices along the scarps and crags of the Mesa Verde and in desolate Chaco Canyon were to remain into perpetuity under the watchful eyes of Uncle Sam. In a roundabout way, the embattled women could take some of the credit.

Hewett suggested that a cliff dwelling that had been spotted on the heels of the documented sighting of Cliff Palace be named Peabody House in honor of Lucy Peabody, who had emerged as the principal proponent for federal control.[9] Probably to calm the political waters riled by the public dispute between the two women, the name later reverted to that the Wetherills used, Square Tower House. This tag referred to a surviving four-story part of a larger structure that had fallen away from a vertical cliff face of Chapin Mesa.

One individual who bridged the eras of collecting for profit and/or fun and of emerging insight into the cultural background of regional antiquities was T. Mitchell Prudden. He was an eminent pathologist engaged in research in the realm of public health at the Rockefeller Institute in New York. He also was an occasional lecturer at Yale University (class of 1872) and Columbia

University. A bachelor with few friends, he was what today would be termed a workaholic, glued to his desk and microscope.

Unglued once in the summer of 1892, he made the pilgrimage to the Alamo Ranch near Mancos and took the Wetherill tour to the newly publicized Mesa Verde ruins. His curiosity was so piqued by what he saw there that he asked Clayton to take him to other prehistoric places in the vicinity. The older Wetherill brothers were busy getting specimens together for the Columbian Exposition.

For several weeks Clayton and Prudden rode over the valleys skirting the Mesa Verde, pausing here and there to prowl around formless heaps of earth and rocks that once had been standing buildings. At night as they lay in their bedrolls gazing up at the stars overhead, the two men pondered the mysteries of life that once had resounded through these homes of a long lost people. At the end of the tour Prudden was invigorated by unaccustomed physical activity, intellectually stimulated by the evidence all around of a past which until his own time had been erased from memory, and in the companionship of a young man of the frontier. He was so pleased with the experience that he returned to do it again almost annually for twenty more summers.

The prehistoric sites that Prudden and Clayton visited were on level ground and generally were overgrown with sage, scrub, and clumps of yucca. Most were so inconspicuous that an inattentive traveler would have passed them by unnoticed. Only rarely were there sections of walls visible above the drifts of crudely shaped sandstone blocks and adobe clods that had been part of contiguous, cellular rooms that could be traced, as could the shallow depressions out front which Prudden assumed must have been subterranean kivas. Local farmers called them "reservoirs" because of water standing in their bottoms after rains. Still further removed was a midden of household sweepings, broken stone implements, grinding stones worn through, and a paving of potsherds. Almost all such middens had been potholed by pothunters because that was where the dead frequently were placed with offerings.

For many seasons Prudden and Clayton confined their efforts to a far-reaching reconnaissance over most of the northern San Juan district. They purposefully sought out small house sites clustered along heads of drainages where there often were springs or others on open mesa tops. Near some of these ruins were aboriginal reservoirs still being used by cattlemen. In focusing on one aspect of the subject, Prudden was foreshadowing a future problem-solving orientation in regional research. Probably the two men explored more of such ruins than anyone before or since. Prudden estimated that they saw four hundred of them and over one thousand associated kivas. It was obvious to them that the cliff dwellings with which their experience in prehistory began had a very limited role in the "big picture" of the ancient pageant.

Even though he referred to himself as "a poacher on archaeological preserves,"[10] Prudden mapped the area, located site groupings on it, noted their characteristics, studied the total environment, took photographs, and made models. These data were presented over the years in a popular magazine article, three technical papers submitted to anthropological journals, and a book for the general public.[11]

Prudden quickly realized that there was an amazing standardization of the small house sites. All had three components in uniform orientation. One was a bank of rooms in single or double rows along the north side of occupation. These were rather tiny, one-story rooms that Prudden liked to describe using a medical term as "congeries." Occasional wings of rooms were added at either end of the row. To the south of the roomblock was an underground kiva that frequently had a tunnel from its encircling bench into the floor of a surface room. The walls of the kiva were lined with masonry of higher quality than that of the rooms. The trash midden was placed to the southeast of the living space.

The use of one wall to serve two rooms obviously conserved resources and labor, but the close, communal living thus afforded and the standardized arrangement of site after site suggested to Prudden some kind of overriding social or religious organization that persisted over an unknown but presumably lengthy period of time. He called these small house sites *units*, with villages being made up of several units, each with its own three components. The unit concept remains the basis by which modern archaeologists define this type of settlement.

Prudden's years of concern with unimposing sites having scant attraction for any but the seekers of curiosities were devoted solely to the pursuit of knowledge and his personal satisfaction in it. He sought no institutional backing or funding but did share his observations in print. In a modest way, he helped lay the foundation for recognition of one phase of the past of the Mesa Verde Province. This now would be termed Pueblo II–Early Pueblo III. Prudden's systematic surface recording foreshadowed future survey archaeology.

In the aftermath of the antiquities legislation, Hewett showed himself to be part romantic scientist and part shrewd politician. His stature in Washington was so enhanced that he had no trouble getting permits for favorite schemes. He could carry them out with funds from the

Archaeological Institute of America, whose board in 1907 made him the first director of the new School of American Archaeology (later the School of American Research) to be headquartered in Santa Fe, New Mexico. Most often he relied on the help of others because he felt compelled to rush off to promote something else. The summer of 1907 was an example.

Hewett recruited three Harvard undergraduates to conduct an archaeological survey of what were scores of ruins in a parched, broken land spread over thousands of acres of the high desert separating southwestern Colorado and southeastern Utah. And they were to do it in three weeks. Surprising coming from one who prided himself on being an educator, it was a typical Hewett sink-or-swim approach that sometimes worked.

The chosen three were Sylvanus (Vay) Morley, Alfred (Ted) Kidder, and John Gould Fletcher. As Kidder later commented, they were selected because no one else applied. Morley was the only one who had been west. He had spent some of his childhood in Buena Vista, Colorado. But none of the three had any field experience. It is a testimony to their ignorance of its impossibility that they did not bolt once they saw the lay of the land and learned of their ridiculous assignment. As twenty year olds, they were not out for career defining moments. The austere grandeur of the setting, with its miles of unobstructed emptiness framed by a ring of distant mountains, probably was lost on callow youths.

Hewett set the novice crew up in a tent next to a haystack on a ranch in the lower McElmo Canyon. It was a run-down adobe hovel swarming with seven small children, assorted dogs and chickens, and clouds of annoying flies. To compensate, the rancher's wife was a good cook who fed the men well. She could do nothing about the searing heat that radiated off the canyon's bare talus slopes and rimrock.

Morley was the designated leader because he had obtained an engineering degree before transferring to Harvard and could read a compass.[12] Characteristically, he tackled the task with gusto, instructing his helpers to take as complete notes, measurements, and photographs, without excavation, as was possible in the time allotted. He would keep the notes, Kidder would measure, and Fletcher would hold the end of the cloth tape that Hewett provided. Kidder's reminiscences express the youthful joy of discovery as the three galloped their skittish horses down canyon and scrambled up the heights encountering, as they went, one derelict ruin after another. Some were in a totally dilapidated state of jumbled rocks, tumbleweeds, and an occasional rattlesnake or jackrabbit. Others were amazingly well-preserved with thirty-foot-high walls braced against the wind and beams grayed with age, warped but still in place. They found roomblocks teetering precariously on mesa edges overlooking sheer drop-offs. Others straddled isolated boulders defying gravity and entrance. Some small rooms huddled along cramped ledges. Circular or square towers stood as silent sentinels on tablelands that now are part of Hovenweep National Monument.

Jackson and Holmes had commented on some of these places three decades earlier, but the report of the 1907 survey, not published until ten years later, not only added information about sites in the Yellow Jacket and McElmo drainages, but displayed respectable skills by untrained observers.[13] Hewett's gamble paid off. Despite its discomforts for city dwellers, it was an exhilarating introductory experience upon which Morley and Kidder would build. Fletcher was a dropout, having learned that he preferred being a poet in the familiar ambience of his beloved Arkansas or the sophisticated social circles in Europe.

Kidder fondly described his lifelong friend Morley as a cheerful bundle of energy who was also a stumblebum.[14] Being very nearsighted, he lurched around like a hobbled horse about to break a leg or fall over a cliff. Short in stature, he fancied a very large, broad-brimmed hat when in the field, which made him look like an overgrown toadstool. But he had a contagious love of life and a gift of gab that endeared him to all. After the survey season and another excavating Cannonball Ruin, a late classic Pueblo site in the same region, Hewett gave Morley the opportunity to get to his favorite topic. From 1909 until 1914 in Yucatan, Mexico, and in Guatemala, he helped excavate and repair Maya ruins. Those endeavors eventually led into a long career of recording and trying to interpret Maya hieroglyphics. For many of his adult years he stumbled through the tropical forests of Central America, witnessing a murder on the trail and discovering the huge Maya site of Uaxactún.[15] At the end of his life, he returned to his home in Santa Fe as director of the Museum of New Mexico, an institution founded in 1909 by the tireless Hewett as a subsidiary to his School of American Archaeology.

As for Kidder, he, too, participated in several more projects in the Mesa Verde Province but expanded his field of inquiry into the Kayenta and northern Rio Grande areas. In the former he helped identify the earliest phases of the ancestral Pueblos, the Basketmakers; in the latter he delineated its later protohistoric expression at the large community of Pecos Pueblo. Very perceptive, articulate, and with a great sense of humor and personal charm, he led the way in ordering what had been a disparate body of information into a social science with structure and goals. During the last half of his productive career, he also went south to work in excavation and finally in administration with the Carnegie Institution of Washington. In that position, on paper at least, he was Morley's boss.

After Hewett left the unenlightened three in McElmo Canyon, he went to Bluff City and on to Butler Wash farther west to meet with Byron Cummings. With the help of two engineering students, Cummings had just completed a topographical map of a portion of upper White Canyon northwest of Cedar Mesa. His party was an odd assortment. Besides the surveyors, there was a minister, a newspaper reporter, and a pair of students in a new course in anthropology. One of the latter was Cummings's nephew Neil Judd. After finishing his schooling several years later, Judd worked for the U.S. National Museum, under the supervision of William Holmes, and contributed to important projects in areas south of the San Juan. A notable one was in Chaco Canyon.

Cummings was a professor of classical history at the University of Utah. He was inspired to explore southeastern parts of his territory by visitors who told him of its wondrous natural beauty and the presence of Indian ruins. On this, his first of a number of exploratory trips through the wilderness, he brought his scraggly band by train from Salt Lake City to a jumping-off spot out in the middle of nowhere called Thompson's Spring. There they were met by a rancher who loaded them and their baggage onto a wagon, in between bales of hay for his horses and kegs of water, and took off. For six days their route took them mile after dreary mile over a grassless, waterless plain that shimmered with heat waves. They crossed the Grand River, later renamed the Colorado River, on a cable ferry. Then they bounced through the tiny Mormon settlements of Moab and Monticello, eventually to descend into the green oasis that Bluff City had become.

Judd's reason for being along was to locate rumored ruins near three natural, high, stone bridges known to be in the upper extension of White Canyon and Armstrong Canyon. The bridges, now called Owachomo, Kachina, and Sipapu, had been seen in the early 1880s by prospectors placering for gold on the banks of the Colorado River into which White Canyon debouches. Judd and his partner were successful in this effort.[16] Cummings imprecisely placed the locations of a half-dozen sites on his now lost map. It is to be regretted that at the time no detailed report was written by a knowledgeable observer because some of the structures at the base of the bridges or nearby gave the impression that their residents had departed yesterday and would be back tomorrow. Their roofs and entrance ladders were intact, and things used in domestic life were untidily scattered about. Other sites already had been vandalized. In 1907 the young students were rank green-horns in archaeology who had never been face to face with a ruin, and for all his years in the field, Cummings suffered from acute writer's block and left few accounts of his labors or impressions gleaned from them.[17]

It is not known now whether it was the minister's prayers, the journalist's accounts, or Cummings's map, but in 1908 Natural Bridges National Monument was included in a rash of Theodore Roosevelt's monument creations. That made it the third archaeological zone in the Mesa Verde Province to come under federal protection, although in this case the primary reason for the designation were the impressive bridges created by howling winds, plunging waters, and the abrasion of sand.

Meanwhile, back at Mesa Verde there was a problem. The boundary survey and the bill sponsored by Congressman Herschel M. Hogg of Colorado and Senator Thomas Patterson, which President Roosevelt used as a basis for his proclamation, was found to be faulty. It did not encompass several of the most important cliff dwellings, including Cliff Palace. The Brooks-Leupp amendment was hastily added to the legislation, undoubtedly with some embarrassment, to put all ruins within a five-mile radius of the proposed boundaries under federal jurisdiction.[18] The secretary of the interior then asked Hewett to initiate a more comprehensive archaeological survey, including high-quality photographs, of all notable sites that should be brought into the park. Obviously, with hindsight, this should have been done prior to the initial legislation. After years of pros and cons over the park's establishment, some officials were too hasty in bringing an end to the matter.

It was a ticklish situation because, from the beginning of consideration of a possible preserve, the Utes had been reluctant to give up any of their reservation even though they had been assured that they would be granted other lands in exchange. Aside from distrust of the government, their hunting and gathering subsistence base was threatened. To arbitrarily add more of the mesa to the park would cause further resentment.

As a reflection of the lack of qualified people to carry out such critically important work as was requested, Hewett turned to Kidder, Morley, and another young fellow Jesse Nusbaum.[19] In the few weeks previously, Kidder and Morley had acquired meager site mapping abilities; Nusbaum had no field experience but enjoyed photography as a hobby. All had been caught in Hewett's web by life's little quirks—Kidder and Morley in answering an ad in the *Harvard Crimson* and Nusbaum through a chance encounter.

As background, it should be noted that Jesse Nusbaum's parents had followed Horace Greeley's advice and gone west to settle in a town bearing his name.[20] Jesse's father was a brick maker and mason and built some of the first sturdy buildings for the colony and passed his skills on to his son. Jesse's first job away from home was as a manual arts instructor at the New Mexico Normal School. Earlier he had met Hewett when he was head of the training department at the Colorado Normal School in Greeley and learned there was a subject such as archaeology. Those two things were to change his life.

One requirement for the Mesa Verde job was that Nusbaum furnish a five by seven camera with regular, wide-angle, and telephoto lenses and carry a pair of binoculars to better observe the cliff dwellings from afar. This equipment cost him about four times the fifty-dollars-and-keep pay he was to receive, but in retrospect, he realized that the work might set the stage for much of his future.[21]

During parts of the summers of 1907 and 1908, as did all early workers at the park, the men set up camp near Spruce Tree House because of a nearby spring. Daily they put cans of sardines and boxes of crackers in knapsacks, filled their canvas-covered canteens, pocketed Kidder's cheap compass, and slung the photographic impedimenta over their shoulders. They had the advantage of Wetherill trails as they climbed over Chapin and Wetherill Mesas. It was in their favor also that they did not recognize their shortcomings as they went about their business. In the end Hewett was satisfied with the results.

A report by the newly appointed superintendent of the park, Hans Randolph, referred to a group of Hewett's students spending time there in 1908.[22] Probably the students were Kidder and Nusbaum.

By 1911 the Indians and the government finally came to an exchange agreement. And then it was realized that Balcony House still was omitted from the final survey. So back to the transits. Seven years after the first designation, in 1913 the troublesome affair was settled at last. The park expanded to over 50,000 acres. The Weeminuche band of Utes gained almost twice the amount of land that they relinquished. It was at the foot of Ute Mountain to the west of the Mesa Verde. From then on they were to be known as the Ute Mountain Utes.

Two expeditions occurred in the western part of the Mesa Verde Province in the summer of 1908. One was at Cannonball Pueblo. This is a large, compact, split-level set of rooms, kivas, and towers on two sides of a canyon head between Yellow Jacket and McElmo drainages. With funding from the Archaeological Institute of America and the help of a crew of five Harvard shovel-hands, Morley cleared a portion of the site on the south side of the canyon. He promptly reported upon it. The work represented a limited study of a masonry complex of thirty rooms and seven kivas dating from the final years of ancestral Pueblo occupation of this region. Understandably, the site report lacks the chronological and descriptive refinements that could only come through future research. The comparatively low yield of specimens, typical for sites in the open, emphasizes the richness of the protected Mesa Verde alcoves.

With his new institutional and supervisory status, Hewett was on the way to becoming the architect of archaeological endeavors in the northern Southwest for the ensuing four decades. Consequently, in July 1908 he arrived at a site on Alkali Ridge in southeastern Utah that Cummings was preparing to dig. He had his two new protégés—Kidder and Nusbaum—in tow. In his customary self-assertive manner (which unknown to him earned him the nickname of El Toro), he pre-empted Cummings's authority. He put Kidder in charge, Judd as his assistant, and Nusbaum as project photographer. Cummings meekly became cook and camp tender.

It really did not matter who was directing the work because none of them had ever put a shovel or trowel into the hard dirt of a ruin. Nor were there yet any guidelines about how to proceed. Still, with the aid of a few drifters, including two young Harvard students out West on vacation, it was full steam ahead.[23]

The site was a wide mound with no standing walls. In five weeks the rookie crew members cleared a sample of thirteen rooms and three kivas. These remains proved comparable to those being worked that summer by Morley at Cannonball Pueblo. That is, they were classic ancestral Puebloan in age, although nobody had a clue as to what that was. Kidder was left to write a report a year later, while Cummings, accompanied by Judd, went off to locate the legendary Rainbow Bridge.

While boundary negotiations were going on at Mesa Verde, efforts commenced to get the cliff dwellings cleared of rubble and repaired. For the first time the federal government was involved with archaeological matters. Beginning in 1907 and continuing into the 1920s, Jesse Walter Fewkes was in charge of this endeavor.[24]

Like his contemporaries Hewett (educator) and Prudden (physician), Fewkes came to archaeology from another discipline. He enjoyed a distinguished career in marine zoology culminating in nine years as an assistant in the Museum of Comparative Zoology at Harvard, where he earned a Ph.D. in 1877. With all that expertise at the ready, he then experienced an uncommon life-altering episode that caused him to totally change course. During a train ride on the Atlantic and Pacific Railroad (today's Santa Fe), he had his first glimpse of colorful Pueblo Indians selling their wares on station platforms along the route in New Mexico and Arizona. He was so captivated that he felt compelled to learn more about them.[25]

Fewkes's opportunity came shortly when Mary Hemenway, who was financing a long-term study at Zuni Pueblo in New Mexico, asked him to replace Frank Cushing as project director. Cushing was then in poor health. Fewkes vigorously reveled in the subject that he found far more fascinating than the lower invertebrates in his Cambridge laboratory. He particularly favored Zuni music and ceremonialism.

Later, Fewkes moved to the Hopi villages in northeastern Arizona. Soon he was absorbed in their seasonal cycle of rites. For his many writings about them, the sovereign of Spain gave him an award at the 1892 Columbian Fair in Madrid, where Nordenskiold also was honored. Little did these two men realize that their paths would one day cross in Mesa Verde studies.

During this period, Fewkes carried out his first excavations in the abandoned settlement of Sityatki at the foot of First Mesa, believing that the past revealed there could be explained by the present culture of his Hopi friends. This point of view would direct his future thinking about the ancestral Pueblos of Mesa Verde.

By 1895 as a result of his field research, Fewkes was recognized as a credible ethnologist and was hired by the Bureau of American Ethnology at the Smithsonian Institution. That position eventually took him to Mesa Verde but to engage in less familiar archaeological rather than anthropological studies.

At the park Fewkes hired a small crew of men from Mancos to do the heavy work and put them in a tent camp on Chapin Mesa overlooking Spruce Tree House. Not only was there an accessible spring but this structure was of moderate size and in a better state of preservation than most of the others. It was a good place to begin. Instead of climbing down a tall evergreen in front of the edifice, as Mason had done when he first saw the ruin, the men hacked a crude trail down to it. They carried down a few hand tools and began the laborious assignment of removing centuries of waste.[26]

Clearing defined the house plan of 114 rooms, eight kivas, a balcony, and some storage cells. On a ledge above the house, which could only have been reached by means of a ladder on the roof below, were fourteen tiny closets formed by stone slabs stacked up horizontally without mortar. Never having been disturbed by natural or human agents, the stones were just as they had been placed many centuries before. In the main complex, unstable elements were relaid in cement. Some walls appeared to have been knocked apart in the recent past, a disturbance for which Fewkes blamed the Wetherills. Few artifacts were recovered, another annoyance the crew attributed to previous plunderers. With the emphasis on getting the dwelling ready for visitors, precise record keeping of what was found and where, and what was done and why, was not a priority with Fewkes.

In the following season of 1908 another crew directed by Fewkes treated Cliff Palace in the same way. For that job, camp was made on the mesa above the site. Water for human use and for mixing mortar had to be hauled daily by mules from the Spruce Tree spring. The seep at the rear of the Cliff Palace alcove was inadequate for these purposes. The work was more demanding because of the size of the structure and great piles of debris. Fewkes counted 217 rooms and twenty-three kivas, making Cliff Palace what was then believed to be the largest of all American cliff dwellings.[27] There was further evidence that some damage was recent. Repairs were made where necessary, in the course of which modern stabilizers now believe some modifications to the original plan were made.

In the next few years examinations of other sites were conducted under Fewkes's direction.[28] Among them were Oak Tree House and Fire Temple in a short canyon that now bears Fewkes's name and the Cedar Tree tower and kiva unit on the mesa top. A surface pithouse was partially exposed by student Ralph Linton which would have had considerable importance in the reconstruction of Mesa Verde prehistory had the results been published. Unfortunately, that did not happen. Fewkes had an ugly shed roof put up over the site that some years later collapsed under a heavy load of snow.

Actual excavation, rather than merely cleaning up a standing room and kiva block, was undertaken at Far View Pueblo, Pipe Shrine Pueblo, and Sun Temple. All these surface sites were covered over with ages of blown dirt and house wreckage and posed entirely different problems in their examination than did sheltered cliff openings. Teams of mules pulling scrapers helped with initial removal of the spoil dirt to some out-of-sight dump. The Mancos farmers were adept at this. Again, Fewkes kept few hand-scribbled notes of sufficient detail to be useful to later researchers[29]

Far View Pueblo is the largest surface complex in the park and dominated a community of some fifty smaller dwellings within half a square mile on the northern extension of Chapin Mesa. It is composed of forty ground-level rooms, an unknown number of second-story chambers, and five kivas in a tight square arrangement made possible by the unobstructed mesa top. Fewkes was unaware of certain features that present scholars regard as reflective of influence from Chacoan ancestral Pueblos. Nearby Pipe Shrine

Pueblo, so named for a cache of a dozen clay pipes found in a kiva pit, is a smaller, contemporaneous one-story building. Native Americans confirm that cloud blowing with such pipes likely was a part of aboriginal ritualism that continues today in varied versions.

Sun Temple proved to be a structure whose enclosed design incorporated the foundations of a pair of probable towers. Fewkes felt that the structure was never completed because there was no sign that various components had been erected to a height sufficient to support roofing. The building may have been intended to be a ceremonial center for the large population in the two canyons on either side of it. Perhaps it was a community discouraged and disgruntled that felt it was time to go and that the gods who were to be appealed to there did not listen.

Trained in the Agassiz intellectual background, Fewkes was rooted in scientific concepts of the nineteenth century. He based his considerations of archaeological features largely on aspects of Hopi culture that he had witnessed during his tenure there decades before. This untenable bias, his lack of documentation for work accomplished, and his failure to adjust to refinements and techniques in field methods and interpretations that had become commonplace in Southwestern archaeology now makes his years of involvement with Mesa Verde antiquities almost irrelevant.[30] However, Fewkes is given credit for opening up the attractions and bringing them to public attention through his evening campfire talks at the park and his voluminous though brief writings, more than two dozen of which specifically deal with Mesa Verde prehistory. These papers, turned out almost annually with mechanical regularity, added to his lengthy bibliography but not to scientific knowledge.

In 1910 Hewett brought Nusbaum back to Mesa Verde, not surprisingly for a job at which he had no previous experience. This was to repair Balcony House, which was sliding off the cliff. The task was delicate, costly, and time consuming. Fewkes wisely felt that he could not undertake it. McClurg, as regent general of the Colorado Cliff Dwellers Association, arranged for financial aid and contracted with Hewett, as director of the School of American Archaeology, to be responsible for the work. Hewett knew of Nusbaum's manual arts skills and his recent help in the restoration of the Palace of the Governors in Santa Fe and assumed that he could cope, somehow.[31] No other person had yet tackled ruin repair on this scale.

Balcony House was built in an opening on a ledge midway through the thick sandstone stratum capping the Mesa Verde, instead of at the top of the long slide of talus below as was the most common case. There was a sheer, vertical cliff face dropping off at the very outer edge of the house. Ancient masons laid up a massive retaining wall to buttress the house front. Some of the masonry within the building components was excellent; some was mediocre with the typical weaknesses of lack of bonding of corners and heavy roofing over thin walls. In places the builders erected units on slanting bedrock with poor footing. Two springs at the rear of the alcove seeped water that flowed under walls. After abandonment, an enormous tonnage of the alcove roof crashed down, taking portions of walls to the slopes and canyon floor below and leaving others tottering at the brink or severely cracked. The retaining wall was pried loose. Drifts of spalls and dirt filled kiva depressions, banked lower surfaces, and put pressure on unstable construction. Two-story walls bulged out of line. Even the most experienced engineer would have paled at the challenge this house presented.

But with the confidence and naiveté of a twenty-three year old, Nusbaum plunged ahead, with the help of his construction-wise father and a stone mason from Greeley. He hired two laborers from Cortez, a cook, and a packer. Occasionally, several men digging a well at the park joined the group. They made camp in a shack that Fewkes had put above Cliff Palace and in some tents. These were home and office for the eight-week duration of the project. Nusbaum made arrangements with the operator of the livery stable in Mancos to periodically carry up supplies in his wagon.

The packer's job was to cart water from the Spruce Tree spring three miles away in barrels lashed on the sides of his horses. In order to use this water to mix mortar, the crew slung a hose over the cliff into another barrel in a kiva depression and siphoned down the necessary liquid. For themselves, they secured an iron pipe in the rocks onto which they tied a knotted rope down which they slid to work each day.[32]

In order to make Balcony House secure, it was necessary to remove large amounts of debris; to swing heavy sledges to break up huge slabs that had fallen from the alcove roof; to push underpinning beneath unstable walls; to take down shaky others and relay them with shaped rocks picked up in the alcove or others pulled up from the ledge and talus below. After much consideration, the Nusbaums decided to use iron angles, tie rods, and turnbuckles in order to fasten parts of the building to the stone walls at the back of the alcove and to cinch loose units more tightly. Coats of mud mortar hid these reinforcements. They did this despite predictable criticism of the employment of non-Indian materials. Ripping away the ravages of time was an arduous, dangerous physical undertaking. One workman had to strap himself with a rope to dangle out in space while repairing the retaining wall. One house wall suddenly came down on another crew member. He was quickly removed from the rubbish, unnerved and still chewing a wad of tobacco.

Aside from labors with which the workers were unfamiliar, Nusbaum had to constantly make critical judgments without the benefit of experience. To his great credit, the measures that his team took have stood the test of ninety years without appreciable further maintenance. In contrast, some of Fewkes's work has had to be redone.

Troubles of a more personal nature marred the endeavor for Nusbaum: money ran out. Communications with his superior were difficult due to the isolation of his camp and Hewett's frenetic schedule. Most of the men got sick. A usual golden autumn turned white with deep banks of snow making it impossible for the livery man to replenish supplies. Food was exhausted. The northeast-facing alcove was an icebox. Water in the mortar hose froze. At camp, the crew huddled under blankets around a campfire and wondered if it all was worth their suffering. And, as often happened, Hewett did not arrive on time to inspect the finished product. When he did appear, Nusbaum had to ignite small fires in the structure to facilitate the matter. The next day he and the mason, who drew the first map of the site, threw the remaining equipment down the cliff. It landed in the trees and ancient midden below as another layer of Mesa Verde history. Then they walked for miles through knee-deep snow off the tableland and down to Cortez. Fortunately, Nusbaum carried out photographs and notes of the operation. He was well indoctrinated in the trials of archaeological fieldwork as he wrote, "I never got in quite so bad in all my life before."[33]

The pothunting frenzy of the late nineteenth and early twentieth centuries extended beyond the heartlands of the Mesa Verde Province in Colorado and Utah to its southern sectors along the San Juan, lower Animas, and La Plata Valleys in New Mexico. Scott Morris was one individual there who was inspired to hunt pots for sale. During summers he worked as a freighter in the La Plata Mountains to the north, but periodically in winters he passed his time probing ruins around the southern frontier village of Farmington. He found some pottery vessels, bought others from local collectors, and traded horse gear for still others until he had amassed an assortment of 160 examples of the Mesa Verde styles. In 1891 he sold this collection to Virginia McClurg's husband.[34] He felt especially gratified in beating out McLoyd and Graham, who at the same time were offering their first Grand Gulch collection for sale.[35]

Scott's son Earl, born the year Mesa Verde looting began, was preordained to follow in his daddy's footsteps. His earliest recollection was his father handing him a pickax cut down to his size and telling him to go dig in the yard of the cabin where the family lived. To everyone's surprise, Earl, then about three years old, stirred up the bowl of a black-on-white ladle.[36] That was just the beginning of forty years of reclaiming pots and other artifacts from the sunbaked earth of the Colorado Plateau.

During Earl's boyhood, father and son often climbed into a freight wagon and headed out across country looking for promising spots in which to dig. Some sites were sterile; some were productive. Even so, the excitement of exploration and the thrill of discovery never faded for either.

After his father was killed in an argument with an associate, Earl often went off by himself to continue this familiar routine. Farmers gave him permission to scout their lands, no doubt thinking it a harmless but odd pastime for a young fellow. Slowly, without realizing it, Earl acquired an intuitive sense about where and how to put his shovel into the ground for the greatest returns and an enduring fascination with the ceramic arts of the "Old People," as he called them. Men of his father's generation knew firsthand of many sites, but by the time Earl graduated from Farmington High School, he probably had already visited them and many others and had acquired a personal collection of more than two hundred earthenware vessels.[37] Morris once justified this activity, which he continued throughout his field career, in this way, "Since everyone else who cared to was pothunting along the La Plata, my conscience did not disturb me for unearthing what I might before someone else got to it."[38]

Just as Fewkes was taking on the Mesa Verde cliff dwellings, Morris went off to college. He enrolled at the University of Colorado in Boulder, majoring in psychology because, unlike Harvard, no curriculum in anthropology was offered. He found a student job more to his liking at the university museum and soon became a favorite of Director Junius Henderson. Through this contact Morris was exposed to orderly scientific procedures and points of view. While still an undergraduate, on a train ride back home he heard Hewett being paged. He followed the porter and introduced himself to this now well-known figure. That was step two in becoming a professional archaeologist because two years later Hewett recommended that the university fund Morris's first legitimate fieldwork. The School of American Archaeology, with Hewett in charge, obtained an excavation permit from the Department of the Interior.

In the spring of 1913 Morris, accompanied by three local men having long acquaintance with ancient sites in the region, rode along the La Plata River on the rough wagon road to Durango. The La Plata River heads in the mountain mass that bounds the northern horizon and flows for fifty miles southward, losing elevation as it goes, to empty into the San Juan River at Farmington. It is next to the last permanent river of a dozen primary northern tributaries to the San Juan as one moves from the Piedra River on the east periphery of the Mesa Verde Province to Grand Gulch on the west. At Red Mesa, a tiny Mormon settlement near the point where the river descends into a lower valley, the party turned westward to traverse a broad, rolling, red upland that breaks down in the west into deep, V-shaped, rock-clogged gorges opening into the east side of the Mancos drainage.

One of those declivities is Johnson Canyon. In the 1880s the Wetherills had a line camp near its mouth, and some of their first explorations were in small cliff structures in the vicinity and in the short northern tributary of Lion Canyon. During his stay, they took Nordenskiold to see them. The Wetherills left their names or initials on some walls. Nordenskiold inscribed a site number on one but did not include these places in his book. Since no excavations were carried out there, perhaps he honestly felt that he had not violated his agreement with the Indian agent.

The Morris party made camp at Mancos Springs near the head of the Johnson box canyon. In a period of cyclical drought common in the Four Corners, this was the only source of potable water for themselves and their animals. Making their way down canyon from there, the men came upon several small, deteriorated structures in Spring Canyon and numerous storage constructions in openings along shelflike projections of the canyon face.

Upon rounding the junction of Johnson and Lion Canyons, the explorers spied a little building dramatically placed high in a gash of the upper sandstone stratum, below which spewed a six-hundred-foot-high talus paved with scree and dwarf pinyons. With some difficulty, the men made their way up the incline to the base of the vertical wall of stone in which the house rested. It seemed tantalizingly out of reach. That made Morris all the more determined to get to it. This was his first encounter with a particularly exciting, supposedly inaccessible cliff dwelling, and he was going to make the most of it. By successively lashing four long poles together, he clutched and tugged himself up the sixty-foot face of the rock and into the house. Surely he was the first white person to do so and must have relished the moment. He christened the place Eagle Nest because of its lofty serenity with an extravagant vista out over tiers of wind-scoured escarpments and plateaus toward the distant San

Juan Basin in the haze to the south. His companions hunched down at the foot of the wobbly poles and could not be coaxed to attempt entrance into the ancient home until the next day.[39]

Eagle Nest is made up of eleven rooms and one kiva. Three of the chambers are stacked to two stories. When first observed, one was particularly well preserved with brown wall plaster clinging to the masonry backing and a ceiling of pine beams, smaller cross stringers, and a topping of indurated mud in place. Articles of daily use were tossed about, such as any departing tenant's apartment might be left today. Workers gathered up sandals with bindings rent and heels worn through, pieces of basketry, lengths of yucca cordage, rush matting, fire tinder, a pine needle hair brush, fragments of feather cloth, bundles of herbs, corn cobs tied together or loose, and sharp-edged fragments of pottery.

The Eagle Nest kiva interested Morris the most. The roof had fallen, with the beams still slumped where they came to rest. Morris carefully removed them in order to take photographs of the kiva, something for which he is criticized now but was not considered unethical at the time. The interior of this chamber was decorated with a red dado enhanced by the three-cluster lanceolate pattern which by that time was known in a number of sites. Leaning against one wall were seven pottery vessels, most of them complete. That made Morris's day.

After this unparalleled beginning to the season's program, the explorers found the three moderately sized cliff dwellings farther into the canyon to be of less interest. In most there were obvious signs of previous visitation. Nevertheless, Morris took photographs, made careful measurements and observations, and gathered a small collection of artifacts that the earlier interlopers had missed. At the conclusion of this tour, he concluded that the remains in these canyons were a part of the culture more extensively present up on the Mesa Verde, on the northwest side of the Mancos River. His later report was the first published description of them.[40]

An official permit for this work had been obtained from the Department of the Interior, but there is no record that the Ute Mountain Utes, whose reservation was being entered, were consulted. It was their archaeological assets that were studied, and in present views, exploited.

The following summer Morris and his stalwarts retraced their path out to the evergreen uplands east of the canyons they had worked earlier. Morris had observed some low mounds lined up on ridge tops there through some of which poked tops of sandstone slabs. It looked suspiciously like human handiwork. There was no evidence of disturbance of the ground other than large badger holes because most of the area was pasture land on the newly renamed Ute Mountain Ute Indian Reservation, where there had been little exploration and no white settlement. Again, the Native Americans seem not to have been consulted about outside activity on their land.

Selecting one large mound in an opening in the thick pinyon-juniper cover, the men began shoveling along a line of these slabs. At their bottoms, they encountered a hard living surface that had been smoothed with a layer of mud. Working across this level, they soon exposed a shallow, rectangular pit rimmed with upright stones. Stubs above this foundation of sorts suggested a wall of small poles wedged into upright position by rocks and glued into place by a mud coat (jacal or wattle and daub). There were no interior features other than a fire hearth. Morris speculated that the dwelling must have had a flat roof of poles covered with brush and earth. No doubt about it, this had been a home unlike any these neophyte archaeologists had ever seen. To confirm this kind of occupation, the party investigated parts of twenty-three similar sites. Morris estimated that one mound covered one hundred of these primitive structures making up a dispersed village. Kivas were absent everywhere.

To the south of each mound there was a trash heap of dark earth and household discards. Often it was more extensive than the living zone. Some had been used for burials. To Morris's surprise, the skulls of about a third of exhumed individuals uniformly showed no evidence of the occipital or lambdoidal flattening that resulted from hard-backed "papoose boards." He had never seen this to be the case in the several hundred skulls he had examined during his boyhood years of pothunting.

The pottery uncovered from graves and elsewhere in the sites also was different from the usual Mesa Verde wares so common in the lower La Plata Valley that Morris knew. Black designs painted over a chalky white ground lacked the bold, balanced patterning. The necks of some gray, utilitarian jars with smoothed bodies were sometimes reinforced by unobliterated coils of clay.

In time the party moved east to the middle La Plata Valley south of Red Mesa. They opened several graves in sites there with a team of horses and a scraper. Human remains were turned up whose skulls were not misshapen. This, again, was something new to Morris. What did it mean? He saw that the pottery also seemed somewhat different even from that found in the Ute Pasture. It generally was rough surfaced and more crudely fashioned in a wide variety of relatively small shapes, some of which Morris had never seen. These included ladles that resembled a gourd sliced longitudinally in half, bulbous bowls, and tiny, closed-mouth jars with a lateral spout. Exteriors of some vessels had been coated after firing with a red pigment that rubbed off. While rarely decorated, the thin-lined patterns were ineptly applied, wavy and imprecisely spaced, and seemed to recall those appearing on basketry. This included a small circle in the interior bottom of bowls that copied the initial coil of baskets made by that technique.

These telltale bits of archaeological evidence convinced Morris that he had encountered a cultural phase that was previously unknown in the Mesa Verde Province. Judging from the apparent primitiveness of architecture and ceramics, he was inclined to think it was earlier than that of the Cliff Dwellers. What he did not realize at the time was that he had happened upon not one new horizon but two, that at Long Hollow on the La Plata being the older.[41]

Exactly twenty-five years had passed since the first public awareness of Cliff Palace and its neighbors. With this Morris find, what were then thought to be four cultural manifestations had been superficially identified. The general feeling among a handful of concerned observers was that the multiroomed, surface houseblocks and towers, such as were surveyed by Kidder and Morley, were produced by the same people as those of their kind who chose to live in the cliffs. The Prudden small, unit-type pueblos were different and might not be related either culturally or temporally. Then there were those Basketmakers of Cedar Mesa, who apparently lacked domestic architecture, pottery-making skills, bow and arrow weaponry, and did not modify the soft bones of their babies' heads. Morris could only wonder how and when his distinctive mesa-top culture fit into the evolving regional prehistory. He wanted to associate it with what he termed "pre-Pueblo" pithouse culture, even though the dwellings in question at Ute Pasture were more surface than subterranean.[42] He obviously felt that his home territory was where the Pueblo progression began as he wrote, " . . . it appears that the region north of the San Juan River is the center from which migration carried the true Pueblo culture to the south, southeast, and perhaps to the west."[43] To have made such discoveries as the Ute Pasture and middle La Plata sites represented and to have his account of them appear in a Smithsonian Institution volume was a noteworthy accomplishment for his first professional try. He remained embarrassed that he had not initially detected the distinction between the Ute Pasture and middle La Plata remains.[44]

Morris's appreciation of pottery caused him to arrange an exchange with the University of Colorado Museum for two vessels illustrated in that report.[45] He displayed them in his home for many years, probably for sentimental rather than aesthetic value. After his death, the small bowl and gourd vessel were returned to the museum as part of the Morris Memorial Collection.[46]

While Morris was busy with his pre-Pueblos, two other research efforts had bearing on Richard Wetherill's Basketmaker claims of 1893. Except for one brief, popular article, Richard Wetherill's material had remained unpublished until George Pepper wrote a descriptive account of some of the artifacts the Hyde brothers gave the American Museum of Natural History. Nothing like the Basketmakers had been discovered in the interim and some scholars were beginning to doubt them. In caves in northern Arizona, Kidder and a colleague, Samuel Guernsey, found and documented a similar cultural horizon. Kidder and Guernsey proved that what was present in Cave 7 in Whiskers Draw and in Grand Gulch was not an aberration or figment of Wetherill's imagination.

Secondly, Nels Nelson, curator at the American Museum, working in sites south of Santa Fe, demonstrated the efficacy of stratigraphic observations such as Wetherill applied in his less professional digging. Nelson got the credit for introducing this important method to Southwestern archaeology because of Wetherill's failure to publish his finds and how he determined their relationship to the Cliff Dwellers.

At the beginning of his long, fruitful career, Morris had the good fortune of getting acquainted with Nelson. He was hired to be the older man's field assistant on a dig in the Rio Grande Valley. There he learned of the new stratigraphic method that became a fundamental part of his own tool kit and would shape his thinking about the pre-Pueblos.[47] By happenstance, the American Museum had asked Nelson to select a classic Pueblo site for excavation that would reflect favorably on a prominent patron. When Morris learned of this, he promptly suggested that Nelson consider the two great mounds at Aztec. He had explored these sites with his father years before and retained a strong desire to delve into them. He offered to guide Nelson there at the end of the digging season.

What Nelson saw was a pair of high mounds surrounded by green fields and a young apple orchard. Thorny chico brush, sage, weeds, and sunflowers eight feet tall covered their surfaces, except for several paths that had been chopped through the tangle to intact rooms in the house wreckage. There, spiky wall fragments above the mantle lured the inquisitive. The prospects of getting to the heart of these forsaken heaps of bygone days probably would have seemed daunting to a less experienced person, but the elder scientist recognized their potential. Nelson recommended that the museum undertake a long-term project in the western Aztec mound, that being the least disturbed, and that Morris be named supervisor of the endeavor.

While awaiting approval of this proposal, in late 1915 Morris returned to dig briefly in the La Plata Valley. His mission was to secure display specimens for the University of Colorado Museum. Such collecting excursions were a common practice of the time to build institutional prestige. The educational value of any such assortments was of less concern. On this occasion a landowner gave Morris permission to work over a site on fertile river bottom lands, provided that he level the mounds when he had finished.[48] Morris obliged with a team of horses and a scraper. Later the meandering river finished the job. The structure investigated was a twenty-room, cobblestone house of the late ancestral Pueblo period. Its refuse produced a satisfactory artifact collection.

The following spring Morris was back at work in the La Plata Valley. This time he went to a gravelly terrace on the west side of the river at the Barker Arroyo where piles of debris had attracted relic hunters for years. He found five more-or-less untouched units of a large concentration of mounds that seemed to have been the result of several prolonged occupations. The largest of these was a compact houseblock of two dozen rooms and two incorporated kivas. The architecture was a mix of cobblestone and sandstone masonry. Although at the time Morris did not uncover evidence for usage during a previous period, his report, benefiting from twenty-three years of later experience, indicates a probable use of the terrace from Basketmaker through classic Pueblo times.[49]

In the late spring of 1916 the American Museum signed a lease with the owner of Aztec West, and Nelson came to help Morris get started. Thus, only recently out of school and twenty-seven years old, Morris became an employee of a prestigious national institution and was set to make his name forever synonymous with the most imposing surface site north of the San Juan River.

Because the Aztec mound was in the midst of a farming settlement, it was not necessary to set up a field camp for workers, who daily rode their horses or walked to work. That was both advantageous and troublesome because family members often came to watch the work. Unintentionally, these visits were sometimes disruptive. However, they led to a community-wide, proprietary feeling toward the ruin that furthered its protection.

The unveiling of the great artificial hummock turned into a one-man affair. Morris directed the work, took notes and photographs, catalogued specimens and packed them for shipment to New York, mended pottery, bought supplies, met the payroll, guided local visitors around the diggings, and, when activities paused during the winters from 1916 through 1920, wrote reports on the findings. The American Museum passed the most sensational of them on to the eastern press, and the Animas Valley newspapers had a field day with their local celebrity.

A regional ruin of this magnitude had not been excavated previously (except for Pueblo Bonito in Chaco Canyon, where the circumstances were entirely different). Consequently, Morris's ingenuity was tested in solving tactical problems. Of first concern was how to dispose of the enormous volume of spoil dirt that engulfed the site. Fields of alfalfa, barley, and corn edged up to the site's perimeters and flourished in the area between the west and east mounds. In an odd way the past was reconstructed: the old inhabitants also once looked out over their own gardens of corn, beans, and squash. The museum agreed to reimburse the landowner for any damage to his crops, but Morris naturally wanted to avoid that.

One idea was to take advantage of the sloping gradient of the ground and a sluice box from an irrigation ditch at a higher elevation to wash the presumably sterile overburden to the Animas River. Fortunately, on second thought, Morris realized the limitations and possible losses of that system. He then turned to four mine cars and their tracks so that horses could pull them to the banks of the Animas River several hundred yards away. The small capacity of the cars made that method inefficient. Next, Morris resorted to flat-bedded, horse-drawn wagons which he rented from his farmhands. Some loads were carted to the riverbanks; others were dumped in mudholes in the road from town. Fill from the outer tier of rooms was just shoveled outside the structure, and other overburden was piled wherever possible.[50]

As work progressed, Morris saw a complexity of rooms terraced back from ground level to three stories in places which formed three sides of an expansive courtyard opening to the south. Kivas were incorporated into the houseblock and generally made to appear subterranean by having space around them filled in. Others were placed beneath the surface of the court. One was small Kiva B at the south edge of the clearing. Its walls were finished with cobblestones rather than sandstone blocks. When examined, the kiva contained two burials in a trash litter on the floor. Morris elected to reroof this structure. Apparently he was uncertain of the beam construction he had dismantled at Eagle Nest. So he made the long, horseback trip to Mesa Verde, where Fewkes allowed him to examine two partially intact roofs in kivas at Peabody House. When the reconstruction was done following these models, the roof on Kiva B was at ground level, with a central hatchway for access.

Actually, Morris's Kiva B probably was an earlier pithouse with gray pottery fragments in its fill. Morris failed to recognize that it may have been comparable in time with the materials he had found at Long Hollow, his pre-Pueblos.

The workers recognized many signs of remodeling of the old house. Openings were sealed, partitions added, dirt floors smoothed over one another like a layer cake. Some chambers housed trash deposits ten feet deep. Lower rooms were clogged with cracked timbers forming the ceilings and floor between stories that had pried out a shower of building stones as they plunged earthward.

In 1917 the crew excavated the especially fine Kiva E in the courtyard near the east wing of the house. It was one of the remodeled units, its upper walls made primarily of sandstone but with lenses of cobbles laid up in abundant amounts of mud mortar. Only the foundation stones of the earlier chamber remained. Having successfully reroofed Kiva B the year before, Morris covered this structure with a similar cribbed-beam roof that prominently stood several feet above the ground level. In the back of his mind Morris thought it might be an interesting exhibit for visitors, who could descend a ladder into its dark interior. Or perhaps the kiva could serve as a meeting room.[51]

Fallen debris helped to seal stockpiled resources from centuries of moisture and a fire that Morris believed ended occupation. Bundles of yucca fiber, bunches of herbs, bushels of corn on the cob and shelled, stacked husks and shredded cedar bark, and piles of pottery clay spoke eloquently of daily schedules that somehow were interrupted.[52]

Other kinds of artifacts resembled those recovered from the cliff dwellings and a few surface rooms that had been cleaned out in the early days of exploration in the Mesa Verde Province. These were such things as sandals, baskets, cradleboards, digging sticks and others with carved knobs, textile fragments, feather cloth, reed matting, bone awls, and stone implements that had survived because of the dryness of the site. It was enough of a haul to satisfy Morris's taste for specimens and to show the distant museum donor that he had made a worthwhile investment. Patronage still was the means by which research was done.

Pottery was abundant. Much of it had been crushed as the building fell into itself. Morris carefully saved the fragments and spent many enjoyable evenings trying to put them back together. The thousands of random potsherds that spread throughout the premises were examined and then discarded. Undoubtedly, many went out in wagonloads of dirt. Today this is to be regretted because some of the site's interpretation is based upon pottery.

Morris was most puzzled by the 186 burials (not counting the many disarticulated bones resulting from animal or other agents).[53] It was his past experience in regional sites that the dead were buried in unconsolidated refuse away from living areas or in pits beneath the dirt floors. He equated the former with Chacoan custom and the latter with Mesa Verdean.[54] That duality was not the case at Aztec West. Bodies simply had been laid out on the floors of unused rooms or in rubbish that accumulated in them. Many of the offerings set beside them were utilitarian and service earthenwares typical of the output of potters adhering to a ceramic vocabulary commonly used throughout the Mesa Verde Province. The crew trenched several middens to the southeast of the house and uncultivated plots nearby in a search for other graves, but the results were negligible. Why this very casual disposal of the departed, and why Mesa Verde-style ceramics in a Great House that Morris had come to regard as representative of the Chaco architectural tradition? Where were the Chacoan dead?

Early in the project Morris speculated that he was dealing with a hybrid culture or, less likely, that of two distinct groups of ancestral Pueblos living together. It was not until work was closing down that the answer to that quandary came when he unearthed two superimposed kivas in a previously untouched portion of the site.[55] The upper kiva was typically that of the northern San Juan district, or the Mesa Verde Province, in its features. The lower one was Chacoan and, furthermore, contained a large assortment of Chaco potsherds and thirty whole vessels, including hollow figurines of a hunchback and a spotted deer, both recalling Chaco workmanship. Suddenly it became obvious to Morris that this edifice had been erected by persons familiar with Chacoan architectural conventions. After they moved away for unknown reasons, a group of others with slightly differing traditions in architecture and ceramics occupied portions of the house. He called them Mesa Verdeans, not because he thought they came from the mesa itself but because they shared stylistic modes common across the Mesa Verde Province. They undertook architectural changes, including crudely fashioning cobblestone quarters at the west side of the houseblock where formerly a small Chaco pueblo had been.[56] Cobbles left from ancient glacial moraines spreading down from the San Juan Mountains paved the terraces above the valley and comprised the usual building material for the local Indians. In contrast, Chaco masons were accustomed to using tabular sandstone plentiful in their home territory and therefore sought out similar resources wherever they moved. The Mesa Verdeans painted one room inside the main structure with their customary red dado and nine three-lanceolate clusters and cut a door from this room to their cobblestone "annex," as Morris called it.

The Mesa Verdeans left pottery offerings with their dead whom, for convenience, they deposited in vacant rooms. Why try to dig with a pointed stick, especially when the ground was frozen, when there was inviting, ready-made, enclosed space?

To jump ahead of the 1920s era, one possible explanation to account for graves within the Aztec West pueblo involved the east mound. Morris did some cursory investigation of that site and concluded that it was Mesa Verdean.[57] That view is now modified. The basic structure is Chacoan in design and construction and partially contemporary with its western neighbor. However, it appears that it may have experienced more Mesa Verdean utilization. Large sections of cobblestone walls are visible above the earthen crust of the mound. A number of tree ring samples date to the A.D. 1200s, or post-Chaco period, suggesting remodeling efforts. One basis for Morris's opinion was a consider-able amount of Mesa Verdean potsherds. No burials have been found in the site's intact rooms. If, in fact, the east mound was the center of Mesa Verdean reoccupation of the complex, the residents may intentionally have chosen to leave their decomposing dead in removed, and less used, Aztec West.

Just when the hypothesized sequence of successive utilizations of Aztec West took place or how much time elapsed between occupations were questions Morris could not answer.

Morris recognized that Aztec West was one of a number of Chaco-affiliated sites that were at some distance from Chaco Canyon itself. It proved to be the largest. He did not address the reasons for this dispersal or why, in this case, Chacoans intruded into a region likely already occupied by others. Because little work had been done in Mesa Verde-related sites to the north, he also did not know they produced very little in the way of trade goods. That meant that many of the articles left with the dead at Aztec, other than the Mesa Verde ceramics, were gleaned from Chaco discards. Such items included abalone and eight other kinds of seashells made into beads, pendants, and bracelets; turquoise beads, effigies, and mosaic pieces from New Mexico; Tularosa pottery made south of the San Juan Basin; red ware from the Little Colorado River area in Arizona; and copper bells and some beads from Mexico.[58]

During the 1919 season, Andrew E. Douglass, astronomer from the University of Arizona, came to Aztec to ask for Morris's help.[59] He was deeply committed to research on the eleven-year cycles of sunspots as they were recorded through time on the annual growth rings of pine and fir trees.

He found that wide rings were added to the trunks and limbs of these kinds of trees in wet years and narrow rings reflected distress in times of drought. By becoming familiar with these signatures, he had formulated a growth calendar from the present back in time several centuries. To push that calendar even further into the past, he proposed to study wood used in construction by the prehistoric tribes on the Colorado Plateau.

Time placement being of the essence to archaeology, the exciting possibilities of temporal placement of the area's ruins was not lost on Morris. He gave Douglass several beam sections recovered from Aztec deposits and others that had been picked up by Nelson at Pueblo Bonito. Together the two men devised a tool by which cores could be removed without damaging beams still in place in the great Aztec structure.

Two months later word came from Douglass that the Pueblo Bonito wood was forty years older than that from Aztec West.[60] Just which forty years would not be known for another decade.

Finally in 1929, eight years after Morris had suspended work at Aztec West, Douglass was able to connect the modern sequence of tree rings to what had been a floating prehistoric chronology. The overlap was in the late A.D. 1200s, the exact period when, as would be learned later, the Mesa Verde Province was forever deserted by the ancestral Pueblos.

Douglass announced that Aztec West had been built between A.D. 1111 and 1121! This was exhilarating but surprising news to Morris. He had thought that the site was much older. And it seemed remarkable that the structure of an estimated three hundred rooms and two dozen kivas had been erected in so short a time by primitive masons without use of metal tools or mechanical devices. This knowledge made him a fervent believer in the new discipline of dendrochronology. In the course of his diversified career, he supplied Douglass and his team of experts with more tree ring specimens covering a greater range of time than any other Southwestern archaeologist.

The formal Aztec project ended with the 1920 season. Subsequent funding allowed Morris to excavate and report upon the Aztec Great Kiva, or super-sanctuary. He had always been aware of its large depression in the southern side of the courtyard but chose to concentrate first on the house. In 1921 he was goaded into action by a bit of professional one-upmanship. His friend Neil Judd was launching an excavation program at Pueblo Bonito, where there were two Great Kivas waiting to be examined. The National Geographic Society richly sponsored Judd's work and provided funds for experts in secondary fields, large teams of Zuni and Navajo laborers, and assorted camp amenities. Morris's project always had been a penny-pinching operation paid for by the generosity of one individual. But Morris felt he would have some self-satisfaction in getting the Aztec Great Kiva dug and reported first so that it would serve as the standard by which other Great Kivas, including at least ten in Chaco, would be judged.[61] With that motivation, he set a small crew to work in the month of February, when the ground was frozen, and in another month had his report done.[62] He need not have rushed because thirty years passed before Judd finished his publication on Pueblo Bonito.

The Aztec Great Kiva was a subterranean structure forty-eight feet in diameter surrounded by fifteen ground level rooms.[63] Access to the lower chamber was by means of narrow ladders inset below each room into the kiva walls. A massive, flat roof, supported by four masonry columns seated on ponderous, circular, limestone slabs, had burned and fallen almost as a unit onto the dirt floor below. Morris was able to determine the construction pattern of beams by charred stubs and undisturbed depressions in the dirt. Interior features included an encircling bench; a pair of rectangular, masonry-lined vaults of uncertain usage; and a raised, square firebox. Later study of Great Kivas would show the interior elements to be typical but the number of adjoining surface rooms to be unique.

As he reconstructed the Great Kiva's history, Morris believed it had been built after the house to its north was occupied for some time. The ground into which it was sunk was deep in refuse. The building seemed to have fallen into disuse later and collapsed. Mesa Verdeans refurbished it until flames rendered it a smoldering pile.

Aztec West was just three-fourths excavated when the museum withdrew its support. Understandably, Morris was disappointed. He wrote his superior, Clark Wissler, "My feeling is that our knowledge of the ruin will not be complete until we have found out the condition and contents of every chamber in it."[64] However, further work would not have added much to a database impressive for its time. In retrospect, it is regrettable that Morris did not probe beneath the ground surface on which the masonry house sits because there were hints of an earlier usage of the locale. Since this was an on-the-job learning experience without established standards, Morris may never have considered that.

It is even more unfortunate that Morris did not document the many bottom land ruins that farmers developing their properties and pothunters, himself included, destroyed. This is especially so because some of his interpretations presented twenty years later are suspect.[65]

Early into his Aztec program, Morris contacted the museum to ask permission to explore land near the mound being examined. He explained, "There are many graves beneath the fields which Mr. Abrams [site owner] has in cultivation, and one who knows what to look for can locate many of them when the ground is being plowed."[66] After getting permission to do so, he inspected twelve sites in the immediate vicinity and sent retrieved materials to the museum in New York but without any provenience or descriptive data other than vague site location.[67] Perhaps he felt that his subsequent account of the annex rooms and kivas explained the other valley cobblestone dwellings.

By his own admission, Morris also dug for pleasure in other places around the valley. His memorial pottery collection contains pieces recovered on some of these excursions.[68] Virtually all of it from the Aztec environs is Mesa Verdean in general style. Curiously, in a report published twenty years later, he stated that Chaco pottery was prevalent.[69]

Had Morris saved wood samples or charcoal from these valley bottom ruins, the importance of which he was then unaware, he might have known whether or not these were the remains of homes of natives living there when the Chacoans arrived. Or were they Chacoans? Or were they a part of a later pattern of the drift southwards away from the mesa and canyon country to the north that in time went on to Chaco Canyon? The grave pottery he recovered now seems thirteenth century in age, but that does not preclude an earlier occupation of the lower Animas Valley, much of the evidence for which is now gone.

Morris was personally fortunate in being nominally supervised by Clark Wissler, head curator of archaeology at the American Museum and a leading figure in American anthropology. Wissler was well aware of the propensity of many field men to put off the tedious task of analyzing and reporting. Consequently, he constantly prompted Morris to write up the results of his efforts so as to stake a claim, as it were, on the archaeology of the northern San Juan territory. Morris did complete papers on an overview of Aztec West, its burials, its Great Kiva, and his general prehistorical concepts. All were the first of their kind in depth and content for the late ancestral Pueblo realm. He never got to planned publications on the ceramics or kivas because of the pressures of other work or lost notes. The lack of a pottery analysis is particularly unfortunate. Even so, his claim was well staked.

During the excavation program, Morris lived for a time in a shack thrown up in the courtyard. In 1919 the museum purchased the ruin. With instructions that he was to guard it against vandals and the rancher's cows and sheep who stumbled over exposed walls knocking them awry, Morris built himself a small, four-room house in front of the site, using stockpiled timbers and recovered green and tan stones from the site.[70] He was following a precedent set by Richard Wetherill at Pueblo Bonito. He converted three rooms in the southwest corner of the pueblo for personal use. One cell became the garage for his 1917 Model T that he fondly named Old Joe. To do this, Morris installed a tar paper and frame roof, removed part of an outer wall, and hung a barn door over the opening. The neighboring chamber became his blacksmith shop and an inner one served as the privy for his house.[71] Needless to say, standards of that time were not as refined as those of today.

A footnote should be added to the Morris evaluation of the cultural sequences expressed in the general Aztec complex. First, a survey undertaken in the 1980s by National Park Service archaeologists Peter McKenna and John Stein of the terraces bordering the west side of the lower Animas Valley revealed a considerable concentration of settlement there that was coeval with but less formalized than that at the two large constructions and associated lesser units in the valley below. In the view of these men, the terrace sites were an integral part of the larger community that somehow at least began as a Chaco expression.

Second, an exhaustive tree ring dating effort of all provenienced wood from Aztec West and East carried out by scholar Thomas Windes demonstrated sequential building episodes from the early A.D. 1100s through the A.D. 1200s. The north wing of Aztec West had been raised in the very brief time between A.D. 1111 and 1120, the east wing somewhat later, and the west wing later still. Parts of Aztec East were begun in the mid-A.D. 1100s but most tree ring samples came from the thirteenth century with one cutting date being quite late in that century.

Taking these findings together, current thinking is that the Aztec complex, or parts thereof, was occupied continuously for at least two centuries with no perceptible period of vacancy.[72]

Another interesting study showed that much of the wood used in the monumental sites was long, straight aspen trunks which would have been available only in the high country a long distance to the north. Most likely the logs were processed there and floated downriver to be stockpiled until needed.[73] Such endeavors imply managerial planning and control, as well as great physical outlay.

In 1923 the museum, no longer interested in a field station, deeded the site and an adjoining 4.6 acres to the United States Government as the twenty-sixth national monument. Today the Morris home, with its twelfth-century beams and walls, is an integral part of the Visitor Center.

In 1921 while he was hanging on at Aztec in hopes that the museum would reconsider its abrupt termination of work in the ruin, Morris guided Harry Shapiro, physical anthropologist on the museum staff, to the Long Hollow sites in the middle of the La Plata Valley, where he had reclaimed eleven undeformed skulls in 1914. Shapiro proposed to do a comparative study of the so-called long heads (undeformed) and round heads (deformed). Whether Shapiro completed such a study is unknown. Nevertheless, the conventional wisdom for many years continued to be that the two biological groups were present, the round heads replacing or absorbing the long heads. More skulls were found in 1921. Most were difficult to retrieve because of the very hard earth in which they lay. The skulls of all were undeformed. Pottery associated with them was of the same crude type unearthed earlier. For Morris, these definitely were early pre-Pueblos. Other scholars might have called them "post-Basketmakers," such terminology pointing up the confused nomenclature being used in these formative days of the discipline.

Still uncertain of the relationship, temporally or culturally, to the sites examined in the Ute Pasture, during August and September of 1922 Morris once more rode back to the mesa tops dense with ruins where in 1914 he first came across the early horizon. He deliberately sought out abodes that had burned because he had learned that such places often produced quantities of specimens left when the original residents fled from disaster. Not only were such items found on floors but also in the accumulated deposits above as a consequence of the collapse of roofs that had been used as outdoor work areas.

This effort reconfirmed a surface occupation by builders of randomly scattered rooms and others in linear rows made of vertical stone slabs or thick courses of mud with roughly shaped sandstone blocks stuck into them in a haphazard fashion. Morris paid particular attention to large, shallow pit structures that he termed "proto-kivas," thus anticipating the later consensus that the residential pithouse was the precursor in the province to the ritual kiva of the classic Pueblo period. With some excitement, he wrote Henderson, " . . . we will be able to give the world the first record of the earliest forms of kivas to be found in the San Juan country."[74]

The one hundred pieces of pottery recovered, destined for the University of Colorado Museum, were improved over those seen at Long Hollow in being thinner walled and more frequently decorated, sometimes over a white slip. Plain cooking pots generally had unobliterated coils in the exterior neck area. The skulls of the dead were predominantly flattened.

Putting all these pieces of the prehistoric story together, it was apparent to Morris that chronologically the Ute Pasture people were in between those at Long Hollow and those at Eagle Nest. A date of A.D. 836 detected some years later in the growth rings of one chunk of wood from a similar proto-kiva substantiated this assessment.

As work ended at Aztec, another project got under way in the northeastern periphery of the Colorado Plateau. This was the upper reaches of the Piedra River and the formidable Chimney Rock cuesta at the place where the river valley opens to the south. It is an alpine setting of lush glades, clear, rushing waters, whispering pines, and majestic mountains walling off the northern horizon. Hardly a usual ancestral Pueblo environment and, in fact, prior to the early 1920s the area had not attracted much notice from those interested in Indian remains. There were none of the cliff dwellings, towers, and sprawling constructions of the open country that typified the central and western Mesa Verde Province. Along the river terraces a peppering conglomeration of cobbles, ill-defined slumps, and scattered potsherds were the sole indications of some unknown past. They invited only casual observation. The lone exception was the wreck of a moderate-sized houseblock high up on a spiny ridge at the base of a pair of towering pinnacles, landmarks that could be seen for miles. In 1921, J. A. Jeancon decided to investigate it.[75]

Jeancon had just assumed a curatorial position at the State Historical and Natural History Society in Denver and was eager to commence an archaeological program in Colorado. During the next several seasons he, some Denver University students, and a few local men dug out a small, cobblestone structure on the Piedra terrace and two crude, thick-walled, circular units among one hundred or so that, like mud pots, pockmarked the edges of the Chimney Rock slope. Finally they turned their attention to the ruin that literally clung to a narrow fin of the mesa top.

Jeancon recognized the masonry pueblo there as Chacoan. Whether that was because masons from Chaco had been at work or whether it was a case of local men copying the styles of a more powerful neighbor he could not say. He did think that the pottery present probably was locally made since it was not of the quality of either Chaco or Mesa Verde wares. Like Morris, Jeancon did not question why a Chaco settlement was at least ninety miles from Chaco Canyon and why it was in the middle of an apparently indigenous community of different style and layout. Nor did he speculate about the reasons for its placement one thousand feet above arable land and water sources, surely a strange location to be chosen by farmers. It may have been a defensive outpost, but from what? He did think the masonry houseblock represented the last occupation of the mesa region, with the dwellings along the river being the earliest.

Frank Roberts, one of the students with Jeancon and an assistant at the Historical Society, returned during the summer of 1923 to conduct a reconnaissance of the upper San Juan drainage to the east and south of Chimney Rock. Recalling Hewett's sweeping survey instructions to Morley and Kidder years before, Jeancon thought nothing of asking Roberts to compile an archaeological map covering the 150 square miles between Pagosa Springs at the headwaters of the San Juan River and the Utah border where his Colorado interests ended. Unfazed, Roberts, his brother, and two friends started out on what would be an impossible assignment in the time allowed.[76] Jeancon simply did not know the prehistoric richness of the region.

The era of the Model T touring car for basic scouting had arrived, but that of decent roads had not. The men had to literally make tracks as they went from farm to farm along the San Juan to inquire about any known Indian ruins. To their satisfaction, with and without this help, they found and charted many as far west as the Animas drainage. Holmes, Newberry, Prudden, and Morris had covered ground beyond there. The benches along the Piedra, with numerous sites so unobtrusive that only an archaeologist would appreciate them, seemed an especially promising place for future exploration.

By then on the staff of the Smithsonian's Bureau of American Ethnology (where he remained for thirty-seven years), four years later Roberts returned to further examine Piedra antiquities. He selected Stollsteimer Mesa just to the south of the Chimney Rock cuesta as a place in which to dig. The season previously he had spent his honeymoon exposing a hamlet on a spur of the Chacra Mesa in eastern Chaco Canyon that now is known as the type site for late Basketmakers, although Nusbaum, Morris, Kidder, and Guernsey had earlier opened comparable sites.[77] Roberts hoped to account for the next step upward in cultural advancement through study of the upper Piedra region.

At summer's end Roberts and his Hispanic crew, hired from family farms along the river, had dug out eighty habitations, two kivas, and assorted burial grounds. He had met up with the pre-Pueblos identified by Morris years before on the highlands east of Mesa Verde. But he also had a cultural phase that was a bit more advanced in the two important characteristics of architecture and ceramics. This seemed a connection into the full Pueblo lifeway. Generally the Stollsteimer houses were rectangular, made of jacal, flat roofed, and were either contiguous or detached. They were placed in an arc around a large central depression that usually lacked any kiva features.

Morris might have called them proto-kivas, but Roberts thought them either to be borrow pits for the adobe mortar necessary to cover vertical pole construction or perhaps some sort of dance plaza. He considered the formal houseblock on the Chimney Rock heights to be later and unrelated to the remains lower on the Stollsteimer Mesa. Just where the crater houses on the slopes below the Chimney Rock masonry pueblo dug by Jeancon fit into the temporal scheme would not be determined until subsequent research, but he considered them contemporaneous with the houseblock. Therefore, based upon evidence from the ground, he concluded that in the upper Piedra drainage three stages of ancestral Pueblo development could be delineated that corresponded to the course of events elsewhere in the Mesa Verde Province.[78] If correct, it was a rather surprising Pueblo adjustment to a seventy-five-hundred-foot-plus elevated environment on the cuesta, to short, erratic growing seasons, and to winters that often were bitter. But game was plentiful, foraging was productive, timber for construction and fuel was just out the door, and a breathtaking panorama stretched away from the sacred spires of Chimney Rock, surely to the residents the physical embodiment of the mythological Twin War Gods.

Meanwhile, Nusbaum became superintendent of Mesa Verde National Park despite, as he remarked, that he was a Democrat in Republican territory. He must have felt that he owned this particular piece of archaeological real estate. He had been there at its birth (surveys), nurtured it in its infancy (Balcony House), and now was primed to help it into its maturity. One thing he had learned from his years of association with Hewett was the fine art of promoting one's pet projects. This talent was put to use in developing the park's facilities. First, he charmed a wealthy female visitor to the park to help fund the construction of a more permanent museum than the log cabin Fewkes used.[79] While that was being built through his efforts and those of his wife, Nusbaum got word that John D. Rockefeller and guests were en route to visit the park for several days. Immediately, Nusbaum drove the official Dodge touring car to Mancos in order to escort these notables to Spruce Tree camp and his new house overlooking the ruin.

The next day the Nusbaums and their guests toured the surface and cliff dwellings, ending in late afternoon at Balcony House. While a steak fry was being prepared at a suitable spot on the rim above, Nusbaum and Rockefeller sat together absorbing a grand tableau of the canyon maze lost in purple shadows, their west rims still bathed in hot sunlight, and in the far distance the crenulated La Plata range rearing up against the sky like some ethereal picket fence. They mused about the kind of life that had taken place here so long ago. Just as the culture of the Old People was reaching an apparent climax, what compelled them to imprison themselves in hollows in the cliffs such as the Balcony House cave? Why did they give up? Where did they go? And when?

Taking advantage of these moments of reflection, Nusbaum spoke of his plans to make the legacy of these admirable Pueblos accessible to the visiting public. As if in passing, he mentioned that the museum could not be finished because Congress had not come forth with funds and, furthermore, there were few specimens to exhibit in it. One reason for that was the wholesale gleaning of sites that had gone on in the early days. Such removal of specimens was not restricted to the cowboys and other collectors but sometimes included professionals such as Jeancon and even a renegade ranger. In 1908, two years after the park was established, Jeancon reclaimed a handsome black-on-red pitcher from the talus below Step House and without obvious guilt kept it for himself. After his death, Morris purchased the vessel from Jeancon's widow. As for the ranger, he caused a frightful ruckus with his unauthorized digging in the back country and then adamantly refusing to turn his loot over to the park.[80] Another reason for a dearth of display objects was that a recently enacted law made it mandatory to house all artifacts recovered on federal lands in the United States National Museum in Washington. Undoubtedly, there were still things to be had in ruins in the canyons away from park headquarters, if only there were time and wherewithal to search for them.

Rockefeller listened sympathetically with a growing feeling that this was an endeavor worthy of his support. On the spot he announced that he would fund the completion of the four rooms of the museum then under construction, and he would also sponsor several collecting expeditions. Nusbaum's dreams were coming true. Hewett himself could not have been more successful at subtle persuasion.

The only time Nusbaum felt he could be free to explore was midwinter when snows closed the new Knife Edge road to park visitors. At that time of year fieldwork was certain to be miserable. Nusbaum also had misgivings about the abilities of his available motley crew made up of the chief ranger, the shopkeeper, a Navajo laborer, and his twelve-year-old stepson. He decided to give them some instruction in archaeological methods by working over the deep midden at the rear of Spruce Tree House. The wide recess was dark and frigid in winter because the structure in the front of the alcove blocked the sun. The filthy atmosphere was so unpleasant, in fact, that even the Wetherills had not burrowed into the trash there. Nusbaum rigged up several floodlights, provided his helpers with respirators so that they would not suffer from noxious dust raised at every movement, and welcomed them to the romance of archaeology. Excitement over the residue of past lives recovered by the novices counterbalanced their grumbling.[81]

Prior to taking on the current Mesa Verde job, Nusbaum excavated in a cave near Kanab, Utah, that contained Basketmaker remains. After this experience, he itched to get to the open floor space in Step House on Wetherill Mesa where he thought there might be a related horizon. Both Nordenskiold and the Wetherills had mentioned a few examples of a crude pottery they unearthed there which likely were older than the more typical Cliff Dweller types. This implied an earlier use of the overhang. So far as it was known at that time, the early Basketmakers did not have a pottery-making technology, but according to research by Kidder, Guernsey, and Morris their descendants did indeed understand how to create functional clay containers hardened by fire. Nusbaum's opportunity to study Step House came in February 1926.

Surprisingly not discouraged by their demanding instruction the previous winter, the same men and one boy, with the addition of a wrangler, set out for Wetherill Mesa. On foot, they led horses piled high with tools, tents, and food off Chapin Mesa, down across rocky canyon bottoms, up opposing, slippery slopes where they had to break through shoulder-high drifts of ice-crusted snow, to a relatively dry camping spot above Step House.

The hard ground within the overhang etched out of the cliff face below them bore ample evidence of previous churning. Rude piles of earth surrounded deep holes still littered with potsherds and fragmented items apparently regarded as not worthy of being saved. Nusbaum learned that this disturbance did not seriously intrude upon an occupation that long predated that of the worn-down masonry house in the north end of the alcove. As hoped, his men found and cleared the semisubterranean portions of four pithouses nestled up against the protective back wall of the alcove.[82] Associated with them were examples of the same primitive kind of pottery the earlier explorers had observed, as well as Basketmaker implements. Nusbaum's bunch of amateurs had proved a human presence on the Mesa Verde that subsequent tree ring determinations would place in the late A.D. 500s and early A.D. 600s. Where these first residents had come from, why they migrated to the mesa, or even if they were all of one ethnicity were not then questions of concern. The 1920s diggers must have taken pleasure in the museum exhibits that Mrs. Nusbaum and the wife of the chief ranger prepared of their findings.

During three following years Nusbaum and his crew spent three to four week periods testing other sites in the park. Most of them had been rifled in the last century, but the men did amass a collection of specimens illustrative of the way of life of the ancestral Pueblos in this place. Today, more than seventy years later, it forms the bulk of the display materials in the small park museum.

In themselves, the artifacts are informative. However, the focus of these Nusbaum excursions was not only the addition to specific site data. It was pothunting justified by scientific expedience. Nusbaum's personal contributions to the record of the park's prehistory remains the knowledge of the late Basketmaker use of Step House cave and, by extension, the same usage elsewhere in the Mesa Verde alcoves and on its mesa tops.

A postscript to Nusbaum's introduction of Rockefeller to Southwestern archaeology came at the close of the 1920s. The financier magnanimously endowed a research center in Santa Fe, the Laboratory of Anthropology, with Nusbaum as its director.

In August 1927, a group of individuals interested in the prehistory of the Colorado Plateau met at Pecos Pueblo, where Kidder was finishing his ninth season of excavation.[83] Judd also had ended his long-term efforts at Pueblo Bonito, and Roberts had dug Shabik'eshchee Village. It was time to take stock. Among the gathering were three men who had actively worked in the Mesa Verde Province. They were Nusbaum, Morris, and Roberts, all of whom came into the archaeological profession as students. Morris, of course, was a bit of an exception in having figuratively been born with a trowel in his hip pocket and a shovel over his shoulder. Morley, whose own student efforts were confined to two seasons at the beginning of the century, and Hewett, whose role was that of facilitator rather than excavator, also were present. Fewkes was noticeably absent. Half of those in the audience had done no personal research in the Southwest.

The purpose of the gathering was to pool information and observations resulting from diverse studies during the previous decades and to agree on standardized format and terminology for future inquiries so that all concerned would speak the same mutually understood language. Southwestern archaeology was being systematized. Both Morris and Kidder had published their versions of chronology, and Kidder added the concept of three regional variations. They were Kayenta, Chaco, and Mesa Verde.[84]

Three days of exchanges led to what is now called the Pecos Classification. This was a chronological arrangement of perceived Pueblo cultural evolution through time. In this scheme the two earliest stages were termed *Basketmaker*, and the successive five were *Pueblo*. This distinction reflects the belief then current that two distinct biological groups were present, as Morris referred to them, the "long heads" (Basketmakers) and the "round heads" (Pueblos).

Research continuing after this meeting showed the inherent difficulties in trying to rigidly pigeonhole portions of a progressive cultural continuum. Inevitably there are transitional phases of adaptations curtailed by resistance to change because all peoples do not march in lock step to the same drummer. Nevertheless, the Pecos Classification, with modifications, remains the basic frame of reference in regard to Pueblo culture. Chronological archaeology gave new meaning to the emerging discipline by linking the past to the present and opening the door to anthropological considerations. This is a particularly impressive intellectual achievement by only a dozen persons with experience in the field.

As the designations were understood then, the early horizon that Richard Wetherill first commented upon on the Grand Gulch Plateau was Basketmaker II. Basketmaker I was a hypothetical pre-agricultural background out of which Basketmaker II must have emerged. The pit dwellings in Nusbaum's Step House cave were Basketmaker III. Morris's pre-Pueblos in the middle La Plata valley and the Ute Pasture were Late Basketmaker III and Early Pueblo I. Roberts's settlements on Stollsteimer Mesa were Pueblo I merging into Pueblo II. Prudden's unit houses and Fewkes's Far View Pueblo were Pueblo II. Morley's Cannonball Pueblo and the Mesa Verde, Lion Canyon, and Grand Gulch cliff dwellings were Pueblo III. In 1927, Aztec West was also considered Pueblo III. Present interpretation classifies the Chacoan occupation as Late Pueblo II and the Mesa Verdean occupation as Pueblo III. Pueblo IV (A.D. 1300–1600) and Pueblo V (historic) were not present in the Mesa Verde Province but were of interest to scholars investigating areas to the south and east.

Two years after this Pecos Classification and Conference, the tree ring calendar supplied dates for the stages from the present (Pueblo V) back to A.D. 700 (Pueblo I). In a few years dendrochronologists were able to read even older dates, taking the record back to the earliest occupations at the time of Christ.

Other important events in the late 1920s were the establishment of Departments of Anthropology at the University of Arizona, chaired by Cummings, and the University of New Mexico, chaired by the indefatigable Hewett. A new generation of regional archaeologists, for the first time including women, was about to take the helm.

For much of the 1920s, Morris divided his time between undertaking the first scientific explorations in the Canyon de Chelly area of northeastern

Arizona for the University of Colorado and the American Museum and excavating at the great Maya center of Chichén Itzá in Yucatan for the Carnegie Institution of Washington. In the latter position he was with colleagues Kidder and Morley. In 1927 his assignment in Yucatan finished, and he visited the Roberts dig at Shabik'eshchee Village in Chaco Canyon. This stimulated him to return to his old haunts in the La Plata Valley to try to find something comparable.

For the third time Morris put his shovel down in one of the Long Hollow sites. He was then sponsored by the Carnegie Institution and the University of Colorado. Formerly, he had been most concerned with human remains and pottery, but now he intended to concentrate on architecture. He cleared four units, each with one or more proto-kivas. The units were composed of single or double rows of irregularly shaped rooms made of slabs and mud and placed in a crescentic arrangement. In short, the layout of these buildings was similar to that in the Ute Pasture but not like that at Shabik'eshchee. How all these manifestations of early ancestral Pueblos related to each other remained unclear.

A rock shelter in a gully beyond the site produced some startling indications of probable cannibalism. In a fire pit there were many splinters of broken human bones. Parts of two skulls, one a juvenile and the other an adult, were in a corrugated pot buried close by. According to Morris, all the bones bore evidence of having been cooked at some time after the neighboring site had been abandoned. The Pueblo III dating interpretation was based upon the presence of the corrugated vessel, fragments of Mesa Verde Black-on-White pottery, and the deformation of one of the skulls.[85]

Such sensational news, the first of its kind in the Mesa Verde Province, was buried in Morris's ponderous technical report published with limited distribution twelve years after the find. Therefore, it received no attention from the lay public, and the professionals adopted a long-standing attitude of denial. The notion of the pacific Pueblos, who only cared about next year's harvest, was to remain steadfastly entrenched for the next seventy years.

Determined to solve questions about the chronological sequence of the middle La Plata district, in 1929 Morris doggedly went back to the Ute Pasture area. During a snowy November four years before, while he was reexamining the Johnson–Lion Canyon cliff dwellings in a fruitless attempt to find earlier deposits beneath them, he had come across an exceptionally large concentration of remains there. An intriguing feature was a huge depression suggesting a Great Kiva. Knowing that Roberts had located a Great Kiva at Shabik'eshchee,

Morris hoped this crater might be part of a similar village which the Pecos Classification would denote as Basketmaker III.

Site 33 in the Morris system is on what was a heavily wooded mesa spur south of Johnson Canyon. To Morris, it was a silent world where one felt alone in the universe. A raven might float on the current. Far away in the haze the volcanic Shiprock galleon sailed the placid San Juan seas. On a twisted cedar branch a rusted shovel dangled. Those peripatetic Wetherills of a former generation had been there first.[86] So had various native peoples who had worn a foot path four feet deep in troughs through the site. In the 1920s, Utes still residing in Mancos Canyon several miles away occasionally walked this route to Durango or to the La Plata Mountains. To get his vehicles to the ruin, Morris's laborers had to clear a couple miles of road through the trees and tall sagebrush.

Site 33 was the largest of a half-dozen settlements in the vicinity that at various times Morris had probed. The houses were the same jacal and mud constructions placed in crescentic double rows that had become familiar in the neighboring hamlets with proto-kivas within their arcs.[87]

When work began, the Great Kiva depression was circular, some thirty feet across, and a foot and a half deep. Trees grew in and around its depth. Removal and disposal of the large amount of fill of even part of the pit presented a problem. In his former days, Morris would have resorted to horse power, but in the 1929 "modern age" he relied on a Dodge truck hitched to tackles to pull a scraper to a dump. The cleared interior was about sixty-three feet in diameter. Its walls were smoothed, raw soil or plastered with mud that had hardened. An encircling bench was faced with vertical slabs. The floor was coated with dried mud plaster. A raised firebox and a *sipapu*, sacred opening to the underworld, were in the center of the floor. A narrow tunnel ran from the bench top to the outside.

The large Great Kiva structure had been roofed, as abundant fragments of charred timbers and brush attested. That represented a demanding undertaking for so-called primitive builders. The crew exposed the butt ends of two ponderosa uprights firmly wedged into place by slabs that had supported the weighty superstructure of timbers, brush, and earth. At the time of excavation, the Douglass dendrochronologists could only inform Morris that a sample of one of these charred stubs had a life span of 350 years. The next summer, after the tree ring calendar was consummated, the remains of the other two supports yielded an A.D. 831 date. This corresponded to within five years of another date of A.D. 836 from a nearby proto-kiva.[88]

Morris may have been disappointed not to have a Basketmaker III hamlet but rather one definitely Pueblo I according to the diagnostics proposed in the Pecos Classification. However, Site 33 was important in reaffirming the cultural continuity from one developmental stage to another.

After a lapse of an unknown number of centuries, Pueblo III folks reoccupied the zone. They erected an odd U-shaped masonry building enclosing a kiva in its center. No excavations were done there.

In 1930, Site 41 was the scene of Morris's final formal endeavor in the La Plata region.[89] Incorporated in this site designation, which spread over the terraces above the west side of the La Plata Valley just south of the New Mexico–Colorado border, were at least forty artificial mounds in no definable configuration that made it the largest community in the midvalley. No wonder the attraction of this spot for modest farmers because of fertile river loam below it, perennial water, timbered heights, and a temperate climate. A seam of soft coal at the south end of the terraces was worked in modern times, but there is no sign that the aboriginal inhabitants used it for fuel or ornaments.

Morris made camp near the river for an unusually large body of assistants that included five friends of the Carnegie Institution and Kidder, director of the Historical Division. Mrs. Walter Trumbull became the first woman to participate in a province dig. Morris put her to work taking care of the specimens in a housekeeping role that became the lot of females in the profession. A young University of Colorado student whom Morris befriended was cook. Oscar Tatman and Oley Owens, his indispensable aids from Aztec, and several local youths to do the heavy work rounded out this assorted crew of three experienced workers and a gaggle of adventurers.

Four months saw the contingent work over sixteen of the mounds to clear 170 rooms and ten kivas. Some houseblocks, constructed with a mixture of sandstone and cobblestone masonry, were large; others were rather small. All were of Pueblo III age, although there were indications of both Basketmaker III–Pueblo I pit structures and Pueblo II surface houses having been razed prior to later erections on the same ground.

A number of burials were found under house floors. Morris noted this mode of disposal of the dead as contrasted to the earlier use of trash heaps as cemeteries. A few bodies had been laid out uncovered on floors. As at Aztec, Morris attributed this to possible famine or pestilence that so demoralized the survivors they forsook normal practices.[90]

There was one instance that again raised the possibility of cannibalism.[91] A sizable pit beneath the floor of two rooms in one of the small houses was partially filled with rubbish and disarticulated, cracked, and splintered human bones. Six individuals were accounted for. Three skulls were cracked crosswise as if to remove the brains. Because all these specimens were exceptionally white, Morris thought that they had been boiled. Fragments of a large, corrugated bowl in which this might have occurred lay above the bone deposit. Probably it was deliberately broken after its grisly use. Morris classed it as Early Pueblo III, his Chacoan period, or *circa* A.D. 1100. This instance of violence generally went as unnoticed as that at Long Hollow and for the same reasons.

It was nine years before Morris's impressive report on eight seasons of La Plata excavations and several decades of grubbing about for pots came from the Carnegie Institution Press. It was a landmark contribution to an understanding of the prehistory of the Mesa Verde Province as a whole. In addition to a detailed presentation of architectural data and typology of artifacts, the delay in publication allowed Morris to place the studied sites into the cultural framework afforded by the Pecos Classification and the temporal one of the tree ring calendar.

A survey of the entire gamut of ancestral Pueblo prehistory as it was then known was a scholarly building bit by bit upon a growing corpus of knowledge that Morris had garnered over three decades of virtually nonstop efforts. For explanation of the opening phases of this human experience, he turned to his unpublished work south of the San Juan River along the eastern piedmont of the Chuska Mountains, in the Red Rocks portion of the Carrizos, and in the de Chelly and del Muerto canyons (Kayenta Province). There he had explored Basketmaker II and Basketmaker III remains, although they often were mixed because of human and animal agents. For most of the early phases of the middle La Plata district, he had no precedent. The surface crescentic structures and the proto-kivas had not been found elsewhere other than on Stollsteimer Mesa more than fifty miles to the east. In regard to later Pueblo periods and as a consequence of his recognition of the Chaco–Mesa Verde sequence at Aztec West, he was able to extend Chaco presence, influence, or trade to the lower La Plata Valley during what he considered Early Pueblo III. This material was particularly to be found at the site at Barker Arroyo which he dug in 1916 and at the Holmes Group to the north at the confluence of McDermott Arroyo and the La Plata River that he and other collectors had essentially pothunted out of existence. Added to a number of ordinary kinds of vessels in his personal assortment from the Holmes Group were three effigy pitchers—a toad, a deer, and a civet cat— which he mentioned in his report.[92] They are pieces he exhumed or for which he traded or bought from other gleaners. All are typical of Chaco manufacture. Some of his categorizations have been modified by later research, but the progression through time was fully demonstrated.

Morris detected no breaks such as would have occurred had there been an invasion by round heads. It was his opinion that the stage he considered Basketmaker III, later placed into a Pueblo I grouping, was the basis for all that followed through Pueblo III. He doubted that Pueblo II peoples were in the La Plata area. If so, their stay was brief or their numbers were few. Later research would indicate that a gap in the continuity of occupation of the northern San Juan districts, or a greatly diminished Puebloan presence, occurred during the Early Pueblo II period. The unit pueblo, long regarded as the trademark of that time, extended into much later periods and was the most typical variety of Pueblo III settlement, even while Great Houses were nearby.

The La Plata report contained an exhaustive Morris review of regional pottery based upon visual observations of form, size, and surface treatments.[93] Never before or since has one individual handled so much pottery from its inception on the Colorado Plateau, something Morris once thought might have been inspired by mud liners smeared in parching trays, to the lustrous, densely painted Mesa Verde containers. This presentation incorporated data he would have used had he written an Aztec pottery paper.

Morris identified a limited sample of the La Plata pieces as typical Chaco wares and others he called Chaco-like. These he classed as Early Pueblo III. Most of the pottery from Late Pueblo III, from his reckoning about A.D. 1175 to 1300, was of the classic Mesa Verde tradition. A few black-on-red pieces from Pueblo I sites may have been trade pieces from the west. A different kind of black-on-red among Pueblo II materials likely were made south of the San Juan.

The lengthy consideration of pottery points up its importance to those trying to interpret the past of ancestral Pueblos. Earthenwares surely were essential to their sedentary mode of life, but they constituted just one of an array of household furnishings. However, their durability, abundance, and variability makes them invaluable to researchers.

Paradoxically, the low-fired ancestral Pueblo wares were friable. Whole vessels were easily shattered, but their fragments lasted for centuries. This is due to the chemical change in clays that takes place at a temperature of about six-hundred degrees Celsius which makes resulting earthenware everlasting. Its appearance may be altered, but it is not destroyed by sunlight, moisture, fire, bacteria, or the blasting of desert sands. Hence, because their vessels served many functions but were easily broken through body weakness or hard usage, their pottery production over the centuries was staggering. Some sites are identified solely by a sprinkling of these fragmented materials. On the other hand, the ancestral Pueblo practice of leaving ceramic offerings in graves, drawn from the entire inventory of forms being utilized at any given period, has provided archaeologists with a tremendous resource. Most specimens left in these protected circumstances were complete or restorable so that one can gain insight into their intended functions and the degree of craftsmanship on the part of their makers. One consequence of the rampant grave robbing that has taken place is that more prehistoric, ancestral Pueblo pots now jam institutional or private storage than those of the more recent Spanish colonial period, when the Catholic Church banned grave goods.

Through the 1920s archaeologists made use of pottery stratigraphically and aesthetically. As cultural horizons and regionalizations in style were identified, the pottery pertaining to them became signatures of generalized time and place. As in the case of the La Plata remains, Morris could reasonably attribute a particular rendition to Early Pueblo III Chaco developments and a somewhat differing mode to Late Pueblo III Mesa Verde. He could recognize the red wares as foreign and indicative of patterns of trade.

With the precise dating of individual constructions established by tree rings and the correlation of dated sites with the pottery they contained, the practical importance of ceramics soared. Here was a temporal tool denied to scholars of the past in most of the rest of the world. By 1939 Morris could say that pottery from his proto-kiva in the Ute Pasture was in use in the year A.D. 831, even though it may have been produced before and after that exact date.

The discussions of pottery were greatly augmented by the first technical analysis of the physical properties of regional ceramics. Anna Shepard single-handedly opened up a new dimension in ceramic research.[94] Long after the fieldwork, she undertook this study in her laboratory under the auspices of the Carnegie Institution and the Laboratory of Anthropology. Beyond considering style and workmanship, she tested clays, tempers, pigments, and firing conditions. These were all factors that went into making this product of the ancestral Pueblo women what it was at different points in time. Potsherds were useful for this kind of inspection because they were more easily manipulated than whole vessels and their cores were exposed.

Shepard was one of those persons in the developing discipline of Southwestern archaeology who fell under the spell of Hewett and profited from it.[95] In 1926, shortly after her graduation from the University of Nebraska with a degree in anthropology, Shepard was hired by Hewett to be curator of ethnology at the San Diego Museum of Man. While still filling his dual posts at the School of American Archaeology and the Museum of New Mexico, in an almost inhuman display of entanglements, Hewett founded the San Diego museum, served as its head from 1917 to 1929, and occasionally taught at the San Diego State Teachers School. The two had become acquaintances a few years before when Hewett accepted Shepard as part of an otherwise all-male crew to excavate in the monumental, seventeenth-century Franciscan mission at Gran Quivira in New Mexico. To Hewett's credit, he continued to support women in what most saw as a man's vocation. Shepard was the first.

The Gran Quivira experience so interested Shepard that in 1929 she applied for admission to Hewett's new archaeological field school in Chaco Canyon. Upon Hewett's urging, the state of New Mexico had purchased the eastern half of the Great House of Chetro Ketl which was not part of the national monument, and the staff of the Museum of New Mexico and students from the new Department of Anthropology at the University of New Mexico were set to begin work there.

Shepard's tent mate was Florence Hawley (Ellis), who had just received a master of arts degree as one of Cummings's protégés at the University of Arizona. Other than the fact that both their fathers were chemists, these women had little in common besides a growing interest in pottery which on different levels would be centerpieces of their future careers.

Shepard was motivated by what she learned at Chetro Ketl to go to Claremont College in California to study optical crystallography and general mineralogy. That done, she secured a research position at the Laboratory of Anthropology, under the directorship of Nusbaum, determined to carve a niche for herself in spite of male prejudice. Believing that one way to know the subject was to observe modern Pueblo potters at work, she spent days watching women at several villages near Santa Fe, where Hewett long had encouraged upgrading of craftsmanship. Ultimately, her endeavors were rewarded when Kidder asked her to analyze the mass of glaze-paint wares taken from the deep deposits at Pecos Pueblo. With the success of that project, Kidder then lured her to the staff of the Carnegie Institution, where she remained for the ensuing thirty-two years while carrying out technical studies of Southwestern and Mesoamerican ceramics.

One of the newcomers to Southwestern archaeology during this time was Paul Martin. In 1927 he was appointed to replace Jeancon at the State Historical Society of Colorado, who had resigned in despair over his board's apparent disinterest in the prehistory of southwestern Colorado. Martin's previous background was in the Midwest and for a longer time in the Mayan Yucatan, where he became acquainted with Morley, Kidder, and Morris. He faced serious problems resulting from tropical diseases that forced him to restrict research possibilities. He must have thought that the Southwest was a good place to land. To begin, he hoped to erase the Denverite apathy by transferring studies from its eastern limits, where remains were not dramatic, to the core area of the Mesa Verde Province, where there were antiquities already well publicized. The Society owned the first Wetherill collection from the cliff dwellings. To buttress his efforts, Martin intended to demonstrate parallel developments that had occurred away from the cliffs by following the cultural road map afforded by the Pecos Classification. He had attended the first Pecos Conference as a graduate student from the University of Chicago[96] and, like many others of the time, wanted to add definitive details proposed by its systematic framework through what archaeologists like to call *ground truth*.

While associated with the State Historical Society, Martin began to carry out his intention of studying ruins present in the broad Montezuma Valley west of Cortez. He undertook excavation of a series of masonry houses that in configuration and quality of architecture and pottery conformed to remains that twenty-four years earlier Prudden termed *unit pueblos*. He judged them to be representative of the Pueblo II stage of development dating to the A.D. 1000s.[97]

In 1930 Martin accepted a post at the Field Museum of Natural History in Chicago, his hometown, with assurance that monies were available for fieldwork and its publication. To continue his interest in the Ackmen region of the Montezuma Valley and to ascertain the evolutionary course that followed the unit pueblo period, Martin's next step was to clear Lowry Ruin just a few miles from where he worked earlier. This was the most visibly high pile of rubble, earth, and sagebrush in the midst of numerous other ruins of various sizes and probable ages. It promised to illuminate a zenith period in regional prehistory.

For accommodations, Martin rented space in the log cabin of a neighboring homesteader, whose wife cooked for the party.[98] He was able to hire local workmen through funds supplied by the Depression-era Montezuma County Emergency Relief Administration. In general, they were hard-working farmers in need of even a small cash income. While some may have had a passing interest in their assigned tasks, there was one who quite literally found his future calling. He was Al Lancaster, a bean farmer with a brood of kids and little money. He took to the job with such zest and understanding that shortly Martin made him dig boss.

Another participant from outside the academic archaeological ranks was Watson Smith, a Midwestern lawyer with a hankering to be an archaeologist. At the opposite end of the social and educational spectrum, he, too, saw a future in studies of the Colorado Plateau past.

Martin's opening salvo at Lowry Ruin got off to a rocky start with an altercation with a bellicose settler who wrongly believed that the site was on land upon which he had filed a homestead claim. He blocked the road to the site and threatened Martin with gun in hand. Showdown at old Lowry was an adventure for which Martin had no appetite. He appealed for help from the agent of the Land Office. That official interceded to gain an uneasy peace allowing science to go forward.

When cleared, Lowry Pueblo was shown to be a forty-room, multistoried, compact house of shaped sandstone blocks laid up in puddled adobe mortar. Incorporated in it or encompassed nearby were four kivas. One still bore a full panel of painted geometric designs on a low encircling banquette. Out beyond there was a Great Kiva, the second in the Mesa Verde Province to be exposed. Morris's example at Aztec West remained the type reference.

Martin viewed some of the masonry and pottery as Chaco-like, not up to the standards of the canyon but reminiscent. Most scholars agreed that the Great Kiva likewise was a Chacoan element. Further, there was a second large mound a few yards away of what some suspected would prove to be what was left of a Chaco Great House. A tree ring date of A.D. 1106 from the painted kiva, which is Mesa Verdean in style, suggests that if Chacoans or their influence were in fact present, they must have come prior to that time and been relatively short-lived. Like his colleagues, Martin did not address the question of why this seeming intrusion was so far from the Chaco Province.[99]

Not one to get dirtied in the trenches alongside his men, Martin's 1937 and 1938 budgets allowed him to hire two graduate students to oversee the dig, map and photograph the sites, and tramp over many square miles to make an archaeological survey record.[100] In addition to some persons who had worked for him throughout his various Ackmen-Lowry endeavors, at least three beginning students paid their own way just to have the experience. One of these was Charles DiPeso, who in later years gained recognition for work in the southernmost sectors of the Southwest. According to Watson Smith, it was Martin's habit to return to his quarters each day to take care of paperwork and inspect excavations accomplished by the end of the day.[101] This was fieldwork by delegation.

Work during these two final seasons opened an early horizon with an architectural mix of slab, pole and mud, and rough masonry. Occupations seemed to have been brief, with little remaining refuse. Several sites were large and consisted of many contiguous rooms. Martin had discovered the pre-Pueblos of the Great Sage Plain. He called them "Modified Basketmakers," or Basketmaker III. Based on architecture, pottery, and tree ring dates in the A.D. 700s and 800s, today's scholars place them squarely in the Pueblo I period. Nor was there Chaco influence apparent at that early time, as Martin believed. His conclusion was that Mancos Black-on-White pottery was an import from the south. Subsequent study shows it to be the standard Pueblo II Mesa Verdean type that shared a widespread design repertory. Such revisions of opinions reflect continued study, not criticisms of the abilities of colleagues.

Just as Martin was terminating his work at Lowry Ruin, another expedition was in the works. Its chosen locale was Alkali Ridge, some twenty miles to the west in southeastern Utah. As the name implies, this is a narrow strip of tableland bounded on its west and east sides by a lacing of canyons, some deep and tortuous. They feed southward into the lower San Juan drainage. With the usual atmospheric clarity, the eye can sweep one hundred miles across the burnished, blow-dried terrain to the south of the San Juan around a northern mountain ring that frames the Montezuma Valley and the Great Sage Plain. The topography, elevation, and vegetational overlay are comparable to environmental conditions stretching east to the foot of the Mesa Verde. There was reason to believe that the same cultural sequences would be found here as were becoming known in the nuclear Mesa Verde domain. J. O. Brew, then a Harvard graduate student, was poised to find out with the sponsorship of the Peabody Museum and the advice of Kidder, who had cut his archaeological eyeteeth there.

On his way to Alkali Ridge in a field vehicle named Pecos because it had seen service there, Brew visited the Lowry dig just as it was winding down for the 1931 season. He knew he was a tenderfoot in unfamiliar surroundings contemplating work of an unfamiliar nature. He needed help. He had an intellectual problem to solve but did not know how to go about it. How to identify a promising site and clear it without destroying the evidence?

On Martin's advice, Brew invited Lancaster to accompany him to Alkali Ridge in order to scout the land and plan for future inquiries. He hired two of Martin's laborers and, to make up what he considered a proper expedition, he added a cook. The group drove the miserable furrowed track out to where the Great Sage Plain bumps into the Abajo Mountains and then down a ranch road on the mesa top to a place where they pitched their tents in the lee of a tumbled-down masonry ruin. This place was comparable to another Alkali

Ridge ancestral Pueblo dwelling where twenty-three years before those found-
ing fathers—Kidder, Judd, and Nusbaum—had their baptismal experience in
dirt archaeology. While Brew and Lancaster inspected the old site, the cook set
to work gathering fallen stones from the building to make an oven. Because
the structure appeared to be of Pueblo III age, Brew decided against investigating it. He wanted to locate sites of an earlier period, namely Pueblo II.

Brew and Lancaster were a mismatched duo. One was a pudgy, library-
bound scholar who had scarcely been out of the city and possessed few
manual abilities. The other was a minimally educated, weather-beaten figure
having a range of practical skills necessary for life on the unvarnished edge
of the West. They would learn that their complementary aptitudes made
them an effective team.

Together these men and their helpers spent three weeks locating dozens
of ruins sprinkled across the hinterland, conducting several cursory tests,
and making arrangements for proposed work to take place during the next
two summers. One late November morning they awoke to find their tents
covered with an early snow that obscured the landscape. It was time to leave.

Back the following May, Brew saw to the general operations of getting a
tent camp set up at the same location as the previous fall. Lancaster recruited
a small crew made up of several of his relatives, others who had worked on
Martin's project, and two or three farmers from the nearest Mormon settlements of Monticello and Blanding. All these men were on their home turf
and were comfortable with it. Their way of life had taught them to read the
soil for discolorations or changes in compactness that might mean human
activity. They knew the whereabouts of natural resources possibly used by
ancient peoples. Strenuous physical exertion, putting up with the vicissi-
tudes of weather and camp life, and fending off swarms of biting gnats that
becloud every spring in this high desert were all in a day's work. Quite likely
most of them had engaged in some illicit digging on their own.

Brew's avowed goal was to attempt to define the cultural phase the Pecos
Classification termed Pueblo II but for which there was yet little definitive
information. To some of the small cadre of regional archaeologists, including Morris, it seemed a long stretch between the crude jacal habitations of
Pueblo I, which Morris and Roberts had found in other sectors of the Mesa
Verde Province, and the Pueblo III terraced, masonry houseblocks such as
Cannonball Pueblo reported by Morley. They felt that the Prudden unit
pueblo format of presumed Pueblo II age did not satisfactorily fill this
lacuna in the chronology.

Most of the elevated spots on the ridge had been scenes of Pueblo III construction. These builders must have robbed earlier habitations of stones to reuse in their own buildings. That made it hard in the patchy, juniper-pinyon forest canopy to detect low mounds left from what were flimsy, earlier dwellings. These could only be detected in more cleared ground by a scattering of rocks, hard chunks of adobe, and a littering of potsherds. The country-dwelling diggers suggested that Brew secure a team of horses pulling a doubletree with a chain over the spaces to pull out high stands of sage. These were burned in what appeared to be depressions marking subterranean kivas in a rather blatant disregard for site damage.

Actual excavation was frustrating for both Brew and Lancaster. They sought out places lacking the classical Pueblo III Mesa Verde decorated pottery with the assumption that earlier inhabitants might have lived there. Then they oversaw a series of exploratory trenches dug to define site features. When warranted, the crew entirely cleared these; others were only partly unearthed.

At the end of the 1932 season the men had delved into a dozen sites up and down the mesa, at least nine of which Brew judged to be Pueblo II. He was satisfied with the validity of the Pecos Classification designation, at least so far as it applied to Alkali Ridge. What he learned was that the architecture of that time was a variable mixture of jacal, slabs, and rough masonry courses separated by rounded wads of adobe locally called "turtlebacks." The continued practice of jacal construction at such a late period was surprising. The settlements generally conformed to the unit pueblo plan of a few rooms in a line, a kiva to their south, and a midden farther to the southeast. Fortunately, it was occasionally possible to observe earlier jacal and later masonry elements stratigraphically. Pottery predominately was Mancos Black-on-White. Like Martin, at first Brew regarded it as Chacoan (Chaco-like to Morris) but became convinced that it was a local product.[102]

As often happens, the most significant find came near the end of the 1932 season. Lancaster noticed lines of low ridges and occupational debris of what promised to be a pre-Pueblo II community of possible large size. If so, that would take the Alkali Ridge occupation back further in time. Enough hasty digging there required further exploration the next summer.

Site 13 in the Alkali Ridge series was not an unlucky number. Four months working on it in 1933 uncovered an exceptionally rich archaeological zone. A long shoestring of contiguous, rectangular, jacal units, some only identified by ghostlike impressions of slender poles that had been used in the walls, snaked in a north-south line down the mesa. Some rows were single, and others were double. Three lines of these insubstantial habitations spaced at right angles off to the east created four plaza openings. At least two additional rows of rooms went off to the west from the main stem. Obviously it was an enormous, spread-out site, not all of which was traced. The expedition dug 118 out of a probable 130 rooms that the leaders believed were used only for storage and twenty-five others that contained evidence of having been living quarters.[103]

Following a method recommended by dendrochronologist Douglass, tree ring samples taken from post stubs were impregnated with a solution of paraffin dissolved in gasoline. This was done to harden them so that they would not be damaged in handling. Uniformly, they dated in the late A.D. 700s near the beginning of the tree ring calendar as it had been worked out to that time. This time frame and the architecture confirmed that this was a Pueblo I site.

Another surprise was the kind of turn of events that make archaeology ever provocative. The recovered decorated pottery was not the customary black-on-white type but was orange with a red patterning. That meant an oxidizing firing technique rather than one in which a reduction atmosphere was created by smothering the flames. It also pointed to a clay source that contained significant amounts of iron, a mineral that reddens under heat.

These discoveries at Site 13 extended the range of Pueblo I presence in the Mesa Verde Province almost to its western limits. These people lived in more-or-less the same type of dwellings and subsisted by the same kind of rudimentary agriculture as their contemporaries in the Ackmen-Lowry area, the Ute Pasture, and on Stollsteimer Mesa. It was only in their earthenwares that they differed. The reasons for that would continue to confound students of their culture.

There were further rewards for Brew at Site 13. Fourteen randomly scattered Basketmaker III pithouses were found beneath some of the surface jacal rooms and in open places in the plazas. Although tree ring dates were not yet obtainable for years prior to the A.D. 700 range, Brew considered three of them to be a type predating that period because they were only partially subterranean. The other eleven were deep and larger with various of the usual attributes, including antechambers, ventilator shafts, deflectors, fire hearths, and post holes. Brew classed these eleven as typical Basketmaker III pithouses as described from other sectors of the province but more recent than the shallower example.

The number of these pithouses suggests an occupation of just a few families who may or may not have shared garden plots and labors. Even if all the living rooms in the later jacal community were not used at the same time, an obvious influx of settlers on the ridge had occurred after the Basketmaker period. Where did they come from, and what attracted them to this particular place? When did they decide to dwell on the surface of the ground rather than in its depths? And what prompted them to adopt a communal living pattern? These were engrossing questions for future researchers to consider.

To cap off Brew's first field expedition, the crew cleared a three-room, masonry house that had been erected over parts of five jacal chambers in the north arm of the Pueblo I settlement. Pottery types strewn about this unit were both Pueblo II and Pueblo III in age. Two typical Mesa Verde-style kivas were adjacent. Thus, the entire cultural sequence of the ancestral Pueblos as it was then known for the Mesa Verde Province, excluding Basketmaker II which then was considered to be confined to the Cedar Mesa-Grand Gulch sector, was present in this patch of Alkali Ridge. Brew came to find one stage of the prehistory but ended up with four that might have extended over seven or eight centuries.

Two years after his work on Alkali Ridge, Brew undertook a five-year project in the Hopi territory of northeastern Arizona, with Al Lancaster as his assistant. Lindsay Thompson, who had cooked at Alkali Ridge, joined the Arizona crew in the same capacity. Brew was so taken with both these home-spun men that he later named his two sons after them. That Arizona enterprise and World War II delayed publication of the Alkali Ridge findings for thirteen years. It was a major piece of scholarship that had a significant impact at the time. Today some of the lengthy discussions of nomenclature and biological concerns are no longer relevant. Brew did no further fieldwork in the province.

Action shifted from Alkali Ridge at the western borderlands of the Mesa Verde Province back to the central sector. In 1934 the Public Works Administration (PWA) allocated funds to Aztec Ruins National Monument and Mesa Verde National Park with a two-fold purpose: to create jobs for the public good and to aid persons in dire straits because of the Depression. Specifically, in these two government facilities archaeological resources were to be repaired and more fully interpreted for visitors. At the same time the Civilian Conservation Corps was to upgrade modern facilities to make them more pleasant and hopefully more interesting.

The Aztec custodian, as the superintendent was then called, had three interrelated plans for this specific program. First, he felt that something had to be done about the Great Kiva, which was facing total destruction. For lack of money, it had been left unprotected after Morris's 1921 excavation. Over the years its poorly preserved walls and floor features had eroded into a confused eyesore. Local citizens, who always had civic pride in the monument, pleaded with their congressmen for remedial help but without success. With the new opportunity to attack the problem, rather than just clearing up the weathered debris and installing a roof over what remained of the old structure, National Park Service officers made an unprecedented decision. They voted to rebuild the Great Kiva as a unique example of the engineering and construction abilities of the ancients. That would also demonstrate their religious orientation. They called Morris back to oversee the reconstruction.[104]

Two part-time crews were hired at forty-five cents an hour in order to spread the jobs around among local families. It was a reunion of sorts because many of the men had worked on the original excavation. One of them was Sherman Howe, one of the schoolboys who broke into the ruin in 1881. The crew went at their new tasks with vigor, reopening the floor area. They rebuilt walls, interior elements, and columns with stockpiled building stones from the Great House and others removed from La Plata Site 41. Timbers were brought from a sawmill in the San Juan Mountains to be cut and peeled for a single, massive, flat roof over the central chamber and surrounding surface rooms. Interior walls were plastered, whitewashed, and then painted dark red on the dado and lower elements. When completed five months later, the Great Kiva stood in the southern courtyard much as it had appeared eight hundred years earlier.

The enclosing walls of the resurrected building blocked out brilliant sunshine and the hum of activity in the courtyard. The hushed, darkened interior transformed what had been of little interest to the nonprofessionals into a sanctuary that was imbued with a heavy overlay of theatrics and piety. The fact that no one knows what went on there adds to its mystique. One can only envision costumed figures descending the slot ladders from the encircling surface dressing rooms to rhythmically dance on the two-foot drums (plank-covered floor pits) to guttural chants of a chorus and the plaintive wail of wooden flutes. What is known is that this edifice is a memorial to Earl Morris, whose ashes lie buried in the earthen floor of the old house he unearthed in his youth forty years before.

There were several instances on the Colorado Plateau during the 1930s of National Park Service partial reconstructions of prehistoric buildings.[105] In one case several rooms of the old Wupatki house became quarters for the resident ranger and his bride. Better judgment prevailed in years following with the realization that the original integrity of the edifices might be compromised. Consequently, a new policy was adopted wherein antiquities were to be kept in the state in which they were found but treated in such a way as to maintain them. That process added the new word of *stabilization* to the vocabulary of Southwestern archaeology and led to a specialization within the discipline.

A second PWA project at Aztec was repair of walls that had been damaged by neglect or natural forces. Once the remains of aboriginal structures became covered by accumulated soil and vegetation, they were essentially sealed to last in that condition far into the future. However, as soon as that covering was removed, as in the case of Aztec West, rapid deterioration took place. Moisture from rain and snow on wall tops seeped into cores, loosening facing and dissolving mud mortar. At Aztec West a further detrimental factor was an upslope, irrigated field that caused subsurface water to be brought up into foundations by capillary action. When excavated the site was dry, as shown by the large amount of perishables within it, but by the 1930s water was rising in the kivas that Morris had roofed, and chunks of wall were falling.

During his Aztec project, Morris capped tops of walls and intact roofs with untinted cement, as Fewkes was doing at Mesa Verde. These measures were unsightly and ineffective. Ultimately they had to be removed. The 1930s approach was to reset building stones in cement but to recess the joints. Much of the exterior facade of north and west walls of Aztec West was taken down and relaid in this manner. Roofs were covered with composition materials.[106]

At a later time drainage lines were trenched through the Aztec West courtyard and behind the north tier of rooms, and sump pumps were installed in attempts to divert unwanted water to the Animas River. One of the roofed kivas was completely backfilled. The roof was taken off the other so that it could dry out. To date no measures to permanently preserve this heritage from America's past have been successful. By its very nature, archaeology is destructive.

Another project of archaeological significance pertained to pottery recovered during excavation. Morris reassembled many vessels but simply bagged fragments of others for a future time. In 1934 he brought ceramist Alma Adams to Aztec to put fragments together and restore resulting pots to their original appearance.[107] She had done similar work with his own collection. Adams was so skillful in her techniques that it was impossible to distinguish aboriginal workmanship from her own. For that reason this procedure is now considered improper.

Beautification of the monument precinct was another of the Aztec custodian's goals.[108] Old sheds, a barn, and cross fences left from the days when the ruin was part of a working farm were removed, and a new boundary fence was put up to keep livestock out. Two dozen men working three horse-drawn wagons and a scraper tackled heaps of dirt and rocks left after excavation. These were in the courtyard and along the outside walls of the houseblock. This material was then spread on the dirt road leading from the Animas to the ruin that often was a quagmire in wet weather. In the process, it is possible that earthworks that might have been part of a ceremonial center—something unthought-of in the 1930s—were leveled. Knowingly, a trash dump was scraped away to make space for a parking lot in front of the new Visitor Center and museum that was being erected around what had been the Morris residence.

At the same time Morris was overseeing various aspects of the Aztec face-lift, he was given responsibility for doing the same at Mesa Verde. The emphasis there was on Cliff Palace. With the help of Al Lancaster, who had a temporary job with the National Park Service, Morris dismantled one corner of a four-story component of the house and relaid it. When first found in 1888, this part of the building had completely disintegrated. Fewkes rebuilt it so that the rest of the structure would not come down. His work might not have been entirely true to the original, and the material he used had badly weathered.

For his own information, Morris took time to put a trench into the Mummy Lake depression at the north end of Chapin Mesa to see if it might be another Great Kiva. He decided it was not. Current interpretation defines it as a reservoir for domestic water.[109]

The final chapter of 1930s archaeological investigations in the Mesa Verde Province is of special interest because for the first time Basketmaker II antiquities were found away from the far west. This came about through the illegal activities of an avid pothunter named Zeke Flora. During the 1930s, he was one of a dozen collectors who took to scouring the vicinity of Durango on the upper Animas River, where they learned there were numerous sources for artifacts that archaeologists then classed as Late Basketmaker III, now as Early Pueblo I. But one day in 1937, while Flora and a friend were poking around in a rock shelter north of town, he hit the jackpot. This was a burial deposit with nineteen individuals crammed into a crevice. Some were skeletonized, and some were desiccated. One female was a nearly complete, naturally mummified figure. The offerings and other things in the deposits with the human remains and the absence of pottery told Flora that this was a find predating those he was used to making and from which he had amassed a collection of hundreds of earthenwares. He carried this haul to his home in Durango and contacted Morris.[110]

During the summer of 1938, Morris brought his assistant Robert Burgh along to begin exploration of the Falls Creek overhang where Flora made his discoveries and which he anticipated would be a Basketmaker II site. In this he was not disappointed. Not only was he interested in Basketmaker material culture, with which he already had extensive experience, but he was convinced that someday and somewhere a lucky archaeologist would come across some sort of shelters they had built. Thus far the only constructions that could be attributed to them were cists scooped into the dirt fill of alcoves. Any flimsy structures they might have erected in the open would be found only through the most fortuitous circumstances. The best chance for such a discovery was in a sheltered place such as the alcove at Falls Creek.

Whether it was keen perception sharpened through repeated trial and error or sheer luck, Morris always had the knack of locating special objects or information. The Falls Creek shelter was no exception.

Not only did Morris and his crew expose a variety of cists of different sizes and shapes on the alcove surface but also the use-hardened floors of what undoubtedly must have been habitations. Generally they were ovoid in outline, of modest diameter, and had a central hole in which the diggers speculated heated rocks had been piled for warmth. Not until two seasons later, when work was going on in a contemporaneous site on a nearby hillside, did Morris and Burgh learn that the walls of these simple dwellings had been made of logs laid horizontally and held firm by mud.[111]

In addition to putting residential architecture on the list of Basketmaker II diagnostics, the Falls Creek artifact assortment showed that these Eastern Basketmakers were somewhat different in their crafts from their contemporaries to the west. Morris also believed them to be different physically although in most respects of the same basic stock. Tree ring dates then and corn kernels later dated by radiocarbon accelerator techniques took their occupation back into the several centuries before the Christian Era.[112]

On this high note in 1940, Morris rested his shovel and a trowel that was worn down almost to its handle. He had spent almost all his years in nonstop pursuit of the Old People, and he was ready to use the rest of his life getting caught up with a paper backlog.

Flora's mummy, named Esther, had been taken from Forest Service land without a permit to dig. After years of bitter disputes, the government confiscated her and the items from the burial deposit and placed them in the care of Mesa Verde National Park.

World events soon marked the end of the formative period in regional archaeology. Academically, the body of accrued knowledge, supplemented by research done in adjacent provinces of the Colorado Plateau, was outstanding. More than a millennium of the ancestral Pueblos' prehistory had been defined and given the gift of calendric time. Detailed typologies of the paraphernalia that made their lives function had been delineated in abundant detail. It was recognized that they had not been alone in the Southwest but shared its beneficence and contrariness with desert dwellers named Hohokam. Perhaps others were in the southerly basin and range country—the Mogollon—but they were not yet assuredly accepted. Just as the period was drawing to a close, the biological quandary over the long heads and the round heads was resolved with substantiation of a single Southwest Plateau stock.[113]

All this had been accomplished by only eight or nine men—and it was still a man's world—in a wild, pristine slice of the West. They endured its hardships in exchange for the exhilarating intellectual discoveries. As years passed, greater familiarity with the territory and what to expect in archaeological rewards dulled the feelings of excitement and adventure in doing unusual work in uncharted places. Generally these scholars worked alone or with minimal assistance from a person who could perhaps double as photographer or surveyor. For day wages, local laborers moved dirt, pushed stubborn vehicles stuck in muddy arroyos, or brewed a pot of strong cowboy coffee. To a man, these few archaeologists who had matured together in endeavors in which each was quite absorbed would assure those they considered less fortunate that they enjoyed the best of all lives. Perhaps they did. ✖

# MEANWHILE, BACK ON THE MESA

WHILE SIGNIFICANT INVESTIGATIONS WERE TAKING PLACE in other sectors of the Mesa Verde Province, archaeological activity where it all began was a hit-and-miss affair. Scholars from elsewhere secured some tree ring samples and made a cursory site survey of Chapin Mesa. A quick walk over a fire-burned area at the north end of Wetherill Mesa found a few previously unknown sites. Local staff processed random objects turned up in the course of park developments that disturbed the ground. One pre–World War II excavation carried out by Lancaster, then a full-time employee of the National Park Service, some Civilian Conservation Corps enrollees, and several Navajo workmen was a small pithouse (Pithouse B) that dated to the end of the sixth and beginning of the seventh centuries.[1] That made it coeval with the Basketmaker III structures in the Step House cave and substantiated what was presumed to be the earliest presence of ancestral Pueblos on the mesa. This Chapin Mesa pithouse was near Pithouse A, dug in 1919 and left to crumble under the unsightly roof ordered by Fewkes.

In the spring of 1942, Erik Reed, archaeologist at the National Park Service regional office in Santa Fe, excavated five sites in the lower Mancos Canyon.[2] This was part of the Ute Mountain Ute Indian Reservation that had been traversed by the Jackson and Holmes explorations of the 1870s and was thought to have experienced the same prehistory as the mesa to its northwest. Historic Ute materials were then of little concern. Reed's purpose was to examine Puebloan ruins damaged or threatened by road construction. He was helped by six Navajos and Utes attached to a Civilian Conservation Corps company. In addition to the excavations, Reed visited twenty-four sites in the lower sixteen miles of the canyon floor and north terraces. From these combined efforts, Reed felt that the occupation of this drier periphery lying at the base of the Mesa Verde cuesta, at an elevation of about six thousand feet, had been sparse but extended from Basketmaker III times through the twelfth century. Of particular interest was the amount of red pottery strewn around, causing one ruin near the mouth of the canyon to be named the Red Pottery Site. Reed thought this red ware along with some white ware examples were trade pieces. He discussed the troublesome relationship between the Chaco and Mesa Verde provinces as evidenced in some of this earthenware.

After World War II and the end of gas rationing, America took to the highways. These tourists were pleasure travelers. However, one by-product was an upsurge of interest in archaeology, which during the angst of the Depression generally was regarded as an arcane topic only for those on the outer fringes of the here and now.

Seeing an increase in visitation, the interpretive staff of Mesa Verde recognized that most such tourists did not know there was more to the prehistoric story of the park than the spectacular, highly publicized cliff dwellings. They laid plans to find and expose examples to demonstrate the evolutionary processes in architecture and handicrafts that culminated in those houses and their furnishings.

Don Watson headed the interpretive staff. After graduating from Denver University, he came to Mesa Verde in 1931. He remained there for his entire career with several titles, one of which was "park naturalist." He organized exhibits in the museum completed in 1936 with Works Progress Administration funds, arranged special programs for visitors, and gave count-less campfire talks. He always got a chuckle when he told the audience that they should see the Mesa Verde artifacts the next time they were in Helsinki. Watson did not know that the Nordenskiold collection had not been out of storage since it was received by the National Museum of Finland in the 1890s. Until the 1950s Watson had done no archaeological work in the park, nor was he expected to do so. The official mandate to preserve and protect the antiq-uities, with the implicit instruction of making them understandable to visi-tors, made him and his fellow rangers caretakers not researchers.

Personally, Watson was something of a character. A confirmed bachelor, he seemed to live on popcorn. His other passion was Navajo rugs, which he collected with abandon and piled in stacks around his house. After his retire-ment these rugs, greatly increased in value over the years, formed the basic inventory of a trading post that he opened in Cortez. The enticing aroma of hot popcorn continued to permeate the premises.

Another member of the interpretive staff was Jean Pinkley. Her father-in-law Frank had been the respected founder and administrator of Southwestern National Monuments, a division of the National Park Service. Her husband was lost in a submarine disaster in the Pacific during World War II. Jean had an academic background in archaeology and, with these personal considerations, was given the opportunity to join the male-dominated Park Service ranks as Mesa Verde's first female ranger. She had no prior field experience.

The one person in the lot who knew archaeology firsthand was Lancaster. After his work with Brew at Awatovi in Arizona ended, his talents were so appreciated that Nusbaum created a slot for him at Mesa Verde. Lancaster was not eager to guide visitors around, but give him a practical hands-on job, and he was in his element. For the next quarter of a century any time something involved the park's ruins, it also involved Lancaster.

The two known pithouses were near the start of a one-way gravel road that had been built along a splinter of Chapin Mesa from which visitors could pause to view Navajo Canyon and Echo House shadowed in one of the alcoves, Square Tower House across canyon, and Sun Temple at the end of the two-mile loop. The staff reasoned that if there were two early ruins in the area just two hundred feet apart, there likely were others. Their previous observations indicated that this part of the mesa top, about a mile in width and banked with deep, fertile loess soil, had been densely occupied in former times. It would be fortunate, indeed, if there were remains in chronological sequence from early to late along that road. They were in luck. Soon the road would be named Ruins Road.

In 1947 Deric O'Bryan, stepson of Nusbaum, who as a youngster had worked on the Step House dig and then was associated with the research center of Gila Pueblo in Arizona, moved about a mile down the road toward Sun Temple to excavate two neighboring sites in a place called Twin Trees. One ruin proved to be that of a surface hamlet of adjacent rooms having walls of slabs and probable jacal. Just five chambers were opened, but O'Bryan felt that the line extended another thirty feet. Two very deep, squared pithouses dated to the early to mid-A.D. 800s.

The second hamlet at this locale was a crude, two-room unit of unshaped stones incorporating an incipient unlined kiva that was built a century later.[3] In Pecos Classification terms, these two sites fit into the Late Pueblo I category. That left a gap of some two and a half centuries in the temporal sequence between Pithouse B and these habitations during which time the rangers believed the essential basis for ancestral Puebloan life was established. Three pithouses representing this period already had been cleared as a result of capital improvements in the park.[4] They served as models for the rangers, but they were not accessible to visitors.

So in the summer of 1950, Lancaster and Watson scouted the roadway for promising remains with which to fill the void. This was to be archaeology aimed specifically at public edification. They elected to delve into a depression and sherd scatter among the trees and about a hundred yards off the road between Pithouse B and the two later sites. What they found was not one pithouse but two, both satisfactorily fitting into the desired chronological scheme at about A.D. 700, or terminal Basketmaker III–initial Pueblo I.[5] One structure exhibited a few architectural improvements over Pithouse B. It had been abandoned sometime after having burned. Later it was filled by debris and earth from a second pit structure that cut into it. The more recent dwelling had wing walls separating a work area from the sleeping space, an antechamber for storage or entrance, and a ventilator shaft to the exterior that allowed stale air to flow out and fresh air to come in. Holes in the floor were clues to a four-post, roof support system. The twin houses provided a good example of the reuse through time of the same ground.

Later work would confirm the burning of many pit structures such as these. Flames in open hearths and wood roofing with bark insulation comprised a potentially deadly combination. Even though experimentation suggests that the heavy earth coverings of such construction smothered fires, accidental conflagrations undoubtedly occurred. In a perverse way this was to the benefit of archaeologists centuries later because these dwellings with their earthen walls and floors were sufficiently hardened and reddened so as to make them distinguishable from the surrounding ground into which they were sunk.

In a district lived in for hundreds of years, it was not unexpected to encounter buried antiquities whenever the ground was disturbed. Such was the case at Twin Trees. When parking space was being prepared beside the sites, workers discovered that the original road had been laid over part of a pit dwelling. Lancaster was called upon immediately to clear the remaining two-thirds. His work revealed that the structure was comparable to the squared pithouse in the opened site but not as deep. It had not burned. Its trashy fill suggested that it was a dumping place after abandonment, probably used by the residents of the hamlets at that location. Nearby were a pit and basin of unknown use. All these features were studied and then backfilled.[6]

An even more complex display of such reoccupation of the same bit of land was afforded by Site 16 a short distance down the road.[7] To give others on his staff a chance to participate in this endeavor, Watson sent Pinkley to be Lancaster's assistant. With the help of some Navajos from the maintenance crew, they cleared the remains of three episodes of usage piled indiscriminately one on top of another. At some time in the past a fire had swept across this area burning down the trees. In 1950 it was covered thickly with sagebrush and yucca and locally known as "the glade." A Ute trail from Mancos Canyon to the crest of the mesa passed through the zone. Early-day cowboys using this access stopped to dig in a sizable trash heap alongside the path. Signs of this disturbance were still visible in the 1950s.

Once the cover of vegetation was stripped away from the area, the oldest settlement was seen as an L-shaped complex. Because it had burned and been partially razed by later dwellers, little remained but charred post ends and baked pieces of adobe. A primitive kiva was in front. No tree ring dates were obtained. The team assigned the house an estimated date of A.D. 900, or Early Pueblo II.

Hamlet number two at Site 16 was a three-room group with a kiva to its south. It was placed over what had been the center of the earlier mud and post dwelling. Its walls were composed of single-course masonry. Lancaster and Pinkley pinned its date to a fifty-year period between A.D. 975 and 1025, or middle Pueblo II.

The third complex on this spot was a double-course masonry house of undetermined size. It overlay parts of the second dwelling. Associated with it were the lower walls of three towers. Off to one side was a well-developed kiva having masonry walls, masonry pilasters on an encircling bench upon which a cribbed-beam superstructure would have rested, and a southern recess. These were all features that characterize later kivas on the mesa. A tree ring date of A.D. 1074 established construction within the last stages of Pueblo II.

Another instance of necessary salvage work occurred near Site 16. A previously undetected Basketmaker III pithouse close to the three-village complex was cut into by a trencher laying a pipeline. Lancaster and archaeologist Alden Hayes, in the park on a special project, and their crews finished exposing it, recorded its elements, then lined it with thick, protective cardboard. Finally the depression was obliterated with sterile soil. The structure corresponded in details and date to Pithouse B.[8]

A final exhibit on this architectural tour through time was an Early Pueblo III houseblock named Sun Point Pueblo and studied by Lancaster and Philip Van Cleave of the interpretive staff.[9] It was what was left of a rectangular, double-course masonry houseblock of about a dozen rooms and a tower connected to a kiva by a tunnel. The diggers believed it was similar to hundreds of unexcavated abodes scattered over the mesa. This one obviously had been robbed of its building blocks and timbers by later builders of the cliff structures just a stone's throw away.

A few yards beyond Sun Point Pueblo is an overlook from which one can see twelve cliff dwellings, including Cliff Palace near the head of Cliff Canyon and four prominent ruins in adjoining Fewkes Canyon. The possibly unfinished Sun Temple commands a mesa top across the way.

Thus, the Mesa Verde team was able to provide the visiting public with an unparalleled architectural display of seven sites covering some seven centuries of development that in the course of an hour or so can be viewed virtually from roadside. This "drive-in" arrangement makes Mesa Verde National Park unique among all prehistoric precincts in North America. But only the informed know that what is apparent is a mere sampling of what lies concealed all around.

Lancaster's work along the Ruins Road was not finished. Insubstantial aboriginal buildings had to be protected with expansive roofs, and, in the case of masonry, building blocks at the tops of walls had to be reset in cement. These measures continued an ongoing stabilization program directed by Lancaster and manned by a Navajo crew that he trained.

Watson had advocated an archaeological survey of Chapin Mesa for years but had never received enough funds or time to put his proposal into gear. In the new flush of interest in regional antiquities, he finally was successful but only because he served as supervisor and took care of the inevitable governmental paperwork. Lancaster and several seasonal rangers were the ones who actually tromped over the ground from the southern tip of the plateau to its northern limits.

Fascination with the park's attractions, and with regional prehistory in general, was welcome. More awareness of this American patrimony meant more citizen concern for its preservation. The negative side was that modern facilities meant to accommodate a few hundreds soon were overcrowded with a few thousands. Heavy human traffic through primitive structures of unreinforced mud and stone threatened their survival. Interpreters were assigned to crowd control. Neither visitors nor rangers were pleased.

A further development in the aftermath of World War II was a widely shared curiosity about distant cultures, past and present. Coupled with the GI Bill which allowed many young people to attend college, that interest promoted the creation of new departments of anthropology. One was at the University of Colorado in Boulder. Right after the war, anthropology became part of the curriculum of an unwieldy Department of Social Sciences that also included economics, political science, and sociology.

Swelling enrollment soon separated these four disciplines into more manageable entities.

Robert Lister was the first archaeologist to join the faculty. A native Southwesterner, he had had considerable field experience in archaeology in the Southwest and Mexico as a student and as a ranger-archaeologist for the National Park Service. He was anxious to train another generation in the techniques of his calling. During summers from 1953 through 1956, he directed a field school in archaeology for undergraduates at Mesa Verde National Park.

The headquarters for the summer exercise was a building used during the winters as a one-room elementary school for children of the permanent employees. Alice Lancaster was the teacher. An adjacent building served as bunkhouse for the mixed student body who came from across the country. The young ladies added excitement but few thought of them as potential professionals in a man's vocation. Little did any of these students realize that the usual reality of field archaeology did not include plentiful good food, hot water, electricity, and comfortable beds. Not to mention ready access to a soda fountain, curio shop, bookstore, washing machine, public phones, and a post office. In an abridged version of the Old West, the evening entertainment included campfire talks in a lovely amphitheater overlooking Navajo Canyon, Navajo Indians shuffling perfunctorily around the fire performing a social dance, and a Stetson-wearing wrangler rearing his horse into the circle to describe the available back country trips. But the young folks did know strenuous work in the hot summer sun as they strove at the requisite shoveling, troweling, mapping, and note taking.

Beside his teaching responsibilities, Lister's goal was to augment the park's on-site exhibits and expand its accounts of their prehistoric background. The Far View section at the north end of Chapin Mesa was chosen for investigation. No work had been undertaken there since Fewkes dug early in the century at Far View Pueblo, Pipe Shrine, and a few small structures nearby, all accounts of which were largely unpublished.

The general consensus among knowledgeable observers was that increased population and perhaps over-exploitation of the land toward the southerly ends of the mesa prompted a Puebloan resettlement farther up the cuesta. There the soil is thinner, but the annual precipitation is greater due to somewhat higher elevation of about seventy-one hundred feet. Just when such a shift took place was uncertain, as was how long it lasted.

Over four summers the students exposed three small hamlets to the west of the Chapin Mesa road opposite Far View Pueblo.[10] Because two of them were thought suitable for public inspection, the stabilization team worked alongside the students making repairs.

Sometime during the A.D. 1000s a few Puebloans pioneered a patch of the tableland to form a scattered neighborhood of modest dwellings for a nuclear family or two with garden plots out beyond. At this north end of the mesa the dense, evergreen cover begins to be replaced by big sagebrush and open-grassed areas, suggesting an agricultural environment somewhat variable from that to the south. The kind of houses the settlers erected were similar to the second village at Site 16 on Ruins Road. According to the standards of the time, these builders leveled the ground with low, dirt platforms, laid up house walls for a few adjoining rooms a single stone in width, and roofed them with timbers, brush, and earth. They also dug and roofed one or two pits in front that could be used for rituals. They threw their refuse to the southeast in accord with some sort of building code. Not all these structures were in use at exactly the same time nor were they identical. Nevertheless, they comprised a cohesive grouping that Lister and his associates considered to be of the Early to mid-Pueblo II and Early Pueblo III phases.

After a generation or two, some of the occupants of these houses felt the urge to move. They did not go far, maybe just a quarter of a mile away, but move they did and began again with the same routines and outfittings. A few years later they or others of their kind were back. They salvaged building stones from the original structures that their grandfathers built, laboriously smoothed the ground again, and put new buildings on top of the buried ones without regard to their layout. Construction techniques had advanced somewhat beyond those of former days. The new buildings had walls two stones in width. The builders daringly stacked some rooms to two stories. They placed kivas within the arms of living chambers and lined them with masonry. They dug some tunnels to interconnect them. Occasionally they raised a tower off to one side. This mode was similar to that found at the third house in Site 16, in Late Pueblo II or Early Pueblo III.

Together these three Far View habitations and the one at Site 16 displayed a puzzlingly fluid settlement pattern that had not been noticed so definitively in former digs, but which later research would confirm to be highly characteristic of the ancient Puebloans. Was it a response to the environmental conditions or to nebulous social or political factors?

The defensive appearance of the indrawn architecture of a compact block of more substantial domestic rooms and kivas enclosed in a compound with limited access was undeniable but curious. What was there to fear? Excavators noted no discernible evidence for violence against the residents, with one exception.

Student enthusiasm for digging was aroused one summer when they uncovered a male skeleton who had a sharp, bone awl lodged in his chest cavity. An obvious victim of foul play, his body had been dumped, or merely fallen, helter-skelter onto a kiva floor between the opening to the ventilator shaft and an upright stone slab in front of it.[11] Someone long ago got away with murder. Otherwise, all seemed quiet on the Chapin Mesa front.

Still, all apparently was not right. These small outlying settlements were vacated sometime before about A.D. 1150. Possibly their residents congregated for greater security into the larger Far View Pueblo, if, in fact, they felt the need for strength in numbers. In any case, their stay there was relatively brief because that edifice also was abandoned soon thereafter as the people moved again. This time they went to the southern brink of the tableland where their ancestors had first laid claim to the Mesa Verde six hundred years earlier. The constructions they crammed into every available opening in the cliffs were more far-reaching but just as transitory.

Up until the waning years of the thirteenth century, the repeated moves by the Mesa Verdeans were a periodic shifting over parcels of the terrain at hand: from alcoves to mesa crests, to talus slopes, to canyon bottoms, back to mesa tops. Whether traumatic or merely adjustments, the final move was vastly different because it took these semitransients totally out of the northern San Juan region, leaving behind a myriad of questions.

The University of Colorado field school efforts added considerable new information about Pueblo II and Early Pueblo III periods and the associated material goods in the park. However, the planned display of the sites themselves was put on hold as another more ambitious endeavor unfolded.

For the half century that Mesa Verde had been a national holding all development to make it available to the American people had been confined to Chapin Mesa. And rightly so because that was the broadest of the cuesta fingers and the locale of the ruins that set off the stampede for relics and the tidal surge of publicity that followed. By the 1950s the combined pressures of too many people and too few exposed attractions culminated in a bold, long-term project designed to remedy both problems.

This would be an archaeological program of a magnitude never before attempted on the Colorado Plateau. There had been three or four multiyear investigations but those primarily were focused on a single site. Aztec West was an example. At Mesa Verde the authorities proposed to open and repair three major cliff dwellings and an indefinite number of surface sites on Wetherill Mesa that would represent the total gamut of ancient life in the park as it was then known. Moreover, the enterprise was counter to established park policy not to engage in primary research for which there never had been funding. In this instance it was justified because of its overarching purpose. Congress was sold on the idea that both the public and science would benefit. Antiquities would be reclaimed, and Wetherill Mesa would become a mirror image of Chapin Mesa in terms of modern conveniences. Hopefully these works would relieve congestion and stimulate regional studies.

The proposed project was not to be a solo performance by a lone scientist out to fulfill his dreams. Six trained archaeologists and a collections manager would be brought to the park and housed for the anticipated six-year duration of the inquiry. Government employees would take charge of logistical and stabilization needs. Development of interpretive and comfort facilities would follow to create what today's entrepreneurs might call an archaeological theme park.

Conrad Wirth, director of the National Park Service, appointed an advisory committee of Southwestern scholars that included Emil Haury, chairman of the Department of Anthropology and director of the Arizona State Museum at the University of Arizona; J. O. Brew, director of the Peabody Museum, Harvard University; Frank H. H. Roberts, head of the Bureau of American Ethnology, Smithsonian Institution; and Robert Lister, chairman of the Department of Anthropology, University of Colorado. Lister was the only one of the group having personal acquaintance with Mesa Verde. Wirth also met with the board of trustees of the National Geographic Society, of which he was a member, to invite them to tour Wetherill Mesa and preview the proposal. The result of this sly diplomacy was that the National Geographic Society agreed to fund generously thirty-six ancillary studies to afford a broad and in-depth background for the physical, biological, and cultural milieu that had probable bearing on the lifeways of the Mesa Verdeans. This was tacit recognition of the fact that humans do not live in a vacuum, but in a world whose parameters most archaeologists cannot afford nor have the personal expertise to investigate.

In the fall of 1958 the nucleus of a professional staff was assembled. First to report was Alden Hayes, newly appointed Park Service archaeologist, who was to make a thorough reconnaissance of the prehistoric resources so that sites appropriate for the interpretive program could be examined. This would provide scientific data for the mesa that had never been gathered.

Shortly he was joined by Douglas Osborne, recruited from an academic position in California to be director of the Wetherill Mesa Project. Hayes, Osborne, and Lister had been classmates and personal friends at the University of New Mexico when Hewett was still chairman of the Department of Anthropology. El Toro would have been pleased that three of his trainees were carrying on in the preserve that he had had a critical role in setting aside. Before the fall was over, George Cattanach, Park Service archaeologist, arrived to help arrange a camp and plan the major excavation of Long House. Carroll Burroughs, another University of New Mexico colleague, replaced Watson, who was retired, on the resident professional staff. The clubby atmosphere that had long prevailed in regional archaeology continued with a new crop of enthusiasts.

The following spring and summer largely were devoted to getting ready to begin. A commodious prefabricated building was erected on Chapin Mesa to be used for offices, laboratory, and curation. Out where the fieldwork was to take place, a primitive road over a horse trail down the spine of Wetherill Mesa allowed trucks to cart army surplus matériel to a camp clearing above Long House. There, maintenance crews put up a tent city, latrines, kitchen-mess hall, office, toolshed, electric generators, and water tank to bring a modicum of modern civilization next door to that of the ancestral Puebloans.

The previous fall, Hayes walked over an extensive sector of the north end of Wetherill Mesa in a quest for archaeological remains there. Vegetation consumed in a 1934 fire had not come back. Hayes found more than one hundred sites. But with initiation of the full-blown program, attention shifted to the more heavily occupied central mesa.

Hayes and a five-man crew thrashed through the thick brush understory on the mesa top, scrambled down sloughy drifts of chunky talus, crawled along projecting ledges while trying not to look down into yawning chasms, rappelled over canyon rims with stout ropes coiled about their midsections, and descended the escarpments on swinging steel-wire ladders. On occasion they ascended the heights by throwing their ropes over projecting roof beams of structures above, as had been done by the first explorers in these parts, but their goals were nonetheless daunting and dangerous. Hayes later recounted how more than once they made their way with great difficulty into a seemingly inaccessible ruin to find Wetherill initials or names scrawled on the walls. Once they came across a very cold hearth around which were rusted sardine cans left from Nordenskiold's 1891 camp above Kodak House.[12] Historic finds made prehistoric ones even more interesting.

Between the 1920s and the 1950s there had been only a few hasty investigations and stabilizations on Wetherill Mesa. Little temporal or spatial information resulted. Hayes's surface survey corrected that. It was as thorough as possible without actual digging. The ground was retraced four times. In all, Hayes and his crew tabulated eight hundred archaeological sites in the prescribed area and still were left with the uneasy feeling that they had missed others. Besides habitations, evidence for human activity included towers, shrines, check dams, potsherd scatters, rock art, and piles of rocks someone had stacked up for a reason not now apparent. They may have been boundary markers used by a kinship group to claim its territorial domain. Their placement at precarious cliff edges suggests a more esoteric reason.

By Hayes's calculations, this one tongue of Wetherill Mesa land—ten miles long, less than a mile to three hundred feet in width, with barricades of naked rock and no permanent water source—had supported as many as seven hundred individuals over the course of seven centuries. A onetime rancher himself, Hayes thought that number probably was too high considering the barely adequate nature of the place. But the needs of the ancients certainly were fewer and their expectations far less.

If Hayes's cultural assessments were correct, the peak population came in the A.D. 700–900 interval. This was a time when the blueprints for the Pueblo culture were becoming fixed tenets. As a group, these people preferred to live and farm on a belt of flat, fertile soil that mantles the girth of the mesa.[13] Certainly not by chance, they chose what was the most productive dry farming tract with deep loess soils that fostered their well-being and increased numbers. The southern peripheries of the mesas are too hot and dry; the northern rims have thin residual soil and strong winds.

For whatever reason, a population decline began before the end of the first millennium. This was accompanied by a change in location for those who chose to stay. Some folks remained on the mesa top. Others put their homes in the alcoves, on talus slopes, and in the bottoms of canyons on either side of the mesa. These were localities which researchers had not considered likely before this survey showed otherwise. The numerous cliff-side openings had been attractive to the first arrivals, and they likely continued to represent safe havens in times of trouble. Their use by Pueblo II and earlier peoples had been overlooked previously because subsequent occupation obscured the evidence. Unquestionably, talus drifts were not ideal situations for homes and gardens because so much labor would have to be invested to make them suitable. However, the northeastern orientation of many of the slopes held snow until late spring to provide moisture for seed germination. Summer rains came too late. Pueblo II farmers blocked ravines down the slopes to make tiers that collected soil and water during runoffs and so formed additional usable patches of farmland. Cold air blowing through canyons shortened the growing season at lower elevations, as did fewer hours of sunlight due to the bounding cliffs. These drawbacks were offset by rich alluvium and a higher water table. Astute farmers that they were, the Puebloans made use of all microenvironments.

Even so, in Hayes's view, throughout Pueblo III fewer people were around. Most of those seem to have wanted to retreat back into the overhangs, their hazards and inconveniences notwithstanding. They still maintained farms on the mesa tops. Of the 153 sites the survey recorded for this period, one hundred were in alcoves. The majority were just a few scruffy chambers for daily life or for foodstuffs to sustain it, but others were the ultimate cities of the time. Living cheek by jowl in the larger of the houses meant a dramatic social change with probable stresses. Even if the structures were divided into suites for family groups, as some scientists suggest, it made for an unaccustomed togetherness. Through time, the customary residence of the ancestral Pueblos was a small house with an average of six to nine rooms where parents, offspring, one or two grandparents, and maybe several stray clan or lineage members passed their days. Groups may have come together on special occasions and shared some sort of suprahousehold affiliation, but theirs was essentially a day-to-day dispersed settlement of the land. A degree of independence of spirit is inherent. This supposition is reinforced by the fact that not everyone left the mesa top. One can assume that there were some diehards who refused to budge no matter what their relatives said, or that they already had given up and walked down Mancos Canyon and out of the territory, never to return.

Long House is the featured attraction on Wetherill Mesa. Hence, it received considerable attention during this project. Cattanach got a choice assignment because no Mesa Verde cliff dwelling had been excavated using modern techniques. Here was a challenge at its best.[14] Arthur Rohn and Robert Nichols helped him from time to time. Nichols also served as the resident tree ring specialist. Lancaster was general supervisor for all the digs and stabilization that took place. The days of hiring laborers right off the farm were past. In the late 1950s there was a large pool of male college students eager to participate. Four dozen joined the team, probably comprising a work force larger than that which originally built the house. A number of them were sons of archaeologists. These fellows brought a new exuberance to the job. They did not know the lay of the land the way the locals did, but they had a lively curiosity about what they were experiencing.

Long House was named in 1890 by the Wetherills because it stretches around a lengthy U-shaped alcove at the head of a draw off the east side of Rock Canyon. They did some digging in part of the site and introduced Nordenskiold to it, who did some more. Both parties, and perhaps others, were disappointed in the low artifact returns and the enormous amount of work involved in moving fallen materials. Spalls, clods, brush, and boulders made up a burdensome cover over much of the site. As a result, Long House in 1959 was almost virgin digging territory.

The archaeologists quickly understood the reason for the heavy overburden. In Cattanach's opinion, old workmanship had been shoddy. Not that he expected the Parthenon, but neither was this Mesa Verde at its best. Walls formed of rows of fill provided an unsatisfactory base. Cattanach felt that whole sections had collapsed even while the building was still in use, bringing down a shower of debris. Once the house was emptied and left untended, extensive decay soon followed. Further agents of destruction included a one-hundred-foot-high waterfall that poured over the cliff face during summer thunderstorms and an active seep at the rear of the cave. In regard to the latter, ecologists believe that in times past, when the pinyon-juniper cover was removed for farming and fuel needs, a greater flow of water than at present percolated downward through the sandstone cap rock and out at the fissures. Moisture could have dissolved the mortar and porous rock of the house.

To facilitate getting equipment down to the site and recovered specimens out, the excavators turned to modern devices. A wooden scaffold supporting a commercial derrick was built jutting past the cliff edge. A winch secured there lowered and raised an old mine bucket to and from the work area. Another twenty-foot-high scaffold with a wheelbarrow ramp extending out over the ruin and the trash dump downslope allowed workers to dispose of spoil dirt beyond the house. A heavy-duty hose was connected to a water tank next to the derrick so that several drums in the ruin below could be filled with water for mortar.

As work progressed, laborers found some wood in place. Elements such as doorjambs, lintels, wall pegs, and fallen beams had survived centuries because of the aridity. However, only two partial roofs were present. It was obvious to the crew that someone had ripped out the timbers and disposed of them. The same situation had been observed in other cliff dwellings. If these were the last constructions on the Mesa Verde, as generally believed, who could have been responsible for this robbery? Could the culprits have been the Puebloans themselves? In their dark, last days, maybe cold and surrounded by a landscape that after centuries of exploitation was denuded, they might have had no recourse but to dismantle their own roofs for fuel. If that scenario is correct, it is one filled with the pathos of a bitter end to life in the northern San Juan. In earlier times dwellings may have been burned upon abandonment in a symbolic return to Mother Earth, but this beam removal suggests an act of sheer desperation. Or perhaps lingering residents used this wood.

Tree ring dates, architecture, and pottery enabled Cattanach to define five building enterprises at Long House. Of special interest was his discovery of a Basketmaker III pithouse beneath several later rooms. This was further confirmation of the use of some, if not all, of the alcoves by the first peoples to make Mesa Verde their home. Most of the dated sample at Long House revealed the year A.D. 648 as the time when this Basketmaker III abode was made ready. Chapin Gray pottery scattered through the fill under adjoining rooms was the recognized earthenware of that time.

The diggers unearthed other pottery more typical of Pueblo I and Pueblo II periods, but it could not be correlated with extant constructions. One possible exception was a later kiva that might have been remodeled from a Pueblo I pit dwelling.

The basic erection of Long House took place in a fifty-year span of time from about A.D. 1200 to 1250. Persons taking over the alcove at that time placed rooms in the most suitable flat parts of the opening. During the following two decades, additions took the structure, like malleable putty, into all the odd-shaped crannies of the overhang, outward and upward. The final room count was an estimated 150, some rising to three stories, and twenty-one kivas and work areas. Not here or at any other ancestral Pueblo community were there toilet facilities. The last cutting date for a Long House construction timber is A.D. 1280. This date exactly corresponds to final dates in neighboring cliff dwellings.[15] Doomsday for the ancestral Pueblos of Mesa Verde had arrived.

Recent remapping of Cliff Palace, long considered the largest of the cliff dwellings, has reduced the number of rooms there to 150. That makes Long House and Cliff Palace of equal size. These were two contemporary centers undoubtedly of comparable standing, one east on Chapin Mesa and one west on Wetherill Mesa. What was their relationship, if any?

Two unusual features were highlighted by the work at Long House. Totally unexpected was a fifty-six by thirty-four-foot plaza in the center of the U-arc.

With space in the residence at a premium, such a construction must have had special significance. Cattanach and Lancaster likened it to an unroofed Great Kiva. However, there were no characteristic embellishments other than an unused, raised firebox and two probable benches along walls. There is a similar space at Fire Temple on Chapin Mesa, likewise for an unknown function.

Two small masonry constructions had been stuck up on narrow ledges high above Long House. They now appear stranded because the rooms below from which they were entered have fallen. In themselves, they are not uncommon, but the several dozen windows piercing their outer walls are not typical for Mesa Verde cliff dwellings. Cattanach and his team saw that they were just a foot or two off the floor and positioned to have a view over parts of the house below or the narrow canyon ravine leading up to it. Who were the sentinels and for whom were they watching? These researchers called the openings "breastworks." Nordenskiold said they were loopholes through which arrows could have been shot.[16] Their size and placement makes that doubtful.

Not unexpectedly, pottery was the most abundant of the recovered artifacts. Diggers reclaimed almost three hundred whole or restorable vessels, along with sixty-three thousand fragments. They retrieved a complete inventory of durable stone and bone objects and a wide assortment of more perishable things such as sandals, coiled baskets, cordage, bundles of yucca fibers and leaves, scraps of foodstuffs, prayer sticks, and arrow shafts. The first explorers lamented what they regarded as a dearth of relics, but to current scholars the specimen take was satisfactory. There were no surprises, but the items added to the database and provided in-house collections that had been absent in the past.

Stabilization continued apace with the excavations. Capping stones were reset and cement joints washed with the local red soil. A little weather and elapsed time made today's work indistinguishable from yesterday's. Workmen recribbed one kiva roof in the aboriginal style so that visitors can share the specialness that enclosure creates.

The second Wetherill Mesa cliff dwelling to be made ready for exhibit was Mug House. It also overlooks Rock Canyon at a point north of Long House where the mesa pinches down to a mere 750-foot width. Arable land there obviously was limited, but it was suitable for dry farming so long as the average annual precipitation rate remained at about eighteen inches. To augment their domestic water supply, the natives dug a tank at the base of a sheer, rock cliff face and dammed it with masonry. Summer rains and winter snow melt filled it from the pour-off above.

Excavation of Mug House was the responsibility of Arthur Rohn.[17]

Smaller than Long House, its pre-excavation condition was much the same with comparable tactile problems for workmen. They needed the same sort of jerry-built apparatus to cope with the cliff-side setting of the ruin, access to which was difficult. Generally speaking, Mug House did not differ appreciably from Long House in its architectural details. It was not erected along a preconceived plan, but like the other buildings in the cliffs, grew as needs arose. Ultimately it contained ninety-four rooms, eight kivas, and two towers. Perhaps it housed eighty to one hundred persons at any one time.[18] One kiva still bore patches of painted mud plaster. It was another of the time's split-level houses, with a set of secondary chambers on a ledge above the principal dwelling. Probably first settled in the early AD. 1200s over some Pueblo II occupation, its final construction beam date is A.D. 1277.[19]

The diggers at Mug House found an interesting use of local resources by the aboriginal masons. Eons ago a deep deposit of adobe washed into a nearby recess. Vertical impressions left by digging sticks on the deposit face were clues to old mining operations. Observers believed that several associated pits occurred where the hacked-down earth had been puddled for mortar. Lancaster followed the example of the ancients and made use of the adobe in his stabilization efforts.

Pottery was particularly plentiful at Mug House. In fact, the ruin was named because the Wetherills found four mugs that were tied together by a thong through the handles. Excavations and early collecting produced an assemblage of five hundred complete vessels from this one site, emphasizing the great importance of the pottery-making craft to these people. The Rohn crew unearthed seventeen large, corrugated jars with lids buried to their orifices under the dirt floors.[20] This was not surprising because the storage use of such jars was well-known, perhaps first from Morris's work at Aztec West. Frequently, shelled corn, corn on the cob, beans, and seeds of various wild plants were found in them or sprinkled around. However, the contents of one such jar did seem strange. Some Puebloan housewife had put about one hundred shrews, tiny mouselike creatures, into cold storage. Their dried carcasses were reduced to minute bone splinters and fluffs of fur. Why? For that, the scientists had no answer. One must have had to have been there to understand.

The Step House overhang on the eastern edge of Wetherill Mesa overlooking Long Canyon was to be included in the proposed exhibits because of its uniqueness in having two distinct occupations separated by six centuries that were visible from one vantage point. In the south end are the four late Basketmaker pit dwellings discovered in 1926 by Nusbaum and his crew. In the north end are the badly deteriorated vestiges of a moderate size Pueblo III house.

While stabilizers went to work cleaning up the crumbled pithouses and partially reconstructing one in order to demonstrate its interior and roof composition, Nichols and a small team tackled the masonry house. In practically all instances where the ancestral Pueblos took advantage of the honeycombed nature of the cliffs, they jampacked every bit of available space with their assemblages, if not for bedrooms or kitchens, then for pantries. Why not at this alcove?

One possible explanation may be that it was a cold place to live because the opening faces generally east and is sunless in winter after late morning. The builders crowded their house in the north end and oriented it as far to the south as they could, but that may not have been enough for pleasant tenancy. From the last construction date of A.D. 1226, one might assume that rather soon the builders of the Pueblo III house withdrew to warmer quarters.[21]

Apparently this disadvantage did not bother the earlier Basketmakers. Nichols found three more seventh-century pit dwellings beneath the thirteenth-century house. They may have been snugger, with dirt walls retaining hearth and body heat to a greater degree than the surface habitations of stone.

Regardless of whether Step House was a desirable place in which to live, residents thereabouts converted the rock-strewn slopes below into gardens. Surveyors counted one hundred check dams across small drainage courses coming off the tableland. Some were connected over slopes to make broad, horizontal, contour terraces.[22] Nordenskiold remarked about their similarity to farms in southern Europe, where rocks and gravel often serve as mulch as they did here.

Project planners chose an area on the mesa top near Long House to be developed as a display along the lines of the Ruins Road loop on Chapin Mesa. The archaeological survey indicated this to be a promising plot.

Such an overview is a necessary first step but is not foolproof. No surveyor is sufficiently clairvoyant to be certain of just what lies under the ground. For a variety of reasons, surface indications can be misleading. Or in the case of earliest human presence, there may be no detectable surficial sign of it. A further hindrance at Mesa Verde is the tangle of vegetation on the mesa crest that makes it impossible in many places to have more than thirty to fifty feet of visibility.

Hayes and Lancaster devoted three digging seasons from 1961 through

1963 to extensive excavation of a series of sites scattered over less than seven acres that exemplify ancestral Pueblo occupation from its earliest to its latest manifestations. They felt that there must have been late Basketmakers around, but evidence for them was scant. In fact, the survey listed only nine sites as being of that period. Hayes made the arbitrary decision of classifying questionable early materials as Pueblo I.[23] Since no Basketmaker II horizon had been identified at Mesa Verde, he was especially sorry that he had not been fortunate enough to find it. Nor could he then feel that he had unquestionably come upon its Basketmaker III successor.

Over one low ridge Hayes and his crew had picked up burned sandstone spalls, such as would have been used in construction, and a few gray potsherds of the opening phases of the craft. However, there was no depression or other trash to suggest a buried dwelling. Nevertheless, the place seemed worth investigating. That is when the soil auger became useful. This is a tool like a large corkscrew that can grind out a core of earth. At this spot, then, the laborers twisted up three-foot-long columns of dirt in twenty-five to thirty plugs. Two of them contained bits of charcoal. The archaeologists believed that the tool had tapped into residue of a burned structure or hearth.

The next step was the arduous one of felling woodland growing over and around the zone that was to be tested by shovel, mattock, and trowel. The diggers were rewarded with a typical, shallow, ovoid Basketmaker III pithouse and antechamber. It had burned but enough wood remained to produce a cutting date exactly the same as the pithouse in the Long House alcove just a few hundred yards away. Then, as now, individual preference about where to live must have played a role.

With the success of the auger, further holes were sunk a short distance away. Another charcoal core led to the antechamber of a second pithouse. To Hayes's disgust, the chamber itself was under a hard-packed, dirt service road. He grumbled that it would have been preferable to chop down trees to get to it rather than to dig up that compacted road. But scientist that he was, he continued. The dwelling was a mate to the first pithouse except that a later jacal unit had been put over it. This pithouse dated to the A.D. 600s.[24]

A century later a sprawling surface Pueblo I village existed just to the south. It was a series of contiguous slab and jacal cells that to Hayes were two- to three-room apartments. They spoke of a major change in social structure as well as in architecture. Hayes estimated that all together there were originally some 150 rooms in linear or arc clusters forming a community. Following Morris's nomenclature, he termed a large pit dwelling a proto-kiva, believing it first was a dwelling and later became the scene of group rituals. It did not yet have the traditional kiva features but was on the way to becoming such a construction. General architectural elements and the village arrangement were reminiscent of Pueblo I settlements by then known in other sectors of the Mesa Verde Province.

At Mesa Verde the Pueblo I phase dated to the A.D. 700s and 800s. Taking into consideration a Basketmaker III pit dwelling in the neighborhood, Hayes figured that this locality had been lived in for about two and a half centuries. Over the years structures were burned, then demolished, then buried naturally or purposefully, and then reoccupied by descendants of the pioneers, who made such liberal use of earlier building supplies that they almost obliterated the past.[25]

In the opinion of the experts, sometime during the latter half of the tenth century what had been a large concentration of Mesa Verdeans on this finger of the cuesta dispersed. When they alighted again, their numbers had dwindled. They chose to live in smaller groups and in different sorts of shelters. This was just one stage of the often inexplicable ebb and flow of ancient life in the Mesa Verde Province that keeps scholars engrossed, and employed.

Further south of the Pueblo I village was a house mound with a midden of impressive proportions to its south. It was peppered with pottery fragments of many different styles and times of manufacture. One of the stabilizers called the ruin Kin Naaschiti, or "Badger House," because some of those animals had burrowed in it. Thankfully, the National Park Service opted for the English translation. What was revealed by the excavations was a Pueblo II house whose walls were made up of stones coarsely shaped in a technique archaeologists know as *scabbled*. An incipient kiva also was present. This was like the Pueblo II ruin excavated on Chapin Mesa by the University of Colorado group.

Next came a Late Pueblo III revisit to the location and a full complement of the compound, pecked (dimpled) masonry mode of that time, with a masonry-lined kiva connected by a forty-foot-long tunnel to a tower. Forty-four tree ring dates of A.D. 1257 proved that not all folks in this troubled thirteenth century fled to the caves, but they also did not linger long at Badger House.[26] In his report, Hayes termed these sites the Badger House Community. In so doing, he heralded the future interest in study of settlement patterns.

Two other Pueblo II houses were dug as part of the Wetherill Mesa Project. Big Juniper House near Step House proved to be too complex to make a suitable exhibit because of repeated reuse and rebuilding. Its last construction date was A.D. 1130.[27] The site was backfilled. Two Raven House near Badger House also had been used at two successive times. It was built one hundred years, maybe three generations, before Big Juniper House in A.D. 1032.[28] This ruin was not so confusing, would make a more easily understood exhibit for the lay visitor, and could be readily stabilized. It was retained as an open site for public viewing.

One feature at Two Raven House that was considered unique at the time of study, but which later work shows to be common at various periods, was a palisade. Only the stumps of a fence remained, but when in use it was a line of closely spaced, upright stakes interwoven with branches. The purpose of palisades has been variously interpreted as wind breaks or walls of defense. Or, according to some, they were nothing more than turkey pens.

Ranchers that they were, it came as no surprise to the Wetherills that the soft down of turkey feathers was used by the ancestral Pueblos as padding for their yucca fiber robes. The question since posed by archaeologists and ornithologists is whether the birds were wild or domesticated types, with identification of archaeological remains being inconclusive. A few fragile eggshells and bones of poults may indicate that the birds were actually being bred rather than captured out under the trees. What is certain from the depth of matted droppings is that turkeys were confined in dark, rear yards of most cliff dwellings. Rohn considered one room at Mug House to have been a turkey pen.[29] It stands to reason that residents of houses in the open would have had to devise some sort of enclosure if they did not want rapacious fowl to eat their crops. But there were further considerations. Other than the usefulness of turkey feathers, their bones could be made into handy tools such as awls and needles as well as tubular beads for personal adornment. There has been a long-standing argument about whether turkeys were eaten. Specimens from the Wetherill Mesa Project suggest that at least some were butchered, cooked, and consumed.[30] This probably happened especially near the end of Puebloan stay on the Mesa Verde when larger fauna must have been killed off. Further, there are pixilated signs that these creatures may have had some obscure ritual significance. A turkey in a burial at Long House can be viewed as food meant for the afterlife. But how to explain the intentional burial of two whole turkeys in a trash dump elsewhere on the mesa?[31]

The answer may be found in the mysteries of Mesoamerican iconography. Charmion McKusick, a specialist in the study of prehistoric avian remains, suggests that elements of the complex were introduced into the Southwest along with corn agriculture.[32] She specifically identifies members of the Small Indian Domestic breed as symbolic of Tlaloc, the rain spirit prominent in the pantheon of deities of many Mexican tribes. In McKusick's opinion, the Tlaloc-turkey cult appeared in the Southwest at the inception of the Basketmaker eras but reached its greatest significance in the years between A.D. 1050 and 1275. The Small Indian Domestic turkeys were so fragile that they could not have survived in the wild. In some areas they were depicted on pottery not just as charming decorative motifs but as prayers. McKusick sees numerous headless carcasses as clues to bird sacrifice during unknown rituals, probably those pleading for rain on the high desert of the Colorado Plateau. These particular manifestations of the sacred nature of turkeys to the ancestral Pueblos have not been noted among the antiquities of the expansive region north of the San Juan River. That may have been due to distance from sources of the Tlaloc cult or because the religious or social structure of the Mesa Verdeans did not need Mesoamerican support. Nevertheless, some degree of sacredness must have been attached to these creatures. If so, their being consumed reflects either loss of faith or dire straits.

Throughout the five summers of fieldwork on Wetherill Mesa, recovered materials were transported to the laboratory on Chapin Mesa. There, curator Richard Wheeler trained four local women in museum methods of processing and cataloging so that these resources were ready when the archaeologists moved indoors in the winters.

Without the laboratory work that usually takes more time and diligence than what is spent on one's knees with trowel in hand, there is little justification for archaeology. It is a time when field notes are deciphered before they grow cold, specimens are analyzed, maps and charts are prepared, literature searches are made, and ideas about what one has witnessed are shared with colleagues. The final step is preparation of a report on the results so that others may benefit from the research. The last two years of the Wetherill Mesa Project were devoted to these efforts with a resulting outstanding series of large format, well-illustrated monographs.[33] The Step House work remains unpublished.

The one woman on the staff with professional standing was Carolyn Osborne. She was another Hewett product from the University of New Mexico. Her expertise in textile analysis was called upon to study perishable items from the digs but also in examination of Wetherill collections now housed at the Colorado Historical Society and the University of Pennsylvania Museum.

Dendrochronological studies were of inestimable value in detecting climatic influences in the past and in establishing a chronological table for the Mesa Verde that reached 845 years from A.D. 435 to 1280.[34] To further enhance this remarkable record was an amazing stand of living Douglas firs discovered by Edmund Schulman of the Laboratory of Tree-Ring Research at the University of Arizona. Cores from a hoary tree on a steep slope in a tributary to Navajo Canyon, known to the Wetherill Mesa Project crew as Schulman Old Tree Number One, gave up a date of A.D. 1170 but began to grow four years earlier![35] The huge trunk of this venerable, thirty-five-foot-tall specimen was almost horizontal when found, rather like an old woman with severe osteoporosis. Nichols and Smith, the tree ring experts, suggest that the Indians bent the pliable trunk to encourage a branch to shoot straight upwards. This would have supplied them with a useful construction timber. With this growth ring reading, the modern chronology overlaps the prehistoric one by nearly a century and extends it 793 years. Nowhere else in the world apart from the Colorado Plateau do scientists dealing with culture through time have such temporal specificity with which to work.

However, dates such as these have to be used judiciously for several reasons. One, the Puebloan builders quite possibly occasionally used timber that was already down and could be many years old but still solid. Recycling of building supplies was commonplace. Two, in the first few years of repair work in the park, workmen sometimes used beams from one cliff dwelling in stabilizing features in another. Therefore, tree ring dates do not invariably mean construction dates.

Also exciting to the archaeologists were Lancaster Old Tree Number One and Number Two. Lancaster came upon them in the same grove of Douglas firs. They were long dead, but several of them bore evidence of having been cut (or mangled) by stone axes. He sent samples to the tree ring lab where specialists read pith dates, or germination and young growth, in the first two decades of the thirteenth century and cutting dates in the mid-A.D. 1200s to 1275. These limbs surely ended up in the final building activity at one of the cliff houses. The trees, like the houses in which their parts may rest, now are ghosts of Mesa Verde past.

Variability in the width of growth rings of Douglas fir, pine, and Utah juniper, all of which were used by the Mesa Verdeans, reflect variations in climate. Even discrete monthly changes in precipitation or temperature are recorded on these sensitive plant registers. The studies of wood samples from Mesa Verde tell of prolonged drought conditions from A.D. 1273 through 1285, with the driest seasons ending in A.D. 1278. This is just six years before the last construction date of A.D. 1284 and no doubt signaled trouble ahead. This drought often is cited as a driving force behind ancestral

Pueblo relinquishment of the entire northern San Juan district. However, there were at least ten more intense droughts in the preceding centuries that the farmers somehow survived. Maybe that of the late A.D. 1200s, added to other problems, was the killing blow.[36]

Gustaf Nordenskiold surely would have been flabbergasted to know that his grandson and namesake, Gustaf Arrhenius, was one of the contributors to research centered on the dot on the map that he had named "Wetherills' Mesa" eighty years before. Arrhenius, staff member of the Scripps Institute of Oceanography at La Jolla, California, and a colleague studied the Mesa Verde soils as one of the supporting inquiries of the Wetherill Mesa Project. It was their conclusion that some three thousand to four thousand years ago prevailing southwesterly winds loaded with dust clouds that had been sucked up over Monument Valley dumped them on the lower and middle sectors of the elevated Mesa Verde landform.[37] This Aeolian deposition, now thought to be of Pleistocene age, formed a layer of loess, up to fifteen feet deep in places, over the Cliff House Sandstone stratum that caps the mesa. It is fertile soil, constantly replenished, especially in late spring and early summer. That renewal, limited though it may have been, might explain how the Puebloan farmers were able to till their gardens and harvest their yields for so many centuries without fertilization or crop rotation. Not only was the soil suitable for the low level type of farming in which the Puebloans engaged, but it was readily dug by pointed sticks to make shelters that were partially subterranean. Neither farming nor pit dwellings would have been feasible at the north ends of the mesa where the soil cover is thin, unproductive, decomposed sandstone.

Ecologists devoted to studies that they hoped would contribute to a better understanding of the Mesa Verde prehistoric settlement patterns and land use considered a mélange of other physical matters. These included temperatures in diverse parts of the park, evaporation rates, wind velocities, cold air drainage, precipitation, and solar radiation. Others studied withered foodstuffs such as corn, squash, and beans; nondomesticates like pollen, animal bones, and scat; and human feces retrieved from refuse to learn what plants and animals were present several millennia ago and compare them with present biota. All these important inquiries, added to those concerning climate and soils, substantiated the convictions that the ancestral Puebloans, possibly through trial and error, ultimately selected the most favorable real estate on the cuesta for settlement.

The unanimous conclusion of the ecologists was that the environment the Basketmakers encountered when they clambered up the heights in the seventh century was essentially the same as the environment now extant. When their descendants departed Mesa Verde in the thirteenth century, most likely it was a depleted land stripped of many of its natural resources.

Because the extent of the damage wreaked by the Puebloans is not known, ecologists speculate about the time necessary for environmental rejuvenation to take place. James Erdman's study, done on behalf of the Wetherill Mesa Project, on the return of several Mesa Verde burned areas to former, presumably normal, conditions suggests that the process required four hundred years or more.[38] He found that sunflowers and other annuals reappear within two years after such devastation. Perennial grasses, such as rice-grass and mutton grass, take four years. Gambel oak, serviceberry, and other crown-sprouting shrubs send out shoots and become well established within twenty-five years. Sagebrush invades middens, abandoned gardens, and disturbed ground sooner.

Erdman attributes this kind of chaparral, which blankets the northern tip of the park, to prehistoric fires that took out the original pinyon-juniper forests. Such fires could have been natural phenomena because Mesa Verde—elevated, heavily timbered, and in the shadow of the lofty La Plata Mountains—is in a significant lightning path, as demonstrated by numerous historic fires. Erdman further suggests that the Indians may have set fires in areas they were not farming in order to maintain a bushy blind for game. These ideas have implications for interpreting the Puebloan past at Mesa Verde. Only within the last few decades have researchers become cognizant of any appreciable aboriginal occupation in the northern and eastern part of the park. Prehistoric, out of control wildfires there could have had disastrous consequences for any residents. If those living further down the tablelands cleared their lands for farming, they might not have been so threatened by lightning. Actually, it was a 1959 fire that brought Hayes and Lancaster to the scene to scout the burned over area for sites, of which they recorded fifty-one.[39] Environmental management of the kind Erdman proposes has not been confirmed, although evidence of the occasional burning of spent fields is not uncommon.

Next in the succession of plant growth in a devastated area is a stage that occurs after a century when shrubs shade seedlings of pinyon and juniper. These trees are slower to germinate because they depend on seeds that have low survival rates. Finally, at the end of two further centuries, the dense forests which now profusely green the middle areas, home to most of the ancient Puebloans, flourish.

Dendrochronologists have identified stands on the Mesa Verde of four-hundred-year-old evergreens alive and well at present. One tree ring sample taken in 1965 from Rock Springs at the northwest part of Wetherill Mesa was then 508 years old.[40] It dated to A.D. 1457. A clump of relict, long-lived Ponderosa pines in Bobcat Canyon just east of Badger House might have had members growing when some Pueblos passed by, but it is likely that these trees were burned in the 2000 fire that roared over this part of the park.

Taking these data of a five-hundred-year plant succession rate and moving back in time, the vegetational complex now seen would have commenced about A.D. 1500. That leaves a two-hundred-year void between abandonment and that date, when undoubtedly a resilient nature was struggling to right itself. Moving forward in time from A.D. 1300, a normal biomass might have been in place around A.D. 1800. Either cycle—backwards or forward—surely was interrupted by fire, insect infestation, or porcupines. Regardless of how one postulates the revival, it was not immediate, but it did happen. As a parallel, one might postulate the same for the hapless Indians of Mesa Verde, defeated once but revived into today's vibrant Pueblo societies.

To understand the people themselves, beyond their misshapen skulls, the project sought the insights of a physical anthropologist and an osteologist. They examined 179 burials and 166 incomplete or mixed assortments of human bones.[41] The burials were equally divided between adults and subadults. Curiously, no Basketmaker remains were among them. This must be attributed to the accidents of archaeology. Apparently no explorations were done beyond the limits of the pithouses, where burials might have been found in trash deposits. Remains from Pueblo III contexts were most numerous, although the scholars believed that the Pueblo I population was larger.

From this limited sample of the Mesa Verde dead, the experts described the Puebloans as short, muscular, and stocky. They estimated a very high infant mortality rate. Cause of death could not be determined because of absence of body tissues. However, the scientists suggested that infectious diseases such as pneumonia, diarrhea, gastrointestinal processes, and rickets from dietary deficiencies were the lethal factors. If a child survived to four years of age, it could reasonably expect to live to be thirty or thirty-five.[42] Today this is a short life span, but it is comparable to that of Europeans in the Middle Ages.

Degenerative arthritis was something from which almost all adults suffered. Other associated aches and pains disappeared with the tissues. In view of the broken terrain in which the Mesa Verdeans lived, the doctors were surprised at so little sign of broken bones. Visitors invariably wonder about the safety of small children very literally living on the edge. Caution and a slow pace of life might have been responsible. Those fractures that were detected healed without abnormalities, pointing to some efficacy by medicine men. There were no osseous clues to tuberculosis or syphilis. Nor was there any indication of violent death. Teeth were badly worn, probably from sand loosened from sandstone grinding slabs, and other dental problems were usual. Toothless smiles may have been fashionable.

Several finds of primitive prosthetic devices display ingenuity in dealing with physical (neurological) problems. One is a pair of crutches apparently made for a child because they are just slightly over three feet in length. Each is a slender pole topped with a yucca pad encased in a scrap of leather.[43] According to the Mesa Verde museum records, the crutches were found somewhere on the mesa by Richard Wetherill. Rohn recovered the second device at Mug House. It is a corset made of aspen bark that was softened and while damp was wrapped around a patient's waist and then laced up the front.[44] The osteologist suggests that it may have been intended to help someone with a common backache or a more serious slipped disk.

By analogy with modern Pueblo Indians, an extensive pharmacognosy can be assumed for their antecedents. The mesa flora contained numerous plants having medical value: Gambel oak for insect bites, serviceberry for skin irritations, bitterbrush for childbirth, mountain mahogany for constipation.[45] However, as the doctors point out, by dying early these people avoided many of the old age afflictions of today. No broken hips, no cancer, no hardening of the arteries. In a rather convoluted rationale, the osteologist stated that he considered the ancestral Pueblos of Mesa Verde to have been surprisingly healthy and capable of remarkable physical independence.[46] Otherwise, how could they have slithered up and down those treacherous hand and toe holds? They just died young.

In 1965, shortly after Hayes and Osborne moved out of the Wetherill Mesa Project laboratory, Lister moved in. He was set to direct an innovative program through a memorandum of agreement with the National Park Service and supported by the National Science Foundation which combined an archaeological field school with on-the-job training for advanced students.[47] The first effort of the Mesa Verde Archaeological Research Center students, supervised by David Breternitz and Jack Smith from the University of Colorado faculty, was to salvage archaeological resources that otherwise would be eliminated in the interpretive development of Wetherill Mesa. They would excavate such materials, document them, and retrieve any associated artifacts prior to their being covered with sterile soil. Then they would submit technical reports.[48] The success of this program was demonstrated by both male and female participants who stayed the course to join professional ranks.

The grand plans of the National Park Service called for two constructions in the Long House and Badger House vicinity that required archaeological clearance. One was a proposed elevator at Long House. The entrance to the elevator was to be on the mesa rim to the southeast of the alcove below. The shaft would extend down the cliff face to a platform on top of a talus bed from which a three-hundred-foot surfaced path would lead to the site. There was a suspicious depression on the surface of the talus where the landing would be. Trenching showed it to be a kiva.[49] It was built above ground, its inside wall being the cliff front. The outer wall and some of the interior features were missing. Style of architecture and potsherds in the fill dated the kiva to the Pueblo III period. The excavators speculated that it had been built at the time of the first constructions in Long House next door, that is, A.D. 1200 to 1250. The outer wall may have been dismantled for use in the pueblo during later additions.

The erection of a Visitor Center was planned to the east of Badger House. Two isolated firepits at its location were examined but could not be dated due to lack of specimens or wood.[50] Such random features had been noted in the survey but were considered too insignificant to be studied further. Probably these were places where men fed or warmed themselves while working their gardens.

Traffic patterns to bypass the hundreds of prehistoric sites thickly spread over the mesa crest had to be carefully planned. To engineers, this must have seemed like trying to navigate through a minefield. Another concern was how to circumvent the human and vehicular overcrowding that plagued Chapin Mesa. The solution adopted was to stop visitors at a reception station above Step House and transport them farther down the mesa in electric minitrains with stops at Long House, a pedestrian path through the surface villages, and an overlook at Kodak House. It was anticipated that the minitrain schedule and its size would control the periodic volume of visitation. That and eliminating cars would help maintain a welcome wilderness ambience.

Once the right of way was surveyed, teams from the university research center were called upon to test the route to make sure that no sites were impacted. By putting down postholes at five-foot intervals along the centerline and trenching in the right of ways, teams encountered a firepit, storage pits, and a check dam in addition to several Basketmaker III pithouses. None of these features were visible on the surface.[51]

Similar soil auger tests and trenches were made in the area where a parking lot was to be paved. This was a narrow stretch of the mesa top between Mug House on the west escarpment and Step House on the east escarpment. Hayes recorded many sites in this zone as possibly of Pueblo I age. Others were not seen. The auger plugs followed by trenching laid bare a Basketmaker III village of seven pithouses and storage pits.[52] Their study was the core of a doctoral dissertation written by one of the students.

The access road from the head of Chapin Mesa was realigned and widened. Road machinery scraped away enough of the surface to expose several ruin areas. Again, students from the research center and park staff dug out some small houses, what may have been temporary field houses, and storage cists.[53]

The Wetherill Mesa Project and salvage operations were a boon to regional archaeology, but the Park Service objective to reduce people pollution was not met. A major reason was that when the time came to build the modern facilities, Congress had lost interest in funding them. Consequently, the elaborate plans of the 1950s were scrapped. There would be no Visitor Center, no Long House elevator, no museum, no cafeteria. Moreover, Mug House did not have the popular appeal of Cliff Palace and so was never opened to the public except for a few special tours. As a result only about ten percent of those who enter the park go to Wetherill Mesa. Park administrators succeeded in reducing congestion, but not on Chapin Mesa.

Because expansion of the public attractions to include the two stabilized ruins exposed by the university students in the 1950s also was tabled, a comparable ruin within walking distance of Far View Pueblo on Chapin Mesa was cleared and repaired by the research center to be part of the interpretive program. Now called Coyote House, originally it was thought to be a standard Pueblo III ruin. But like so many houses at Mesa Verde, it had experienced two earlier uses. Its final condition on display represents a typical settlement active around A.D. 1150.

Another endeavor in the Far View group was the exploratory trenching of Mummy Lake, a depression ninety feet in diameter upslope from the primary house and near to two small habitations excavated by Fewkes. The purpose of this work was to attempt to determine if it was a reservoir, an assumption that had been debated for years. Because excavation found an intake but no outlet and sediments obviously laid down under water, the conclusion was that it was a storage tank for domestic water used by families in the concentration of settlements in the sector. Potsherds from water jars of Pueblo II age substantiated this idea.[54] What originally was thought to be a canal going past Mummy Lake for four miles to terminate above Spruce Tree House actually might have been a horse trail that eroded into a shallow channel.

No sooner had a new campground been opened at the head of Morefield Canyon just a few miles inside the park than some tourists entertained themselves by digging in two sites nearby. The research center was called to duty. Students excavated a modest house on a slope that was then backfilled, and hopefully made inconspicuous to thoughtless intruders. The other was an unusual above-ground kiva on the top of a conical hill. It was stabilized and left open for the inspection of the campers.[55]

Further down Morefield Canyon, the research center undertook partial excavations of some small ruins on the slopes, a Great Kiva, and what was judged to be another reservoir for household use.[56] The reason behind this effort was that this part of the park, conveniently near the new campground, was to be developed for visitation. That did not come to pass. However, as work progressed, for the first time at Mesa Verde mechanical equipment, under the supervision of the archaeologists, was employed to remove deep layers of soil that had accumulated over the ruins. Enormous amounts of time and toil were saved, and the ruins were not harmed. New age archaeology was at hand. In the view of the students, this had limitations. After summer thunderstorms, they still had to wade into their waterlogged trenches to bail them out in a bucket brigade.

Other students were south of the park at the invitation of the Ute Mountain Ute Tribe and the Bureau of Indian Affairs to make a reconnaissance of twenty-seven cliff dwellings on their reservation. Neither the Utes nor the scientists were then interested in Ute remains left over a century of use of the district. Some of the Pueblo sites were visited by the Wetherills and Nordenskiold in the 1890s; others were reported by Morris in 1915. This work of the late 1960s and early 1970s was done with the idea that Johnson, Lion, and Mancos Canyons would become part of a tribal park sometime in the future.

An incident perhaps to be remembered by the young students more vividly than archaeological achievements occurred when two Ute policemen arrested them at gunpoint and took them to headquarters in Towaoc. Lister was notified and came posthaste. Apparently there had been no communication between tribal leaders and the police, who thought they had captured a bunch of poachers. The leaders were chagrined. The students first were fearful and then relished their escapade. The director was livid.

Gradually the research center took on jobs outside the park. Lowry Ruin, investigated in the 1930s, was reexcavated and repaired under authorization from the Bureau of Land Management and the direction of Lancaster, who had been on the original crew. A Basketmaker II site near the Falls Creek shelters on the outskirts of Durango, explored by Morris in 1938, was dug. It produced the latest Basketmaker II date of A.D. 372 for the region.[57] A Pueblo I dwelling close to Ignacio was explored by several students from the research center on behalf of the Southern Ute Tribe and supported by the Bureau of Indian Affairs. Originally it was hoped to make it a permanent display. However, prairie dogs had literally had a field day there and destroyed most of what would have constituted an exhibit. Enough of the jacal and cobble foundation and potsherds remained to substantiate the cultural level as corresponding to that of the eastern province examined by Roberts and Eddy.[58]

As the decade of the 1960s drew to a close, Lister unknowingly was initiating a new era in the archaeology of the Mesa Verde Province by expanding the focus of research beyond the boundaries of the national park.[59] Largely because of the glamour of the cliff dwellings in their beautiful but improbable setting, for a century that sector had seemed the center of the ancient Pueblo universe to the north. Not so, as future studies would demonstrate. In 1970 Lister, after two decades of work in the Mesa Verde Province, left the research center to his successor, Breternitz, and turned his administrative talents to another important undertaking in Chaco Canyon. Extensive inquiries there would heighten academic interest in interprovincial relationships between Chaco and Mesa Verde. ✣

# Before Rising Waters

After World War II, two proposals for dam construction on the upper Colorado River drainage system had the potential of impacting regional antiquities. At the western limits of the Mesa Verde Province the Glen Canyon Dam would fill Lake Powell. At the province's eastern side a dam on the San Juan River would create Navajo Reservoir. Consequently, in a climate of growing emphasis on conservation of cultural resources, a newfound American interest in the prehistory of the Colorado Plateau, and with the authority of the 1935 Historic Sites Act, the Department of the Interior initiated emergency research programs during the late 1950s and early 1960s to take place before flooding.

## Glen Canyon and Lake Powell

It would be hard to find any corner of the United States with a more kaleidoscopic modern history than that of the Glen Canyon and its environs.[1] This is all the more astounding when considering that it is still a largely uninhabited region where nature ran amok. The cast of colorful characters that passed through featured Franciscan priests, Mormon converts, explorers, prospectors for gold, oil, and uranium, cattle rustlers and stockmen, entrepreneurs, wandering or trading Indians, river runners, and assorted escapists. Some were merely trying to get across the Colorado River. The aim of others was to get into the canyon, get rich, get out. None got rich. There were those who took advantage of its remoteness to conduct clandestine activities. Still others were captivated by the stark, scenic grandeur of multicolored cliff walls defiantly towering above turbulent waters rushing through a high desert and the brooding solitude that pervades the scene.

The roster of those who came early to the fractured domain east of Glen Canyon includes the names of Clayton and John Wetherill, McLoyd, Judd, and Morris. McLoyd collected specimens but from where is not known. Morris, of course, dug wherever possible.

In 1929 Morris was traveling companion and cultural interpreter for

Charles Bernheimer, a New York businessman and dedicated patron of the American Museum of Natural History.[2] Bernheimer periodically came west to absorb the beauty of the Colorado Plateau and track down its isolated antiquities. As for many before and after, it was a means of recharging his energies and feeding his soul. This season his party included John Wetherill, Morris, and Zeke Johnson, a native of Blanding with intimate knowledge of the San Juan country and at one time the custodian of Natural Bridges National Monument. All had been Bernheimer's guests previously and were accustomed to his persnickety ways and the knickers he wore during the day and the red skating cap he always donned at night. For them the trips through a part of the world with which they were thoroughly attuned were treats. One suspects that Bernheimer was drawn to add this eastern Glen Canyon destination to his trophies because of a melodramatic article written by Judd for the National Geographic Magazine in which he described it as "the dwelling place of evil."[3] What adventurer could resist? To prepare, Bernheimer outdid himself in having Johnson assemble a pack train of forty-four animals. This seems excessive for just five or six men, but many of the beasts just carried oats because browse for the train was expected to be in short supply.

The group assembled at Monticello, rode south of Blanding, and then headed west. They crossed Cedar Mesa, went down Grand Gulch, out through the Clay Hills pass, to the wedge of land between the San Juan on the south and the Colorado on the northwest known as the San Juan Triangle, and on to the upper stretches of the canyons that open westward to the Colorado. It was in Moqui Canyon at an alcove to which Wetherill guided the group, having visited it six years earlier with Judd, that the ever ready Morris had his best chance to dig.

Morris was looking for an unadulterated Basketmaker III site to help him clarify in his own mind the developmental sequence of early phases with which he was working in the La Plata Valley and in Canyon del Muerto in Arizona. At the Moqui Canyon alcove he had to be satisfied with unearthing five Basketmaker II mummies and assorted artifacts including a curved stick probably used in rabbit hunts. At the end of the trip these specimens were divided between the American Museum and Mesa Verde National Park. The back country trek continued north to White Canyon and then eastward up to Natural Bridges, where in 1907 young Judd had his first taste of regional archaeology.

Morris was chagrined to read Bernheimer's subsequent far-fetched interview in the *New York Post* in which he recounted how his extraordinary expedition found the mummified remains of ten-thousand-year-old natives who had used boomerangs because of some dubious ties with ancient Australia in the misty time of biblical King David. Perhaps that explains why Morris never again served as Bernheimer's cultural interpreter.

Although rumors abounded of Indian houses tucked into scarps back in the depths of the canyons, archaeologists paid little further attention to the district. Actually, the very first exploration of Glen Canyon, that of John Wesley Powell in 1869, noted two ruins at the northern limits of the Glen. Sixty years later, Julian Steward, of the University of Utah, floated the river and saw several dozen other sites. However, the general scientific consensus was that the sector was too rugged and arable land insufficient to have attracted Puebloan farmers. Morris's opinion, shared by many, was, "West of Grand Gulch the country is so utterly worthless that the old people pretty much left it alone."[4] He referred to a flattened landscape of slickrock, black bush, and dunes. It took a governmental emergency program to bring the researchers into what for most was terra incognita.

As part of the dam endeavors, in 1956 the University of Utah obtained a long-term contract for archaeological explorations and recovery of data and specimens along the west bank of the Colorado River from the dam site northward 186 miles to the tiny village of Hite at the head of planned Lake Powell. Further, the university took on the responsibility for comparable study of the east bank and tributaries coming into the river gorge from uplands off toward the Nokai Dome and Elk Ridge beyond.[5] The contract was sufficiently flexible to allow work on sites above the anticipated level of Lake Powell and up canyon beyond its limits. This was in order to gather as full a prehistoric accounting as possible.

Limited surveys of the pool area to the east of Glen Canyon were made by Jesse Jennings, director of the Upper Colorado River Basin Archaeological Salvage Program. Robert Lister, taking time away from his Mesa Verde duties so as not to interfere with the Wetherill Mesa Project going on at the same time, devoted his attention to the west bank. Ted Weller and Don Fowler, students at the university, scouted intervening parts of the project area.[6] To everyone's surprise, they concluded that at least three of the canyons in the east central portion of the Glen had considerable promise for archaeological investigations. From north to south they were Moqui (thirty miles long), Lake (eleven miles long), and Slickhorn (two and a half miles long). Other tributaries also merited exploration. They felt that the highlands above the canyon heads and the San Juan Triangle, which in this survey took in the western edge of Cedar Mesa, should be considered even though they were above the pool limits. The west bank was out of the Mesa Verde Province, hence not pertinent to this aerial review.

Jennings was a masterful organizer and a stickler for meticulous detail, as he needed to be for an undertaking demanding sensitive coordination with government authorities and construction engineers and having, in terms of proceeding with proposed scientific goals, enormous logistical complexity. With the expectation of sending crews of young, relatively inexperienced men into the unknown hazards of uncharted territory, cut off from ready contact with the outside world for many days at a time, he had to anticipate all manner of contingencies. Just getting personnel, equipment, and supplies to the jobs variously called for boats with outboard motors, rubber rafts, trucks, four-wheel drive jeeps equipped with winches, horses, and as always heavy-duty leg work. Landlubbers dealing with the capricious river was a haunting concern. Consideration had to be given to lightweight, sturdy camp gear, foods that would not spoil in temperatures often soaring well over one hundred degrees Fahrenheit, and medicines to take care of everything from stomachaches to blisters, twisted ankles to snakebites.

For the professional aspects of the program and to assure uniformity throughout, Jennings drafted an operational manual specifically outlining how he felt that work should be done, records kept, artifacts processed in the field and in the laboratory, and formats followed in descriptive reports. There was to be no interpretation until careful field observations were documented. This proved frustrating to independent-minded staffers but did succeed in producing useful consistency in the results. Salvage operations of this sort take a different approach from those in which sites are to be held for public inspection possibly into perpetuity, as at Mesa Verde, or in which the aim is to investigate a defined academic problem. In the Glen Canyon instance, just a sampling was to be made in the limitations of time allowed by dam construction, but hopefully one that would illuminate the full extent of what was present. That had to be done as carefully as possible under less than ideal circumstances because there would be no going back to double-check ideas or illegible notes. As with the gold rush early in the century, it was a matter of getting in, getting the riches (archaeological data), and getting out. Where that would lead no scholar was then ready to state, but a Mesa Verdean presence in the eastern Glen region was suspected.

In the summer of 1958 and continuing through 1962, crews of male college students ranging from several to twenty in number were led by full-time project employees at various stages in their educations. Among them were William Lipe, Don Fowler, and Floyd Sharrock. They were under the general supervision of Jennings, who served as overseer, instructor, and strict taskmaster. Camps were moved as work progressed, sometimes with the help of laborers and wranglers from Blanding, the nearest outpost ninety miles away. Every two weeks retrieved specimens and notes were sent back to a laboratory organized in a temporary building on the campus of the University of Utah in Salt Lake City.

There, Dee Ann Suhm, with a new Ph.D. in anthropology, was in charge. She was assisted by several young ladies carrying out the routines of management and curation that remained the customary role of females in the discipline. As a further sign of the times, they came to work in dresses, hose, and heels, and they did not feel the need to wear white gloves when handling specimens. After yeoman's service for six years, as a bonus Suhm was permitted to venture into the field for a two-week stint at the end of the project. To her credit, she did not fall off a cliff, get lost, attacked, or whatever else her macho colleagues anticipated.

The field crews found little evidence for prolonged ancient life along the Colorado River itself.[7] There were some small structures next to patches of land that might have been farmed. At one such two-room dwelling the diggers cleared a meager reservoir with a slab-lined outlet that was fed by a spring. There were a few gravel terraces and sandbars where flint knappers might have plied their craft, of what age nobody then knew. Quite possibly some were of a distant time as long as seven thousand years ago that researchers now term *Archaic*. Escarpments with a sheeting or trailing fringe of desert varnish exhibited some iconographic messages to Puebloan gods, their ages then unknown. Campsites identified by scatters of lithics and potsherds and what might have been pits where foods were roasted suggested that the river corridor primarily served as a transportation route. Its steep cliffs were draped like beads in a necklace with lines of hand and toe holds—Moqui steps—which facilitated access from cliff rims to the river. At periods of low water the river could be forded in three or four places. It was apparent the river was a way to get to where prehistoric life was centered, in the bowels of several offshoot canyons on both banks, rather than in the main stem.

Correlated geological studies done as part of the Utah program entirely changed the scientists' preconceptions about this region and its usefulness to primitive horticulturists.[8] These investigations revealed that up until the late nineteenth century, Moqui and Lake Canyons had been filled with rich alluvium from fifty to one hundred feet deep in places. Meandering streams flowed from canyon heads down to the Colorado River. A shallow lake a half mile long was dammed by a huge stabilized dune in the upper end of Lake Canyon. A number of active springs and plentiful subsurface water percolated down through porous sandstone strata to support a growth of cottonwoods, willows, tamarisks, and grasses at an elevation of about thirty-five hundred feet. This was far below the usual range of the ancestral Pueblos. In times past when migrant Pueblos were on the move, these two canyons were inviting green islands in the midst of rolling, red seas of bare rock and contorted crags. The lower elevation meant long growing seasons and warm temperatures that allowed the cultivation of cotton in addition to the ubiquitous corn, beans, and squash.

Around the 1880s nature shifted gears and all across the Colorado Plateau began a vigorous cycle of scouring away soils that for millennia had accumulated over the earth's hard underpinnings. Repeated flash floods boiled down ravines tearing off all topping and vegetation in their paths. From their soggy tents every August afternoon, the field crews witnessed this rampage dressed with wicked lightning that ricocheted off stony walls. As if this were not enough, in 1915 Lake Pagahrit in Lake Canyon breached its buttressing dune and powerfully flushed all before it into the Colorado River. The lapping depths of Lake Powell would only cover the devastation wrought by other waters moving under mighty gravitational force. In the erratic nature of the region, Slickhorn Canyon escaped these onslaughts and thus permitted a dramatic peek into what once had been the environment available to the ancestral Pueblos in the longer, neighboring gorges.

What the crews saw when they hiked into the canyons resembled a battlefield whose wounds were slowly healing. Jagged remnants of the original alluvial canyon bottom hung like cantilevers many feet above the 1960s streambed.[9] Some sections were as much as 250 feet wide. Piled on them was a flotsam of uprooted trees, twisted branches, and other plant debris. At their base spring-fed streams aiming for the mother drainage flowed over sandstone bedrock and in Lake Canyon over high, rocky impediments, "jump-ups" in Utah vernacular, that created waterfalls. Various kinds of flora were beginning to make a comeback that visually softened an otherwise desolate setting. Whatever Puebloan constructions once had been on the canyon floors or their lower slopes were no more. Built of the earth, they returned to the earth without a trace.

It was in bell-shaped alcoves at the point where the alluvium met the cliff, buried in its deposit, that the diggers found what they were after. Other ruins were in openings and along ledges higher up the cliff faces well above the zone of degradation or the eventual level of Lake Powell. These are the sites now visible to boaters on the lake. Some are accessible; others are tantalizingly forever out of reach.

Hundreds of sites of various types were recorded in surveys. Of these more than fifty were tested or excavated. All were uniformly small in size and those with structures were homogeneous in style. Five or six rooms of wet- and dry-laid masonry, with an occasional jacal or roofing element, were typical. Rooms with hearths or mealing bins were considered living quarters. The researchers judged the remainder to have been used for storage. The houses in Lake Canyon were notable for their general lack of kivas.

A site of unusual interest was the alcove in Moqui Canyon, which Morris had probed thirty-two years earlier. Not only was this intersection with the history of regional archaeology significant, but this was one of only three habitation sites in the region where the University of Utah party confirmed Basketmaker II remains. Elsewhere, field men observed a few nonceramic sites, but they remained uncertain of their cultural affiliation. Lipe later would classify them as places where foods or tools were prepared or stored and of probable Basketmaker age.

At this Bernheimer Alcove workers excavated seven Basketmaker II burials accompanied by baskets, fiber bag shrouds, and cradleboards diagnostic of the period.[10] On those cradleboards lay five tiny infants, a poignant testimony to the transitory nature of Basketmaker life. All skulls were undeformed. No pottery was present (nor were there any "boomerangs"). At some time, perhaps even during the Basketmaker tenancy, massive chunks of the natural roof crashed down directly on the use area. That may have been the reason for the departure of the Basketmakers, but it certainly thwarted additional clearing by the archaeologists.

The Bernheimer Alcove was another instance where there was a second occupation centuries later. A small, masonry structure of the same type as those in other locales in the canyons was in one end of the opening. It had not been damaged by the fall, hinting that it was erected after that event. The site's location at the upper limits of the alluvial deposit in the canyon likely was at the terminus of suitable farming land.

The fellows who took a summer job on the Glen Canyon project soon learned that it was not all a lark. There was the pleasant camp comradeship and the new experiences in part of the country where none of their peers had been. But they had come to a savage land where sometimes it must have seemed that it was not meant for humans. Middays in the closed-in canyons were broiling hot. One group swore they had seen a rattlesnake coiled up in a sagebrush to get away from heated slickrock scorching its skin. There were huge, sucking sand dunes to slog through and pockets of sucking quicksand to avoid. Of the latter, Judd said, "Beneath each thin vibrant surface lay slow, cruel death for the unrescued."[11] Moreover, the best ruins always seemed the most unreachable, up snagging crannies, often requiring ropes, and over tortuous humps of detritus.

Little wonder that the diggers christened one site the Rehab Center.[12] Its huge, wide mouth opened onto a rock ledge at the base of a massive stratum of red Navajo Sandstone and a clump of Gambel oak. The deep, darkened recess was a welcome refuge from relentless sun and wind. At the rear of it was a spring of cool, drinkable water that gurgled into a pool rimmed with maidenhair ferns, reeds, and moss. One can imagine the men wearily dumping their packs and sprawling on the loose fill that covered the alcove floor to luxuriate in these refreshing, sensual pleasures. They soon learned that they were in the company of two rattlesnakes.

To top it off, those venerable Basketmakers also had tarried in the alcove long enough to bury four of their own with appropriate offerings. Three bodies were laid together in one cist. The Moqui Canyon alcoves were grouped just a half mile apart and probably were where a small overflow from the considerable Basketmaker occupation on Cedar Mesa to the east occasionally camped.

Pueblo families moved into Rehab Center in the twelfth and thirteenth centuries. They erected three units of mud and stone and one of jacal. Then they moved away leaving their trash strewn about. Less-inhabited gorges such as Red, Forgotten, Wilson (Iceberg), and Slickhorn were examined and several dozen sites excavated.[13]

The Glen Canyon project also worked nine sites in the uplands east of the Lake Powell limits. The only additional data garnered was one ruin at the western edge of Cedar Mesa that was then thought to be of Basketmaker III–Pueblo I age. If that were the case, it is the outermost western extension in the Mesa Verde Province of Puebloan occupation of this period. Morris was not wrong in his 1929 assessment that he conveyed to Kidder, "Thus it would seem that the whole triangle between the San Juan and the Colorado was practically untenanted during the period in question [Basketmaker III]. It seems not unnatural that such should have been the case in view of the utter barrenness and general worthlessness of the country."[14] To Morris, absence of prehistoric places in the San Juan Triangle equaled something archaeologically akin to the notorious Bermuda Triangle. It should be noted that the Glen Canyon project survey took in a more extensive, favorable plateau than Morris considered and that later investigations have confirmed a prevailing absence of Basketmaker III people.

At the end of the fieldwork the scholars felt they had demonstrated a minor Basketmaker II use of the upper part of one area canyon and a plateau to the east. That was followed by many centuries when the eastern flanks of Glen Canyon were devoid of human life. Sometime around the beginning of the second millennium there was an influx of ancestral Pueblo families who took possession of sheltered cavities in the cliffs and had field houses and gardens along the bottoms of canyons. The style of architecture and ceramics indicate that they had achieved a level of advancement that, for convenience, archaeologists term Late Pueblo II and Pueblo III.

At the beginning of investigations, the crews expected to find that Mesa Verdeans had been in these borderlands of their customary territory. They did not anticipate that Kayentans also had taken up residence there. That was a blind spot that grew out of the province concept and an unconscious acceptance of boundaries between them. However, if the pottery classification was reasonably accurate, there was an important thrust of contemporary Puebloans north from the Kayenta Province. Presumably they forded the San Juan River and made their way along the east bank of Glen Canyon to turn up into the southern gorges. They especially dominated Lake Canyon and others to the south. Aside from ceramics, the evidence for this is the use of jacal construction and the near total lack of kivas. Unlike Chacoan Pueblos who invaded the Mesa Verde Province at the same time, they moved into a part of the domain that was unoccupied.

Mainly in Moqui Canyon but elsewhere, too, the Kayentans met Mesa Verdeans infiltrating the region from the east. The scientists did not detect any violence between these two entities such as might have occurred in disputes over scarce land, even though the placement of some houses suggests a need for defense. They must have dwelt as neighbors, engaging in a lively exchange in ceramics. Their modes of life were comparable with a few provincial variations. This is not an unrealistic interpretation. In historical times similar juxtaposition is known for Pueblo groups who speak different languages and have variant ritualistic preferences. Scientists speculate that population pressures in the core areas of the two provinces were responsible for the movement of ancestral Pueblos into the "outback" where climatic changes produced conditions favorable for agriculture.

Studies of the west bank in Glen Canyon and in the highlands beyond the extent of Lake Powell showed that Kayentans also penetrated the home territory of another group. These were the Fremont, who roamed over much of Utah west of the Colorado River. Again, diggers found no sign of conflict. In the late A.D. 1000s and early A.D. 1100s, Kayentans took over the lower Escalante drainage and the hanging valley at the foot of the Aquarius Plateau. At the latter place, in 1958 and 1959 Lister, his student Richard Ambler, and a University of Colorado field school group dug a typical Kayenta jacal, masonry, and pithouse village that lacked kivas. A total of eighty-one structures were cleared, most of which had burned. The recovered ceramics were Kayenta wares, local copies of them, and trade vessels from the Fremont tribes and others in southwest Utah. Archaeologists know the ruin as the Coombs Site. To the visitors it is now the Anasazi Village State Park.[15]

The mighty Colorado River obviously was not a barrier to the movement of native peoples, as once thought. However, it was a west boundary of the Mesa Verde Province. The west bank survey conducted by Lister and others did not identify any Mesa Verde structure and only a handful of Mesa Verde potsherds on that side of the river.

The staff was troubled by concerns over precise dating. To their disappointment, dendrochronological examinations failed to date any of the wood samples submitted from the reservoir area. All were unusable juniper or deciduous woods such as cottonwood. Additionally, some material items of the ancestral Puebloans generally do not lend themselves to discrete dating because of an exceptional continuity of style through many centuries. Little change in axes, points, and other items occurred during the period of the Glen Canyon occupation.

That left dating based on pottery, which did change stylistically and physically over time. This depended upon dates established for specific types in the nuclear areas. There was no assurance that potters in outlying settlements kept in step with their sisters back home. Nonetheless, there was nothing other than a widely used manual with physical descriptions and dating then accepted upon which to base judgments about the Glen Canyon pottery. Research done after the project was completed suggested that some styles, particularly those in vogue in the Kayenta Province, were made for a longer time than scholars previously believed. This new schedule would place the east Glen Canyon occupation from *circa* A.D. 1100 into the late A.D. 1200s. The proposed A.D. 1275 date as one concluding the occupation of the Coombs Site corresponds to that now being postulated for the central Mesa Verde Province. Most likely, at that general time settlers in Moqui, Lake, and

Slickhorn Canyons and other Colorado River tributaries loaded up their burden baskets, strapped babies on their cradleboards, and headed south across the San Juan River and eventually on to the Hopi mesas. Many diverse groups from all directions were beginning to converge there during the fourteenth century. Once more, cohabitation seems to have been peaceful.

The east bank of the Glen Canyon reverted back to being a lonesome, silent place for centuries, visited only occasionally by a few Hopi, Navajo, and Paiute hunting parties.

Mourn not for the dozens of prehistoric, often ephemeral, sites left undug and doomed to watery extinction. Total recovery was not practical given the time limitations and redundancy of data. The scientists were satisfied that they had amassed a sufficiently adequate sample from which researchers in the future would gain some understanding of the hazy yesteryears of ancestral Pueblos. A few more hammerstones, worn sandals, or potsherds would have added little to the discourse. In retrospect, it is regrettable that radiocarbon dating (still at the time not always reliable) was not done on some samples from excavated strata that lacked pottery in order to determine their possible Archaic age and that little attention beyond mere recognition was given to historical Indian or Euroamerican remains. Those areas of study were not part of the archaeological agendas of the time.

The Museum of Northern Arizona carried out a comparable archaeological project as part of the encompassing Glen Canyon energy developments. Its territory was the Kayenta Province on the east bank of the Colorado River from the dam site north to the confluence with the San Juan tributary. The museum's efforts and those of the University of Utah teams represented a worthwhile, but sometimes controversial, tangent to traditional archaeology. The motivation to scientifically examine so vast a region that had been previously neglected, reclaim whatever there was to be had before it was lost forever, and to do it expeditiously with long-term government funding far in excess of any that the usual academic sponsors could invest produced significant intellectual returns. Although there was some later criticism of the lack of conceptual evaluations, contract stipulations regarding documentation, curation, and prompt reporting of the results set exemplary standards for the future of regional archaeology.

A very important by-product of the Glen Canyon archaeological program was the training and focus it gave to a new generation of scholars. It was a practical, hands-on field school experience without college credit but with a modest paycheck. At least a dozen individuals involved to some degree with the work continued in the profession, some in the Southwest and others elsewhere but all to the benefit of American science. William Lipe was one of those whose future professional direction was determined by participation in the Glen Canyon project. In later years he credited Lister's report at the 1957 Pecos Conference on the west bank survey for prompting him to apply to Jennings for a job while still a graduate student. For most of the next three years Lipe met the physical and intellectual challenges of the work that culminated a few years later in a doctoral dissertation at Yale University. This study was a response to an emerging interest by Southwestern prehistorians in using the descriptive base of traditional archaeology together with examination of the physical world in which regional cultures evolved to gain insight into their intangible social fabrics.[16]

In addition to considerations of the functional applications of various categories of artifacts and presumed purpose of the diverse structures present, Lipe reasoned that two primary ecological factors molded Puebloan adaptations to the demanding Glen Canyon country. One was cyclical climatic changes characteristic of the Colorado Plateau. Favorable conditions of precipitation and temperature in the third, twelfth, and thirteenth centuries fostered occupation of the less than benign Glen environments. Longer stretches of austere weather, causing reduced rainfall that dried up springs at the base of permeable sandstone strata and resulting in severe erosion of arable soils, made sedentary life impossible for centuries at a time. During periods of use, hot summers and relatively balmy winters made open camps preferable to more substantial dwellings. Seasonality of occupation also may have been responsible for this pattern, or it may have been a simple disinterest in the architectural refinements exhibited in other areas.

Topographic features, such as limited and patchy parcels of land suitable for farming, allowed only a few families to be in residence at any one time. They necessarily were dispersed. That, in turn, meant little communal interaction, with each small unit remaining somewhat independent and isolated. There was no gathering of the clans into compact communities such as occurred elsewhere in the Mesa Verde Province. The comparative scarcity of kivas suggests limited emphasis on group ritualism.

Dissatisfaction with the implied rigidity of the Pecos Classification led Lipe to suggest regional names for the identified temporal stages of cultural development. Comparable phase nomenclature was being used concurrently by the Wetherill Mesa Project and by another salvage activity on the San

Juan River. Three different names for the same coeval period resulted, all then being correlated by the researchers back to the original Pecos Classification. The Basketmaker II occupation of the Red Rock Plateau, the same region Morris knew as the horrid San Juan Triangle, was the White Dog Phase (*circa* A.D. 200–300). Lipe divided the Pueblo periods into the Klethla Phase (*circa* A.D. 1100–1150) and the Horsefly Hollow Phase (*circa* A.D. 1210–1260), both being Pueblo III in his opinion. Later workers would place the Klethla Phase into the Pueblo II category. Through architectural and ceramic analyses, he interpreted the Klethla people as being migrants from the Kayenta Province and the Horsefly Hollow peoples as being from two distinct groups: one out of the southern Kayenta Province and the other originating in the eastern Mesa Verde Province. They were all ancestral Pueblos but with modest differences in material goods and perhaps social orientation. They met in central Red Rock Plateau zones but did not merge. Only after their departure from the canyons did they possibly blend as they drifted south of the San Juan River to meet new circumstances and to prove once again that adaptability was their greatest cultural strength.

## SAN JUAN RIVER AND NAVAJO RESERVOIR

Salvage archaeology was first initiated in the eastern Mesa Verde Province in 1950 and the person responsible was Jesse Nusbaum. In his position as consulting archaeologist for the Department of the Interior, it was his duty to inform the El Paso Natural Gas Company that under provisions of the 1906 Antiquities Act it was necessary for the company to secure excavation permits for the 451-mile pipeline it proposed to lay from the southern edge of the state of Colorado across the Colorado Plateau to the Colorado River. As the promoter that he had learned to be through the example of his mentor Hewett, he further advised the company leadership that it would be a public relations coup if they were to hire archaeologists to monitor the pipeline trenches so as to bypass any archaeological sites or reclaim those that were impacted. He emphasized that this region was the heartland of the ancient Pueblos and contained thousands of their remains. The officers took the hint and generously funded fieldwork and publication. Their voluntary support soon became mandatory for any developmental disturbance of public lands. This included roads, power plants, phone lines, geological explorations, and, as indicated above, dam construction. Thus, Southwestern salvage archaeology was born and in various mutations has continued to underwrite many regional inquiries.

For starters, in 1950 the El Paso Natural Gas Company hired men from the Museum of New Mexico to examine what appeared to be an archaeological site that heavy equipment being used to clear land for a gas line field station at Ignacio, Colorado had exposed.[17] The scientific value of this sort of emergency reaction was brought home to the business and professional personnel involved when it was determined that the site was the first Basketmaker II hamlet found on level, open ground and so far to the east. It is safe to say that under earlier circumstances the seventeen-hundred-year-old site would have been leveled without further ado.

At the same time that the Glen Canyon Dam was being built, a second dam was under construction on the San Juan River upstream from Farmington as part of the Upper Colorado River Storage Program. Engineers anticipated that it would back water up the north side Pine and Piedra tributaries and up a number of lesser canyons with intermittent streams opening to the main river from the southeast. At full pool the dam would form a lake thirty-four miles long that would cover twenty-three square miles. Two small modern villages would be literally liquidated. A road and a stretch of the Denver and Rio Grande Western Railroad would have to be realigned. What prehistoric settlements might be drowned or obliterated by the new transportation routes was unknown. During the 1920s and 1930s there had been limited investigations to the north in the Mesa Verde Province and to the south in the Chaco Province, but the river valley itself was largely an untapped zone.

As a preliminary measure, in 1956 the Department of the Interior asked the Museum of New Mexico to do a quick overview of the area to be affected by the dam in order to ascertain whether a full-blown archaeological study was warranted. This two man team concluded that the projected pool area had potential importance in unraveling the prehistoric past. In contrast to the situation in Glen Canyon, preliminary observations suggested possible sporadic human presence over many centuries culminating in that of historic Native Americans. Soon the Laboratory of Anthropology and the Museum of New Mexico were awarded a joint contract to make the necessary survey assessments and to undertake selected excavations of representative sites.[18]

Alfred (Ed) Dittert was the overall director of the Navajo Reservoir Project. During the survey part of the effort, he was variously assisted by five or six college students. When the excavation phase was reached, laborers from local communities and Taos Pueblo were hired. These parties were in the field for different lengths of time from 1957 through 1963. The full-time staff spent winters at the museum in Santa Fe trying to keep abreast of analyses and reports. Following the conclusion of the fieldwork, an additional year was devoted to final synthesis of results. Dittert's organization of the project as a whole was not as structured as that of Jennings. His own written contributions were so splintered into finite districts, phases, components, and minutiae as to be perplexing to most nonprofessionals. Nevertheless, the scientific data presented were enlightening on many levels. They were supplemented by what had become requisite relevant environmental, biological, and geological studies.

Understandably, dam builders choose to plant their works in canyons whose walls can serve as buttresses. Such locations pose a challenge to those whose job it is to scout the surroundings. Approaches often mean poor or no roads and strenuous clambering. But that was overlooked when the 1957 museum crew arrived at the dam location to observe that the mechanical monsters roaring and cutting the river bed for dam fill had already taken out sixteen sites.[19] With a marked sense of urgency, more professional observations and unearthing began.

The terrain near the site of the dam was a sheer-walled, deep, narrow canyon topped by flat-bedded mesas rising well above the sixty-one-hundred-foot contour of the high waters of the reservoir. Work in this region was arduous but necessary to complete rapidly before the waters rose. Salvage operations concentrated on the construction zone, along the river bed, and where borrow pits were to be hollowed out. The district just above the dam which encompassed the mouths of Frances Canyon on the east and the Pine River on the north was a first priority.

The San Juan Canyon and the lower Frances Canyon had not been suitable for ancestral Pueblo farmers because of lack of arable land. Surveyors had more luck in the upper portion of Frances Canyon where they counted sixty sites, half of which were simple Pueblo I jacal rooms. Since this gorge reaches into what was traditional Navajo territory until the mid-A.D. 1700s, it was no surprise to find their remains here and there. That hiatus in occupation meant that this particular locale had been devoid of human presence for as much as six hundred years.

The Pine River Valley entering the San Juan channel from the north just above Frances Canyon was slated to receive reservoir waters for some thirteen miles of its extent. Because of being very deep but less than one half mile wide in its middle course, it presented the most trying field conditions. The expedition jeep was able to use gas exploration and homesteader roads to get the crews to access points. A vertical extension on its exhaust pipe allowed drivers to navigate the canyon floor and its waters, the first, perhaps only, amphibious field vehicle used in regional archaeology. Mostly it was a matter of hiking the benches, scrambling up talus slopes, wading back and forth across the meandering stream, and always being on the lookout for human signs.

These were concentrated at the juncture of the Pine and San Juan and north toward what would be the head of the lake. Of a total of ninety-two sites counted, the same two cultural stages were represented as in the Frances sector: Pueblo I and historic Navajo. However, later excavations would reveal a surprise bonus confined to the Pine drainage.

During the survey period, camps were moved as work progressed. In 1959 with the commencement of excavations, a base was established at the tiny town of Allison on the north highlands between the Pine and Piedra Rivers. Supplies were readily available, living conditions were comfortable, work space was suitable for processing artifacts coming in from the various digs, and workers could commute to work.

Frank Eddy was put in charge of one of the opening rounds of excavations. He elected to begin with sites in the upper stretch of the Pine River that had puzzled Dittert and associates from the time they were discovered during surveys. In one of those, the fellows walked over a terrace above the river that was suspiciously darkened from decomposed organic matter and sprinkled with bits and pieces of man made objects—*sheet trash* to the archaeologists. No habitation debris was present. There was a patch of cobblestones partially buried under grass and weeds that seemed to spread out into a broad circle, the center of which was empty. The men dismissed this as unusual but a natural phenomenon until they went upslope a bit. Under trees and sagebrush, they saw another ring of large river cobbles. From there as the team worked further along the benches bordering the Pine River, they came across another cobble ring, then another, until ultimately they counted twenty-eight of them.[20] It was obvious that these rings were part of some kind of construction, but what was it? Another curious thing was that the survey did not notice any potsherds among the refuse. Could they have been so fortunate as to have discovered a previously unknown cultural manifestation? That was what Eddy meant to find out. Science would be enriched, but it would be a personal boon to a career that was just beginning.

The selected site was on a high terrace beyond the limits of the reservoir. Eddy called it the Power Pole Site because such a modern feature incongruously had been put at the edge of one of the mysterious circles.[21] He gave one workman the hard-on-the-knees job of using his trowel to grub out clumps of grass and loose soil between the cobbles in order to get a clear idea of the stone configuration. Others went to work with picks and shovels to skim off the empty surface within the figure-eight circle. Then they, too, knelt down to trowel the ground carefully to reach an earthen floor just a foot below the surface that had been compacted by many years of use. Around the perimeter of this presumed floor the diggers uncovered some logs laid end to end and casts in the earth where others had been. The considerable size of the floor, up to seven hundred square feet, seemed to have been divided by jacal partitions into distinct functional areas. A central, shallow basin in the floor was reddened and contained pieces of burned rock that apparently had supplied the radiant heat of the day. Other, larger, subfloor cists of various sizes and shapes pockmarked the floor. Probably once they had contained stockpiled foodstuffs. They may have been dug within the living space for convenience or to keep the contents from being frozen in winter. Or perhaps it was to protect precious comestibles from the ravages of raiders. It came as no surprise to the diggers that some of these pits had seen secondary use as burial places. The severed dog carcass placed with one human was unexpected. These Pine River folks did have their idiosyncrasies!

To laymen, this spot would have looked like nothing more than a jumble of rocks, dirt, and holes. To archaeologists Dittert and Eddy, it was a grand prize. They realized they had an unexpected example of a milestone in the cultural evolution of the ancestral Pueblos; perhaps the very first kind of shelter they devised to protect themselves from the elements.

Taking a clue from the recently published report by Morris and Burgh on Basketmaker II houses in the Durango region of the upper Animas and that at Ignacio on the upper Pine River salvaged just six years before, the scientists saw comparable evidence in those rotting logs around the outer edge of the floor as the base of cribbed log construction. Without nails, bolts, or tenons for fasteners, the builders could not have merely stacked log on top of log to make secure standing walls. By diagonally placing logs across the junctures of rows of underlying logs, they could raise a wall held in place by balance and weight. This cribbing method dictated the circular shape of the structure as each layer of shorter logs reduced the circumference. Eddy speculated that such construction was domed overhead and that irregularly spaced holes in the floor were sockets for upright bracing poles. The end product was a crude but ingenious solution by Stone Age people of a human need.

Clearing of the cobble ring surrounding the house showed a paved apron from five to six uniform-sized stones in width. One explanation for it was that it was meant to divert moisture away from the wood building. No similar cobblestone ring has been noted elsewhere in the Mesa Verde Province.

The Navajo Reservoir Project researchers were so pleased with the promise of the Power Pole Site that over parts of the next three seasons crews dug at other places on the Pine River seemingly used by some of the same peoples.[22] A total of twenty-four structures were examined. Thirteen of them were encircled by cobble rings. The others lacking the paving were covered abundantly with hardened clods of mud that had been used as chinking to fill spaces between cribbing logs that otherwise would have allowed wind and rain to invade the shelters. Corncobs, tatters of worn baskets, and other fibers had been stuffed into interstices as binding. Their impressions were still plainly visible to the excavators. They found evidence that the cribbed domes had been slathered with moist mud daub inside and out. Some units were extraordinarily large in size and may have been for the use of the total community. The final construction of the Pine River Basketmaker II builders was a hard, dry-weather membrane over a wooden skeleton that would have had to be refurbished seasonally. From a distance the cluster of half-round dwellings must have looked like a melon patch on the vine. It was a chicken-and-egg dilemma as to whether one architectural style preceded another or whether they were coeval. At least in part, the latter seemed to have been the case.

If the interior floor basins held only heated rocks and not open flames, one would think that the structures were not apt to catch fire. However, all the chinking clods had baked to a bricklike consistency that endured for centuries, and most of the logs were charred. As was the case with a high percentage of all ancestral Pueblo habitations, the last chapter was a fiery one—whether purposefully or accidentally one could not say.

Away from the dwellings, excavators discovered clusters of more than three dozen deep pits that once had sandstone lids. Some were five feet deep, many cubic feet in capacity, and retained grooves on walls made by the digging sticks used to gouge them out. They were of two kinds: one straight sided and the other narrow mouthed with a bulbous lower body. The interior of the latter typically had been fire hardened. Eddy believed that these pits had served as ovens. Other observers felt that they had been hardened to reduce moisture or rodent activity. In either case, so many storage facilities, added to those in the houses, is confirmation of what appears to have been successful farming and gathering enterprises and staunch commitment to harboring the returns for the future. Exterior pit storage to this degree remains a unique prehistoric attribute of the San Juan River region. Although Basketmaker II alcove sites were rich in artifacts, these items were scarce in the open Pine River sites. Primarily they were stone tool grinding implements, a limited amount of projectile points, and the debitage left from their manufacture.

An important compensation was the presence of some pottery. By the cultural phase definition of the Pecos Classification, Basketmaker II people did not have pottery. But here it was, just a handful of fragments and almost over-looked because their brown color was that of the ground around. The scholars' first explanation was that it must have been trade ware from the area to the south, where rough brown pottery was then being produced. Later ceramic specialists rejected that idea but concluded that the Pine River people and those upriver but a little later in time were experimenting with pottery made from the river silt. Regardless, the pottery is the oldest in the Mesa Verde Province.

From several radiocarbon dates, stratigraphy, and architectural and specimen assemblages, Eddy placed the house rings in a developmental stage extending from the A.D. 200s to the 400s. He called it the Los Pinos Phase.[23] It was a discretely defined horizon because there had been no later occupa-tion of the area, other than that of historic Navajos hunting in the region. In more traditional terms, the phase was Basketmaker II merging into Basketmaker III. The Pine River and lower reservoir area was then deserted as the scene of action shifted upriver.

In their reports neither Dittert nor Eddy addressed the perplexing ques-tions about where these Basketmakers came from or why and what might have been their history wherever that was. Were they heirs of nebulous Basketmaker I tribes postulated in the Pecos Classification? When did they turn to farming to supplement hunting and gathering? Even lacking these considerations, Eddy's career got off to an enviable start with his reading in the soil the opening chapter in the saga of sedentary Pueblo life, complete with the largest representation of these pioneers then known and their first attempts to make houses out of trees and containers out of earth.

Assumed subsequent cultural continuity in some sectors of the prescribed Navajo Reservoir study area could not be confirmed by the surveyors for two reasons. One was that there was no surface evidence for an intermediate step between the log houses and later occupations. No house walls or foundations, no depressions. Second, the river must have cleaned away daily discards of living with a resulting absence of middens. Moreover, apparently there had been only scant use of the San Juan Valley for several centuries, and the small, shallow pithouses in vogue during the intervening centuries had been overlaid with later constructions. Had there been no excavations, the presence of possible descendants of the first San Juan–Pine River peoples would never have been recognized.

These latecomers, who may or may not have been inheritors of residual cultural attributes of conventional Basketmakers, put their semisubter-ranean dwellings at the front edges of gravelly benches above the middle sector of the San Juan channel, where presumably they overlooked farm fields on the bottom lands.[24] It was here that sheer cliffs receded several miles to allow a modest valley to form. The largest complex of these abodes consisted of seven pit dwellings and four exterior pits. Whether all were in use contemporaneously is doubtful.

Some of the building elements in five cleared sites, the presence of a few groupings of one pit larger than the rest that recalled an early form of the Great Kiva, and the increased appearance of brown pottery suggested to some scholars that influence or colonists from the south had reached the San Juan. Probably the source was to be found in the Mogollon culture that had been acknowledged during the 1940s.

A tie to the local past was the greater use of exterior pits. Some were near occupied zones and others were at a distance. If the numbers of these settlers accounted for no more than small sites a mile apart lived in by just one or two families, why was there need for forty-five such pits in one locality?[25] Did these folks enjoy occasional communal cookouts, if the pits were indeed ovens? Or were the pit gougers compulsively banking their hard-earned agricultural and gathering rewards for some future dismal day?

In either case, these presumed latter-day Basketmakers found unused pits to be handy places in which to lay their departed to rest.[26] Not only that, but one body generally was accompanied by several more placed side by side or one on top of another. Multiple burials were not uncommon elsewhere in the province. The Wetherills and McLoyd and Graham had seen them in stor-age pits in Grand Gulch. What was unusual on the San Juan was that one or more dogs also had been deposited in the graves. The animals had been decap-itated or sliced in half either as an effective way of killing them or to make them fit space available. Today's animal rights protagonists would surely find this inhumanly offensive. Others might conclude that, on the whole, sacrificing one's pet or hunting partner was preferable to doing in kin or retainers, as was the practice in some presumably more advanced societies. Customary Puebloan offerings of pottery and other household objects would seem a more morally acceptable way of meeting an underlying human urge to ease the way into a mysterious unknown. Actually, such offerings of material things were made by the San Juan Basketmakers, canine contributions being additional tribute. Of a total of twenty-two dogs, some were so prized that a few received their own burials. They, too, were sent off in sets.

The addition to the list of stone and clay artifacts and the absence of others, and the fact that the true pithouse replaced surface cribbed domiciles, led Eddy to suggest a period from A.D. 400 to 700 as having been a bridge into that of the identifiable Pueblos.[26]

Archaeologists were realizing that in the two centuries centering on A.D. 850 the native population of the Mesa Verde Province reached its peak. Later research work would show that those who came to the banks of the San Juan River in the central reservoir district were fewer in number than those in the core area. They chose Pleistocene-age benches left by ancient geological degradation as suitable dwelling spots above gardens on the modern floodplain. At its zenith the largest of their settlements was made up of nineteen pithouses, thirteen jacal surface rooms, and five exterior pits. Archaeologist Eddy named it the Sambrito Village after a nearby creek.[27] It represented a typical occupational pattern for the entire time these people and their descendants were in the region. With a sparse population, the single family dwelling and assorted outdoor work and storage units were most common.

The everyday hardware of these residents resembled that of other provincial Pueblo I persons, including gray ware pottery. They were more fortunate than others in that they enjoyed a permanent water supply. In the high desert environment, that was a plus. If the river could not be turned onto hillocks of corn, beans, and squash, it could be counted on to occasionally overflow and the water table remain high. Possibly because of this resource, topographical limitations on population growth, and distance from larger concentrations of other Pueblos, the locals remained complacent and content with the status quo. For several hundred years there was little change in the rhythm and apparatus of life. That included lack of masonry, absence of kivas, and only rare use of the corrugated pottery, all of which became ubiquitous elsewhere by the end of the first millennium.

The physical advantage that the river afforded disappeared over time as the river ate deeper into its bed. Bordering fields were flushed away, and others were literally left high and dry. As headward erosion ensued, the erstwhile farmers were forced to move upstream. Those affected first bypassed neighbors farther up the river who still had not faced this problem and took up residence beyond in what Eddy termed a "hopscotch mode."[28]

By the end of the A.D. 900s the San Juan families were crowded on open ground and slopes at the confluence of the Piedra and San Juan Rivers near the upper limits of the anticipated reservoir. Their stay there was brief. Some migrated up the Piedra River Valley. Forty years before the Navajo Reservoir Project, Roberts encountered rubble of their homes on the terraces of that river and on Stollsteimer Mesa. By the mid-A.D. 1000s they were ensconced on the shoulders of the Chimney Rock cuesta at the head of the Piedra Valley.

Some of those who departed the San Juan vicinity probably moved east to the Gallina area of northern New Mexico. Tapered-based pottery jars with diagonal grooving on exteriors which the Piedrans produced show a latent connection to tribes there. Others may have been drawn southward into the cultural maelstrom that archaeologists now know as the Chaco Phenomenon.

One possible cause for the departure of people from the reservoir district was tension within the group due to scarcity of available farming land. That became increasingly troublesome as the river took charge. Eddy pointed to the erection around some sites of a pole "stockade" that may have been a refuge from attack. To him, most structures likely were torched by adversaries. The multiple burials that continued through the Pueblo period, in his view, may have been those of victims of raids. Two piles of cracked human bones at Sambrito Village were evidence of probable cannibalism.[29] These remains dated to the mid-A.D. 900s, or Pueblo II. Not all observers agreed with these interpretations, but if they were correct, they reaffirm the undercurrent of violence that from its inception was part of ancestral Pueblo life.

Several aspects of the fieldwork were harbingers of the future in Southwestern archaeology. Two female professionals joined the field parties. One was Beth Dickey, who participated in excavations and artifact analyses. The other was Polly Schaafsma. With a background in art as well as anthropology, she undertook study of the rock art present within the proposed pool area. Both had been Lister's students at the University of Colorado.

The other innovation was the employment of a backhoe to scoop away sterile overburden that had been deposited naturally over sites. Fred Wendorf, then at the Fort Bergwin Research Center near Taos, New Mexico, operated the equipment judiciously so as not to do harm to the antiquities. When the cultural level was reached, it was back to the trusty shovels and trowels. Without doubt weary excavators with sore muscles welcomed this heretofore undreamed of help, but it was available only so long as the machine worked. Field notes indicate periods of frustration when there were mechanical failures. Handwork, the handmaiden of dirt archaeologists, is not subject to that problem.

Navajo utilization of the reservoir district was not unexpected because their traditional homeland through the seventeenth and first half of the eighteenth centuries was the broken Gobernador and Largo headlands just to the south of the river. The number of sites that the survey crew tabulated was somewhat surprising. Conventional wisdom of the time was that the San Juan had been a recognized dividing line between Utes to the north and Navajos to the south which was breached only by random skirmishes back and forth leaving few cultural footprints on the landscape.

One hundred seventy-one Navajo-related features were counted. They were forked-stick hogans, sweat lodges, storage bins, shallow refuse drifts in rock shelters, and a scattering of distinctive potsherds and lithics.[30] These remains were most prevalent near the dam site, up the Pine, in the midcourse of the San Juan, and where the Piedra met the main drainage. Frequently these were the places lived in centuries earlier by Puebloans, and the Navajos made use of their discards.

James Hester took the study of the Navajo occupation as his responsibility. He was assisted by museum staff member Joel Shiner. Schaafsma's pictograph and petroglyph review added an esoteric dimension not generally recognizable archaeologically.[31]

In brief, these examinations revealed that the Navajo time in the study area dated to the so-called Refugee Period *circa* A.D. 1700–1750. That was when some Pueblo Indians, fearing the Spaniards who reclaimed New Mexico after a native revolt, fled to the protection of the Navajo. That in itself was one of those odd historic accommodations because for the previous one hundred years they had been enemies: mounted, basically nomadic Navajos preying on pedestrian, settled Pueblo farmers. But since both had been oppressed by the Spaniards, they became allies, at least temporarily. The Pueblo thrust into Navajo land may have precipitated an accelerated movement to the peripheries of the usual Navajo range. Consequently, in the San Juan district the Navajos, like the ancestral Pueblos of former times, were essentially marginalized from their cultural base. The absence of Spanish and Pueblo goods and the feeling of perhaps seasonal presence in the reservoir area support this hypothesis.

Curiously, no Ute sites were noted by the team working through these canyons. That must be attributed to lack of recognition rather than their absence. These Native Americans have been roaming around this part of

Colorado since at least the early A.D. 1600s, if not earlier.

Just as in the Glen Canyon project, this one nourished a new corps of students of the past. In a very meaningful way, directors passed the torch. Eddy and Hester became members of the University of Colorado faculty. Schaafsma grew into a specialist in regional rock art. ❊

# A Time of Transitions

THE THREE DECADES THAT CLOSED THE SECOND MILLENNIUM saw the young adulthood of Mesa Verde regional archaeology blossom into full maturity with all its complications. As the tempo of the search for knowledge accelerated, the tone changed. The once wild frontier had been tamed with a cobweb of roads and trails. Inevitably that meant few visible ruins unexplored by either scavengers dredging recklessly through the wreckage of the past or a new breed of scientifically trained individuals intent on other goals. The kinds of prehistoric sites likely to be encountered and their probable contents were anticipated, thus reducing the addictive thrill of discovery. "Doing archaeology" transformed into a nuts and bolts business while retaining a sufficient dose of the extraordinary to appeal to a new troop of scholars numbering into the hundreds. The typical modus operandi for pure research was a professor providing on-site instruction for college students while satisfying his or her own intellectuality. Science profited by attracting many bright, young minds who would continue to enrich regional studies. In this category were endeavors such as those of Arthur Rohn (Wichita State University) and Joe Ben Wheat (University of Colorado) in the Montezuma Valley, John Ives (Fort Lewis College) in the Ridges Basin south of Durango, and Joseph Winter (San Jose State University) at Hovenweep National Monument. Some funding was through a federal grant from the National Science Foundation.

This era also signaled the acceptance of professional women into what had long been almost exclusively male turf. Up until 1970 just five females had published on any aspect of provincial archaeology: Shepard on La Plata ceramics, Dickey and Schaafsma on topics related to the Navajo Reservoir Project, and Suhm and Florence Lister on Glen Canyon subjects.

A complexity of external issues not intrinsically part of the discipline shaped the perception and pursuit of much of the work that was done otherwise. Usually these efforts were paid for by monies from governmental or private industry sources.

Field methods kept in step with technological advancements. Remote sensing, whereby magnetometer readings indicated subsurface anomalies of possible human origin, determined various excavations. It made some digging unnecessary. The use of mechanical, earth-moving equipment was routinely done without any hand wringing, but hand tools remained necessities. Aerial photography, total station, and Global Positioning Systems for topographical and contour maps produced the ground record. Brunton compasses, alidades, and plane tables were obsolete. Archaeomagnetic and thermoluminescence dating helped bring remote times into the present, but dendrochronology remained the diggers' best friend. Most pervasive was the introduction of computers to store and manipulate data recovered by these other means. The typewriter was doomed to extinction. The mouse threatened the trowel.

Loaded into the computer age, which hit with a vengeance in the 1980s, was a jargon baggage of software, websites, downloading, simulations, histograms, and spreadsheets. Theoretical models, probabilistic sampling, and reams of numbing statistics and charts became the order of the day. Artifact analyses were ever more finite to the point that they almost became an end in themselves. Mapping, publishing, and thinking turned electronic.

The lexicon of the profession underwent semantic adjustments. Architecture was revamped as *facilities technology*. Ceramic analyses were considered *additive technology*. The study of lithics became one of *reductive technology*. *Ecofact*, a word coined to contrast with *artifact*, reflected an increased interest in environmental indicators. Salvage archaeology, with implied indiscriminate collection of imperiled antiquities, was reborn as *mitigation* through data recovery. This designation seemed more germane (or highbrow) to monitored control of federal lands.

In the intellectual sphere, there was a notable, albeit measured, shift of emphasis in the discipline to attempt to gain anthropological meaning through the archaeological evidence. Hard-earned historical and taxonomic data gleaned from the hard earth during the previous century formed the foundation for new age processual theory, ecological evaluations, social identity, and sometimes obscure sociological interpretations. A nebulous something called the "human system" became the pivot upon which scholarly attention turned. In murky terms not easily understood by those without relevant academic backgrounds, it described the whys and wherefores of those who left no written language with which to explain themselves. This enlivened a long held feeling among some lay persons that archaeologists in general were disdainful of them and otherwise arrogant. Trouble ahead.

Projects for which Lister had done preliminary groundwork got the new phase of regional archaeology well launched. The dam projects at the borderlands of the province initiated contract archaeology, but a series of other endeavors by the Mesa Verde Archaeological Research Center introduced that means of inquiry to the heartlands.

## Mancos Canyon, Ute Domain

In addition to some survey and stabilization of cliff dwellings on Ute lands by the Mesa Verde Archaeologicaı Research Center, other antiquities had to be examined because threatened by further road construction in Mancos Canyon. During this enterprise, continuing between 1972 and 1976, evidence of possible cannibalism of seventeen adults and twelve children was found in a Pueblo III site.[1] Long bones were splintered to extract the marrow. Heads were removed, roasted, and broken open. Other bones bore cut marks from butchering or having been boiled. Unlike the La Plata incidents noted by Morris in the 1920s and 1930s, this one forty years later did get attention from journalists, from physical anthropologists, and eventually from filmmakers. Quiet, now empty, Mancos Canyon was where some primitive orgy had taken place. Recognition of this episode was a prelude to what was to come.

In tandem with the Mancos Canyon archaeology was planning of the proposed Ute Mountain Ute Tribal Park.[2] After observing the popularity of Mesa Verde National Park just to their north, the Utes began to think of the cliff dwellings on their property as a possible source of income. Some elders were opposed to opening up the reservation that had been closed to outsiders for a hundred years. For other tribal members money talked, as it did for their Anglo neighbors.

Lister's son Frank directed the establishment of trails, picnic places, and a campground with the help of a group of Ute youth. The National Park Service sent a team of Navajo stabilizers to train them in ruin repair. The aim was to make as little change as possible in the condition of the ruins and the surrounding landscape so that visitors might have a feeling of stepping back into the time of the first white explorers. They could hike along the Lion Canyon escarpment to visit four cliff dwellings still swallowed in fallen building debris and peppered with fragmentary Puebloan goods. A primitive path would lead them over boulders, around stumps, past clumps of poison ivy, to end at a tall, wobbly ladder that reached to a narrow ledge along which they could walk in single file into Eagle Nest. From there they could look over broken, shadowed mesas toward Shiprock, the stony galleon still riding at anchor, and ponder why and how the Old People lived here eight hundred years ago.

One of the external factors affecting archaeology was the promotion of tourism in the Four Corners country. It encouraged development of heritage attractions as recreational and economic assets. In response, during the 1970s the Bureau of Land Management and San Juan National Forest officials contracted with the Mesa Verde Archaeological Research Center to undertake the preparation for public inspection of three archaeological zones in distinctive locations. All were known in the earliest recognition of a prehistory having graced this sector of the Colorado Plateau and, incidentally, all had Chacoan implications combined with a Mesa Verdean base. They were Chimney Rock, Lowry, and Escalante.

### Back to Chimney Rock

In the eastern borderland of the Mesa Verde Province, Eddy was enabled to further study the upper Piedra River Valley district with which he had become acquainted during the Navajo Reservoir Project. Forest Service administrators wanted to set aside some six square miles surrounding the Chimney Rock cuesta as an archaeological preserve and open the most obvious concentration of old structures to visitors.

Thus, aided by several University of Colorado students, for two seasons from 1971 through 1972 Eddy dug out the story of the Puebloans on the upper Piedra. He had read the opening chapter with those Pine River Basketmakers who thought up the unusual cobblestone-ringed, cribbed log–walled type of dwelling unlike any others used by contemporaries and made brown pottery when no one else did. In the next chapter, he followed the travails of their descendants up the San Juan Valley as they moved into pithouses, gouged out huge exterior pits for unknown purposes, and had a special fondness for dogs. Driven by natural forces beyond their control, after some centuries they were at the junction of the San Juan and Piedra Rivers. These hapless farmers still were residing in pits with closets outside, when other Mesa Verdeans had substantial houses of stone, and eschewing whatever ceremonies that demanded kivas. Furthermore, they made a crude, gray earthenware unlike that produced by fellow Mesa Verdeans to the west. All in all, they seemed out of step with neighbors. Were they iconoclasts or just hayseeds? Besides that, the river upon which they depended disappeared into its channel. As this chapter in their dreary saga ended, Eddy saw them at a cultural rock bottom. That is where he left them as the Navajo Reservoir Project ended.

When Eddy next met some of these strange, eastern Mesa Verde people, they had abandoned the San Juan vicinity and moved north up the more welcoming Piedra Valley until blocked by the continental backbone reared up by the majestic San Juan Mountains. No place else to go but up, they ascended the Chimney Rock cuesta. That is where Eddy proposed to bring their tale to its climactic last chapter.[3]

As the University of Colorado diggers revealed, the houses of the Chimney Rock settlers were circular to resemble their traditional pit dwellings but, because of the impossibility of digging into the crusty cap rock with only pointed sticks, were placed on its surface.[4] Their walls of roughly shaped sandstone blocks were inordinately thick as a hedge against frigid winters at a higher elevation than that to which the migrants had been accustomed. Most habitations were single structures, but a few were multiple, round rooms with some rectangular storage units attached.

By the A.D. 1070s a hundred of these domiciles, most suitable for no more than mother, father, offspring, and perhaps a grandparent, inched up the ridge of the upland and spilled down its sides. Eddy identified seven groupings of households that he regarded as comprising an interacting upper Piedra community and through which he sought clues as to probable social organization. In their midst Puebloans erected a modified communal Great Kiva, as apparently religion had gained a foothold. Still eccentric as compared to the Mesa Verde norm, they varied its internal features from the more common format. The residents of these complexes farmed patches of land on the heights but also made use of terraces by the Piedra and the flatlands next to a small tributary. The soils up on the plateau were thin and rocky, but there was sufficient precipitation for dry farming, and the winters were a bit milder than down in the valleys. The women still favored that strange, tapered, textured gray ware but attempted to copy decorative styles on white wares that must have been inspired by the works of other Mesa Verdean potters.

Because archaeologists necessarily place so much emphasis in their cultural interpretations on architecture and ceramics, the uniqueness of the Piedran expression may be overstated.[5] It could have resulted from their relative isolation from the stimulus of larger centers of Mesa Verde life. Or it could be that this whole district was taken over by peoples who shared much of the same agrarian subsistence orientation as other Mesa Verdeans but originated from a different Southwestern base. In any case, they were introduced to the highest form of ancestral Puebloan ethos: the Chacoans arrived.

Judging from a large tree ring sample, in the A.D. 1090s masons versed in

Chaco architectural style moved to Chimney Rock to raise a compact house-block that differed totally from the dwellings of the local residents. It was a multistory, fifty-five-room building of sandstone core-and-veneer masonry. Two kivas were incorporated within its heart. The edifice sits on the upper-most platform of the cuesta as close to the feet of the two pinnacles as possi-ble with the mesa dropping off sharply on either side. Helicopters delivered sand and cement to a Navajo stabilization crew that went to work as soon as Eddy's team finished reworking the building that had badly deteriorated after the 1920s excavations by Jeancon and Roberts. Forest Service employees ran a water line more than a mile from the river in order to mix the mortar for reset-ting walls. Without these advantages, the reasons why the builders chose this location are hard to find: no water, little work space, no arable land, just a breathtaking view from a barren, windswept prominence.

The questions raised by this outpost are manifold and took on added importance ignored by the pioneer researchers because of a large scale project also begun in the early 1970s in Chaco Canyon. What could have prompted Chacoans to come nearly one hundred miles from their home territory to an environment in sharp contrast to that which they left? And why did they elect to invade a region already long occupied by others? Did they do so by force or through persuasion? Did they usurp farmland on the lower floodplain or did they rely on support from an oppressed, less aggres-sive people? One hint of trouble on the mesa was calcined human bones mixed with household discards in a nearby depression. Cannibalism has been attributed to Chacoans, but the available literature on Chimney Rock does not consider that possibility.[6]

The most obvious explanation for the site was the magnetic draw of the powerful anthropomorphism that turned the chimneys into the Twin War Gods. To both modern Pueblos and Navajos, these are prominent figures in their pantheons of supernaturals and probably were so in the past. Those burned bones may have been the residue of ritual activity associated with these deities.

A second theory comes from the discipline of astronomy. In the 1970s as part of a growing concern with human behavior as illuminated archaeologically, scientists shifted from concentration exclusively on what lay in the earth to noting natural phenomena in the sky that undoubtedly were observed aborigi-nally. Behind this viewpoint was extensive publicity about a pair of spiral petro-glyphs on a butte in Chaco Canyon that were pierced by a shaft of light for twenty-five minutes at summer solstice and for almost three hours at winter solstice.[7] This observation was followed by a flurry of interest in identifying architectural and horizon features that could have been used to foretell or mark such rhythmic natural events so critical to agrarian societies worldwide. Professional and avocational archaeoastronomers, as they came to be called, flocked to relevant places across the Colorado Plateau every June and December to see if they functioned as predicted. Cloudless skies were prized.

Astronomer Kim Malville, of the University of Colorado, presented an alternate intriguing idea about the placement of the Chimney Rock Great House.[8] In his view, its primary reason for being where it is was not merely as an observation point for solar cycles but for lunar ones. He was cognizant of a period every 18.6 years when the moon reaches its northernmost declination and remains there for an interval of about two years. Calibrating back in time, he found that such a standstill took place at exactly the year in which the house was built, or in Eddy's judgment, was remodeled. What a coincidence! He then witnessed such an occurrence in August of 1988 to substantiate his hunch that as one looked eastward the moonrise was visibly framed by the stony chimneys like some divine portrait. One can envision a golden radiance bathing the Great House on its lonely summit while spellbound onlookers stood transfixed. According to Malville, that unquestionably was the reason for the building's placement.

But there were other events that must have made the natives uneasy. A total eclipse of the sun that occurred in this period on July 11, 1097, darkened a long swath of the Colorado Plateau and moved across Chimney Rock.[9] Moreover, the decade of the A.D. 1090s was one of prolonged, severe drought when the rains did not come and corn stalks withered.[10] What was happening to the Piedrans' world?

After having observed the lunar spectacle once or twice, if, in fact, they were permitted to enter what might have been restricted sacred precincts, the Piedrans gave up. Atypical to the end, they had something the others did not, but it did them little good. By A.D. 1130 their story was written.

Presumably the Chacoans went home and then onward. Getting reacquainted with them in this 1970s return to Chimney Rock was to spark revived interest in their presence in the northern San Juan districts and how it affected the indigenous population there.

As part of the modern development of the Chimney Rock preserve, the Forest Service built a winding road up the south side of the cuesta to the group of Piedran habitations dug by the university crew. Facilities were installed and a loop trail prepared. The steep path struggling up to the Chacoan Great House was left unimproved. Shortly thereafter a pair of peregrine falcons nested at the base of the pinnacles and could be seen from the ruin and a high fire tower erected at its side. These birds were on the endangered species list. The park was closed. It would seem that the Twin War Gods had returned in another guise.[11]

### Lowry Ruin, Again

A second precinct to receive attention in this 1970s initiative by government agencies was at Lowry Ruin on the Great Sage Plain. When it was originally excavated in the early 1930s, an interior kiva wall was found to be decorated with a painted band of repeated geometric motifs. The kiva was backfilled as a preservative measure and remained so during a second excavation and stabilization effort in the 1960s. Subsequently, as part of observances of the nation's Bicentennial, the Bureau of Land Management decided to add the painted kiva to the monument's visible attractions. There had been other kivas at the Lowry settlement and elsewhere that were similarly decorated when in use, but the near total survival for some 850 years of this mural made it a unique feature.

Breternitz and Lancaster instructed eight advanced University of Colorado students in the exacting work of ruins stabilization. In this venture, which took place during the summers of 1974 and 1975, it was necessary to remove a badly deteriorated kiva on the second-floor level of the houseblock in order to probe down to the painted kiva in a room compound on ground level. That done, the pilasters to support a new roof were rebuilt, each slightly varied according to the abilities of the novice masons. Such minor variation in aboriginal architecture surely was due to the same causes. A skylight in the new roof substituted for the hatchway that would have been the means of access originally, and a new opening through the southern recess permitted viewing of the interior. Visitors could peer into a quiet, darkened chamber to gain some sense of the sacredness with which the Old People must have regarded it and the rituals that transpired there.

Whatever such reflections were, they were relatively short-lived. In just a dozen years a combination of destructive factors saw the mural become a disheartening ring of plaster crumbs on the kiva floor. All the twentieth-century conservation skills, technologies, and chemicals could not save what were just mud plaster and clay pigment. Comparable erosional forces were held in check in the twelfth century by routine refurbishing that is now counter to administrative policy.[12]

### Escalante, the House on the Hill

The house on the hill now named Escalante Ruin commands a wondrous view.

To its north is the Dolores River valley now glistening with waters of the McPhee Reservoir. Its backdrop are forested foothills reaching upward to the spiky, lofty La Plata Mountains. In the opposite direction the Montezuma Valley stretches off to the western horizon. Directly south is the passageway between the Mesa Verde heights and Ute Mountain that slopes several thousand feet down to the silty San Juan River. Beyond lies the bleakness of the Chaco Province.

It was fitting that Escalante be excavated and made ready for the Bicentennial celebrations. It had first been noted by Fray Vélez de Escalante in 1776, the year of the nation's birth.

Again, University of Colorado students under the supervision of Breternitz and Lancaster went to work in 1975 and 1976 to partially clear the site. Working out of a field camp next to the ruin, they uncovered a single houseblock of twenty-three rooms surrounding a central kiva.[13] The unexcavated portions of the mound concealed a settlement of considerably larger extent. Domestic and kiva architectural styles identified this structure as yet another Chaco settlement, but in contrast to that at Chimney Rock, it was used in its final days by Mesa Verdeans who made some modifications to the original plan. As was often the case with these Chacoan intrusions into outlying regions, the Escalante Great House was placed on a prominence above a scattering of perhaps a dozen indigenous dwellings built in a less-refined way reminiscent of some Early Pueblo II buildings at Mesa Verde. One of these was excavated and named Dominguez after the leader of the Franciscan entourage of 1776. Tree ring dates in the early decades of the A.D. 1100s confirm the general contemporaneity of all these remains.

From the size of the hilltop structure, its ordered sophistication as opposed to a confused adding on as needs arose, and its situation, one might infer political, social, or religious dominance of invading Chacoans over local Mesa Verdeans. If that meant a better standard of living by the intruders, archaeology provided no confirmation. Even though ten or so families might have dwelt in the modest houses on the slopes below, they did not comprise a reasonably adequate support base for those living above. With the exception of a few trade items at the Great House, it appears that life for all inhabitants of the district was on the same low level of survival with limited food, scant physical comfort, and few luxuries. Nevertheless, some observers favor a hierarchical social structure operating here. Others argue that probably egalitarianism and privation prevailed, both of which may have prompted eventual emigration.

There was one known, puzzling exception. A female burial lay in a four-room Dominguez dwelling at the base of the knoll upon which Escalante

Ruin stands. In the fill just above her was what was left of an infant judged to be less than four months old. Both bodies had been dusted with red hematite. This makes for a touching story. Were they related? Did they die at the same time and from the same causes? Food for thought are analyses of X-rays of the infant's bones that reveal two periods of arrested growth probably from protein deficiencies. The woman's bones indicate trauma from giving birth. It may be that she succumbed from childbirth and, for lack of mother's milk or other problems, her baby soon perished.[14]

Even more curious was the abundance of special goods placed with the woman.[15] There were sixty-nine hundred beads of shell, turquoise, jet, and shale scattered about her remains. The shell would have been traded from the Pacific coast. Turquoise from north central New Mexico was processed in Chaco Canyon. Neither material is commonly found in the Mesa Verde Province. Also present were three pendants. One was made of abalone shell in the form of a toad. A duplicate in jet was recovered by Richard Wetherill in the 1890s digging at Pueblo Bonito, suggesting that this was a symbolic specialty of that community or others in Chaco Canyon. Several black-on-white pottery vessels of Mesa Verde Pueblo II types were in the grave along with some bone tools and a burial mat.

The woman's burial was surprising on several counts. It was the richest in terms of offerings in a region where status graves are as yet unknown. It was beneath the dirt floor of a presumably empty, humble house. And it was a female in what is generally thought to have been a male-dominated society. One interpretation is that she may have been the beloved mate of a prominent figure living in the Chaco house on the hill who placed her body, and perhaps that of her offspring, nearby with special tokens of devotion that he acquired from sources in his Chaco homeland. In essence, this was the human system in action.

In a pattern repeated endlessly throughout the province, the Chacoan residents of the Escalante Great House moved on in the twelfth century after a stay of perhaps no more than thirty years. Probably they trudged south through the gateway to the eastern flanks of the Chuska Mountains, from which they may have migrated originally, and then on to areas of the upper Little Colorado River drainage or to the Hopi mesas. If so, their descendants contributed to a remarkable rejuvenation there of Pueblo culture that carries through to the present.

### Salmon Ruin, Port of Entry

Cynthia Irwin-Williams and her younger brother Henry were destined from adolescence to become archaeologists when they grew up. Their mother, Mama Kay, and her good friend Marie Wormington, curator of archaeology at the Denver Museum of Natural History, saw to that. Books, excursions, conversations, and behind the scenes, small tasks at the museum were deliberately planned to orient the juveniles in that direction. They obligingly responded well. When the time came for higher education, they enrolled in Radcliffe College and Harvard University, Wormington's schools. While undergraduates, they applied Wormington's tutoring on several digs in the foothills near Denver that focused on preceramic cultures. In due time they both earned doctorates from Harvard. Both inaugurated their initial professional studies working in France with Paleolithic materials. France, coincidentally, was Wormington's ancestral home. By the late 1960s Henry was teaching at Washington State University and Cynthia was at Eastern New Mexico University. In that position the female part of this unusual sibling team, with her trademark French beret, emerged as a respected student of Archaic and ancestral Pueblo prehistory after extensive study with even earlier cultural manifestations in Wyoming and central Mexico.[16]

In 1969 San Juan County, New Mexico, took the insightful step of purchasing a piece of land on the north bank of the San Juan River near Bloomfield that had been the late-nineteenth-century homestead of George Salmon. A few tumbled-down buildings and sheds of that period remained and were of historic interest. However, the reason for the purchase was a large, mounded ruin that officials thought worthy of development as a cultural and financial investment. This recalled the American Museum of Natural History's acquisition of Aztec West just ten miles to the north. Fortuitously, the Salmon property was next to a main valley highway that might funnel tourists to it. Local citizens could feel good about high-minded heritage preservation while making it pay.

With that proposition in mind, staff members of the San Juan County Museum Association contacted Irwin-Williams to ask if she would consider directing excavation of Salmon Ruin. She had visited Aztec and Mesa Verde as a child but had no academic experience in the archaeology of the northern San Juan region. Still, she was interested enough to go to Bloomfield to see what was being proposed. Upon viewing the huge pile of earth obscured by sagebrush, tumbleweeds, and assorted trash, she was so unimpressed that she reportedly asked, "Where is it?" all the time standing on the ruin.

As Irwin-Williams mulled it over during the following winter, she came to realize that very likely the Salmon site might have some relationship with

Aztec West. If that were the case, it might also have connection to the settlements in Chaco Canyon which at that very time were being intensively investigated by a joint program mounted by the National Park Service and the University of New Mexico. These probable relationships played into her abiding interest in regional systems, one of which she called the "Chaco phenomenon."

Irwin-Williams was at that time committed to instructing Eastern New Mexico University field school students on the forlorn benches along the Rio Puerco west of Albuquerque about Archaic hunting-gathering remains that she considered to be rootlets from which the later ancestral Pueblo culture grew. When the 1970 session was over, she took fifteen of her students back to Salmon Ruin to attempt to assess its potential as a meaningful study and exhibit.[17]

Since this was to be a relatively brief inspection, arrangements were made to house the group in the Navajo Indian School in Aztec, not then being used, and later in a Farmington church. Museum members supplied the camp cook with fresh garden produce and on occasion took the party to cafeterias. This was archaeology on the cheap, but it gave nonprofessionals a feeling of satisfaction in being part of an intellectual exercise. To reciprocate, the students, there on a volunteer basis, chipped in by putting on a pit barbecue and fundraiser. It helped that several of the fellows had been army cooks. As was her custom, Irwin-Williams personally took care of other extra expenses.

In the months following Irwin-Williams's first visit, museum members managing the site under lease arrangements with the county prevailed upon a Boy Scout troop to clear the mound surface of plants and rubbish. Other than potholes left by vandals, most of the mound was in pristine condition and far more interesting to the archaeologist than when first seen.

Exploratory testing in 1970 and again in 1971 showed great promise for the proposed project. In an admirable display of public enthusiasm for regional antiquity, or perhaps for its hoped-for financial returns, the San Juan County Museum Association successfully lobbied for a bond issue and other funding to pay on a long-term basis for excavation of the site and to erect an administration building with a small museum, research library, laboratories, and storage space for the anticipated haul of specimens. A number of prefabricated cabins for single crew or staff, a barracks for married couples, an open air shower, cook shack, and indoor and outdoor mess halls of a sort were put conveniently beside the site.

Irwin-Williams transferred her field school to Salmon Ruin in 1972 and continued working there seasonally for the next six years. Thus, she became the first female to direct a major excavation in the Mesa Verde Province. Some years there were as many as one hundred people involved in various aspects of the project, making for lively camp life. With her pleasant memories of France, Irwin-Williams always gave a big party on Bastille Day with abundant food and a concocted drink that the jocular participants referred to as "clang juice." If imbibed in sufficient quantity, one's ears rang resoundingly. Long live France! To wrap up each season there was a gala pit barbecue for crew and numerous invited guests prepared by none other than the San Juan County sheriff. Such attention must be classed as public involvement beyond the call of duty.

The ways in which Morris excavated Aztec West and the 1970s all-out assault on Salmon Ruin could not have been more different. Morris's work was virtually a solo performance with a half-dozen untrained family men who went home at night and forgot the day's chores. In contrast, Irwin-Williams marshaled a small army of eager young people, many of whom intended to make archaeology their life's work. While she dealt with a blizzard of administrative and logistical paperwork, Lonnie Pippin and Rex Adams served as her on-site lieutenants. Ten advanced students were crew chiefs directing eight or more diggers in some assigned portion of the mound. In addition, from time to time various specialists contributed their expertise. Just as at Aztec fifty years previously, a proprietary feeling about Salmon Ruin brought curious visitors to watch the uncommon activities.

Salmon Ruin met high expectations. It was, in fact, another Chaco Great House with the same ground plan as Aztec West but on a somewhat smaller scale.[18] It was built in the typical Chacoan core-and-veneer manner but the surfaces were not as finely finished because of the lower quality of the available sandstone. As was the case at Aztec West, the western arm of the building was not cleared. What remained were approximately two hundred or more rooms laid out in an E-shaped pattern opening to the south toward the river and the winter sun. The north side of the structure rose to two, possibly three, stories and encompassed a spacious, buttressed kiva on the upper level. A Great Kiva was sunk into the southern part of the courtyard. There were no intact rooms hidden beneath the earthen rind of the mound. Tree ring dates ranged from A.D. 1068 to 1116. This was a relatively short construction time considering the size of the building and the primitive methods used. A managed work force, highly motivated, was responsible.

At an elevation of fifty-four hundred feet, in a sheltered valley with rich river loam, and with permanent water to channel onto it and bring in storage jars to kitchen hearths, the migrants settling into housekeeping at

Salmon Ruin must have found a pleasant place to live. No doubt they wondered why they had tarried so long in bleak Chaco Canyon.

The importance of Salmon Ruin was underscored by remote sensing studies being carried out by the concurrent Chaco project that identified an aboriginal road running north from the canyon toward the San Juan River. Ground examinations took it some thirty miles as far as Kutz Canyon, but from there to the river no trace of it could be detected. Nevertheless, it can be assumed with a fair degree of certainty that this so-called Great North Road continued on to a river crossing at or near the Salmon Ruin location where Kutz Canyon begins its course through barren headlands to the east. In addition to taking care of themselves, the Salmon Ruin residents may have had a mission of either producing foodstuffs and other commodities for the resource-deficient parent communities to the south or for overseeing such shipments garnered from the local populace, perhaps in some form of tribute. Their probable success in this regard encouraged successive Chaco colonists or waves of influence to come northward into the Mesa Verde Province. The Chimney Rock Great House was built as construction work at Salmon Ruin was completed. The complex at Aztec followed a decade later and perhaps was erected in part by Salmonite masons. At the same time traders were busy getting Chaco pottery delivered to hamlets along the lower La Plata Valley after being imported via the Salmon port of entry.

Archaeologists investigating Salmon Ruin concluded that the Chacoans left this dwelling by about A.D. 1115.[19] Despite their investment of considerable labor in it, they used the house for little more than a generation. After they left, a few squatters moved in, their numbers swelling in the late twelfth century. Remodeling activities were evident in that small circular kivas were put into original rectangular rooms and other living rooms were reduced in size. Even though these changes and pottery of Pueblo III Mesa Verde types confirm a secondary use by people following those traditions, no part of the structure had been converted into tombs for their dead, as at Aztec West. Burials may have been put into a trash midden that was washed downstream long before excavators arrived.

However, the diggers at Salmon Ruin did find human remains. These were calcined bones of children and adults scattered over the roof of the tower kiva. The possibility of an intentional act of violence cannot be ignored. Whatever it was, it took place during the last years of the A.D. 1200s, a time when discouraged Mesa Verdeans were withdrawing from the province. Could the children have been sacrificed to appease the gods and make a troubled world right again? We will never know what dark, tragic turn the human system might have taken on the banks of the San Juan.

Currently, new investigations are reexamining data gathered in the 1970s in light of research accomplished since then. One goal is to estimate the importance in the valley of Salmon Ruin and its possible ties to other settlements there. Unlike the Animas Valley adjacent to the Aztec complex, there are only four small settlements near Salmon Ruin that can now be seen. Others may be buried under alluvium. Further downriver there are several fifty-room structures that possibly had some ties to Salmon Ruin.[20]

## REPRISE OF MESA VERDE

Beginning with the first white encounters with Mesa Verde, there had been various attempts to count and classify archaeological sites on Chapin and Wetherill Mesas. These two slices of the tableland comprise just a quarter of the national park. Certainly because there were no large cliff dwellings replete with treasures present, its northern and eastern sectors, some thirty-nine thousand acres, remained essentially unknown in terms of lesser archaeological specifics. That lacuna in the record was about to be filled when in 1970 President Nixon issued an executive order that federal agencies compile an inventory of their cultural resources. That put the Mesa Verde Archaeological Research Center in the survey business under the field direction of staff member Jack Smith. This was government bookkeeping having nothing to do with recreational or economic concerns but it did further scientific inquiries.

Armed with cameras, field books, topographic maps, two-way radios, binoculars, collection bags, and first aid kits, Smith and company took to the field. Each season from 1971 through 1977 Smith organized a nine-person team divided into three crews to walk and rewalk the sector designated to be examined. The combined personnel roster for the seven summers lists 104 men and women.[21] With nine actually engaged at a time, that number exemplified the continual dropping out of inexperienced helpers and the bringing in of inexperienced new ones that Smith ruefully attempted to indoctrinate. The rigors of breaking through rough terrain mantled with nearly impenetrable, snagging brush and sloughy talus, the annoyance of swarms of stinging gnats, summer heat, and general camp discomforts soon sent many of them packing. However, about a fourth of them later continued to be involved in some aspects of archaeology and may have looked back on the experience as a prerequisite test of stamina and perseverance, both essential qualities for competent field archaeologists.

Portions or all of twenty mesa tops and canyons were examined to record eighteen hundred prehistoric sites, bringing the total number of known sites to well over forty-three hundred.[22] Mere artifact scatters, mounded middens, and habitations that ranged from pit depressions to small cliff houses made up the tabulation. They covered the full continuum of ancestral Pueblo existence in the Mesa Verde Province from Pueblo I times through Pueblo III, or some six hundred years. Although presumed to have been there, pre-Pueblo I sites could not be identified positively because of lack of surface clues. As Hayes had learned years earlier in his Wetherill Mesa survey, only excavation could reliably determine temporal placement of these early sites. The years between A.D. 1050 and 1150 presumably were those of peak population. As elsewhere, the restless natives periodically shifted about over the landscape like grains of sand before a wind, but a total hiatus of the district at any one period seems not to have occurred. Such continuity has not yet been noted elsewhere in the province although it likely occurred.

Smith's survey included ninety-six examples of historic homestead presence, such as fences, corrals, cabins, windmills, and trash. There also were Navajo hogans and sweat lodges used by park employees. These were in the bottoms of eastern canyons that opened to the Mancos drainage or where road construction had taken place. No Ute sites were identified.

During the 1990s and early 2000s, major lightning-ignited fires roared over Mesa Verde turning what had been the "green table" into a moonscape of ghostly, black tree trunks and twisted branches silhouetted grotesquely against the sky. The positive side of such destruction was that in burning off the layer of vegetation hundreds of unknown prehistoric sites were exposed. Most were surface sheet trash or rubble mounds that once had been small habitations. They were superficially tabulated and left unexcavated as part of a reserve for scientists of the future. Some sites on the lower elevations will be obscured again in a few decades as brush thickets come to life. Those higher up will not because the evergreens that surrounded them take centuries to germinate and mature. The surface houses and cliff dwellings on Wetherill Mesa and Chapin Mesa, where the fires were especially hot and extensive, escaped severe damage. The modern service buildings and roofs over some excavations were a total loss but are replaceable.

In December 1988 the superintendent of Mesa Verde National Park, assisted by local historians Richard Ellis and Duane Smith, brought a number of Wetherill heirs to the park in recognition of the centennial of the Wetherill-Mason first sighting of Cliff Palace. For two days they shared family recollections of the exciting days following that event. It was a pleasant, informative affair open to all interested persons until the pervasive Park Service condemnation of the nineteenth-century Wetherill activities in the cliff dwellings resurfaced. Many on the government staff have habitually ignored the prevailing circumstances of those "unenlightened" days and seem uninformed of the fruitless efforts of the father of the clan to get the Smithsonian Institution interested in overseeing the work. Not surprisingly, the Wetherills at this meeting took umbrage over what they considered an affront.

In a few years when they realized the historical value of their combined memorabilia from the exploratory era, they pointedly chose not to deposit the collection at Mesa Verde.[23] That was a considerable loss because the old letters, notes, and photographs would have enriched the park archives.

The grandson of Gustaf Nordenskiold, who had been a soil consultant for the Wetherill Mesa Project, attended this meeting for a touching connection of two families generations later. He heard no criticism from the park staff over his forbear having walked off with barrels of loot including human remains. On the contrary, Nordenskiold seems to be the golden boy of the park. Three years later a traveling exhibit was mounted honoring the one hundredth anniversary of his 1891 work. Included were a few finer specimens that were returned on loan from the National Museum of Finland, some photographs donated years earlier by Nordenskiold's aging daughter, and excerpts from his classic book, *The Cliff Dwellers of Mesa Verde*, an original copy of which is in the park research library. Also on display was a recently annotated edition of Nordenskiold's field journal presented to the park by the son-in-law after he translated it from Swedish into English.[24]

A flurry of research activity began at Mesa Verde National Park as the twentieth century was winding down, and it continued for several years. The White House Millennium Council in cooperation with the National Trust for Historic Preservation established a mission to repair and upgrade places of special historical importance. It was called Save America's Treasures and was funded by the government and the private sector. Mesa Verde was one of sixty-two recipients, probably because it earlier was named one of the world's outstanding examples of antiquity that is most endangered. Hillary Rodham Clinton traveled to the park, inspected Cliff Palace, and gave a laudatory, open-air talk on a hot May morning in 1999. It was appropriate that Native Americans participated in the program. A large audience of other citizens drove the fifteen miles up to the Far View area to see and hear the first lady, but more importantly to show their interest and pride in the renowned installation in their midst.

The Mesa Verde plan for judicious use of this windfall was twofold. One endeavor was devoted to what staffers called the "front country." That was Chapin Mesa, where most visitors went. The other effort was in the "back country," all off limits to the public except for Wetherill Mesa.

As for the front country project, the park's centerpiece—Cliff Palace—was an obvious choice for attention, with Spruce Tree House to follow. Larry Nordby, chief archaeologist, chose these venues as his turf. Joel Brisbin, a graduate of two long-term regional archaeological programs, helped him. For Nordby, to work in these sites was something of a sentimental journey. Three decades earlier he had his early field training in the park as part of a student crew working for the Mesa Verde Archaeological Research Center. Like his peers, he fell under the spell of the ancient buildings dappled with shadows in their alcoves that almost seemed to be waiting for his tender loving care. He knew that their study, the first step of which was mapping them in painstaking detail for the first time, was going to be the culmination of his long career and that it would demand all his acquired observational and technical skills.

Originally Cliff Palace had been built over a span of years by an unknown number of masons. Consequently, there was little construction uniformity from one part of the structure to another or from room to room, although the same materials were utilized throughout. Overall it was a complex medley of chambers with and without apertures, one square and one round tower, and kivas placed on several levels. Some units were atop huge chunks of fallen alcove roof and others were stranded on a narrow ledge high above the main house. In modern times repeated stabilizations were done for which there are no or incomplete records. All these factors complicate unraveling the structure's history.

Nordby's multilevel approach to the task of mapping Cliff Palace and Spruce Tree House was one of excruciating computerized detail about every conceivable facet of the buildings. No stone, mortar joint, plaster patch, wall segment, or wood element remained unexamined or unrecorded in tabular and graphic databases. When the men finished, these two cliff dwellings, representing standing thirteenth-century artifacts, were subjected to closer examinations than any in the Southwest have been or may ever be in the future.

Just as important as it is to know how Cliff Palace grew is how it was used by its residents. To recapture that seemingly intangible part of the story required matching physical evidence with educated inference. In this case, those deductions had to be made solely on architecture because telling artifacts were stripped away long ago. Rooms with hearths and occasionally with soot stains left from hearth use were considered living rooms. The lack of specimens meant work spaces were speculative. A large percentage of the chambers of Cliff Palace have no interior features or evidence of domestic fires. Some lack exterior openings. Nordby decided that these had been where an inordinate amount of foodstuffs or resources had been stacked and guarded.

Nordby's final map showed that the 223 room count published by Fewkes early in the twentieth century and unequivocally accepted thereafter was erroneous. His new map indicated just 150 rooms.[25] Apparently there had been a bit of Fewkes's creative reconstruction with walls added where he thought they might have been. Thus, Cliff Palace is not the largest of all Southwestern cliff dwellings, as has been endlessly repeated, but is actually the same size as Long House on Wetherill Mesa.

Because of the reduced size of Cliff Palace, Nordby estimated a much lower population than the former exaggerated number of about a hundred individuals, most of whom he suspected stayed in the settlement only periodically. The large number of rooms just used for storage transformed Cliff Palace into a mere warehouse and distribution center for the many dwellings in the vicinity, with a handful of caretakers as full-time tenants of Cliff Palace. There is no evidence that this or any of the other cliff dwellings were defensive constructions, although the tenor of the A.D. 1200s apparently was one of anxiety over natural or human circumstances. Alas, for the romantics among us, Nordby's point of view sadly demystified Cliff Palace into a commonplace relic. However, his interpretation is open to question.

What really caught Nordby's attention was a wall running through the center of the structure dividing it into two parts. That element had been overlooked previously because of room walls abutting it on either side that obscured its significance. This led Nordby to suggest a duality in the social organization signifying what ethnologists know as a *moiety system*.[26] This will remain an interesting but controversial idea. However, other large Puebloan sites were divided in a similar manner, and some present Pueblo tribes ascribe to a moiety arrangement wherein the two bodies seasonally alternate in ritual responsibilities. The question is whether present practices are analogous to those of the past.

One part of the front country project was to find and document both Indian and Euroamerican inscriptions that were scratched into the soft plaster of old structures or on rocky surfaces nearby. When some of the sites were first being prepared for visitation, rangers made a concerted effort to rub off what they then regarded as unsightly graffiti. Fortunately they missed some native rock art and quite a few names, initials, and dates left by Euroamerican trespassers. Sally Cole, rock art specialist, reports hundreds of such works that were previously overlooked, and Fred Blackburn has found approximately two thousand historical inscriptions of which a very small percentage are still readable.[27] Most interesting are about twenty that predate 1888, thereby confirming white man's presence on the Mesa Verde before the Wetherills unofficially claimed it.

Back country work was more diversified. Three women were lead archaeologists in assessing the condition of scores of sites peering out of alcoves along canyon walls, in documenting them, and in carrying out preservation measures where necessary. In some of the more inaccessible sectors, crews and equipment, under the direction of female stabilizer Kathy Fiero, were taken in by helicopter because of the ruggedness of the terrain. After a century, the total extent of the park's antiquities finally is recorded and hopefully reinforced to withstand whatever may come.

### Towers, Sunrise, and Sunset at Hovenweep

From the eighth century when the Pueblo system began to coalesce, Mesa Verdean builders combined circular (semisubterranean) and rectangular (surficial) forms in their habitation zones. After a further one hundred years of the evolutionary process in architecture, masons added circular features above ground. Some of them were incorporated into what had become a consolidated block of contiguous, rectangular rooms and were connected to the subsurface, round rooms, or kivas, by a tunnel beneath the ground. A major construction advancement was sturdier walls two sandstone blocks in width that allowed workmen to take the daring step of stacking rectangular units one on top of another and circular components similarly placed one above another to create multistoried houses. This construction format furthered social integration of the group. Even bolder was the masons' growing penchant for making the circular units, or towers, freestanding and often in isolated situations. Fortunately the province is not subject to earth tremors or the unreinforced, unbonded constructions quickly would have crashed into heaps of rubble.

It is the towers, particularly those that were set apart from dwellings, that have intrigued observers since the earliest explorations of the Four Corners country. Some loom tall and defiantly above a flattened landscape, often precariously perched on the drop-off of a mesa edge or molded like hot lava atop a huge boulder. Without hoists, cranes, other lifting mechanisms, or human harnesses, their erection was a challenge. When they first appeared in Late Pueblo II times, towers generally were circular with a single chamber on the ground and perhaps an upper level. Over time they were elaborated into square or D-shapes enclosing a series of connected rooms in as many as three stories.

The reasons behind the perceived need for towers are baffling. Combinations of curved and straight lines at differing elevations added aesthetic interest to a building's silhouette and in a subtle way translated stone and mud into a metaphor of the natural, geometrically aligned environment in which the Mesa Verdeans lived. This harmony with nature continues to inspire Southwestern architects via the Pueblo-Spanish Revival impetus. While ancestral Pueblos demonstrated remarkable artistic sensitivities in all their handiwork, that hardly seems a compelling raison d'être for towers.

Those towers connected to kivas by tunnels can be considered to have had a ritualistic purpose. Perhaps they served as dressing rooms or shrines for particular rites whose participants emerged dramatically into kivas. A more easily built rectangular room would have sufficed for those functions, but through centuries of association of circular cells with religion, the mind-set of the builders called for this addition to the sacred complex to be round. Rina Swentzel, a native of Santa Clara Pueblo and a student of her tribe's architecture, sees the tunnel-kiva combination in sexual terms.[28] To her, the tower symbolizes the male reproductive organ and the kiva that of a woman, or the womb of Mother Earth. That interpretation and its consequences might have perked up pages of prosaic technical reports. But more pragmatic archaeologists suggest a variety of practical functions or mixtures of them, such as fortifications, lookouts, dwellings, silos, or observatories. None of the above are entirely convincing. Maybe Swentzel is right.

Enigmatic towers are found across the central Mesa Verde Province. Those on Cajon Mesa, a finger of the Great Sage Plain, are most notable.[29] There are one or more towers rising amidst nineteen groupings of small communities, five of which are within Hovenweep National Monument. The remainders are tenuously protected by the emptiness of a deeply furrowed, beautiful but tempestuous land with few all-weather roads. Many of the towers and domestic structures near them are so well preserved that their massive walls still rear up as bulwarks thirty or more feet high. That makes them unusual in a region where most old prehistoric structures in the open have dwindled to their foundations. To support the tonnage of stone utilized in them, they were built on bedrock sometimes with walls three blocks wide. This monumentality is emphasized by a prevailing scarcity of apertures that caused some visitors,

Fewkes among them, to liken the buildings to European castles.

Cajon Mesa and environs were some of the province localities to be archaeologically studied first. Names such as Morley, Kidder, Fewkes, Prudden, Martin, and Brew are associated with sites there. In a broad sense what these men learned is now essentially repeated in the developmental sequences of other sectors.

From about the Basketmaker III period to the mid-A.D. 1000s, the settlers here shifted across the tableland from ridges to swales, from pinyon-juniper forests to sagebrush flats. They left behind telltale traces of their passage and small habitations of the unit pueblo type. They were reaching their greatest numbers around A.D. 1130 and had made that possible by an assortment of ways to control or direct whatever precipitation came their way. Then, almost in concert with ancestral Pueblos in the Montezuma Valley to their east, the Cajones made a final, decisive relocation. Possibly because of successive dry years or population pressures, they moved to the mesa lips and heads of narrow canyons that cut back into the plateau. They also spilled down talus slopes and onto canyon bottom lands, where they put homes and gardens. Without doubt the attraction was dripping springs and slowly gurgling seeps at the base of the porous Dakota Sandstone cliffs.

It is also without doubt that conflicts over water rights or threats of them that have beclouded the modern history of the arid West began with the introduction into the Southwest of agriculture and sedentism several millennia ago. That provides one explanation for the enthusiastic embrace on Cajon Mesa of the tower concept. The defensive aura surrounding these monuments might well have been suggestive of action rather than its perpetration. As prominently displayed claim stakes, they said to those outsiders who dared approach with water jars in hand, "Private property. Absolutely no trespassing." A single tree ring date of A.D. 1277 secured from one tower beam implies determination by some to fight to the finish.[30] And that was fast approaching.

The search for other answers to the question of functions of the towers was part of a three season (1974–1976) project at Hovenweep National Monument carried out by Joseph Winter and students from San Jose University.[31] During their work in eight towers, they unearthed enough domestic paraphernalia and plant and pollen remains to convince them that some everyday life had taken place in what would seem to have been exceedingly uncomfortable, inconvenient spaces with difficult entry through ceiling hatchways, little light or air because of almost complete closure, and severe winter chill penetrating and remaining in thick stone walls. But then, across the world Spaniards, Frenchmen, and Englishmen put up with comparable discomforts in their coeval castles.

In anticipation of the upcoming summer solstice one June in the late 1970s, astronomer Ray Williamson and a graduate student assistant arrived at Hovenweep National Monument with scientific equipment and high hopes. As part of a study of the cosmology of Native Americans, Williamson wanted to learn whether or not some seemingly randomly placed openings in a few tower facades had an astronomical purpose. With permission from the monument superintendent, the men walked across the monument parking lot and into Hovenweep Castle where Williamson intended to begin his inquiries. He could not have chosen a more favorable place.

Hovenweep Castle is the most imposing of all the structures in the monument. Although parts of it have fallen, its enormous mass remains formidable. Once three storied and multiroomed with two D-shaped towers, it is at the very edge of a mesa and overlooks a talus house that has cascaded down into Little Ruin Canyon. At the head of this rather shallow, narrow declivity is a spring that supplied domestic water for a number of habitations now in ruin beneath the canyon rim. Farther down the canyon is a modest square tower that presumably guarded a second spring and for which the community now is named.

At some time an equally high, ten-room addition was erected on the south side of the primary tower of Hovenweep Castle. It was one first-floor room in the addition that interested the astronomer because of two high portholes in its outer wall and what was the only ground-level doorway in the entire building. And what a doorway it is! If a person inside the building went out through it, he would have plunged straight down into the canyon or onto a roof of the talus house because there is nothing beyond but space. How to explain that?

Working diligently with their transit and calculations, by the end of the first day Williamson and his assistant had confirmed their suspicions. The ports were aligned in such a way that at specific times of the yearly cycle and at specific times of the day, shafts of light would pour through them to strike an opposing wall thereby alerting a sun-watcher priest of a particular solar event.[32]

During the next year further work and personal observations at the appropriate times revealed that summer and winter solstices and spring and autumn equinoxes could be indicated by the portholes and doorway of this room. Depending on the direction in which these and the openings elsewhere were oriented, either at sunrise or sunset the beams of light shining through them and onto interior walls would have been wakeup calls telling the priests when in March it was time to take the digging sticks to prepare the fields and when in September the burden baskets should be readied to reap the harvests. Ceremonies could be planned around the June and December solstices. In short, this room was a solar calendar and a sacred calendar. The creation of it presupposes generations of priests observing the sun's movements and keeping track of the number of days between events. It was one thing to use a physical feature on the horizon for sighting but a far greater intellectual feat to calculate correct alignments by artificial means, in this instance the built environment of architecture. The astronomers called the viewing station a "sun room" rather than an "observatory." Nor did they detect anything about the towers themselves to justify the latter designation or a cosmological orientation. To quell skeptics, Williamson figured that the odds against the accuracy of the openings being accidental at 1 to 216,000.[33]

Continued research identified the Cajon community in the extreme southern part of the mesa as having two buildings arranged so that shadows between them defined a solar calendar. A small habitation glued to the top of a boulder near Hovenweep Castle had three peepholes properly oriented for solstice observations.[34]

Sun-watching priests among other Mesa Verdeans might have been as clever as those at Hovenweep. Any sign of their having worked out similar devices for predicting or observing the solar cycle vanished with their walls. Williamson tried to make a case that several openings in the walls of the structures in Chaco Canyon had astronomical purposes. Archaeologists generally reject them as likely candidates because of the probability that architectural elements, now absent but present when the buildings were in use, would have blocked outside light from shining on interior surfaces. However, the buildings themselves may have been purposefully oriented in cardinal directions. Thus, the Hovenweep sun rooms remain unique. They continue to perform as intended but their audiences are gone. That is, except for eager archaeoastronomers who regularly make the pilgrimage to lonely Hovenweep to witness the fleeting capture of an eternal celestial episode.

A modern interpretation of Hovenweep sun watching through architecture now can be enjoyed at the Center of Southwest Studies on the campus of Fort Lewis College in Durango. When this edifice was under construction, an artist was commissioned to design a version of the wall ports. He encountered considerable technical difficulties working through the thick cement blocks of the building and figuring out the correct angles of an opening. His finished work consists of a glass-covered opening in the upper eastern exterior wall of the building in which is secured a steel plate cut in a spiral pattern, an iconographically meaningful motif to the ancestral Pueblos. On June 21 as the sun rises over the mountains to the east of the campus, a brilliant ray of sunlight streams through the port to cast a silhouetted spiral pattern on an opposite wall of the gallery. As the sun moves higher in the sky, the pattern elongates until it finally fades away but will come again a year hence. The ingenuity, indeed the spirit, of the old Cajones is commemorated in an inspirational way.

## CEDAR MESA REVISITED

William Lipe spearheaded the transition from the traditional way of looking at archaeology, concerned with single sites, to a more regionally oriented method in his first postgraduate project. He returned to the western periphery of the Mesa Verde Province where he began his career. While on the staff of the University of New York at Bingingham, he launched a seven-year inquiry into the prehistory of Cedar Mesa. Subsequently, after moving to the Museum of Northern Arizona, he teamed up with R. G. Matson, Northern Arizona University, and William Haase, Bureau of Land Management. Lipe's Red Rock Plateau work during the Glen Canyon Project pointed to a linkage of the two adjacent regions in the early and late years of the ancestral Pueblo sequence that were separated by a lengthy void in occupation. Cedar Mesa was a place of importance in the first public awareness in the 1890s of regional antiquities through the rifling exploits of McLoyd, Graham, the Wetherills, and others. However, even though many parties tramped over the ground in the years following and made a few cursory observations, no serious examinations had been done there.

Lipe and associates were not out to rescue threatened Puebloan remains or to make others available to tourists. They had specific academic questions in mind and decided that a survey of Cedar Mesa would be the best means of finding answers to them. Obviously, reconnaissances permit spatial overviews that site-specific work does not. The Cedar Mesa Project, which included college student helpers, set up a field camp near a spring on the mesa top which provided cool, potable water fed into a livestock tank. Every June it was open season for annoying gnats from which there is no escape. Otherwise it was an enjoyable place to spend the summers. It is a place of untrammeled natural beauty whose remoteness has secured a prehistoric microcosm from large-scale ravages of modern exploitation.

The plan of attack proposed for the main phase of the project (1972–1975) was to select five quadrats (or sampling plots) in various settings across the five mesa watersheds to be fully examined in order to determine where, why, how, and when people at different levels of advancement had settled there and how they adjusted to environmental limitations. An inventory of associated canyon sites was to be done. Some of these were where the 1890s intrepid few made large artifact collections.

The Cedar Mesa landscape is much like that of Mesa Verde. It is a flat plateau averaging six thousand to seven thousand feet in elevation, sliced by deep, sheer-walled gashes opening to the south, and having no running water except in some of the fissures. It is blanketed with the same Aeolian soils deposited by winds whirling out of Monument Valley and a dense pinyon-juniper forest that merges with taller timber in the uplands. It was expected that in both places comparable modes of sedentary life existed at comparable times. However, Cedar Mesa research showed significant differences.

Of outstanding interest was the Basketmaker II horizon absent at Mesa Verde. Previously, no sites of that time had been noted on open ground in the western parts of the Mesa Verde Province other than one tested by Lister during a brief overview of the San Juan Triangle when he noted vertical slabs that were possibly part of a dwelling. Sharrock and Lipe excavated the site later as part of the Glen Canyon Project.

The Lipe-Matson team was fortunate to encounter 130 sites which they considered to be of Basketmaker II age, or their postulated Grand Gulch Phase.[35] Surveyors soon learned that living spots were announced by nothing more than seemingly insignificant, fire-reddened, limestone rocks. Less aware individuals would, and probably did, pass them by without a thought. But this group recognized those rocks as clues to home-cooked meals. Sometime in the hoary past the Basketmakers or their predecessors, both without pottery-making know-how, discovered the use of heated rocks as a way to boil water or parch seeds in tightly woven baskets.

Sure enough, where there were limestone rocks on the sandstone Cedar Mesa uplift, there were barely discernible depressions signaling dwellings. Half of the sites observed were thought to include habitations, an inference supported by excavation of several. These were shallow pits of modest size entered by lateral passages lined with vertical slabs. The absence of pottery, the presence of grinding stones meant to be used by one hand, and a few stray projectile points of size and shape suitable for use on atlatl-propelled darts were hallmarks of the Basketmaker phase.

Away from the dwellings were places where farmers may have camped near their gardens or fashioned stone tools or other objects. The appearance of corn plant parts indicated that maize agriculture was practiced in the midmesa elevations where the wooded cover meant fertile soil.

The Cedar Mesa staff postulated that the primitive dwelling most likely had a use-life of about ten years or less and housed no more than five family members. If the occupation extended over about a century and a half during the period from *circa* A.D. 200 to 400, they placed the average number of persons present at any one time at 334, or up to a total of 880 for the entire period. Add that figure to whatever were the number of contemporary residents on the unsurveyed parts of the mesa and in the canyon alcoves and it is obvious that the Cedar Mesa district was a major staging area for those at the dawn of Puebloan history. They moved away by the fifth century. Further, this work demonstrated that the Cedar Mesa shelters were unlike those of Basketmaker II groups found in the eastern Mesa Verde Province by Morris and Eddy, again suggesting divergent cultural roots.

Two hundred fifty years later somewhat more culturally advanced Basketmakers returned to take up residence on Cedar Mesa and farm plots a bit higher up the tableland. They continued to live in pit dwellings but also erected surface structures of slabs and jacal. They had a tendency to loosely arrange them into small hamlets. No limestone rocks for them because they had gray pottery as part of their household furnishings. That is, they were cooking in pottery jars and not in parching trays. Apparently circumstances were not conducive to their staying put for more than seventy-five years. The territory was again emptied, this time for an estimated 335 years. If there were such a thing as a homing instinct, it was then short circuited.

According to the scholars, around A.D. 1060 a new wave of migrants arrived at Cedar Mesa. By that time their material culture had evolved to a stage archaeologists know as Pueblo II, but their daily way of life was not much elaborated over that of the first settlers some eight hundred years before. Showing a preference for the higher shoulders of the landform, they built small masonry houses on the surface, a few of which were accompanied by kivas. In the course of time their pottery indicated a Pueblo III developmental phase. It was at that time when some of them moved into the canyons, where they erected houses and granaries in alcoves. Although there was not much arable land, available domestic water was an advantage. The departure from the region by these Pueblos coincided with that elsewhere in the northern San Juan at about A.D. 1270–1280.

The maximum population of the whole mesa in any period was never more than fifteen hundred individuals. Generally they lived in single family units in a dispersed pattern so as to work patches of suitable land. Consequently, one might assume limited social cohesion and scant concern with group ritualism. Although abandonment and reoccupation of some areas was common throughout Pueblo presence in the north, the researchers thought the long gaps between periods of use of the Cedar Mesa were excessive. They speculated that the reasons for these periods of absence were to be found in fluctuations of the paleoclimate, deforestation as the residents burned or used up the timber resource, and depletion of soil nutrients from centuries of use without giving back to Mother Earth some of the exploited riches. Added to that was cultural depression which produced little change in lifeways for a thousand years. When conditions seemed to improve, farmers, the most optimistic of the species, returned to try again. The men concluded, as Jennings had earlier from the Glen Canyon experience, that a small population, scattered rather than clustered, was the most viable solution to the vagaries of marginal agricultural surroundings known for unpredictable fits of wetness and dryness, heat and cold. Having little investment in material things or monuments, they could pick up and move along with the tides of fortune, or misfortune.

An interesting fact that emerged from the Cedar Mesa Project is that, as well as in the Glen Canyon gorges, during the early and late A.D. 1000s and early A.D. 1100s, Kayentans moved northward into that promised land. A much later survey of Natural Bridges National Monument just to the northwest of Cedar Mesa revealed the same infiltration.[36] By definition of the province concept, the then empty northern terrain was not theirs but belonged to the Mesa Verdeans beside whom they lived for several centuries. What was the motivation for the Kayenta *entrada*? Too many mouths to feed in a resource-starved zone south of the San Juan or perhaps the temptation of greener pastures and prospects of a better life beyond the horizon? Looking back from here, there are some submerged currents in the human experience that do not change.

### Pots in Trenches

During the last decades of the twentieth century, the need for inventories of cultural materials on public lands and those associated with energy developments, both of which are extensive in the Mesa Verde Province, put archaeology on a business footing and took it in a direction in sharp contrast to the more traditional grant-based endeavors. Some of those engaged in this side of the profession are young people with appropriate educational backgrounds but who choose not to invest the many years and large sums of money now needed to earn doctorate degrees in anthropology in order to join professorial ranks. A growing number do have advanced degrees but reject academic life. Both groups enjoy the physical and mental challenges of dirt archaeology but wish to remain independent. And, it is fair to say, some are not especially drawn to the theoretical problem-solving exercises that appeal to many academics. One typical pattern is for one or two persons to form a company to bid on contracts issued by government or industry agents and then employ transient crews to help fulfill incurred obligations. Presently, larger companies with full-time staffs are becoming common. A number of regional universities now have teams of archaeologists for hire. Also engineering firms sometimes engage the services of archaeologists to provide information that may help avoid threatened antiquities.

Thus, archaeology has been seduced from the ivory tower into commercialism. As in any business, there have been instances of mismanagement and friction between competitors. Nevertheless, there is little to criticize about contract archaeology. First, it offers gainful employment to troops of aspiring scientists which educational institutions continue to turn out and for whom professional jobs are limited. Second, the contracts usually specify investigations in localities that have not received prior attention or, in some cases, ever would. That assures expanded knowledge. Third, jobs are completed expeditiously because they are full-time assignments that do not have to be worked around a teaching schedule. And to counter academe's habitual lack of reporting of work accomplished, contracts require approved documentation before final payment. Unfortunately, this usually is not widely disseminated.

An outstanding example of new information resulting from this approach to the general theme of regional prehistory occurred during the early 1980s when the Celsius Energy Corporation and the Shell/Mobil Company hired Complete Archaeological Services Associates, a small local company, to monitor areas around well pads prepared for gas, oil, and carbon dioxide explorations.[37] These installations were on Woods Mesa, a fingerlike tableland between Woods and Yellow Jacket Canyons about sixteen miles northwest of Cortez. It was uninhabited back country administered by the Bureau of Land Management. Over several seasons, Steven Fuller and Laurens and Nancy Hammack, contractors, made remarkable discoveries of a number of places where thirteenth-century potters, presumably women, had fired their vessels. The archaeologists incorrectly called them "kilns." Technically, a *kiln* is an enclosed chamber, such as an oven or furnace, which allows the attainment of high temperatures. What was seen on Woods Mesa were rectangular or subrectangular trenches just below ground surface averaging three feet in width and varying in length from six to more than fifteen feet that contained lower layers of ash, charcoal, and burned sandstone cobbles.[38] The only objects associated with the trenches or on the surrounding ground were assorted pottery fragments that obviously were pieces left from firing mishaps or used to cover the load within the trench. Prior to these finds a few similar trenches had been noticed around the province that generally were thought to have been food-processing stations or roasting pits. And so they might have been. Nevertheless, the volume of ceramic remains in the Woods Mesa features secured their identification as ceramic-firing trenches. This was further substantiated through the excavation of eight of them at one site.

The reason why such features had not been discovered in a hundred years of archaeological probing in the Mesa Verde Province was that the trenches are uniformly located at considerable distances from known Pueblo settlements where investigations have concentrated. They cannot be linked to specific habitation sites. If it had not been for the mandated impact observations and the vigorous energy explorations taking place in sectors of southwestern Colorado and southeastern Utah that were not otherwise developed, this fascinating part of the Puebloan story would not be known.

The scientists reasoned that the firing trenches were located where they are because after centuries of occupation, fuels near Puebloan settlements had been exhausted. In this scenario, it was easier for potters to take fragile, unfired vessels to distant trenches than to cart wood to homes. There is no evidence that pottery was fashioned at the trench locations. Pottery making probably was a warm weather activity so that moist pieces would dry properly and transporting them across country to the trenches would be facilitated.

The trenches, called "thermal features" by the archaeologists, typically were on the soils of north-facing slopes of the mesa or shallow drainages off it where pinyon, juniper, and brush were plentiful and where at certain times of the day cold air blowing downward into the canyons could aid in the firing process.

Firing is the most critical step in pottery manufacture. Numerous things can go wrong to spoil days of labor. Many superstitious artisans worldwide place good luck tokens beside their kilns. No such objects are known to have been used by the ancestral Puebloans, but perhaps they should have been. The trenches produced many examples of failures, with vessels being overfired, underfired, unfired, cracked, or warped. In one trench there were thirty-five restorable pots that for one reason or another disappointed some woman who must have trudged home empty handed to try again another day.[39]

All the wasters found around or in these trenches were of two stylistic types characteristic of Pueblo III workmanship. They primarily were black-on-white bowls.[40] However, Pueblo II period trenches now have been found. Firing in them meant technological changes over earlier methods of stacking pots on open ground with fuel mounded under and over them. Benefits from the new technique were that the depressions retained heat, required less fuel, and perhaps enhanced a reducing atmosphere.

In reconstructions of use of the trenches, researchers suggest that firing pottery in them may have been a yearly cooperative endeavor by household groups of potters. The smaller trenches could accommodate two dozen or fewer vessels intended for immediate family use. Larger trenches could contain up to two hundred vessels, a high percentage of which may have been used in trade.[41]

The initial discovery of the firing trenches was followed by dozens of others as seismic and further energy operations brought out contract archaeologists and colleagues. Nine were uncovered on the Mesa Verde when a new waterline was being laid. It is evident that numerous clusters of trenches are present and widespread. Their exact number likely will never be known. Considering the millions of pots these people produced over time, it must have been a Dantean spectacle of hellish, blazing fires lighting up the evening or early morning sky and sending plumes of smoldering smoke upward.

This discovery of Mesa Verdean firing methods stimulated modern craftsmen and researchers to attempt replication of the ancient pottery. The Crow Canyon Archaeological Center conducted experimental conferences in the early to mid-1990s for this purpose. The participants assiduously dug clay and temper materials, hand coiled pots and decorated them with natural pigments, and wood fired them in slab-lined trenches. New insight was gained about resources used and techniques developed by the ancestral Puebloan potters, but they also learned that the Mesa Verdean women took some basic craft secrets with them when they walked away.[42]

## DOLORES RIVER AND McPHEE RESERVOIR

For years there was talk of throwing a dam across the Dolores River to impound irrigation water in order to turn the red ground of the Great Sage Plain green with alfalfa and other crops and to honor a century-old water treaty with the Ute Mountain Utes. In the 1880s an audacious irrigation system some one hundred miles in extent took the river's bounty to the new waterless town of Cortez and environs. No one knew or cared how many sites were sliced in that construction. In the early 1970s no one knew how many such sites might be flooded by any proposed dam on the Dolores. Because there were no noticeable ruins, such as cliff dwellings or towers, the Dolores Valley had been largely ignored archaeologically. One sprawling, presumably early site on Grass Mesa had been mapped in the 1950s, and Escalante Pueblo and another ruin to its east of a later period were known. Otherwise the shadowy past of this particular sector of the province was a blank.

The possibility that a dam and canals feeding from a created reservoir might be in the future led to preliminary reconnaissances to determine cultural resources that might be impacted. On behalf of the National Park Service, University of Colorado teams variously led by Allen Kane and Charles Adams surveyed far-reaching sectors north and west of the proposed reservoir district where canals might be dug. A surprising total of 556 previously unsuspected sites of differing importance was recorded.[43] That information prompted the Bureau of Reclamation, under whose control any dam would be raised, to sponsor further the assessment of antiquities that might be present and develop a recovery plan as required by law. In 1978 this was formalized through compliance with a series of existing pieces of legislation, the most recent of which was the Archaeological and Historical Preservation Act of 1974. Arrangements were also made with the Bureau of Land Management to curate data and materials recovered in a museum-research installation that was to be built near the affected sector.

As a representative of the University of Colorado, Breternitz then submitted a proposal to the Bureau of Reclamation to undertake the necessary cultural mitigation, as it was then called. The university was a logical choice for the planned endeavor since for the preceding decade a major part of work with antiquities in this provincial center had been carried out by archaeologists from that institution. Much of that effort after 1970 had been directed by Breternitz. He was known to colleagues as a hard worker with a wry sense of humor and unusual sartorial taste.

Knowing the wheels of government turn slowly, Breternitz was taken by some surprise when in June 1978 the agent for the Bureau of Reclamation contacted him to sign a contract as representative of the University of Colorado. Neither party to this agreement was prepared logistically or mentally.

Breternitz was aware of the need to adhere to dam construction schedules and budgetary limitations, both of which understandably were top priorities for the Bureau.[44] He was not prepared for the lack of understanding by some administrators in that agency of the procedures and goals of regional archaeology as they had evolved. He needed time to arrange facilities and to formulate practical and theoretical research designs for the long-term, in-depth enterprise that was anticipated. Lack of a definite plan of action was the equivalent of starting on a journey into the unknown without a road map. Although his words were carefully chosen, Breternitz's later writings about the project show that the men in the federal offices and the man in the field were not infrequently at loggerheads for the seven and a half year duration of the work.[45] It was an oil and water conundrum: government bureaucracy and academic research do not readily mix.

The first shock came immediately. Not recognizing the need to undertake preliminary preparations, the Bureau demanded that digging begin at once and at a site of its choosing. This was McPhee Village, where some wall remnants had attracted pothunters. The site had not been included in the preliminary survey by professionals because at the time it was on privately owned land. In June 1978 the Bureau already had a contract crew working at a portion of it and surveying lands that would be affected. As members of a Youth Conservation Corps, they were being overseen by one of the veterans of the university field school, but they themselves were thirty teenagers untrained and just doing a summer job.[46] Breternitz felt that their record keeping would not mesh with whatever one was developed for the formal project, and, furthermore, that all the archaeological work should be under his control as principal investigator and not under that of the Bureau or some outside contractor. Discontent aside, he tacitly agreed to put a seven-person crew into the field just two weeks after the contract became valid. The next year he insisted that the Youth Conservation Corps work through him.

Tents for the crew were set up in the trees on the upslope near the site. A few weeks later public health officers closed the camp on grounds of unsanitary conditions.[47] With that, Breternitz decided that a field camp was unnecessary. Also, as work would stretch out through the ten-mile designated area, even a centrally situated camp would not be satisfactory. There were rentals and houses for sale in the surrounding county where employees could fend for themselves and commute to work. The elimination of a field camp would save money and headaches for the management. To old-timers, it lessened the luster of "doing archaeology" and the special camaraderie of shared camp life.

Well, not entirely. As the crew of young people grew exponentially, there was a round of frequent parties. An important one was an annual summer pig roast when a dressed carcass was placed in a deep pit and allowed to bake overnight. The midwinter gala was a dress-up day. Breternitz wore a dress that showed a bit of leg. Beside being pleasurable, such frivolity cemented the esprit de corps. So much so, in fact, that a dozen romantic relationships and marriages resulted. Some lasted.

The youthful vigor of these various crews found vent in Cortez's recreational activities. The trophies they won from softball and other sports are housed at the Anasazi Heritage Center along with the scientific artifacts they unearthed.

A problem for Breternitz was the Bureau's idea of a headquarters for the project. This was a rented trailer in Cortez that was office space and no more.[48] During the next six months, a half-dozen excavators shoveling and troweling their way through old houses and middens brought in a flood of specimens that remained unexamined and stored wherever possible. Nor was there room for the work of individuals hired for specialized tasks. Even though the Bureau had agreed to furnish a laboratory, there was an amazing lack of comprehension on its part as to what that involved.

Meanwhile at the end of the 1977 season when the Mesa Verde Archaeological Research Center left the headquarters in the park, which it had utilized for twelve years, Breternitz bought a small country house on the outskirts of Dove Creek, thirty-five miles west of Cortez. Although relieved for the duration of the project of his teaching duties on the campus of the University of Colorado in Boulder, for the next three summers Breternitz continued to run a reduced field school operation from there, while at the same time trying to get the Dolores Archaeological Program on track. The students worked on archaeological surveys for a Shell Oil Company carbon dioxide development in the Great Sage Plain and for the Dolores project.[49]

The 1978 season ended with few positive results for the Dolores investigations. The Youth Conservation Corps opened up ten surface rooms and several pit structures at McPhee Village to reveal at least two episodes of occupation. The contributions of the Dolores Archaeological Program were primarily magnetometer sweeps, which indicated two sizable horseshoe-shaped units and some rubble, and plans for future work. No surface collections were made.[50]

The start of the next field cycle seemed more promising when the Bureau announced that at last it had secured a laboratory. Breternitz was dismayed when he went to inspect what he assumed was going to be a fully equipped facility.[51] What he saw was a large, metal-sided building on a farm that the government had purchased. Formerly, it had been a shed where apples were processed for juice. It had a cement floor and the necessary utilities but no furniture, storage shelves, darkroom, microscopes, or sinks for cleaning artifacts. It was up to the project to make the so-called laboratory operational. In time that was accomplished and the building was then the heart of the endeavor for the next six years. Eventually three trailers were parked next door to provide space for the necessary administrative, reporting, and computer functions.

Computerization of data was just beginning to be a basic tool of research. Although Irwin-Williams had used a primitive computer card process at Salmon Ruin, the Dolores Archaeological Program was the first regional study to adopt the technology that had more fully advanced. And not without considerable frustration. Working out suitable programs for all aspects of standardization, entering, and retrieving data consumed the efforts of several years and a growing work force. One operational difficulty arose immediately. The computer programmer was required to transmit the data to the government mainframe in Denver. That mainframe served all federal agencies west of the Mississippi River, including in Hawaii and Alaska. The only hours available for the Dolores Archaeological Program were at night. Therefore, throughout the lifetime of the project a lonely operator next to the apple shed worked the darkness to dawn shift while an electric fan brought from home cooled the machine.

Lipe signed on as a co-principal investigator for the Dolores Archaeological Program. He was one of only three, other than Breternitz, who stayed for the entire time of the project, although he went home during the winters. One stalwart was Allen Kane, a Colorado graduate student responsible for field operations and general reporting. The other was Paul Farley, the tireless laboratory director and computer guru. Lipe's title changed as work progressed, but his significant impact on the theoretical direction the project took is unquestioned. For three summers (1979, 1980, and 1982) he directed a field school for Washington State University as part of the Dolores Archaeological Program. For two sessions the students were housed in tents by an abandoned ranch house near to where they were introduced to the shovel of proper weight and the all-purpose trowel.[52] During the 1982 summer, Lipe put the students in tents on the grounds of what would become the Crow Canyon Archaeological Center. Many of them became ill when *Giardia* contaminated the camp water supply. That inevitably reduced their pleasure in the field experience.

Over the course of the project the number of people involved grew enormously as needs arose according to the stage of investigations. Timothy Kohler, Washington State University, joined the senior staff. In addition to excavators and surveyors, the roster included photographers, draftsmen, word processors, editors, computer programmers, data managers, and specialists in pottery and lithic analysis, environmental studies, and magnetometer and archaeomagnetic calculations.[53]

A good deal of fieldwork is not the exciting stuff of fiction and nothing like that of Indiana Jones. This is particularly true of basic laboratory processes, historically the part of the enterprise allotted to women. In this case, there were a few individuals who did not see themselves as servile workers doomed to spend dreary days washing potsherds or putting catalog numbers on specimens with fine-pointed pens and India ink. Their work became so careless that Farley replaced them with several handicapped persons recommended by the Cortez Sheltered Workshop.[54] Their work was beyond reproach. So much for the rarefied atmosphere of the classroom.

Professional consultants as subcontractors dealt with soil, faunal, pollen, and human physical analyses, dendrochronological determinations, obsidian dating, geology, and other topics that in some way were relevant to the archaeological studies.

Most employees in the project proper were young men and women with at least a bachelor's degree in anthropology and one or two years of field experience. Some had been Breternitz or Lipe students. Others applied for jobs after having read about the work in newspapers or hearing about it from friends or faculty. Breternitz and Kane devised an elaborate hierarchical framework of chiefs and subordinates, each with specific assignments, that must have pleased the structured federal employees of the Bureau of Reclamation. At the conclusion of the work in December 1985, they tallied almost six hundred participants. Some remained in the program three or four years and provided a needed continuity to the effort. Many others came and went.

Through much of its course, which was to be flooded, the Dolores River Valley was a comparatively restricted declivity that formed the northern boundary of the ancestral Pueblo domain. Meadows and riparian growth of cottonwoods and willows covered bottom lands and alluvial fans. The terrain rose rather abruptly along the river's north banks, as one moved downstream from the town of Dolores at the east mouth of the valley, to recede back into a mountain mass where tall timber was abundant. The heights bordering the left bank were lower, their slopes supporting the characteristic clumps of pinyon and juniper. On top were undulating grasslands dotted with sagebrush, scrub oak, and rabbitbush. Low, rolling ridges reaching westward from the La Plata Mountains separated this valley region from the Mancos Valley to the southeast and the Montezuma Valley to the southwest.

The pool area to be explored by the archaeologists was 4,470 acres in extent. Obviously that encompassed river terraces and bounding cliffs. The federal government acquired an additional 11,507 adjacent acres primarily on the southern tableland to form a buffer zone next to the reservoir that would be developed for recreational purposes and for a wildlife refuge.[55] This parcel was called the "takeline" because the government arbitrarily took it in exchange for reasonable compensation to landowners. Archaeological clearance for the takeline was to be included in the mitigation process.

Survey work, in this project called *settlement archaeology*, continued while sampling or excavations got under way. The pool area was considered satisfactorily inventoried by 1980; the takeline survey was completed in 1981. When all the numbers were added up, it came to a total of 1,626 sites where just a decade previously only several were known.[56]

In traditional archaeological thinking, a *site* is any place that exhibits former human presence. This can be a scattering of the debitage left from flint knapping or fragments of what once was a cook pot. Or a site can be post stumps left from a temporary shelter or a fire-reddened hearth. The distinction between these two categories is hazy. The Dolores Archaeological Program classified them either as *seasonal stations* or *limited activity sites*. Other sites might be the remains of one or more large hamlets or small or large villages.[57]

Unlike the Glen Canyon and Navajo Reservoir projects that began at the dam construction, and in the case of the Navajo Reservoir work happened to proceed upstream temporally, the Dolores Archaeological Program was engaged from the beginning throughout the prescribed zone. McPhee Village, for example, was at midsection. At times as many as ten crews were digging at widely separated, varied sites. That made coordination of methods and data gathering critical. Given the constraints of time, money, and the ever watchful Bureau, there never could be excavation of all the sites, nor was that desirable. The temporal placement or function of a majority of the smaller sites could not be determined. Consequently, fundamental decisions had to be made as to which other sites should be exposed partially or fully, which should just be accounted for by survey or controlled surface collecting, and what kinds and how many artifacts should be retained and processed.[58] Where possible in sites that were to be randomly tested in a technique known as *probabilistic sampling*, heavy equipment was used to remove overburden. It often was guided by magnetometer-generated maps that indicated the presence of subsurface features and whether they had burned. Those sites and others that were to be completely cleared then called for more discrete hand shoveling and troweling, the down and dirty part of archaeology. Kristin Kuckelman, prominent among the twelve females who conducted excavations, made history when she learned to use a backhoe on her assigned sites.[59] That was archaeology's answer to a current cigarette advertisement that said, "You've come a long way, baby."

As the project evolved, investigations fell into three stages. Although they got off to a slow start because of lack of advance planning, the first three years were a matter of securing the data, classifying and analyzing the specimens, and writing descriptive reports. By the conclusion of this period, the researchers had an idea of exactly what the occupation of the district had been and when it had occurred. Some materials and information pertaining to the intellectual aims set out by Breternitz and his senior staff had been attained. The next three years expanded upon that base with a conscious effort directed toward securing archaeological materials and data that hopefully would be useful in answering some of the posed anthropological questions. The last two years at headquarters were devoted to cultural interpretations afforded by accumulated data and observations.[60]

When fieldwork ceased at the end of 1983, 101 sites had been fully or partially excavated. Nearly half of those had been subjected to intense scrutiny.[61] They were found on or near the river's floodplain, its benches, and the enclosing cliffs, adjacent mesas, and tablelands of the takeline. All sites were numbered in accordance with the Smithsonian system and also were given names that were easier to remember. Crew members were creative, leaving the records filled with references to Casa de Nada, Windy Wheat, Tres Bobos, Poco Tiempo, and Standing Pipe. Sites were classified by presumed function and time of use.

The Dolores occupational time span was divided into four prehistoric phases.[62] For more finite study of cultural modifications within those phases, eight subphases were postulated. In the years of greatest occupation, these were just twenty years in length to allow close detection of change. So that persons not associated with the project would know how these categories fit into the standard, widely used chronology, the phases were correlated with the Pecos Classification.

The crews learned that a very few transients had passed through the Dolores area in the little known pre-Christian Era. Others came later and took seasonal refuge in Cougar Springs Cave up a side tributary. In Pecos Classification terms, they were believed to have been Basketmaker II people, probably culturally affiliated with others identified in the eastern part of the province.

Beginning in the early to mid-A.D. 600s, some Puebloan families began infiltrating the project area to settle as farmers. Where they had been before that remained unknown, as was how and when they had acquired the complement of Basketmaker III traits that they brought with them. Here and there they settled down in the same kind of distributed, shallow pithouses as others were using up on the Mesa Verde banking the southern horizon. They made the same kind of rough, gray pottery, used the same range of household goods, and subsisted on the same general diet. About the middle of the eighth century, their numbers started to rise either from births within the group or from others attracted to the promise of the Dolores River area. They began to gather closer together into hamlets made up of larger, deeper pithouses outfitted with ventilators and jacal surface storage rooms. The Pueblo I period was about to emerge.

The next step up the cultural ladder was the dramatic but sporadic abandonment of nights and surely some days in quarters partially below ground to others above. The builders made contiguous, rectangular rooms based on foundations of unshaped sandstone blocks or slabs sealed in place by mud, with upper walls of jacal, and arranged in double rows in an arc around a pit out front and a trash dump beyond. Small hamlets consisted of a household of up to eighteen or twenty rooms and one to three pits which the builders squared up. This was the most common type of settlement. Large villages, of which there may have been at least seven, incorporated one to fifteen roomblocks of thirty or more chambers each and as many as five pit structures. Generally these dated to the A.D. 800s.

In time the pits took on the identifiable attributes of kivas with floor vaults and sipapus. A local innovation were small floor holes filled with sand that possibly had been where prayer sticks were stuck around a portable altar. The sand may have been used in some ceremonies. Without documentation, these suggestions remain speculative.

Great Kivas made an impressive showing. The greatest was at an overhang named Singing Shelter.[63] It was notable for its eight hundred square feet of floor space, by far the largest such structure of comparable age in the province. The overhang ceiling made roofing unnecessary, even if the Pueblo I builders had been capable of putting one in place. Surface rooms at one side were the earliest example of this attribute, one that was occasionally present in Great Kivas of the classic Pueblo periods. The Singing Shelter Great Kiva may have been the primary gathering place for those ninth-century residents of the central valley.

The archaeologists concluded that the peak level of Dolores population was reached between A.D. 840 and 880. At that time there were sixty-six large and small settlements made up of an estimated 629 households, or a population of approximately 1,250 individuals.[64] It must not have been mere coincidence that this was a period most favorable for the kind of dry farming that the Puebloans practiced. After that came a prolonged period of cold temperatures and a gradual vacating of the land. By the beginning of the first millennium, the Dolores Puebloans had emigrated to other locations in or out of the province. There was some evidence that before they left, they laid pairs of their dead on room floors, placed offerings beside them, collapsed the roofs, and set the structures on fire. Ashes to ashes, dust to dust. When the Chacoans arrived, their only neighbors in the Escalante vicinity were those on the downslopes of the hill and in the Reservoir Site a short distance away.

The archaeological investigations concentrated on two main groupings of structures. One included McPhee Village, where the initial work began and continued for three more seasons. It was located on a wide, sloping terrace above the west (left) side of the river several miles downstream from the town of Dolores. A steep cliff dotted with the usual pinyon-juniper woodland amid rock outcroppings formed a pleasant backdrop. An old ranch road along the front of the site then being used by the dam builders made access easy.

McPhee Village was a grouping of two surface houseblocks of unique, double horseshoe layout embracing partially subterranean pit structures. The west horseshoe, where the Dolores Archaeological Program carried out most of its examinations, was made up of some fifty rooms of fairly large size. Close by were twenty-seven other houseblocks of fewer rooms that constituted a sizable village.[65] There may have been as many as 850 people living in the vicinity when it was at its zenith.

The west wall of the Dolores canyon broke down in the vicinity to open out to the Sagehen Flats that provided an easy entrance into the canyon. Another ninety-two habitations, field houses, and limited activity sites were in that area. Surrounding territory that might have been farmed or where some kinds of resources were obtained added the word *catchment* to the growing archaeological vocabulary.

McPhee Village's history extended from perhaps as early as A.D. 760 into the late A.D. 900s but was not continuous. The second episode of use was its heyday when immigration from outside the province area took place or when there was a slow resettlement from the northern sector into the central valley where the McPhee Village was expanding. The last two occupations were a few straggling families who did some remodeling but lingered only for brief periods.[66]

The second locale of special interest to the Dolores Archaeological Program was an entrenched cut in the canyon about ten miles downriver from Dolores. It was a place layered with history. First, some 1,250 years ago, Native Americans settled on the point of a flat-topped bluff on the northeast (right) bank that descended precipitously down to the Dolores River on one side and the Beaver Creek drainage on the other. They stayed there off and on for perhaps two centuries beginning in the early A.D. 700s. They probably raised crops of corn, squash, and beans on stabilized floodplains and alluvial fans bordering these two permanent water sources. They used hand and toe holds down the steep escarpment to get from homes to fields. Since the growing season there was apt to be shortened by cold air wafting down canyon, other pieces of ground higher up likely were tilled.

The next human activity came in 1885 when white cowboys determined to take the West as theirs killed six men, women, and children in a Ute hunting party camped at the mouth of Beaver Creek.[67] That untoward act, which went into the records as the Beaver Creek Massacre, set off a frenzy of recriminations that for some time threatened any settlement stability. Increasingly, the worrisome Utes were confined to their reservation on the Mesa Verde.

Next, during the early twentieth century ranchers used the mesa top as a corral for livestock. The animals did the ancient remains little good. Fence post holes and a trail up the cliff used during this time were still apparent when the archaeologists later arrived.

The final historical chapter came with the erection of a mighty dam just a half-mile away that in the unforeseeable future would change the economy and landscape of this sector of southwestern Colorado. As diggers at the Indian site they knew as Grass Mesa Village shoveled and troweled into the past, they could peer down into bustling equipment yards and constantly hear the construction cacophony. It was an incongruous intersection of the best of two worlds. Had any of the hard-hatted workmen left their giant earth grubbers and climbed the cliff to see what those quixotic folks above were doing, they doubtless would have been aghast, if not amused, at the sight of unyielding, rocky soil being moved inch by inch by hand tools. Several seasons into the project, the Bureau prevailed upon some of them to grade a narrow road up the heights so that a backhoe could speed trenching.

Grass Mesa Village had been known locally since the time of those murderous pioneers. Sheets of artifacts of all sorts spread over the humped, sagebrush-shaded surface attracted relic collectors, who generally called their trophies "Aztecan." The site was first reported somewhat officially in 1919 by Fewkes while he made a brief foray to the north and west of Mesa Verde in search of antiquities. In the 1950s, Joe Ben Wheat more formally noted it in a survey. Men doing the preliminary reconnaissance for the proposed dam project also visited the site.

Four seasons of work in surface collecting, sampling, trenching, and intensive excavating confirmed that Grass Mesa Village had more structures of a specific period and yielded more specimens than any other of the project sites and at times must have had a greater, densely packed population.[68] There was solid evidence of several occupational periods, with later materials covering or disturbing earlier ones. That made this bit of archaeological exploration the most taxing and complex.

The evolutionary sequence of architecture was comparable to that known in the other sites. It was carefully defined temporally to clarify changes through time.

In the period from A.D. 760 to 850 an estimated thirty-eight to fifty-eight households were established on the mesa. If at any given time there were one or two able-bodied males in each, that was enough manpower to erect a Great Kiva having four hundred square meters of floor space. Some scholars calculate that its excavation and roofing required the muscles of twenty laborers working long hours for two months. That, in turn, implied some sort of managerial apparatus, as well as the perceived need for such a community center.

There were a few outlying settlements in the surrounding reaches that interacted with the main village. All ceased to be early in the A.D. 900s. Precise dating could not be determined because builders at that time did not use woods with readable growth rings. Unlike McPhee Village, Grass Mesa Village was not reoccupied.

It is hard enough to appreciate the pulse of activities, the noises, and the pungent smells of daily life in crumbling dwellings with fragmented standing walls as in, for instance, a cliff dwelling, or even in the rooms at Aztec West with their original ceilings still in place and patches of adobe plaster clinging to interior surfaces. To recreate the panorama of life in the Pueblo I houses as they appeared after being unearthed verges on the impossible. What was exposed were rectangular spaces framed by two or three courses of rough stone, holes in corners of dirt floors where roof supports had been positioned, shallow depressions that confined smoldering cook fires, perhaps a few cists scooped out of the floor, and slab-lined basins in some corners. Where the outlines were complete, there did not seem to be doorways. Did the residents have to climb a ladder to enter through a roof hatch? If upper walls were composites of daub turtlebacks or jacal, there might have been ground-level doorways at one time. Now there is no way to surely determine the general appearance of these houses or their elevations. With all these unknowns, the indomitable Dolores staffers aimed to try to put this seemingly sterile display into a human context. To some extent artifacts *in situ* could explain room functions, but they sought further insights.

In his original proposal, Breternitz reflected the transition from traditional descriptive archaeology of the past to the new emphasis on possible anthropological explanations to illuminate the immediate study and to drive future research. Accordingly, he noted problem areas that he felt the project could address.[69] He listed them as the economy of the local populace, how they developed it, and how they adjusted to difficult situations. What were the environmental factors at the time and how did they affect life on the Dolores River; could botanical remains from hearths, post holes, or burials be reliable clues to former human ecology; what was the social organization that sustained the group; and what contacts, if any, did these people have with contemporaries elsewhere? Once those aspects were considered, could the causes of and the responses to cultural change be detected?

To Breternitz and his associates these were valid considerations necessary for scientific justification of the project. Contrarily, Bureau officials, who originally had agreed to this generalized outline of goals, balked when the time came to confront them. They felt the need to rein in the scientists who might stray into "pure" research that, in their view, more properly should be left to another time and place. Through lack of mutual understanding at the outset, the Bureau's commitment and that of the researchers were at odds. Therein lay the seeds for controversy.

Added to that problem was funding that was likely to run out before the final wrap-up. Virtually at the last minute, Colorado and Washington state senators persuaded Congress to increase monies allotted.

When reconstruction in human detail of the Dolores past was at hand, Lipe and other team members were expectant as they immersed themselves in theoretical models and variables and computer simulations to determine sociocultural processes.[70] The Dolores Archaeological Program brought a bevy of young scholars into a fresh, sometimes bewildering, but creative perspective on regional prehistory. Through the basic archaeological databases, they sought answers to such questions as whether the small houseblocks were those of the rank and file citizens. Were the larger units those of an administrative hierarchy, or corporate group, as the researchers liked to think of it? Did that group allot farmland, dictate who was responsible for securing certain resources, and determine who processed them? Who decided when it was time to plant and time to celebrate? How were open spaces within the settlements used? Architects like to ponder the aesthetic contrasts between mass and voids, but it is unlikely that Pueblo I builders had any purposes other than utilitarian ones in using these spaces as outdoor rooms for daily activities. How did families interact? Did they share the duties of maintenance, the burdens of failure, the satisfactions of success? Could craft specialization be verified? Did the increase or decrease of faunal remains correlate with agricultural productivity? There were a myriad of other matters to which the responses of Pueblo I people, then in a formative phase of their cultural development, would mold their future.

As the Dolores Archaeological Program concluded, Lipe, Kane, and others outfoxed the Bureau by including this "pure" social science in four hundred pages of the final synthetic report on the project. Further, like children who are told, "no, you can't," some project campaigners on their own time produced the largest volume of publications on elements of the project's inquiries than ever covered any piece of Southwestern antiquity.

There was a long-standing but shortsighted feeling among Southwestern scholars that archaeologists should not venture into documented times that customarily were the research territory of historians. In the 1970s that attitude was another one in transition with the realization that both disciplines were charged with understanding the human experience which was continuous whether or not scribes recorded it. A dividing line between them was meaningless. Formal history could be enlivened by groundwork and vice versa. The Bureau recognized that an accounting of the postancestral Pueblo presence in the Dolores Valley was an appropriate component of the overall process of mitigation of the loss of all the cultural resources in the proposed dam and reservoir areas. Its contract with the University of Colorado therefore allotted funds for historical research.

Generally the Dolores environs were empty and silent for five centuries after the ancestral Pueblos left them. They were visited infrequently by Hopi and Shoshone hunters or others gathering natural resources. Sometimes these parties camped along canyon rims and left behind calling cards in the form of sherds from broken pots or chips from broken projectile points. Judging from objects recovered by the Dolores Archaeological Program field hands, they buried several kinfolk in convenient crevices. Crews could not date these scant remains when they encountered them because often they were not diagnostic of any particular group and were mixed with known ancestral Pueblo materials which they recycled. The best guess estimates were that these uncertain clues could date this protohistoric period anywhere between A.D. 1500 and 1850.[71]

As part of the Dolores Archaeological Program, Duane Smith, history professor at Fort Lewis College, compiled a general background of the non-Indian use of the Dolores Valley from the time of the Spanish friars Dominguez and Escalante to the present.[72] In another approach, crew members interviewed several families displaced by the dam endeavors to record their memories. Excavations at some known historic spots were planned but not yet implemented when the Bureau abruptly voided the historical part of the contract.[73] Either the administrators were unhappy over delays in getting these inquiries further along or they had second thoughts about archaeology's legitimate role. In either case, they turned the historical research over to the National Park Service.

The Historic American Buildings Survey, a department within the National Park Service, sent seven students and an architecture professor into the field in 1981 to document and make scale drawings of ranch buildings in the Dolores Valley that would be inundated. Others wrote essays about the 1880s irrigation project, the history of local ranching and farming, and the establishment and fiery end of a 1920s lumber mill that brought fourteen hundred workers into the valley and gave the name of the company town to the reservoir.[74]

All those historical facts notwithstanding, it was unfortunate that archaeological work was not part of the package because possibly it could have added a personal flavor to the dry record. That would have been particularly true of the late nineteenth century when there were interesting parallels and contrasts between the Euroamerican and Pueblo I stories, although the material possessions and attitudes of each were centuries and worlds apart.

Attracted by the same unsullied, uninhabited grasslands as had lured the Pueblo Indians to the northern peripheries of the Colorado Plateau, in the late 1870s a few white families traveled westward from Durango to establish themselves in the Dolores Valley. They were all of one race—Caucasian—and shared a general Western European historical background but may have represented diverse ethnicities and spoken several languages other than, or in addition to, English. German immigrants are known to have been among them. Research has established comparable racial homogeneity and ethnic diversity for the ancestral Pueblos. Given the latter, and the situation among modern Pueblo tribes, linguistic plurality is also possible.

The white settlers took up residence along the benches and upper slopes of the Dolores River Valley with consideration for range for livestock, as well as for soil suitable for cultivation of grains and a large variety of fruits and vegetables. The animals and plants were introductions that had not been available to the Indians. The white holdings were individual homesteads of 160 acres that were scattered, as were those of the Pueblos. Occasionally they incorporated land that once had been occupied and farmed by their long-vanished predecessors.

The nineteenth-century newcomers erected dwellings, barns, storage sheds, and outhouses, but no places of worship. They dug water wells. Their work was done with the help of metal tools, nails, and hardware they brought from outside the area. Their architecture was dictated by preconceptions transferred from past experiences in Europe or in other parts of America about how their establishments should be. One ranch headquarters looked much like another, but they were not identical. In contrast, eighth-century builders, working with stone implements and easily available local materials, fashioned domiciles, storage units, and places of worship, but no outhouses. Their structures were created according to ideas that presumably were worked out somewhere else. They were standardized and duplicated as though builders were leery of experimentation and quite surely followed a format established in response to social organization. If they were resourceful enough to exploit the high water table in the valley bottom, evidence for that eroded away with the passage of time.

The scattered settlement pattern of both groups demanded a high degree of self-sufficiency in order to survive in what was an unforgiving region blessed with scenic beauty but one reluctant to nurture agricultural productiveness. Cold air settling down in the valley depression, infertile soils, and unpredictable rains or snows were shared hardships. The Euroamericans had two other problems to overcome. One was fear of Indian attacks. The other was the region's isolation from other settlers and trading centers. When deep snows blocked the mountain passes, they became depressed that they could not get supplies of what they considered the necessities of coffee, sugar, tobacco, and mail. Before the century was over they, too, came together in a rough-and-ready huddle of clapboards and log cabins at a bend in the river. This tiny outpost of Big Bend lasted just thirteen years, about the same life span as many Puebloan communities.

Some settlers endured; many did not. Out on the frontier, their cultural disposition was that they had to go it alone or find another base. Nor did they have any deep-rooted emotional tie to this land. Those who moved away from ranches generally left the region entirely and may have turned to other occupations. Their abandoned houses, their trash, and their weedy gardens soon were enveloped in the wistful sadness of failure as they formed yet another archaeological deposit. Some of those who deserted the village by the river moved to the new town of Dolores, where their descendants still reside. The valley downriver again was an untenanted wilderness until a lumber mill arrived in the 1920s.

The social climate of the ancestral Pueblos differed. Not only were there many more of them, but they were supported by an interrelated group. If one dwelling spot proved unsatisfactory, they took up residence nearby without interrupting their connections to kinsmen or associates. Whatever the drawbacks, they hung on in the Dolores area for two centuries. They surely had a sensitive involvement with this land because they knew no other. When they did leave, they regrouped with others of the same ilk and continued the same customary lifestyle.

The labors of years and the expenditures of huge sums of money that the Dolores Archaeological Program entailed did not produce a grand monument: no Cliff Palace, no Aztec West. What was gained instead was a small, elegant museum, the Anasazi Heritage Center, which made the findings of this endeavor and others on regional federal lands available to the public and to professionals alike for years to come. If local citizens wanted economic and cultural benefits from the county's archaeological richness, this was it. Science likewise benefited. An unintended but rewarding by-product of the program was its role as an incubator for a new generation of social scientists, the methods of their craft, and ardent intellectual curiosities which they would continue to pursue. The Dolores Archaeological Program laid bare the greatest abundance of the beginning stages of the long ancestral Pueblo sequence and in more multifaceted complexity than any previous provincial explorations.

## IRRIGATED ANTIQUITIES

As waters began to lap along the shores of McPhee Reservoir in 1985, the Bureau of Reclamation implemented the delivery systems to customers more than fifty miles away. Planned routes of lengthy open canals and piped feeders coming off them like octopus tentacles had to be examined for possible antiquities to be recorded and excavated when deemed potentially informative. The Bureau turned to small noninstitutional companies to carry out a proposed Four Corners Archaeological Program that would continue over a number of years as construction proceeded on particular sections of the far-flung system.

As a prelude to any work, the government secured legal easements through parcels of privately owned land that would be crossed by any part of the network and asked for agreements from land owners to allow archaeological probing of these affected properties. Some farmers gave permission for this work, but others did not. Behind this refusal may have been a latent suspicion by country folks of those better educated than they or the fear of reckless damage to crops or land. Some agreed with the stipulation that any recovered artifacts would be returned to them after study.

The Bureau of Reclamation contracted with Complete Archaeological Services Associates, owned by the husband and wife team of Laurens and Nancy Hammack, to survey and partially or totally excavate selected sites along three canal routes and several laterals. From 1988 through 1992 this company worked almost one hundred sites representative of the entire ancestral Pueblo continuum then known for the region. A number of their crews had spent time in the Dolores Archaeological Program and so brought regional experiences to this stepchild endeavor. Laboratory analyses and preparation of reports were done in exhaustive detail at the company facilities in Cortez. The restricted nature of the work limited reporting to descriptive accounts of settlement patterns, subsistence, and material culture, which met Bureau commitments and avoided the unfortunate adversarial climate associated with the Dolores Archaeological Program. All artifacts, other than those given to property owners, were deposited at the Anasazi Heritage Center.

These projects posed a new kind of archaeology that surgically opened cross sections of the ancestral Pueblo heartland.[75] Investigations were done linearly and sequentially over many miles instead of being localized at one discrete spot. It was rather like riding the chuck line in the Old West when a traveler feasted at one stop and then moved on to repeat it at the next welcoming one. In some zones large tracts had been cleared, plowed, planted, compacted by county or ranch roads, grazed by livestock, or occupied in modern times, all factors that influenced procedures. Surface collecting of site areas could be done, but digging was strictly confined to right of ways. Tantalizing remnants of sites might be beyond those boundaries but could not be touched, although cognizance of them had to be made in broad cultural interpretations.

Generally, excavation methods were those formulated during previous years. These included recording surface collections by grid, surface clearing, auger testing for buried features, backhoe trenching to learn stratigraphic deposition, digging, troweling, and screening.

The nature of some work to be done and time constraints placed upon it fostered methodological innovations. In sites with no visible surface structures, mechanical help in the form of a road grader was put to use in taking off the top plow zone. The exposed surface was then cleaned smooth with shovels. Any indicated objects of possible archaeological value were flagged for future reference and then covered with sheets of black plastic so that they would not dry out. Otherwise a truck with water tank was on site so that crew members could use hoses to lightly sprinkle the surface. Moisture highlighted buried features. Summer rains were helpful in this process so long as the ground was not muddy. On their hands and knees and moving as a team, the workers used their trowels to scrape the defined area. Whatever would old-timers Kidder and Morris have thought of that scene! The final step was to record place of deposition and then unearth any revealed construction elements or specimens.

Two locations at opposite ends of the McPhee irrigation system stand out because of unique features in sites there. One was in the far west.

In 1988 Complete Archaeological Services Associates arrived at a location which the twenty-three-person crew christened Knobby Knee Stockade. They were inspired by a Kokopeli figure on a pot. The site was on a farmed rise at the northern extent of Cajon Mesa that was to receive water from the Hovenweep Lateral. This feeder connected to the South Canal flowing southwestward from near the town of Pleasant View some ten miles distant.[76] At one time a small masonry houseblock had been present at Knobby Knee that, with the exception of the lower masonry courses of two partial rooms, had been leveled by plow or a county road and borrow pits that cut through the site. The crew believed many sherds lying around were left from a probable Pueblo II period, but others were definitely earlier although there was no surface hint of any structure of that age. Excavations below the bladed area soon verified that indeed there had been two distinct uses of this small chunk of what once was wooded real estate and that the site would be a demanding but fruitful dig.

The often mysterious impetus behind aboriginal human events on the Colorado Plateau caused a couple of Basketmaker III families to decide to live at Knobby Knee about the beginning of the seventh century. Where they came from and what drew them to this place perhaps will never be known. What is known is that they were not solitary vagabonds. Other Basketmaker III parties also were migrating into regions north of the San Juan River during this time.

Once at Knobby Knee, these settlers literally dug in. They sunk pithouses and raised a few pole and surface units.[77] They set about making the objects necessary for their mode of life. Having arrived in a period of sufficient moisture for farming without a perennial water source, they prepared and tended gardens out on the red loess soil. Their efforts were successful enough to permit a modest increase in their numbers and expansion of their little hamlet.

What the archaeologists found almost in the center of the lateral right of way was a confused cluster of seven pithouses, thirteen surface rooms, and over fifty pits of varied sizes and shapes and all of unknown purpose. Not all structures were contemporaneous. Some later ones were superimposed like flapjacks over earlier ones. Abandoned early pits were filled with later trash.

Of special importance was a wide ring of closely spaced post holes left from a substantial fence of upright poles that enclosed the entire compound. The crew called it a "stockade." That may be an inapt term that implies a need for defense for which there is no evidence. The significance of this stockade was its great size and remarkable delineation. Comparable features now are known to have been erected from Basketmaker III through Pueblo II times.

By the end of the A.D. 600s another of those undetermined motivations prompted the people at Knobby Knee to torch their homes and move. Perhaps they joined other Basketmakers, such as those in the Dove Creek environs, in drifting northeastward to somewhat higher elevations that were better watered. Maybe they were among those who reached the Dolores River valley and climbed up Grass Mesa.

Five hundred years passed before another group of ancestral Pueblos came to Knobby Knee. Like their predecessors, they were trying to subsist by the same rudimentary kind of dry farming supplemented by foraging and hunting. The archaeologists classified the site as a farmstead used by one or two families. Their style of architecture, however, had greatly improved over the intervening centuries. At this place they erected what may have been a six-room, double-rowed, masonry houseblock. The foundations cut down into an earlier structure on the same spot. This did not surprise the new builders because they saw the many fragments of old pottery distributed all around. More confirmation of previous occupation came when they began to put a kiva out front. Its depression sank through the floor of a large Basketmaker III pithouse and went six feet deeper into the subsoil.[78] That undisturbed stratum formed the walls of a Mesa Verde-style kiva complete with six pilasters, ventilator shaft, deflector, encircling bench, hearth, and sipapu. The tops of the pilasters were at the level of the pithouse floor. Excavators speculated that the floor had braced the kiva's cribbed roof.

Pottery and tree ring dates placed construction of the intrusive kiva about A.D. 1193, with its abandonment coming just twenty or so years later.[79] That made it Early Pueblo III in the Pecos Classification. Upon abandonment the kiva was burned and its roof destroyed. When the diggers worked down through the deposits that ultimately filled the structure, they learned that many specimens had either fallen with the roof or been left in the kiva interior when the Puebloans departed. Possibly they represented domestic use of the kiva.

Two turkey burials and many turkey eggshells and bones unearthed in the precincts of the compound are evidence of the importance of the bird to the inhabitants.[80]

The Knobby Knee kiva yielded a big bonus in having portions of at least four superimposed murals on the plastered faces of its bench and pilasters.[81] Bold geometric elements, such as triangles, frets, scrolls, and horizontal frame lines, were painted in bright red and white, and on one panel there was a tiny bit of green and yellow pigments. The patterns were comparable to those on coeval black-on-white pottery and must have made a dazzling display when fresh. The labor invested in these murals suggests a ritual use of the kiva outweighing that of a domestic nature. The surface layer had been damaged by the fire, but conservators from the Anasazi Heritage Center were able to strip layers beneath it, reconstruct the designs, and remove some samples.

These Knobby Knee murals gain added significance because of the site's proximity to Lowry Ruin and its painted kiva.[82] In addition to the notable one with a completely intact mural, there were traces of other murals in several less-preserved kivas there. For fifty years archaeologists thought them a special attribute of Lowry. The Knobby Knee finds suggest this decorative mode was a Great Sage Plain trait of the Early Pueblo III developmental phase. Kiva painting elsewhere in the province differed in portraying red dados with clusters of three lanceolates projecting upward on a white background.

Very likely when these Puebloans left Knobby Knee, they joined colleagues in the movement toward the canyon heads of Cajon Mesa and built the enigmatic towers. If upon leaving the Mesa Verde Province for good, those groups from the western reaches went south to the Hopi area, their descendants might well have contributed their inherited mural painting talents to the great artistic flowering expressed in exuberant depictions associated with the kachina cult.

The second district of particular interest to the Complete Archaeological Services Associates is south of Ute Mountain where evergreen uplands descend to the San Juan River and meet the barren, windswept high desert.

Sagebrush, shadscale, and bunch grass replace pinyons and junipers. The unobstructed vistas there are on a grand scale. The eye can sweep from the vertical, wrinkled face of the Mesa Verde, south to the "rock with wings" (Shiprock) with its hollows and crags a mélange of shadow and sunlight, around to the hulking Carrizo Mountains, and off west in the haze the surreal landscape of Monument Valley. The stark contrasts and utter emptiness lift the human spirit, but man cannot live on scenery alone. It would seem a place uninviting to farmers.

Whether that was the case was not known until fairly recently because the strip north along the brown San Juan was closed territory. Early in the twentieth century it was given to the Ute Mountain Utes as part of their reservation in exchange for acreage on Mesa Verde. Only when rumblings began to circulate about a possible irrigation system from the Dolores River were archaeological surveys by outsiders allowed. Thus in 1974 and 1975 the Mesa Verde Archaeological Research Center confirmed that ancestral Pueblos of some past time had tested their agricultural skills there. Fifteen prehistoric sites were noted from surface clues.[83]

The third reach of the Towaoc Canal was slated to run south beyond the Ute Mountain Ute headquarters and then angle more than twenty miles west across gravelly piedmonts spilling down from Ute Mountain. Seasonally, water flows along five or six shallow channels cutting from the mountain to the San Juan, but of greater importance are a few springs in the foothills that are fed from the heights. Fourteen years after the first survey, Complete Archaeological Services Associates recorded thirty-four prehistoric sites in the canal easement that crosses this terrain. Only two of them had been indicated previously. In 1990 and again in 1992 they selected eight of these sites for intensive excavation.[84] This was new archeological territory in the province.

Diggers uncovered evidence of limited Basketmaker III presence in the early periods and some reoccupation in the waning years of the ancestral Pueblo stay in the northern San Juan area. Five of the eight sites investigated dated to a fifty-year transitional interval between Late Pueblo II and Early Pueblo III phases. Tree rings and ceramics placed this brief occupation between A.D. 1125 and 1175. The observable rubble mounds were those of small habitations loosely scattered on low ridges close to the ephemeral washes that they hoped would overflow occasionally to keep gardens growing. The buildings each were suitable only for one or two families. The harsh environment did not encourage close neighborliness. Structures were of crude slabs set in lots of mud mortar. Their partitions were jacal. Outside were simple ramada-shaded work areas. Nearby were Mesa Verde-style kivas for both domestic and ritual use and tiny subterranean rooms presumably used for storage and processing foods roasted in slab-lined pits. The number of the roasting pits reflected heavy reliance on foraging. The nature of the settlements suggested a low-level existence that was impoverished and sporadic. If there were a need for storage, the underground rooms could be sealed and obscured by a layer of dirt when residents were away.

The surprise in the ceramic assemblage was the unexpected appearance of pottery imported from the Chuska region along the western periphery of the San Juan Basin about one hundred miles south of the proposed Towaoc Canal. Such pottery had not been noticed earlier in the Mesa Verde Province. The Chuskan Pueblos dwelt in a similar setting at the base of the mountains between New Mexico and Arizona. They were important to the central Chaco towns some forty miles to the east as suppliers of utilitarian pottery and chert for flaked implements. So much so that a Chaco colony was put at Skunk Springs near the foot of the Chuska Mountains. The volume of Chuskan pottery at the piedmont sites, up to thirty percent in one instance, hints at the possibility of a few migrants coming north. They might have brought not only their own pottery but some wares from Chaco. There is no concrete evidence for that; the pottery simply may have been the result of a vigorous trade network. It is of interest that this Chuskan pottery included decorated types whereas that going to Chaco predominately was plain gray. Perhaps this was an example of marketing strategy.

Another surprising discovery on surface room and kiva floors of four sites were masses of human bones in their fill.[85] Some were disarticulated; others were left in chunks of fleshed body parts. The report's author, Mary Errickson, delicately described them as "culturally modified." In plainer English, they were cut, splintered, fragmented, burned, powdered, and so thoroughly mistreated that identification of sex, age, or number of victims was problematical. One estimate was that fifteen persons were represented, but that number likely is too low. No whole skulls were recovered. They were smashed into bits and pieces, uprooting teeth like popcorn in the process. Dark stains on the ground were suspected of being from pools of human blood. The archaeologists thought the sharp-edged, flaked tools recovered from the dirt around the bones had been used to cut up and deflesh human bodies or, as they unemotionally said, to "process" them. Blunted anvils, hammerstones, and manos served heavier duty. The killers either grabbed up whatever household objects were handy, or they had the forethought to bring their own complement of weapons of mass Puebloan destruction. If the latter case were true, they shared the same material culture as the dead. There was little doubt but that those who had been slaughtered or parts thereof had been eaten, but these investigations provided no proof. To cover the scenes of the crimes, the roofs of some structures were set on fire, in several instances leaving a considerable amount of objects to be buried in fallen debris.

The horrendous attacks must have been carried out simultaneously at all the dwellings, which were short distances apart between Aztec and Cowboy Washes, by a sizable gang of men and boys in order to slay so many. Maybe they were killed elsewhere and bodies were dragged indoors to be "processed." There is some evidence that one kiva already was abandoned when it became a dumping ground for the remains. Or perhaps victims were trapped in the kivas by blocked hatchways and ventilators so that they could not escape.

The reasons for what obviously were premeditated murders and who was responsible for them are unfathomable. Did the locals rise up against Chuskan invaders, if, in fact, there were any? Did bloodthirsty foreigners with a grudge or intent on raiding take it out on helpless settlers? Why? There was little food and no prized resources to steal. Warfare seems unlikely; attackers would not have paused to do such damage. Was religious fanaticism to blame? It is thought provoking that many of the bones were on kiva floors or in their southern recesses, but they were dumped and not arranged in a symbolic fashion. Furthermore, the kivas were being used for daily activities, not just for ceremonies. Punishment for perceived witches usually was meted out to single individuals and not to families. Some scholars attribute the ruthless violence to dissolution of the Chacoan efflorescence that incited social unrest.[86] However, if the end of this occupation was about A.D. 1175, the Chacoans had been gone for a generation or more. Admittedly, repercussions of their meteoric rise and abrupt fall could have lingered, but relating this incident to those factors remains hypothetical.

The most compelling explanation for the piedmont killings is unvarnished starvation, the kind of desperate circumstance that spurs otherwise civilized persons into unthinkable misconduct. The piedmont dwellers had the misfortune of trying to establish themselves in what in the best of times was a generally hostile sector. In the mid-A.D. 1100s it was gripped by a severe drought. Paleoclimatic studies show that this drought was the worse by far of any in the human history of the northern San Juan region.[87] It continued relentlessly for fifty years from A.D. 1130 to 1180. Presumably less than the usual ten inches of annual precipitation was available on the Ute piedmont. On all these points it was more life threatening than the so-called Great Drought of the late thirteenth century which many scholars think caused the final exodus from the northern Colorado Plateau.

Undoubtedly, washes and springs went dry. Searing winds and blazing sun in a locale without even the comfort of a tree made life more miserable. If crops sprouted at all, they were stunted, yielded little, or withered. The marginality of the farming base probably meant few or no stockpiles of seeds for planting or food to sustain the populace from year to year. Pollen and flotation samples from the digs showed little corn being used and a substantial dependence on weedy and wild plants. Bones of large animals were notably absent in trash heaps. Those of jackrabbits, rodents, and other small creatures were more common. Turkeys were not plentiful. In the final analysis, the excavations projected a pitiable picture of demoralizing hunger.

An opposing point of view is that the unusually high percentage of fleshed body parts present argues against starvation being the motivation.[88] Could it be that the "processing" was somehow interrupted before the job was finished?

In former times affected groups found solutions to crises by moving elsewhere. That may not have been an option this time with unrelenting drought being widespread and not just afflicting the piedmont folks. In the A.D. 1150s and later those in Mancos Canyon, near Cortez, and in the Yellow Jacket district were similarly victimized. If starvation were the reason for this wholesale rampage, the unanswered question is why were those Mesa Verdeans having stockpiles of foodstuffs spared?

The twelfth-century catastrophic events on the piedmont would have been sensational news abroad and made the efforts of Complete Archaeological Services Associates known nationwide. If the name Aztec Wash, the locality of several of the sites, was publicized, the public immediately would have conjured up mental images of altars dripping with the blood of sacrificed slaves or captives. However, Complete Archaeological Services Associates did not make its findings known until the Bureau of Reclamation finally printed the site reports four years after the work was completed.[89] A recent listing of ancestral Pueblo sites showing evidence of possible cannibalism overlooked those on Aztec Wash.[90]

Beyond the end of the Towaoc Canal lay seventy-six hundred flattened acres that were to be converted into fertile fields through the miracle of waters born in the high Rocky Mountains. That required archaeological clearance and the formation of the Ute Mountain Ute Irrigated Lands

Archaeological Project. Soil Systems, Inc. of Phoenix, Arizona, owned by Breternitz's son Cory, was awarded the contract for the work.

Because a field camp could not be set up on the Ute Reservation, Soil Systems bought a house in Cortez to use as headquarters and temporary laboratory. Final analyses and writing took place at the company offices in Phoenix.

Soil Systems crews, directed by Brian Billman, were in the field during digging seasons from 1992 to 1998. They had the advantage of working in a broad, neatly defined area rather than being limited to a narrow, linear easement. This permitted more far-reaching studies of settlement pattern and agricultural adjustments. Their surveys tabulated forty-two Pueblo sites, sixteen Archaic sites, and five historic Ute sites. The substantial Archaic presence was a new piece of information because it had not been previously confirmed. However, the most energizing discovery was four pithouses in a community complex on Cowboy Wash with the dismembered and muti- lated bones of a total of twenty-four individuals.[91] It remained uncertain whether this was the same violent episode for which Complete Archaeological Services Associates previously had uncovered significant sign, but it did occur in the mid-A.D. 1100s not far from where the other finds were made. There was more telling evidence of humans eating humans at the Soil Systems digs.

Presumed stone butchering tools lay near stacks of human bones. Several tested positive for traces of human blood.[92] They had been used to hack and deflesh corpses. In one kiva, workers recovered fragments of a large earthenware container scattered near an ashy hearth. Some of them tested positive for human myoglobin, a protein molecule from the heart and skeletal muscle. This was undeniable evidence that victims had been cooked, or to use archaeological jargon, *thermally altered*. Perhaps some were boiled and some were roasted on spits. Eaten? Yes. A single coprolite was retrieved from the hearth. Biochemists confirmed that it was from a human and also contained myoglobin. Someone had sampled another's body part and remained long enough to digest and defecate it in a contemptuous manner. That implies a gruesome affair that lasted for hours or days.

The archaeologists speculated that only two-thirds of the residents of these four pithouses had met this fate. What happened to the rest? Did they turn on fellow piedmonters, or did they flee?

The most sobering fact is that the carnage probably was much greater than these diggers exposed. A number of other dwellings in the environs and of the same age were not dug by either contract group.

There is nothing like gory details of human misbehavior to excite the media and its followers, and what better than cannibalism? Particularly when it involves someone else's race and culture. Quickly there was an overdose of headlines and TV bytes about Cowboy Wash, a name recalling the romantic West (that everyone knows was wild) with considerably more zing than just Site 5MT10010. Cowboy Wash was Mesa Verdeans' Donner Pass. Neither did the Soil Systems staff hesitate in making their findings known through impassive professional talks and writings. For others, ancestral Pueblo archaeology suddenly turned melodramatic with loose talk of Mexican mercenaries and death squads. When the news cooled, researchers took a calmer view of cannibalism and recognized that the long-held concept of the ever peaceful ancestral Pueblos was passé. What had once seemed to be isolated incidents was part of a pattern of violence (not all cannibalistic) that had its fieriest outburst in the Mesa Verdean Dark Ages of A.D. 1125 to 1175, most in the final twenty-five years. As did the drought.

### ALPINE BASKETMAKERS

A half century ago when Morris and Burgh worked at the Talus Village site, the upper Animas Valley was bordered by sparsely settled, wooded benches hemming in herds of elk lazily browsing grassy meadows through which the river meanders southward. Off to the north are the crenellated battlements of the San Juan Mountains and the fastness of the Weeminuche Wilderness. It was a bucolic but awesome scene that likely also was known to Talus Villagers at the inception of the Christian Era. Today, as the town of Durango has expanded up the valley, strip malls, houses, gardens, and horse corrals cover the slopes and compete with the elk for uncluttered bottom lands to use as glider pads, golf courses, and trophy homes. It was just a matter of time until this omnipresent, visible development encountered the hidden one of the past already identified in the locality.

In the fall of 1998 an operator of a backhoe gouging a depression in a hillside for a house foundation noticed that his machine had uncovered some bones. He stopped work immediately in accordance with a Colorado law requiring official notification of unmarked graves on private property and summoned the county sheriff. Through a series of inspections, the bones were determined to be human and lay in a prehistoric context. In due time archaeologist Mona Charles from Fort Lewis College and some students obtained permits and funding from the Colorado Historical

Society to conduct emergency excavations at the site, which they named Darkmold in a transliteration of the owner's name, Mark Dolt.[93]

Further preparations for the house construction revealed a total of eleven burials. Their removal and analyses prior to final reburial were the primary reasons for the hurried excavations. Their cultural interpretation meant as much examination of the surrounding premises as the ongoing building activity allowed, but obviously it was not going to be a normal dig. Fortunately, the owner understood the need to reconcile critical data collection with his desire for haste in fieldwork.

Trench profiles indicated an ancient midden, assorted cists of varying sizes and shapes, some of which had been used secondarily for burials, and stone and bone specimens. Unfortunately, ground disturbance eradicated any evidence of habitation.

Darkmold turned out to be primarily a Basketmaker II hamlet occupied at various times over the course of several centuries by people dependent to some degree on high altitude maize agriculture. The material culture and the cists conformed to those at Talus Village in an identical setting just a half-mile to the north. It is probable that at least the west side of this stretch of the Animas Valley was home to other Basketmaker II settlements that have been destroyed and unreported as contemporary American occupation has taken hold. Some evidence for a limited post-Basketmaker II presence is in line with what is known elsewhere in the valley.

The study of the human remains by Debra Martin, Hampshire College, was especially enticing because Eastern Basketmakers are few. Earlier finds had not received such anatomical attention or were in too poor of a condition to be analyzed. It was disappointing, therefore, that the small size of the sample, its fragmentary state, and the unreliability of cranial and dental metric analyses allowed only broad generalizations about this Basketmaker population.[94] They were short in stature, muscular, and subject to nutritional stresses. Nothing unexpected there. Martin and her assistant Michael Margolis could only say that they were of indigenous Native American stock; they could not determine more explicit genetic ancestry. Had such information been forthcoming, it might have provided a clue as to whether these particular Eastern Basketmakers had originally come out of the Great Basin to the northwest, the southern districts now straddling the United States–Mexico border, or had evolved out of an *in situ* Archaic base. Each of these diversities might have had biological distinctions while sharing a common cultural orientation. This is a problem for the future to solve.

## Confrontation, Accommodation, Education

These various wide ranging finds by the archaeologists augmented a passion for things Indian that swept the country as the twentieth century was drawing to a close. By this time archaeology had colored the Southwestern identity and, for some, converted it into something semimystical.

As years passed, domestic and foreign heritage tourism increasingly overran the six national parks and monuments of the Four Corners. A blitz of archaeological publications made Cliff Palace the most photographed ruin in the world, a World Heritage Site in 1976, and according to some journalists, the most important historical place in the world. What would the Wetherills have thought of that! *Anasazi* (ancestral Pueblo) became a household word. Back country recreation reached Cedar Mesa, Grand Gulch, and the Great Sage Plain. The Bureau of Land Management, the Forest Service, and the National Park Service hired a few archaeologists to serve primarily as caretakers and interpreters for the thousands of sites under their jurisdiction and contracted with outsiders to inventory them as mandated by the 1969 National Historical Preservation Act. The Edge of the Cedars Museum was built in Blanding in 1978. A small ruin outside the back door dating from Pueblo I through Pueblo III times could be visited, as could a restored kiva. Fort Lewis College added a Department of Anthropology and for several years operated a small field school in the Durango area.

Such attention to the antiquities was appreciated, and those with authority on federal lands tried to accommodate it within their budgetary limitations. But there was a down side. Traffic through the sites unintentionally caused damage to fragile structures, and artifacts such as potsherds, which visitors placed on "museum rocks" for others to see, lost their scientific value by being moved. Worse yet was a firestorm of pothunting, endemic in the region with the arrival of white men, that was reignited by reports of extravagant sums being paid for specimens by galleries and auction houses. There were no legal restrictions against digging into ruins on private property, but the Society for American Archaeology lobbied hardpressed government officials to revise the 1906 Antiquities Act with stiffer penalties for violators on public lands. Instead, a new Archaeological Resources Protection Act was passed in 1978 that, in addition to fines, provided for the confiscation of looters' vehicles, payments for repairing any damage, and jail time. Senseless vandalism, such as knocking down walls, spray painting rock art panels, or riddling directional signs with bullet holes, caused some spots to be restricted or access to them eliminated.

Administrators and the citizens they served grew increasingly antagonistic.

There were those among the laymen who regarded archaeologists as an aloof elite treating the ruins as their exclusive fiefdoms and locking away artifacts for their personal enjoyment. As taxpayers, they resented not being allowed free rein on public lands. An undercurrent of Western antifederal sentiment nourished their discontent. Harassed officials and some in the scientific community viewed the general public as a threat best warded off by not revealing the whereabouts of sites that were difficult to monitor. These opposing views deteriorated into a standoff that simmered for years.

In their advocacy for conservation of archaeological resources, the scientists faced their own quandary. Federal officials took their charge to preserve antiquities so seriously that it became increasingly impossible for legitimate investigations to be conducted on public lands. The archaeologists' rationale was that ruins without interpretation, which could come only through in-depth, in the ground study, were essentially just piles of rocks.

The other side of the coin was that archaeologists were slow to realize that it was their responsibility to turn enemies into allies. To begin, they needed to stop referring to this concerned but sometimes disgruntled group as amateurs because that carried a tone of condescension. Rather, they should be called "avocational archaeologists" with the recognition that they came from many workaday walks of life but had a genuine desire to learn about peoples in other times who had lived in this Four Corners of the nation. They were the hordes at the gate waiting to be invited in. Even if the scientists felt constrained by tightened federal controls, they needed to reach out to the avocational groups through lectures about their work and its importance, through popular writings in nontechnical terms, and through field and museum trips for persons of all ages. They had to admit the value of volunteers' help in routine tasks and in site stewardship. Above all, they had to assure this motivated group that they were an important part of a crusade to understand and safeguard an irreplaceable national patrimony. For all citizens, including those who owned lands containing archaeological remains, cultural resource management had to be the mantra of the day.

Over the final decades of the twentieth century, the response from the public was heartwarming. Membership in archaeological and conservation societies burgeoned, and volunteerism soared. One outstanding example of the latter is at Chimney Rock. After the falcons finally flew away, thereby allowing the park to reopen, volunteers donated and erected a new entrance station. They collect fees on behalf of the Forest Service and lead tours during the summer months. Pothunting has been curtailed, but unfortunately not eliminated. The public is asked to report such illegal activity, as well as damage to sites from natural causes, whenever they are observed. Preservation has to be a team effort. The healing of old wounds and misunderstandings is a slow process that requires patience and mutual respect.

A test of this attitude came near the end of President Clinton's administration when he proclaimed the Canyon of the Ancients National Monument that takes in 164,000 acres of the Great Sage Plain where the ancients by the tens of thousands once lived. Cattlemen and farmers are irate. Archaeologists are fearful of another round of site destruction. Bureau of Land Managers remain stunned by the enormity of their assignment to protect such a site-rich, dauntingly broken territory with limited budgets and personnel. Businessmen and civic leaders are hopeful that somehow public involvement and academic scholarship can be a fruitful partnership. Only time will tell.

Another difficult situation for American archaeologists generally is not conflict with dissatisfied travelers or backpackers but one that pits them against minority Native Americans whose legacy has provided a century or more of mental stimulation. Their voices finally being heard about past insensitivity toward matters they regard as sacrosanct, the Native Americans were offered soothing accommodation through the 1990 passage of the federal Native American Graves Protection and Repatriation Act (NAGPRA). This was followed by varying state laws regarding treatment of Indian or other burials.

The federal legislation has two parts. The protection section states that, if possible, burial grounds are to be avoided by archaeologists. If such places are encountered unavoidably, human remains should be treated with due respect and immediate consultation with potentially affiliated tribes should ensue in order to decide whether *in situ* or other disposition is desirable. This harks back to a long history in the Mesa Verde Province, as well as elsewhere, of human bones being bagged up and sent off to some distant institutional storage place, where they remained unstudied for years as just another batch of goods taking up space. Or of skulls lined up on mantelpieces as curiosities, their humanness being virtually ignored.

The repatriation part of the federal law stipulates that if requesting tribes can show lineal descent or cultural connection, all museums receiving government funds shall return human remains, funerary goods, or sacred objects to these petitioners. This requirement has placed an oversized burden on understaffed, underfunded institutions in order to make necessary inventories of vaults jammed with hundreds of thousands of accumulated specimens. It also has hindered or halted some physical analyses such as DNA determinations. However, its implementation also has worthiness in that it forces both the petitioners and the scientists to more seriously than ever examine geographic, kinship, archaeological, anthropological, linguistic, folkloric, historical, and oral traditional information to substantiate claims. Education for all parties must surely emerge from these reviews.

As for the Mesa Verde Province, appropriate repatriations have been made followed by tribal reburials and rites performed by religious leaders. Other resolutions are still pending more than a decade after the act's passage. Confirming cultural identities and securing mutual agreements between native entities, curators, and administrators has proved troublesome, but amends are being made.

### Crow Canyon Archaeological Center

It was at this critical time in the troubled relationships between various interested parties that Stuart Struever arrived on the scene with what to some observers was a novel idea and to others a questionable one. During a sabbatical leave from Northwestern University spent in Telluride, he became convinced that southwestern Colorado was just the place for what he envisioned as a combination scientific research and public educational center focused on Mesa Verdean archaeology. The plethora of nearby ruins could entertain scientists for years to come and lay participants in their endeavors could learn about regional archaeology and how and why it is done. It was his conviction that such education was a good way to help curtail the loss of prehistoric resources. In his rosiest dreams Struever saw charitable foundations and corporations and the largess of monied citizens funding plant facilities, government agencies supporting ongoing inquiries, and fees paid by those who joined the program providing the operational wherewithal. He knew it would work because previously he had founded and successfully directed a similar institution in Illinois. In fact, the Colorado equivalent would be a western branch of his Midwest Center for American Archaeology. With the fervor of a proselytizer, he set about looking for a suitable home for his new brainchild.

In 1982, Struever found and arranged purchase of a seventy-acre plot of rural land on the western outskirts of Cortez along with the collection of rustic shelters that had been used for a program of experiential outdoor education for high school students. The location had the advantage of being secluded but near a main east-west highway and a small airport, as well as a source of supply in Cortez. However, only a visionary like Struever could have seen much potential in the layout. Except for an inspiring view eastward toward the La Plata Mountains and an evergreen backdrop, no attempts at beautification of the premises had been made by the previous owners. Three shopworn house trailers and an attached one-room, jerry-built, frame building could temporarily serve as office, laboratory, and dormitory. A makeshift cook shack and an outdoor shower using pond water were available. Any overflow of young students surely would revel in sleeping in several teepees pitched in a meadow in front of these ramshackle constructions. Several secondhand carryalls for group transport went with the sale. Without doubt this was to be a no-frills institutional building.

Against this inauspicious background, the first two seasons (1983 and 1984) were challenging learning experiences. From the beginning the center's mission was two-fold: conduct relevant scientific research and encourage lay persons of all age groups to take part in it. And, of course, pay for the privilege. Many scientists were skeptical of this radical plan thinking it inappropriate to include untrained individuals, particularly schoolchildren, in basic fieldwork. The opportunities for mistakes in digging and data collection were many. Nevertheless, as this dual program got under way, Charles Adams, Bruce Bradley, and Ricky Lightfoot, young archaeologists with backgrounds in regional prehistory, were hired to oversee work at an ancestral Pueblo site a short drive away. They were familiar with their assignments of excavating and caring for any recovered specimens. Perhaps they were not as prepared for being instructors, but archaeologists who do not thrive on talking about their projects to captive audiences are rare indeed. Being nighttime chaperons for underage kids was another matter but came with the territory.

National advertising brought a parade of the curious for one-week stints in the unglamorous, blister-producing chores of removing firm, sun-baked earth from pit depressions and lines of upright stone slabs. A commonly held human pleasure in groveling in the dirt and the anticipation of hidden treasures combined to make their pursuit of the past sufficiently exciting to create a troop of disciplined followers who would return year after year as alumni. Over the five-year endeavor at this ruin several thousand lay persons had some experience with it.

Crow Canyon's multifaceted approach to accomplishing archaeological goals was breaking new philosophical ground, but the first site chosen to be investigated was done so because of its convenient location, its modest size suitable for Crow Canyon's admittedly tenuous beginning, and the opportunity to expand on earlier work. Lightfoot took control of excavations there from 1985 through 1987. He was a graduate of the Dolores Archaeological Program and had worked with similar materials. The site was named Duckfoot because on the first day of work diggers recovered an earthenware figurine fragment that seemed to resemble that of a splayfooted fowl. Four years later as work was ending for good, the second foot was uncovered. Unfortunately, no identifiable body parts were found that might have shown how what must have been a modeled hollow body (probably a pitcher) was balanced on these two stubby appendages.

When finally completely cleared, Duckfoot consisted of a double row of nineteen continuous, jacal surface rooms, four pit structures to their south, and a large trash mound beyond. Its architectural style and configuration, its artifacts, and its ample tree ring sample placed it squarely in the second half of the A.D. 800s, or the Pueblo I phase.[95] Obviously, it was part of the same occupational sequence as the villages concentrated in the Dolores River Valley and was vacated at about the same time. Most units had burned with numerous, nonflammable specimens left on the floors whose analyses added to the growing Pueblo I database. A particularly interesting topic concerned the probable number of pottery vessels a household used and broke annually and then tossed out on the expansive dump. The rate of accumulation might indicate length of occupation. After study, the specimen assemblage was deposited at the Anasazi Heritage Center through arrangements with the landowners. Site interpretations formed part of Lightfoot's doctoral dissertation at Washington State University.

Meanwhile, Adams and Bradley selected Sand Canyon Pueblo for a second project, thus jumping the focus of inquiry approximately four centuries forward in time. This Pueblo III site is on Bureau of Land Management woodlands along the V-shape of two escarpments and talus slopes at the head of a small tributary to Sand Canyon, which cuts from the Montezuma Valley south down to the lower McElmo drainage. The ancestral Pueblos' choice of this location was not unique but was common to numerous other province villages at the mid- to late A.D. 1200s. Goodman Point Ruin, officially recognized as important in 1889 when it was set aside as part of a federal archaeological preserve, was a probable contemporary nearby center in similar environmental circumstances.

A practical advantage to working Sand Canyon Pueblo was that it was just off a maintained county road that made it easy for the participants to be taken to work in several old school buses. Trailers for water, lunches, and other supplies could be parked under trees. Volunteers associated with the

Amaterra organization out of Tucson built trails and facilities for the crews.

Compared to any Mesa Verde Province site previously investigated, Sand Canyon Pueblo was a metropolis that archaeologists now call a *nucleated village*. It was appealing for study because surface indications were that it had enjoyed a single period use, not one with episode piled on top of episode. Mapping done by Adams and Bradley using what later would be regarded as the old-fashioned plane table and alidade method suggested 420 masonry rooms, ninety kivas, fourteen towers, a Great Kiva, a central courtyard, and a multiwalled, D-shaped structure.[96] The whole building complex was massively walled on three sides. Scholars were interested to learn whether it grew piecemeal or in one concerted effort, whether there were changes related to social stratification that could be demonstrated through architecture or ground plan, how the pueblo related to others in the vicinity, and how and why it was eventually forsaken.

Sand Canyon Pueblo was not totally excavated nor was there any intention of doing so. Its size and importance demanded that much be left for future, hopefully more advanced, investigations. Crow Canyon's plan devised by staff members Adams and Bradley was to sample fourteen blocks of the settlement exhibiting a cross section of its varied components.

At the end of the project, Bradley, in charge after the first season, saw the east arm of the pueblo as being one of habitations and the opposite west section, with its more numerous kivas and special constructions, as being the ritual center of the village although also where people lived. Tree ring dating ranging from A.D. 1250 to 1277 confirmed a relatively brief use life after what must have been considerable expenditure of effort in the pueblo's erection.[97] Bradley speculated that 157 individuals working forty-hour weeks for a year could have done the job either communally or individually as needs arose.[98] It goes without saying that the forty-hour work week is a modern concept unrecognized by persons of any time who till the land. Michael Adler, who joined the staff, put forth a population estimate for Sand Canyon Pueblo at about 750 persons.[99] If these figures are anywhere near accurate, it would seem that few tenants had deep-rooted ties and hence would not have regretted leaving this one spot; abandonment of the land of their ancestors would have been more distressing. The scientists remained uncertain about how that occurred, but the consensus was that it came late and somewhat abruptly in the thirteenth century. Some rooms were ceremonially shut down by fire with nonportable goods left where they lay. At least eight individuals died violent deaths that may have taken place in the final days at Sand Canyon Pueblo.[100]

The prolonged fieldwork at Sand Canyon Pueblo exposed only one-tenth of the site. Doing archaeology Crow Canyon's way, with weekly or biweekly turnover of inexperienced diggers needing instruction and oversight, is necessarily slow. Compensatory rewards come from sharing a mental and physical experience with those who otherwise might never have such an opportunity.

While work continued at the two sites of Duckfoot and Sand Canyon Pueblo, in 1985 the tie to the Illinois group was severed. What was its western offshoot became the independent Crow Canyon Archaeological Center. The new status meant getting the fledgling institution more structured and purposefully directed. Struever took over as president with offices in Denver, and Ian "Sandy" Thompson, a prominent local resident, assumed the on-site directorship.

Struever's forte was promotion of and fund-raising for the new not-for-profit organization. In addition to outright solicitation of foundations and corporations, he brought prospective private donors to the Center to observe archaeology firsthand and to review proposed physical improvements of headquarters. Many donations were forthcoming, but some efforts went awry. Staffers recall the time a prospective contributor was quartered in the frame building with its resident skunk. No check was in the mail following his abrupt departure.

Another Struever approach was to treat selected groups to treks across the Colorado Plateau for the express purpose of exposing them to its natural and cultural diversity as explained by experts in the region's history, archaeology, geology, and native peoples. A considerable number of these invited guests were from the Chicago area and had been supporters of the Center for American Archaeology but knew little about the Southwest or its attractions. Fortunately the high quality of these so-called seminars had popular appeal and did loosen some purse strings.

Struever's tireless efforts gradually made capital improvements and grounds developments possible. The campus was transformed into an attractive, functional facility totally belying its humble beginnings.

Thompson proved to be an able administrator who set the tone for the Center's evolution into a highly respected adjunct to Cortez and surrounding county. He assembled a staff with a wide variety of talents essential to keeping a one-of-a-kind, self-sufficient academic body functioning. Clerical, marketing, financial, housekeeping, kitchen, landscaping, and automotive help backed up the two primary parts of the program: research and education. Together Thompson and Struever created a board of directors composed of influential persons with corporate and legal experience. The one archaeologist in the group was Alden Hayes, then retired from the National Park Service. It was he who successfully opposed having the Center operate only during summers. He insisted that if the Center was to have scientific significance, each field season had to be followed by a season of laboratory analysis and reporting.

With the Center's new independence, William Lipe, who had served on the advisory committee during its establishment, assumed the role of director of the research around which other activities would revolve. He saw a challenge tailor-made to his grander visions of unraveling cultural processes in a more advanced society such as that which must have existed at Sand Canyon Pueblo. Ignoring tight budgets but encouraged by enthusiastic public response exceeding expectations, he proposed a long-term look at the A.D. 1150 to 1300 occupation (Pueblo III) of some two hundred square kilometers west of Cortez virtually bursting with inviting ruins awaiting shovels, trowels, and the intellectual prowess of his small band of converts to problem-solving archaeology. Coincidentally, the Dolores Archaeological Program was ending just as the Crow Canyon Archaeological Center geared up thus providing a pool of well-versed researchers from which to draw.

First, Lipe initiated an intensive survey of the uplands and lower Sand Canyon in order to determine the extent of the Puebloan presence there in the twelfth and thirteenth centuries. Michael Adler, later at Southern Methodist University, was responsible for the most important reconnaissance. Secondly, thirteen small Pueblo III sites on public and private lands were tested (probabilistic sampling) in an effort to understand their relationships, if any, to the Sand Canyon Pueblo. Mark Varien and Kristin Kuckelman, both having been involved with the Dolores research, directed this work. They were assisted by James Kleidon, also formerly part of the Dolores program. Portions of the results went into Varien's doctoral dissertation at Arizona State University for which he received a merit award from the Society for American Archaeology.

Auxiliary studies were made of the paleoenvironment that would have affected the populace. A sign of the enlightened times was that two women were key players. Carla Van West, previously on the National Park Service roster working for Lister, undertook a comprehensive soil and precipitation study that led to her doctoral dissertation from Washington State University. Karen Adams, primary administrative assistant to Irwin-Williams at the Salmon Ruin, engaged in biotic research that grew into an archaeoenvironmental department at Crow Canyon.[101]

There are small structures tucked into recesses along Sand Canyon as it descends to the McElmo River of interest to the Sand Canyon Project. The most significant of these is a grouping of rooms and kivas hugging the slopes and crannies of an isolated pinnacle named Castle Rock at the mouth of the declivity. One's first impression is that there was scant reason for the settlement's unusual placement when more suitable flat land spreads away from the spire. Still, motives often are hidden in the veiling of time and its earthy deposits.

Seldom does archaeology actually verify legendary accounts of past events, but archaeologists Lightfoot and Kuckelman did just that. And more.[102] According to a story recounted to early-day explorer William Henry Jackson, a battle had taken place long ago at Castle Rock Pueblo.[103] The diggers gave little credence to this tale until their probabilistic test pits exposed disarticulated, fractured, reamed, and mutilated bones of forty-one men, women, and children primarily scattered through kiva fill. Indeed a battle occurred at the village that must have taken the lives of most, if not all, of its estimated 75 to 150 residents. Kuckelman and Lightfoot felt that this tragedy completely wiped out the village. More startling was a re-examination of the physical remains that showed the same kinds of treatment after death as had been discovered a few miles away at Aztec and Cowboy Washes and elsewhere in the Mesa Verde core area but which dated a century or more earlier than the late A.D. 1200s when Castle Rock Pueblo was in use. Some instances of cannibalism, or more technically *anthropophagy*, were confirmed by analyses revealing human myoglobin on stone implements and three pottery vessels.

Again the motivation for such hostility cannot be ascertained. The post-A.D. 1274 event, as calculated by the researchers, was in another time of devastating drought that might have driven some persons to excessive survival measures. Violence may have come easily to a culture now recognized to have occasionally inflicted severe trauma on victims. The widespread shift in the late A.D. 1200s into large settlements at the canyon rims—and at Castle Rock Pueblo to the protection of a natural citadel— implies a climate of fear and the perceived need for defense. But from what and from whom? In any case, departure from the northern San Juan district was imminent and underlying causes may have been seated therein.

In part to compensate for not accomplishing a historical study during the Dolores Archaeological Program, Lipe agreed to educator Margie Connolly taking on the task of researching the initial period of white occupation of the valley adjacent to Sand Canyon Pueblo and Goodman Point Ruin.[104] Although it was recognized that homesteading here came some three decades later than in the Dolores River Valley, it was hoped that dryland farming methods of the early twentieth century would shed light on those of the prehistoric eras. Further, it would be interesting to know how this agricultural development had affected the valley's antiquities and what the settlers thought about the ancient culture with which by chance they had contact.

From interviews with fifteen persons whose parents or other relatives had settled in the Goodman Point environs shortly after land became available, Connolly learned that, except for metal implements, at that time ways for clearing and planting were not much advanced over those of the Puebloans. It was still rigorous hand labor to some extent ameliorated through the help of draft animals. North slope sage land was preferred because the brush did not present the removal difficulty of trees and soil moisture was retained later into the spring. Very likely these also were factors important to ancestral Pueblo farmers. Corn was the first crop to be planted, but it was used primarily as feed for introduced livestock. However, as for the Puebloans, some corn had to be stored over the winter to be sown in the following planting cycle. The settlers' other vegetables and fruits had not been known to the Indians, including the pinto bean variety which subsequently became the main cash crop of the Montezuma Valley.[105] For the Whites, as it surely had been for their predecessors, the need for sufficient seasonal precipitation was critical, but this group could not recall that any of the early years resulted in a total crop failure.

Those interviewed remembered about a hundred rubble mounds of which several dozen were knowingly robbed of stones for fencing and construction or were plowed under or pushed aside. They knew of at least one aboriginal road, several reservoirs, and a terraced garden plot. It was their general opinion that the antiquities meant little to their forbears, and in the late 1980s, although most had artifact collections, they, too, were markedly, but pleasantly, disinterested. As one person casually remarked, "It's fine for people who like it."[106] These were not among the people who fought government agents for unrestricted rights to the Four Corners storehouse of ruins.

To further understand demographic, social, and political adjustments that Mesa Verdeans might have made during their final centuries in the northern San Juan region, the Crow Canyon scholars took their inquiries beyond the Sand Canyon Pueblo locale to do limited examinations at a tiny fraction of the ninety-six known communities having more than fifty rooms. Woods Canyon Pueblo, Yellow Jacket Pueblo, and the Hedley Ruin, all in a sector bounded on the south by the McElmo drainage and on the west by the Montezuma drainage, were part of their Pueblo III Big Site Project.[107]

Researchers reasoned that there were three basic settlement modes. The first revolved around a village with a large house modeled on a Chacoan prototype. The second was a clustering of the linear unit-type pueblos. The climax pattern was a dense concentration at the rims of canyons. Mapping and limited testing at the three sites showed that while they shared many elements, they were not clones. Woods Canyon Pueblo contains two hundred surface rooms, fifty kivas, architecture used by the community rather than by individual families, and agricultural and water management features. It had grown from mid-twelfth-century occupation at the canyon bottom and had moved upward to the rim a hundred years later.[108]

Yellow Jacket Pueblo is the largest of all settlements in the northern San Juan region and spreads over uplands, canyon rim, and talus slopes. It also was the first of these core pueblos to be described by Newberry in the 1859 report and has been worked over legitimately and illegitimately in hit-and-miss fashion ever since. Crow Canyon crews mapped the entire one hundred-acre complex to estimate approximately six hundred rooms, 194 kivas, a Great Kiva, eighteen towers, one tower kiva, five dams, and a large reservoir. It was indeed a place of importance. Test pits were sunk beside each of the forty-two roomblocks to determine stratigraphy and architectural change through time. Pottery from test pits in middens helped in dating various episodes of occupation. Together the architecture and the pottery pegged the life span of Yellow Jacket Pueblo between A.D. 1050 and 1300.[109]

It was at the Hedley Site, actually a complex of three large settlements incorporating seven hundred surface rooms, 160 kivas, and a large reservoir, that the Crow Canyon staff and participants crossed paths with Prudden, who had dug there before World War I. He was not alone, however, but was followed in the 1930s by Leonard Leh, of the University of Colorado, and more recently by zealous pothunters. Using the same procedures of mapping and sampling, the Crow Canyon scholars felt that their three-stage settlement growth concept was most clearly demonstrated at Hedley.[110] Unlike Sand Canyon Pueblo and Castle Rock Pueblo, these three sites evolved over long periods of time. Their histories may have differed, but they shared features such as enclosing walls, towers, multiwalled buildings, blocked-in kivas, siting on the rims of canyons, and their use until the near end of the thirteenth century.

The next phase of continuing investigations embraced a triad of problems as its name Communities Through Time: Migration, Cooperation, and Conflict suggests.[111] In the captivating way that some research whets the

appetite for further research, these studies prompted interest in broad sociological questions, or to researchers the "human system." Did villagers coop-
erate with each other and with neighbors? As their numbers swelled, were
there disputes over arable land? Did their catchments have to incorporate less
fertile tracts? Why did they move from scattered farmsteads into large,
congested structures? How to account for the almost tidal movements of some
folks into the region in the A.D. 600s, out of it in the A.D. 900s, back into it in
the A.D. 1000s and 1100s and finally in the twilight of the A.D. 1200s, out of it
forever? And, furthermore, could dirt archaeology provide demonstrable
answers to such illusive questions? Lipe and company obviously thought so as
they probed the extensive Shields and Albert Porter sites, adding the degree of
Chacoan presence or influence to their mounting list of concerns.

As has been pointed out, archaeology is destructive. Once the covering of
a site that has accumulated over the centuries is removed or churned up in
any way, elemental forces hasten its eradication as a meaningful entity. Hence
the approach to Crow Canyon's work can best be termed *conservation archaeology*. Lipe and his disciples choose selective methods of studying the Mesa
Verde core ruins in keeping with their problem-oriented inquiries, as well as
recognizing the duality of their mission to include public education.
Carefully choosing places that hold potential answers to their academic questions, they plug them in key spots with test pits or trenches. Observations of
revealed architecture and ceramics establish any stratigraphic deposition and
temporal placement with minimal disturbance of the site as a whole.

Some critics of such sampling argue that a site to be studied should be
totally excavated in order to understand its complex history and so as not to
miss the rare unexpected feature. That would be impractical in the case of
these extraordinarily large communities because of the huge expense, the
great amount of manpower and time involved, and the resulting problem of
preservation. Further, the kind of region-wide questions the Crow Canyon
scholars are addressing cannot be answered through examination of just one
or two villages. An added value to their approach is that it reinforces the
lessons of conservation the Center aims to pass on to its participants.

The teaching component of the Crow Canyon Archaeological Center
agenda did not get started formally for several years. It was a new concept
for which in the early 1980s there were many doubts and no models. The
overarching themes were to be how former peoples lived in the Mesa Verde
Province and how today's Native Americans join in mainstream American
culture but retain their inherited identities. The person given the responsibility

for determining how to proceed with presenting these complexities was Margaret Heath. With an academic background in anthropology and education and some teaching experience with the Ute Mountain Ute Tribe, she set to work on the demanding task of devising plans for informing and entertaining students ranging from early childhood to old age who represent diverse ethnicities and cultural backgrounds.

Following Heath's curricula, at Crow Canyon edification takes many forms for different age groups. The program begins with fourth graders. These ten year olds do not actually dig in a site (to the relief of the skeptical critics) but are introduced by accredited teachers with training in archaeology or Native American studies to techniques of observation in large sandboxes salted with a few specimens of the sort that might be found in a ruin. Unlike real life, each grid has at least one artifact so that a child will not be disappointed. The children have a chance to experience a model pithouse and a pueblo-style classroom, attempt to throw a spear with an atlatl, try to make fire with a pump drill, or weave fiber cordage. The routines resemble summer camp with the aim of instilling in the minds of the young an appreciation of Indian life and history. To many adults, education beginning with youngsters like these is the only way to ever solve the problem of ruin depredation. Similar but more advanced programs are designed for middle school students who experience Puebloan lifestyles and technologies, tour Mesa Verde National Park, and work in a simulated site.

High school students from all over the country are given the opportunity during a three-week session to dig in an actual site under the supervision of a staff member. For most, this is the best part. Then comes what some consider the humdrum laboratory work, even more boring reporting and lectures, fun-filled field trips, and a weekend camp out. The Center's aim is not to encourage the teenagers to consider archaeology as a possible career avenue but to expose them to hands-on contact with a past with which they may not have been familiar previously. Over the years a few have returned several times; some have become stimulated to continue anthropological studies in college. Scholarships are awarded to deserving local students, as well as to Native Americans from regional tribes. Some stipends come from a lecture series sponsored by citizens known as Friends of Crow Canyon.

For adults there are week-long programs that include field and laboratory exercises and evening talks about work in progress. Many of these persons become so engrossed in what is going on that they return repeatedly. Sessions also are arranged for families to learn together. The educators host seminars in native handicrafts and arrange special courses for teachers of social studies, geography, history, and science so that they can better design inquiry-based curricula for their students.

Another part of the adult education offerings grew out of the tour seminars of the early days. A department of Cultural Explorations, headed by Dottie Peacock with travel agency experience and boundless appreciation for far-off places that might interest clients, offers a variety of domestic and foreign trips to points with archaeological or contemporary ethnic significance. Some destinations are remote and physically difficult. Some are not far from comfortable hotels and fine restaurants. All are rewarding as interpreted by scholars with the most current insights.

On an academic level, the Crow Canyon Archaeological Center has evolved to now being able to award thirteen annual, competitive graduate internships in laboratory, field, and education areas. These broaden the reach of the Center's goals well beyond the confines of the Mesa Verde Province to the archaeological profession at large.

Individuals attempting to learn about the ancestral Pueblo past enjoy the enviable advantage of having descendants of these peoples still living in close proximity. However, there are obvious pitfalls in attempting to correlate former practices with those of a present overlaid with a heavy coating of westernization. Moreover, for a century Euroamerican observers have tended to dismiss those whose physical and material remains with which they are involved as unaccountably irrelevant. For one thing, the native versions of histories about how they came to be what they are and where they came from often do not coincide with archaeologically demonstrated fact. It is a matter of divergent viewpoints about the fundamental human role in this universe.

With considerable perspicacity, since 1995 Crow Canyon has been leading the way into fuller understanding between interested entities through bringing together representatives of ten Native American groups to offer their perspectives about their tribal histories and give advice on culturally sensitive issues that those with different roots might not realize as sacred. These face-to-face encounters have fostered friendships between the white academics and native tribal members who often have felt shunned and misunderstood. To carry racial and social relationships further, a Ute Mountain Ute teacher, Rebecca Hammond, has joined the staff to lend her input about the cultural matrix that makes the Four Corners past and present so fascinating. Native American scholars also participate in Cultural Explorations, lecture offerings, and craft workshops.

Understanding that archaeology without sharing its results with colleagues has no value, the exceptional team of diggers and teachers engage in active publication and professional meeting activities that have brought Crow Canyon Archaeological Center national recognition and awards. Further, more than fifty thousand lay persons have taken part in some aspects of the program. As the Center's twentieth anniversary is at hand, three archaeological stalwarts, Lightfoot, Varien, and Kuckelman, fill important posts in the high hierarchy. Richard Wilshusen was on the staff for a time. Mary Etzkorn, Louise Schmidlap, and Angela Schwab, all transfers from the Dolores program, carry on with editorial, computer, and organizational functions. Others of the fifty-member staff have joined the ranks as replacements or as added goals necessitated. The naysayers who were certain that this unrealistic enterprise was doomed to quick extinction now admit that this institution is here to stay.

With invigorating research now being carried out by Crow Canyon, the National Park Service, a number of contract companies, and advanced students, plus widespread public involvement and the input of Native Americans, the first century of Mesa Verdean archaeology ends on a high note. ✶

# VISTAS OF MESA VERDEAN PAST

A century and a quarter has now passed since America learned of its unexpectedly rich tapestry of ancient life in the far West. No region was more consequential in this revelation or afforded more opportunities for a wide range of studies than the Mesa Verde Province. The lost civilization romanticism had become unemotional objectivity. Site-focused inquiry with its bounty of specimen analyses provided the foundation for anthropological considerations on a regional level. The Crow Canyon Archaeological Center scholars felt it was time to take stock of that cultural fabric which scores of men and women had woven together. The following résumé relies heavily upon their exhaustive assessments of what has been learned thus far; questions for the future are left there. These writers divided the Colorado antiquities into seven major drainage units, a convenient format followed in this text. Information about the peripheries in New Mexico and Utah is provided when relevant. To avoid overloading the account, the Crow Canyon encompassing references are cited.

These, then, are vistas across a broad spectrum of the human landscape as it evolved during several millennia.

## PALEOINDIAN[1] 10,000 B.C.–6,000 B.C.

Preambles to the human drama in the Southwest usually deal with Paleoindian hunters on the prowl for a variety of huge beasts that are now extinct in the dimly illuminated eras some twelve thousand years ago. Diligent troweling of a floor at Grass Mesa Village uncovered the partial skeleton of an extinct species of musk ox buried in deep loess soil. It dated from the end of the ice age in southwestern Colorado about sixteen thousand years ago. That predated any known human presence in the Southwest.

There is little basis for that introduction to life in the Mesa Verde Province because neither these individuals nor their prey seem to have been especially attracted to the region. Only a mere nineteen of their spear points have been found in the Colorado portion of the province and less than a half-dozen of them are said to have been recovered in southeastern Utah. The dearth of specimens may be due to the needle-in-the-haystack dilemma of finding such small objects in the sweeping countryside. Or it may merely reflect an unfavorable environment or few persons in those days. Considering the twenty-five hundred years of the late Paleolithic period to which these points pertain, the tiny sample is hardly significant. The finds were concentrated near Ute Mountain in the lower elevations and higher up in the Dolores drainage. That suggests some possible seasonal mobility. However, there is no assurance that Paleoindians were actually on the scene. Later peoples might have found the points elsewhere and then discarded them where found.

## ARCHAIC[2] 6,000 B.C.–1,000 B.C.

The peopling of the Colorado Plateau essentially began in the sixth millennium before Christ. Small family groups drifted across the empty high desert and uplands. They likely came from all directions and represented divergent biological and linguistic stocks but were united in the common goal of finding enough to eat. That quest focused on hunting modern faunal species and whatever edible plant foods they could gather or grub out of the hard ground. That kept them on the move over large tracts of the plateau, although in propitious times they could linger for perhaps a season. Somehow over the course of centuries they amassed an incredible fund of knowledge about their natural world and its bountiful resources which they could use to their advantage. They learned which plants they could eat, which had medicinal value, which could produce dyes, and which were fibrous. They became skilled weavers of cordage, netting, snares, sandals, and baskets. They knapped sharp-edged points from chert, quartzite, or obsidian which they attached to wood staffs propelled with the leverage afforded by atlatls. They ground down other kinds of rock in order to pulverize seeds. They came together in small bands because solitary figures could not survive in this often hostile wilderness. And they felt the need for protection by some amorphous supernatural powers to whom they addressed prayerful messages on rocky cliff faces. Some twisted split twigs into tiny, quadruped figures to magically ensure success in the hunt. Bit by bit they were building a lifestyle that would underpin the future.

As regional archaeology began to accelerate to full throttle in the 1920s, researchers postulated a formative base such as this for the long Puebloan continuum. They reasoned that the Basketmakers identified by Wetherill and then by Kidder and Guernsey could not have arrived with their full complement of hardware unless there had been some earlier evolutionary stage. In their Pecos Classification they proposed it as the ambiguous Basketmaker I. Today this is known as the primitive Archaic—Early, Middle, and Late.

For many years few scholars tried to precisely define the Archaic period. With so many more tangible remains to explore, the scanty Archaic record had little appeal despite its acknowledged importance. For those accustomed to dendrochronological specificity, the eons back behind the nether end of the tree ring calendar in the first century before Christ were a black hole. Slowly developmental sequences based almost solely upon spear point typology—size, shape, corner or side notched, stemmed—were made, but they could not be satisfactorily tethered in time. Nothing is more distressing to those attempting to securely place their subjects in the chain of events than not knowing their datable niche.

That problem was being solved by the 1970s when radiocarbon dating became more accurately refined. It was at this juncture that pack rat (more correctly wood rat) middens were found to be useful. They were a new archaeological tool that for the fastidious diminished any lingering romantic illusions about a dazzling chase after the past. Even so, the collecting instincts of these rodents, who moved into dust-dry alcoves as soon as Archaic campers moved out, saved such garbage as cactus pads, dropseeds, withered tubers and roots, nut shells, stems, and other plant residue once used by humans that through the miracle of modern science could then be dated.

As if that were not distasteful enough for the romantically inclined, human coprolites, or dried feces, offered a very intimate insight into what people at any period ate and discharged. Without any sort of formal, private closets for bodily functions, such materials found in quantity "out back" assumed significance in reconstructing dietary habits. It is of interest that in 1891 Nordenskiold was the first of the fledgling archaeologists to have the foresight to save such items for analysis.

Dating of the two primary components of regional prehistory differs widely. The evolving Puebloan culture has to be studied in relatively brief increments in order to chart cultural change. Sometimes these are no more than twenty-five or fifty year phases. In contrast, the lengthy, static Archaic period, when change came ever so slowly, is theoretically divided into developmental segments several thousand years in length.

In his investigations of the Archaic period along the western fringes of the Mesa Verde Province, Phil Geib, Arizona archaeologist, sees small groups following hunting and gathering subsistence patterns moving out of the harshness of the Great Basin of Utah into the Glen Canyon corridor of the Colorado

River. Over many thousands of years beginning in the 5000s B.C. (or Early Archaic), they took shelter in some of the cliff-side alcoves that thirty years previously the University of Utah teams found utilized by later peoples. Or they squatted on the river's gravelly banks to fashion their weapons. Others settled in the eastern reaches of Cedar Mesa. Excavators found Old Man Cave there to contain stratified deposits of several episodes of use. Undoubtedly times of unfavorable climate prompted considerable shifting about over this vast, broken territory with some camps or places where limited processing occurred being repeatedly used, abandoned, and reused. Thanks to the tidiness of the pack rats, radiocarbon dates suggest a population increase in the closing centuries of the Archaic from *circa* 2000 B.C. to A.D. 1 (Late Archaic). Geib's reconstruction proposes far-ranging, summer foraging cycles followed by colder, drier winter residency in more-or-less permanent bases. At last change was in the air.

Archaic remains are not as common in the central Mesa Verde Province and even less so further east, perhaps because there has not been as much research into this period as in adjacent areas. Nevertheless, by 1998, 413 Archaic-age materials were noted mostly in sites with subsequent occupation.[3] The Middle Archaic stage (4,000 B.C.–2,000 B.C.) was typical in sites showing a preference at that time for sandy, low elevations where a variety of grasses and shrubs mature at differing intervals and where antelope, mountain sheep, and jackrabbits could be bagged. One favorite locale was the lower Cajon Mesa in the Montezuma-McElmo drainage where centuries later the regional ancestral Pueblos met what must have been a turbulent end. A total of eighty sites with Archaic specimens have been recorded there. Another sector that attracted the Archaic bands of some four thousand years ago was the piedmont slopes south of Ute Mountain, scene of twelfth-century cannibalism. The Colorado state files list 137 Archaic sites, the largest number for any of the seven province drainages in the state but still representing only slightly more than twelve percent of the total number of known sites in that district and probably all with a very small population.

During later years the bands spread into surrounding uplands. Personnel in the Dolores Archaeological Program partially excavated two sites with Late Archaic materials, but fifty-nine sites are also listed for that drainage at somewhat higher elevations than earlier sites and with a differing pinyon-juniper biotic environment. More adventuresome bands made their way into the lofty La Plata Mountains stalking elk, deer, and bear.[4] Energetic hunting parties expended arsenals of spear or dart points that have been recovered scattered over ridges above the timber line. The amount of time and effort it took to secure raw materials and then to flake the points has to be balanced against raw expenditure of finished products. For the sake of hungry women and children back in camp, one hopes it was worth it. The upper Animas drainage also was visited by Late Archaic groups. Surveys during the 1980s counted about four dozen camp sites having scattered lithic debris, milling stones, and reddened hearth rocks.[5]

These uplanders were unaware that other bands in southern Arizona in a more direct trajectory from higher cultures in central Mexico were about to make prehistory. They were toying with maize agriculture, living in constructed dwellings, and producing pottery around 2000 B.C. It was just a matter of time until those practices would spread northward to cause students of culture considerable consternation.

### BASKETMAKER II[6] 1,000 B.C.–A.D. 500

Classificatory systems as applied to cultural elaborations through time have drawbacks as well as benefits. Sharp demarcation lines, particularly those proposed in early stages of investigation, often have to bend in light of further inquiry. That is the way science builds on itself. A case in point is the transitional period about three thousand years ago when some Colorado Plateau groups in what turned out to be a cultural hot spot south of the San Juan River, while still clinging to the ageless hunting-gathering way of life, began experimenting with raising corn as a buffer against hard times.[7] Whether this was an idea diffused to them, along with actual seed kernels, or whether migrants from the south, who already were familiar with maize agriculture, moved into their territory is uncertain. Either way, this practice intruded upon the changed subsistence system that the 1927 Pecos Classification doctrine reserved for early Basketmakers. Archaeological pigeonholers were stymied. Were they dealing with Late Archaic folks or with the more immediate forefathers of the ancestral Pueblo tradition?

Lipe was one of those who recognized that semantic adjustments had to be made for the sake of taxonomic orderliness.[8] If there was agriculture, it was Basketmaker. Further, its time frame should be pushed back a thousand years from its originally stated inception at the beginning of the Christian Era, making the Basketmaker II period fifteen hundred years in length. That radical idea emphasized the slowness with which Pueblo culture took shape. By the same token, it also pointed up the rapidity with which the remainder of the ancestral Pueblo sequence evolved, by most arbitrary schemes used by scholars in two-hundred-year increments.

If the proposed long chronology is a standard, twelve hundred years ensued before the Basketmaker II cultural stage appeared in the northern San Juan region, and then it differed from that south of the San Juan in being two distinct expressions some two hundred miles apart.

Most like southern developments was the grouping in Grand Gulch and on Cedar Mesa, generally called the "classic" Basketmaker because it was the first recognized. Work on Cedar Mesa suggested that its earliest dates were in the A.D. 200s.[9] According to Matson, it was a late part of the northeastern Arizona Marsh Pass–Black Mesa Basketmaker complex and consequentially heir to distant relationships of tribes in southern Arizona.[10] Quite possibly these Western Basketmakers in Utah actually derived from local Late Archaic peoples now believed to have been in the area.

A second body of peoples at a similar level of advancement settled in the upper Animas drainage in the A.D. 200s or a bit earlier. They, too, might have had connection to Late Archaic bands there, but they also seem to have had ties to early Fremont tribes to the northwest. Perhaps shortly another contingent came to the upper Pine River terraces. Because they made pottery, Eddy believed they may have had some sort of linkage with Mogollon groups far south of the Colorado Plateau.[11]

Regardless of derivation, what was significant was that these groups had corn as a cornerstone upon which their well-being and that of those who followed so wholeheartedly depended. Without corn cultivation and consumption there would have been no Pueblo civilization because the Archaic hunting-gathering means of survival was severely restrictive and in time was doomed to run its course. Quite literally, human life would have come to a dead end.

Corn, or maize (*Zea mays*), was domesticated eight thousand years ago from a wild teosinte grass native to southern Mexico, Guatemala, and Honduras.[12] It became such a crucial staple for the Mesoamericans that the plant was deified. So much so that the sixteenth-century invading Spaniards tried to eradicate all representations of it as symbols of paganism.

This cereal is not a temperamental plant, but it will not reproduce itself in the wild. In addition to human care, to mature it needs fertile soil, sunshine, moisture, and a minimum of 110 to 120 frost-free days, all of which were in more abundance in the southlands than in the north. It can be used in many ways: eaten raw, boiled, parched, or roasted. When dried, it can be ground into meal to make gruel or some kind of bread. The Indians did not realize that it also could be fermented to produce whiskey. They used its stalks as trellises for runners of squash or beans, its tassels as padding for cradleboards, its cobs for fuel. A particularly valuable asset was that when dried, if kept free of weevils and rodents, corn on the cob or shelled could be stored for long periods to be planted later, to nourish an expanding population, or to be eaten in times of crisis. That quality promoted a new mindset of looking toward the future. And ultimately corn gave science the gift of time because today it can be dated with remarkable precision.

The earliest dated corn thus far known in the Mesa Verde Province came from deposits in the Eastern Basketmaker site of North Shelter in Falls Creek. Samples have been dated by accelerator mass spectrometry to the fourth and second centuries B.C. One interpretation of this corn is that Late Archaic novice farmers made use of the alcove long before the Eastern Basketmakers took over.[13]

The corn from the upper Animas drainage was a number of types from more original northern and eastern sources instead of being raised further south. It must also have been adapted to higher elevations. Furthermore, in the Animas and Pine drainages it could be grown by floodwater irrigation in addition to dryland farming on upper benches, whereas dry farming methods were customary in most of the south and west.

Corn not only was responsible for at least seasonal sedentism but for domestic and storage architecture, the latter being the most essential. In the provincial west the Basketmakers used natural overhangs in cliffs as places to protect storage cists, some of which secondarily contained human burials. Apparently these people felt no need for shelters for themselves in these same alcoves but were content to camp in the open. Their peers up on the mesa tops did erect rudimentary single-family habitations with nearby surface storage rooms of poles and mud. At least in the North Shelter in Falls Creek the Eastern Basketmakers put up domiciles within the alcove incorporating interior cists of various sizes and shapes. It is debatable whether enclosed storage was desired as protection from the elements or from raiders. Others in the area placed their house structures in the open but with interior cists. The log wall construction was unlike anything in the west. The Eastern Basketmakers on the Pine River varied the format in making use of large exterior pits for storage and building dwellings with log walls but surrounding them with cobblestone rings. Thus, while architecture had become a necessity of settled life, it differed regionally.

A notable difference was that at the North Shelter and Talus Village in the upper Animas Valley residential remains were close together and not dispersed. Large structures on the Pine River could have been gathering centers for a number of families. Without doubt social organization was still in a state of flux, but there are hints that Eastern Basketmakers were moving toward a clustered settlement pattern and a communal bias.

The rhythms of daily routines in east and west were geared to those of the seasons. When gardens were dormant, there was time to weave baskets, matting, sandals, or cordage, to knap projectile points, to drill and string stone or bone beads, to slap another coat of mud on house walls, to scout for edible wild things, and surely to congregate occasionally to ponder their place and time in the universe as they perceived it. The produced articles were meant for the same purposes but were not stylistically identical, reaffirming deviant roots.[14] In regard to this, one intriguing question concerns the physical identity of the Eastern Basketmakers. Morris was convinced that their skull and facial appearances were very different from the other Basketmakers with whom he had worked.[15] In neither instance was skull deformation practiced. Christy Turner, physical anthropologist then at Arizona State University, found their dentition to be distinctive.[16] Hopefully this matter can be further explored through analyses of burials recovered at the Animas Valley Darkmold site. Since it is on private land and not subject to federal law, consulted Native Americans have not expressed reservations about such study.

The great mysterious void that separates man from the natural world surrounding him continued to wrap its mysteries in a metaphysical vocabulary expressed in painted and etched phantom anthropomorphic, quadrupedic, and geometric figures on rocky palettes. On escarpments beside the San Juan and Colorado Rivers, in the protection of overhangs in Grand Gulch, and high above the tiny log and mud domiciles in the upper Animas Valley are testimonials of their beliefs in some controlling powers beyond themselves. Variant artistic styles and scales unquestionably stem from divergent backgrounds of ethnic groups and now are arbitrarily cobbled together into the one Basketmaker II category. Offerings left with their dead, humble but the best they had to give, show sensitive peoples with a belief in a spiritual afterlife regardless of where they may have originated.

There seems to have been a kind of no man's land between Western and Eastern Basketmaker enclaves. In spite of considerable work in the Mesa Verde core domain during the past three decades, archaeologists have noted few sites of the period. They are difficult to spot from faint surface signs, are often overlaid by later occupation, and in actuality may not have been present. Although sixty-three components have been identified in the Mesa Verde–Mancos, Ute, Montezuma–McElmo, and Dolores drainage units, just four small sites have been excavated. Not unexpectedly, those to the west had characteristics of the Western Basketmakers and those in more eastern locations were allied to the expression there. What is most interesting is that they appeared prior to the larger complexes. Were they left by Late Archaic families or those aspiring to be early Basketmakers?

By the beginning of the fourth century A.D. what always was a thin, relatively shadowy population, calculated at less than one percent of the known prehistoric totals, faded away to parts unknown. The potential for growing corn had brought the two entities to the province. When adverse climatic conditions made that impossible, it was necessary to leave because the gathering of nondomesticates also was no longer an option. The forsaken northern San Juan region then lay essentially empty for several centuries until a new tide of humanity flowed back in to begin again with the raising of corn, by then the unchallenged basis of Puebloan life.

## BASKETMAKER III[17] A.D. 500–750

To the trait list for Basketmaker II add a new style of architecture, pottery technology, bows and arrows to replace atlatls and darts, cultivation of beans and you have Basketmaker III, or Modified Basketmaker to some. Add further a great increase in population and a marked, but probably superficial, cultural homogeneity from provincial border to border. Of course, this description is too simplistic in many aspects but fits others. Framers of the Pecos Classification regarded Basketmaker III as the most important of all the proposed progressive stages. Today scholars recognize that these groups were inheritors from those who went before of a mélange of survival skills and means to enhance them.

Compared to what transpired in Basketmaker II days, beginning in the late sixth century there was a veritable land rush into the Mesa Verde Province. Within seventy-five years or so an estimated one thousand persons were spread over the countryside. That number likely doubled in another seventy-five years. They tended to cluster on the Great Sage Plain, which was little occupied by their predecessors, or up on Mesa Verde, thought to have been devoid of humans previously. Still others reached the Dolores Valley. Surveyors have counted a total of 1,902 Basketmaker III sites in these localities.[18] The upper La Plata Valley at Long Hollow was where Morris began his distinguished career first discovering the Basketmaker III horizon. Off to the west, a small Basketmaker III presence was noted on Cedar Mesa and its eastern slopes.

These Basketmaker III immigrants seem to have come from out of nowhere, that being unidentified refuges to the south of the San Juan River. What drew them to this northern sector that had been silent for so long? Perhaps its emptiness. Furthermore, according to paleoenvironmentalist Kenneth Petersen, the period between A.D. 570 and 700 was one of benign weather with few droughts or killing frosts over much of this portion of the Southwest. In essence, the Basketmaker III immigration was the first of the human tidal surges that swept over the north country from time to time.

Although presumably the new settlers came from dissimilar places that were widely scattered across the Colorado Plateau, they had advanced in such comparable ways that single-family dwellings on the Mesa Verde Ruins Road or in the Step House alcove were much like those at Knobby Knee on Cajon Mesa or on Grass Mesa above the Dolores River. They varied in size. Some had antechambers and some did not. But their basic features were predictable: circular or oval in shape, semisubterranean with central hearth, wing walls, and four roof support post holes indicated. The pits were provided with a ventilator shaft as the stage wore on, but otherwise there was modest alteration of style. That conservatism has hampered students trying to distinguish early from late construction. Most sites were places where just a family or two lived. It was the occasional grouping into hamlets of five to as many as nine pithouses that signaled an incipient village settlement pattern that would typify the future.

Heightened emphasis on farming entailed greater concern for adequate storage for the future. This is shown by numerous differing kinds of constructions, some above ground and some below, that were randomly placed near the pithouses. Excavators were able to define spots where preparations of foodstuffs or raw materials had taken place. On the Great Sage Plain stockades similar to that encircling Knobby Knee were fashionable for undetermined reasons. Whatever else, it would seem they instilled a sense of community.

The people of the A.D. 600s had become full-time farmers concentrating on three vegetables, corn, beans, and squash, but also making use of volunteer wild plants that sprouted in their gardens. Tansy mustard, goosefoot, amaranth, and bee plant quickly germinated in disturbed ground and just as quickly ended up in cooking pots to supply vitamins lacking in the usual triad. However, just to have a further measure of security, the settlers chose locations with an eye toward water sources and woodlands that might be exploited for plants or animals. Over time the meat supply inevitably diminished, as reflected by decreased numbers of projectile points recovered archaeologically. Ironically, with improved weaponry for the hunt, there were fewer targets.

Dependence upon agriculture and the large investment in time and effort to build granaries may have caused these Basketmakers to stay in one place for more extended periods than elsewhere. If the climate was conducive to successful farming, there was no reason to pack up and move over to the next inviting ridge. Still, archaeologist Wilshusen thinks the hamlets may have been lived in no more than fifteen years and the protovillages no more than forty years.

The addition of beans to the diet was made possible through the manufacture of earthenware vessels in which they could be boiled for a long time. The prepottery cooking method of parching foods in basketry trays with hot rocks did not work with beans at elevations hovering around seven thousand feet. Having containers that could be placed directly over heat also contributed to other culinary experimentations, such as stewed meat, soups, or boiled greens.

The brown pottery made from unaltered alluvial clays first discovered in Pine and San Juan river sites has now been shown to have been in use by many Colorado Plateau tribes and in the San Juan River drainage throughout the Basketmaker III interval. In the late A.D. 500s it was replaced in the central and western portions of the province by a ware that incorporated temper additives and fired to a dull gray or off-white color. This was fashioned into a variety of undecorated, small forms for many utilitarian purposes. It made up about ninety percent of the total output. Some innovative potters dabbled with painting loosely structured designs on small, deep bowls using a mineral pigment that turned black under heat. It was obvious beginner's work but served such useful household needs that pottery became an indispensable furnishing for its users and of inestimable value to modern investigators of regional prehistory as a hallmark of temporal and functional progression.

As the curtain was coming down on the Basketmaker III periods, a red pottery made its appearance. It was a relatively short-lived special production of artisans in the southwestern part of the province that was traded into the heartlands.

After two centuries the slow-paced Basketmaker III began to give way to allow another rung up the cultural ladder. Many questions about its origins, agricultural intensification, and social cohesion remain as fodder for future inquiry.

## PUEBLO I[19] A.D. 750–900

Continuity of the cultural statement blurs distinctions between the Basketmaker III period and Pueblo I. It was still a simple, agrarian way of life but demographic, material, and social changes were imminent. Sites considered in the formative years of regional archaeology as being of the earlier stage now are seen as part of the opening rounds of the later one. Some researchers avoid being specific by using the hyphenated designation of Basketmaker III–Pueblo I. Crow Canyon Archaeological Center scholars prefer adjusting the traditional time frame by making Basketmaker III fifty years longer and Pueblo I fifty years shorter in order to accommodate gradual, rather than abrupt, modifications. Everlasting life flows along, but scientists need to dissect time into manageable segments so as to explain the course of events. In 1914 at the very beginning of Mesa Verdean archaeological studies, Morris happened upon sites in the Ute Pasture southeast of Mesa Verde that later fit into the Pueblo I category. In that same year he also had the good fortune of digging into earlier deposits at Long Hollow. At the time, Morris was puzzled, as subsequent observers have been, about how to distinguish transitional stages between these two phases.

Between Morris's discoveries and the definitive inquiries into the period made by the Dolores Archaeological Program and the Crow Canyon Archaeological Center some seven decades later, other diggers exposed Pueblo I presence across the entire Mesa Verde Province: Roberts on Stollsteimer Mesa in the east; Brew on Alkali Ridge in the west; Martin at Ackmen; and Lancaster, O'Bryan, and Hayes at Mesa Verde in the central zone. Those finds, together with the late 1970s and early 1980s excavations in the Dolores and Montezuma Valleys, confirm a large-scale influx of people moving north of the San Juan River to merge with an indigenous population long content with the status quo and bringing in a yeasty mix of new ideas probably derived from varied sources in New Mexico, Arizona, and Utah that were to mold Puebloan lifeways for generations to come.

Current thinking by some researchers is that the Pueblo I population of the Mesa Verde Province may have been the largest of any during the eight hundred years of ancestral Pueblo presence there. Others believe they were far fewer than Pueblo III groups. The Pueblo I population peaked just before the closing years of this stage at an estimated and phenomenal ten thousand persons. Early in their stay, these peoples concentrated along the upper San Juan and Piedra drainages, around the Durango environs on the Animas, and in the western sectors of the Great Sage Plain. Toward the end of their time in the northlands they were situated in the latter and on Mesa Verde. They avoided Cedar Mesa in Utah but preferred the more exposed lower Alkali Ridge to the east.

Sites of this period have suffered much destruction. Because of their barely discernible surface evidence, they have been plowed under by twentieth-century farmers attempting to use the same piece of land. Furthermore, they have been ripped apart by relic collectors, especially in the heights around Durango in the

1930s when hundreds of pots were taken from burials.[20] Fortunately, enough have escaped depredations to show that, as undistinguished as it might appear, this was a time of consequential foment and redirection.

One very noticeable change was the practice of skull deformation. Was it at first an accident that dismayed an infant's parents but was subsequently perpetuated? Did the immigrants bring this custom with them? And why? It is a prehistoric example of beauty being in the eye of the beholder.

Architecture most explicitly mirrors new ways in which eighth-century ancestral Pueblos then were viewing their lives. They began living on the surface of the ground rather than halfway down in it. Rather than considerations of health benefits, it most likely was a matter of conserving energy and resources. Construction of rectangular cells was variable but most commonly was of jacal walls on upright slab foundations. This model was nothing new to the builders because in smaller, often less substantial, versions it had been used since the time when storage units were first needed. What was new was that the rooms adjoined each other in linear or arced layout so that a number of families dwelt side by side rather than in scattered quarters. They shared plazas, central pit structures, and middens. Conservative almost to a fault, these units typically were in the same relationships to each other. Moreover, various numbers of these households were grouped together to comprise villages on average of 125 rooms but up to 400. Given the unsubstantial construction, most rooms probably were usable for little more than a generation. Nor were all rooms occupied contemporaneously.

The villages and outlying field houses and work spaces made up communities with surrounding agricultural and resource territories, or to the Crow Canyon archaeologists, catchments. This housing style and arrangement indicates an emerging, structured social organization that would form the communal basis of future Puebloan society. At the same time, small family clusters continued to dwell apart from the villages, not all identical but generally comparable.

Architecture reveals that these groups were adopting a religious orientation that continues to dominate their thoughts. The partially underground chamber was retained, squared up, and dug deeper. While residents continued to use it for living space, as indicated by household items left on floors, the kiva was more decisively meant for special functions for families or clans. The sipapu was standard, and in some instances shallow floor holes were sockets for prayer sticks placed around temporary altars. Much more spacious semisubterranean chambers, or Great Kivas, few in number and restricted in distribution, were designed for group use. In addition to integrating communities, they are another clue to greater interest in probable personification of esoteric knowledge enriched by outward material display. Without documentation and surviving trappings, what these ceremonies were cannot be known, but the richness of modern Puebloan ritual must have begun then, as did a priestly class to oversee it. That does not seem to have been the case throughout the province as one indication of diversity among immigrant groups.

In consideration of ceramic assemblages, Crow Canyon researchers postulate three distinct assemblages in the province during this time. The wares in common use were stylistically dissimilar. Made by the same procedures to serve the same purposes, their composition and decorations were sufficiently different to hint at variant histories of the makers. Off to the west was a Bluff red ware production; in the central province a decorated type named Piedra Black-on-White dominated; the eastern group made Rosa Black-on-White. In all zones utilitarian gray pottery was predominate, frequently distinguished from Basketmaker III grays by exterior coils left at the neck areas of jars.

Favorable climatic conditions in the A.D. 700s and 800s and rich loess soils in the uplands invited these farmers. Huge outlays of toil were needed, but to prosper they depended on winter snows, summer rains, and long, warm growing days. Their success led to more people than the land could support. The last two decades of the A.D. 800s then saw a downturn for them when weather patterns altered again, the farming belt shrank, and their survival was at risk. A slow exodus ensued that took some further south into lower elevations near the San Juan River and perhaps out into the great interior basin where the Chacoan florescence was to shine. Their leavings became the stuff of archaeology. The thousands who had thrived in the province were reduced to no more than twenty-five hundred by century's end.

## Pueblo II[21] A.D. 900–1150

The "bust" part of the boom-and-bust cycle of early Mesa Verdean occupation came in the first half of the tenth century. Those who did not leave the province as times worsened in the late A.D. 800s spread thinly across the region to find pockets of refuge here and there for a few years and then move on in a seemingly endless search for something better. Slowly, harsh natural conditions mitigated; the hardy souls survived and multiplied; and unknowingly the Pecos Classification's Pueblo II period arrived.

The Crow Canyon review lists sixteen of the best known sites left from the early one hundred-year portion of this period (A.D. 950–1050). They are equally divided between the Montezuma-McElmo and Mesa Verde–Mancos drainages. That tabulation probably reflects more archaeological work accomplished there than actual distribution of the ancestral Pueblos at that time. A hundred miles or more to the east, other peoples were hanging on near the confluence of the San Juan and Piedra Rivers and upstream of the latter. Otherwise, present research suggests that most of the northern San Juan region was untenanted.

The residential plan of the hangers-on was that of the past. An extended family or two joined forces to erect a double row of contiguous surface rooms of jacal for domestic and storage use, a circular kiva in front, randomly placed work areas, perhaps a tiny, subterranean mealing room, an outlying equivalent of a modern landfill, and occasionally an encircling stockade. This was Prudden's unit pueblo layout identified a century ago. The gradual increase in sandstone masonry brought the complex closer to his model. Great Kivas were more common than previously and probably contributed a necessary sense of cultural stability.

The pottery-making craft flourished. The basic coiling method remained unchanged. Recent observations at Mesa Verde National Park and on the Ute Reservation to the south confirm the early use of the stone-lined trench for firing.[22] Tactile dexterity, use of variable nonplastic tempers, and bolder geometric patterning with mixtures of mineral and vegetal pigments doubtless stemmed from generations of experience that always was strongly controlled by convention and functional requirements. The most significant addition to the ceramic repertory, and one that would endure for the remainder of the ancestral Pueblo history in the northlands, was the introduction of textured exterior surfaces on utilitarian gray ware. Without doubt, this treatment, now called *corrugation*, grew out of the earlier habit of leaving a few coils at the neck area of jars unsmoothed on their exteriors, decoratively incidental but functionally important as reinforcement for a vulnerable part of the vessel. In the corrugation mode, the exterior coils on the entire exterior surface not only were not scraped smooth as in the earlier gray wares but were precisely pinched horizontally coil by coil as the pot was being formed from the bottom up. The pinching pressure helped weld construction coils together but also allowed more of a pot's surface to be exposed to the heat of cook fires. The roughened surfaces also facilitated handling a large, filled container. Carefully executed corrugation created a handsome, uniquely ancestral Puebloan statement, with fingerprints often left as permanent maker's marks.

Despite this ceramic high point that may have begun about the middle A.D.

900s, the early stage of the Pueblo II period in the north appears to have been one of a small populace struggling through a time of general cultural stagnation.

Good times began to return as the eleventh century unfolded. With a long history of ready mobility, people on the move again headed north of the San Juan to relocate on the uplands, sometimes on the same spot where their ancestors had lived long before. The Crow Canyon tabulations of best known sites of the A.D. 1050–1150 time frame show a continued preference for the central heartlands. Other migrants settled back on Cedar Mesa to the west, down the lower La Plata and Animas Valleys, and up the Chimney Rock cuesta at the foot of the San Juan Mountains. Very likely the new wave of settlers spilled out of various districts to the south or east and once again revitalized a stalled developmental sequence.

There always are aggressive and regressive individuals in any culture. That is well illustrated in Pueblo II Mesa Verdean architecture. Some builders gradually adopted the use of sandstone blocks set in mud mortar for surface walls. Easily fractured sandstone strata comprise the primary geological structure of the Colorado Plateau, making that material a valuable, virtually inexhaustible resource for substantial construction. At first such walls were a single stone in width with those stones being only roughly shaped. As the style evolved, walls became two shaped stones in width which supported upper levels. In some localities the faces of the blocks were pecked, or "dimpled," so that mud plaster, another element that came into use, would more securely adhere to the backing. In other places the masons did not bother with this step. Meanwhile, some workers maintained the venerable jacal construction for surface rooms, apparently thinking that the effort and time to secure and process stone were not worth it, particularly if they did not anticipate a lengthy occupation. Or maybe it was mere resistance to change.

Both those ready to move ahead and those not continued to dig small, underground rooms where women in cool darkness could kneel before their metates in bins to tediously do their daily chores of grinding the staff of life.

While kivas were a standard element of most settlements, some continued to have earthen walls and others were carefully masonry lined. Some acquired new features, such as masonry pilasters on encircling benches as roof supports and more pronounced recesses on their southern flanks. Others did not.

Not all masonry was sandstone. In the Aztec area builders made use of cobblestones that pave the river terraces. Obviously this is less stable building material that could not be stacked up to more than one story and soon collapsed once steady maintenance ceased.

In the core area the usual architectural layout as it developed was a compact houseblock of a number of rooms, some several stories in height, kivas incorporated into the building mass, and circular towers either isolated or connected by an underground passageway to a kiva.

Regardless of materials utilized, the small family unit was most widespread but sometimes with enough close association for interaction that culminated in communal gathering places such as Great Kivas.

Dryland farming was the rule, but in the central sectors it was augmented by terraced gardens on talus slopes, check dams across minor drainages, and reservoirs to collect runoff waters or direct and store stream flows. These features were seldom adopted in other parts of the province where topographical features were not suitable. Flood waters along the Piedra and La Plata Rivers must have been important. Farmers in the Aztec area depended to some extent on irrigation canals off the Animas River. There may have been times of severe drought when the water level was too low for them to have been useful. Even in the best of times, farming in the province was unpredictable.

Pottery production kept apace, with enormous quantities made and broken annually. The black-on-white decorative mode commanded the output of service vessels. Corrugated types overwhelmed plain grays in the utilitarian category. Small quantities of red pottery were present.

About the mid-A.D. 1000s further incursions occurred at opposite ends of the province. Kayentans moved into the Glen Canyon and Cedar Mesa areas, where they continued their customary architectural and ceramic processes while living as neighbors next to unassimilated Mesa Verdeans. They probably were responsible for the small assemblages of Tsegi Orange Ware that reached the center province.

A more singular migration into the province was by groups from the Gallina-Jemez Mountain stretches of northern New Mexico who went to the Chimney Rock cuesta on the upper Piedra River. Presumably a remnant population was absorbed by the invaders who introduced their unique house and pottery styles.

Not to be outdone, at the end of the eleventh century Chacoans joined the tide flowing northward. They followed three migration routes. One crossed the middle course of the San Juan River, went a bit further north into the lower Animas Valley, and branched off to the extreme eastern periphery of the Colorado Plateau. Salmon Ruin at the crossing, Aztec East and West on the Animas, and Chimney Rock Pueblo at the head of the Piedra Valley resulted.

A second route was northwest out of Chaco Canyon, following the Chaco drainage to its confluence with the San Juan, north through the pass between Ute Mountain and Mesa Verde, and out into the broad Montezuma Valley. A string of colonies was planted from Escalante on the east to Lowry in the west.

A third way Chacoans or their influence came into the province was down the San Juan as far as Bluff and then angling north up Cottonwood Wash and other canyons along the east side of Cedar Mesa. One settlement at Bluff and several others further inland were established.

In their review of regional prehistory, Crow Canyon scholars expanded by fifty years the usual time allotted to the Pueblo II period in order to include the Chacoan era. Thus far they have been unable to satisfactorily assess the impact those incursions might have had on the local scene.

Researchers have proposed many motivations for this Chacoan expansion beyond the San Juan Basin. One idea is that Salmon Ruin and the Aztec sites may have served as administrative facilities for an economic system designed to gather and send desired resources south to headquarters in Chaco Canyon. These centers were the largest of the northern outliers and more than any resembled the canyon Great Houses in layout; they were downtown Chaco transferred to the suburbs. Traders from them distributed quantities of Chaco-style ceramics to locals in the La Plata Valley, but what might have been carted south over the Great North Road is unknown. A welcoming natural setting with a large indigenous population persuaded or coerced to support the Chaco system likely made the Aztec community so powerful it challenged or usurped central authority.

A third center resulting from this easternmost migration was Chimney Rock Pueblo. Built in a compact style typical of modest-sized outliers in the southern parts of the San Juan Basin, it was the only known northern one with an avowed religious purpose. Initially that purpose may not have been to celebrate an astronomical phenomenon but rather the stony embodiments of dual supernaturals, the realization of the added attraction of the lunar standstills coming later. One can assume that the aim was to satisfy Chacoan spirituality and not necessarily to convert the natives.

The central outliers in the Montezuma Valley were generally in prominent locations. That and their formal appearance in contrast to the Late Pueblo II Mesa Verdean architectural styles implies an intent to impress or dominate a more humble populace for social, political, or economic reasons. Contrarily, it may have been a mere ethnic attitude of how one should properly live. These persons may have had no reason for being there other than to make a living after Chaco itself became overcrowded. Other than introducing more trade goods than had been in circulation earlier, they do not seem to have had serious impact on the Mesa Verdeans other than in their architecture. Whether these buildings were erected by migrants from Chaco or whether local masons copied a popular style is still an open question. Crow Canyon scientists refer to them as Chaco-era Great Houses.

The outliers to the far west appear more Chacoesque than Chacoan. Perhaps they were a kind of backwoods attempt to emulate the powerful and prestigious.

The Chaco interlude lasted for just thirty or fewer years. When the center in the San Juan Basin collapsed, the northern satellites were deserted. A few were later reoccupied but others were forever stilled.

Coeval with the Chaco migrations, peoples from the Chuska region at the west border of the San Juan Basin also may have crossed the San Juan and moved onto the Ute Mountain piedmont. However, that notion is based solely on pottery recovered there and not on solid indication of actual settlement.

Whether the violence that now has been verified to have occurred in the central province during the mid-A.D. 1100s can be attributed to the death throes of the Chaco Phenomenon is a matter of continuing debate. Regardless, there was obvious unrest exacerbated by a worsening of climatic conditions. Some emigration from the province resulted. A notable example was the complete depopulation of the entire eastern third of the province when the residents there are thought to have rejoined their relatives in the Gallina and northern Rio Grande domains. A few tree ring dates for construction timbers in the central and western districts reflect a dramatic decrease there in new housing. A probable hiatus in occupation of Cedar Mesa and Red Rock Plateau occurred in the mid-A.D. 1100s. Thus, the Pueblo II period ended as it began in a time of depression.

## PUEBLO III[23] A.D. 1150–1300

The repetitive cycle of immigration and emigration in the prehistoric record of the ancestral Puebloan Mesa Verde Province assured renewal of cultural vitality. Incomers had hope, ambition, and ideas. This was demonstrated once again by those who left in the A.D. 1150s, then reconsidered, regrouped, and returned thirty years later with a new body of relatives. Many claimed unoccupied patches of good agricultural land amidst homesteaders and villagers on the mesas of the Montezuma-McElmo and Mesa Verde–Mancos drainage units. Some went back to Cedar Mesa and Glen Canyon. More moved into the three river district of La Plata, Animas, and San Juan now called Totah. They took advantage of the vacated Chaco Great Houses at Salmon and Aztec and remodeled them to suit their own tastes. The northern La Plata and Animas Valleys and all the province eastward were left vacant.

The small, unit pueblo houseblock with a kiva and trash dump continued to be the most common in dispersed settings. On occasion several houseblocks were at a single site. More frequently through time, they were grouped into communities of fifty or more structures with one cluster having specialized elements such as a Great Kiva, D-shaped or multiwalled structure, or towers which the Crow Canyon archaeologists now term *public architecture*. These presumed centers perhaps were a sort of county seat where disputes over land use, such as surely arose as the population dramatically increased and parcels worked by individual villages overlapped or adjoined, were arbitrated. Further, they were where scattered residents came together for obligatory rituals to satisfy religiosity and for conviviality to satisfy sexuality that most likely led to some mating. Then back to the farm.

The Crow Canyon review lists thirty-six sites of Early Pueblo III period from A.D. 1150 to 1225. For the remainder of the thirteenth century, the same review lists sixty-two sites or clusters of sites. It goes without saying that prosperity had brought many persons into the province. However, by the mid-thirteenth century most were not living in their own peaceful space but in densely packed villages of an average of 125 rooms. This observation does not apply to those out west who remained dispersed.

The question of how many individuals were residing in these numerous structures and others as yet unknown has a special appeal because of its associated intangibles, all of which can shed light on interpretive contexts. How long were these places occupied? Could that be judged by the extent and depth of the pile of rubbish left behind or by construction materials or methods? What was the total room count? Real or estimated? How many of them were habitations? How many were for storage? Did one room or suite of rooms equate with one family? What was the average size of the families? The scholars working on these perplexing problems devised elaborate formulas based on several databases and their own observations. They came up with widely varying population estimates ranging from ten thousand persons to thirty thousand with perhaps up to fifteen thousand having been present at any one given time. Whether these figures are accurate for the core area, which does not include the middle San Juan district and the western borderlands, there is little doubt but that the Mesa Verde Province was the homeland for a century and a half of more ancestral Pueblos than any other sector of the Colorado Plateau.

The Pueblo III population growth made intensification of agriculture critical. More land was cleared and planted for dryland farming of corn, beans, and squash. These vegetables were supplemented by wild plants that typically invade disturbed ground. Some hastily built shelters may have been field houses. Water control assumed even greater importance for both domestic and farming needs.

About the mid-thirteenth century some community centers relocated from open mesa tops to the often bifurcated rims of the many canyons that slice the territory, and others shifted up from canyon bottoms or talus. Still others moved into natural cliff-side alcoves. That is where white settlers some 650 years later first met up with them and indirectly opened up the new science of Southwestern archaeology.

One result of this compacting of residences was stimulation of the pottery craft. Staggering amounts of utilitarian and decorated service vessels were made and fired in trenches that could accommodate hundreds of objects. Couple mass production and large population with the practice of leaving pottery as offerings in graves and an irresistible magnet for relic collectors was created.

No longer was it just a matter of a woman and her daughters siting in the shade of a ramada and coiling up a pot or two in their leisure time, if, in fact, there was such a thing. Even building on generations of experience, it had to be an immensely time-consuming activity to seek out and prepare raw materials, fashion dozens of receptacles for various functions over a period of time, set them aside to dry, then hand carry fragile greenware over rough ground to some distant firing trench, cut fuel, stack the trench, tend the fire, and anxiously wait. No other handicraft is wrought with comparable anxiety.

The concentration of numerous artisans must have meant lively exchange of ideas and a spirit of competition. Human nature said that products had to be superior to those of one's neighbors. Even though the vessels were destined for daily routines, the powerful aesthetic vigor of their makers demanded beauty as well as utility. The Mesa Verde Black-on-Whites reached a pinnacle of excellence with bold, geometric, balanced patterns displaying skilled draftsmanship. Students of art might see that the design grammar and its execution came from a passive society comfortable with itself that through this medium was translating the angularity of the physical world surrounding it.

A specialized work force may have developed within or between communities with familial groups banding together for joint firings. After the Chacoans departed, virtually all the pottery in use was a home product.

One exception was in the western borderlands where Kayentans settled and introduced their customary ceramic assemblage and passed some of it on to Mesa Verdean neighbors.

The mug shape in large and small size was added to the form repertory. Some had false bottoms with clay pellets to rattle between them. Others had modeled animal figures playfully crawling up handles. It is of some interest that the use to which these mugs were put is uncertain because a beverage of any kind has not been identified. It is possible that archaeologists have wrongly associated the form with what would have been Western usage. Maybe the mugs were clan icons not intended as drinking vessels. Another innovation was the so-called kiva jar. Its bulbous body was outfitted with a flanged orifice topped with a knobbed lid and surely had some special use, such as in a kiva.

Some undercurrent of trouble beset the Mesa Verde Province in the three decades between A.D. 1250 and 1280. Paradise was about to be lost. Most of the ancestral Pueblos no longer chose to live isolated and unprotected out on open land. They shared the trials of close quarters in the canyon rim communities at Goodman Point, Sand Canyon, and southern Cajon Mesa enclosed by low walls, warned by sentinels in towers, or jealously guarding springs. Others were in the cliff dwellings at Mesa Verde and Lion and Johnson Canyons where they could huddle or could have been starved out. Whether turmoil came from humans against humans within or without the grouping probably will remain one of the mysteries. Bodies that were not formally buried as noted in a few sites, traumatized female remains, possible cannibalism, widespread destruction of structures by fire, and locations that can be interpreted as having been selected for defensive considerations are archaeologically demonstrated clues to an increasingly difficult environment. Less discernible archaeologically are the social footprints of cultural exhaustion: discontent, uncertainty, hunger, and fear. And then there was the drought of A.D. 1276–1299.

That factor traditionally has been considered the cause for final abandonment. Other environmental problems such as shortened growing seasons due to a colder than normal period, depleted natural resources, infertility of overused farm lands, and water shortages all could have added to the distress of the ancestral Pueblos.[24]

Researchers are in disagreement over the time of withdrawal. Some see a drift away from the province starting as early as the beginning of the thirteenth century.[25] Others prefer a more gradual exodus coming late in the century. Lipe advocates a rapid abandonment around A.D. 1280, the latest construction date according to tree ring samples from Mesa Verde. Nor do the scientists know where the emigrants may have gone. A ray of hope for some may have been the rise of a religious stimulus in the kachina cult emerging among Pueblo peoples to the south. Another probable draw was kin relationships to inhabitants of the northern Rio Grande where providential waters always flowed. These may have been what Lipe calls the seductive "pull" factors that countered the negative "push" factors of hard times. Whatever the bundle of man-made or nature-inflicted causes, by A.D. 1300 it was ancestral Pueblo emigration from the Mesa Verde Province for the last time.

### THEN, THE NOMADS[26]

For two hundred years the land lay deserted and ghostly. Winds out of Monument Valley continued to drop their load of fine Aeolian soil to mantle the red ground of the Great Sage Plain. Tumbleweeds raced before them until captured by kiva depressions. Sagebrush and thistles peppered garden plots and took root in fertile middens. Slowly, dwelling walls on mesa tops crumbled into formless hillocks of rocks and solidified earthen clods. Hovenweep towers stubbornly clung to the brinks and lost their roofs. Mesa Verde cliff dwellings transformed into hollow-eyed, haunted houses with spirits of the remarkable Old People omnipresent.

It was those spirits that kept the province ruins from being violated by nomadic peoples who began infiltrating the northern San Juan region by the A.D. 1500s or possibly earlier. Ute Indian tribes may have come first. They were followed shortly by the Navajos.

Cultural historians believe that the Ute Indians wandered eastward out of the Great Basin of Utah and Nevada but when remains uncertain for a variety of reasons. Typically, nomads leave little telltale evidence of their passing because it is transitory, any shelters are flimsy, their material wealth is sparse, and their numbers are few. Further, little archaeological investigation of the Ute past has been done and virtually none in this province. Added to that is the problem of distinguishing old Ute from old Navajo remains because their lifestyles and accoutrements were very similar.

Ute presence in the Mesa Verde Province cannot be demonstrated to have intersected with that of the Late Pueblo III ancestral Pueblos. However, bands of Utes may have been just to the north in about A.D. 1100 and could well have hunted and even raided further south.

Archaeological surveys have identified (but not excavated) 116 Ute sites in the Mesa Verde Province. They are concentrated in the eastern drainages of the upper San Juan–Piedra, Animas, and La Plata. That distribution is not surprising because the San Luis Valley on the east side of the Rockies was their more traditional protohistoric territory. Ute residential sites are made up of a few wickiups, which are conical arrangements of upright poles covered with brush or animal skins. Hearths and a small trash scatter of several kinds of stone projectile points and crude brown pottery may be present. These were camps used once or repeatedly. Most interesting are historic-era places where the Utes stripped the bark from ponderosa pines for food or medicine.

Spanish documents indicate that Utes were in the general vicinity of their control in the A.D. 1600s. Some Utes left the very upper San Juan reaches to spend winters in the New Mexican Chama Valley, where they were given rations. By then they had acquired horses through trade or stealth and dramatically turned into bellicose warriors who regarded Navajos as their particular enemies. Their newly appreciated means of transportation put them in contact with Plains Indians from whom they adopted teepees, skin garments, feather headdresses, and beadwork.

Today there are two Ute reservations in the Mesa Verde Province: the Southern Ute in the east and the Ute Mountain Ute in the core area and a small detached zone in southeast Utah. The latter tribe owns a significant chunk of the ancestral Pueblo past to which they are racially but not cultur-ally related. It operates a preserve to show off four cliff dwellings first explored by the likes of the Wetherills, Nordenskiold, and Morris. Ute guides have learned something about their predecessors; several work as rangers at Mesa Verde National Park. The tribe also controls irrigated farmland where Archaic hunters-gatherers tarried and where some twelfth-century Puebloans were cooked and eaten.

Roughly contemporaneous with prehistoric Utes were Athabaskan-speak-ing nomads who came down the Great Plains from Canada. Upon reaching the greater Southwest, they split into Navajo and Apache bands. Perhaps in the early A.D. 1500s, the Navajos gradually went into the eastern drainages of the Mesa Verde Province, where they competed for resources with the Utes. Archaeologists have identified 162 Navajo sites from prehistoric into historic times, a majority of them there. The debris marking these sites is a paltry sample of grey potsherds, stone projectile points, a few forked-stick hogans, storage pits, and sweat lodges. By A.D. 1700 the Utes had driven them south of the San Juan River and out of the Mesa Verde Province. Today they have returned to a tiny patch of reservation land north of the San Juan just inside the Utah border.

Thus far the once nomads now semipastoral tribes of the Mesa Verde Province have not seriously met the archaeologists' trowels. ❈

# Epilogue

Exactly one hundred years after the first known sighting of Cliff Palace, residents of the Four Corners experienced the same combination of unfavorable environmental circumstances that may have driven the ancestral Pueblos away from the northern San Juan region. Successive years for more than a decade of less than normal precipitation left the land tinder dry, inviting repeated, fierce lightning strikes to set it ablaze. Thousands of acres of wooded landscape went up in stifling smoke and clouds of gray ash.

Scientists have long considered drought to be a major cause for the Puebloan abandonment of this area. They now add extreme violence to the list of demoralizing factors. The current spectacle of the rampages of nature show that fire was another of the multiple problems besetting these thirteenth-century peoples. With out-of-control wildfires that left the ground so baked that plants could not grow and which may, in fact, have consumed some dwellings, they must have thought that Mother Earth and Father Sky were telling them that it was time to go and never to return.

Lightning-ignited wildfires are a natural phenomenon in the Mesa Verde Province that accompany the late summer monsoonal flow. The first superintendent of the newly established Mesa Verde National Park stated in his initial 1907 report, probably with relief, that there had been no fires in the preserve that year.[1] He surely would be stunned to know that three-fourths of the park (some sixty square miles) would be incinerated within less than a century. In times past conflagrations just burned themselves out, but with the development of the park, it became imperative to control them as expeditiously as possible in order to protect the ruins and the visitors who came to see them. That has been an enormously difficult task because of the rugged, roadless terrain. It has involved hundreds of firefighters, airborne slurry, heavy land equipment, and archaeologists trying to guide the activities away from prehistoric sites that might be damaged. Seared vegetation on most mesas will remain for centuries as a reminder of the relentless power of natural forces. Fortunately, the antiquities have remained relatively unharmed—toasted here and there but still present. There is little aboriginal surface material in open sites to be eradicated. The cliff-side alcoves without vegetation and the houses they shelter remain intact thus far. One positive aspect of the fires is that they have exposed many previously unknown artifact scatters and small house mounds. These contribute little information about the lifeways of the Pueblos but do add to the tally and reveal usage of parts of the park and adjacent Ute land not studied earlier. An unanticipated result of public interest in regional archaeological attractions was a local economic crisis when the park had to be closed at the height of tourist season because of fire damage and threat to personal safety.

In the summer of 2002 fires raced across the Ute Pasture, where Earl Morris began his fieldwork, and Talus Village on the upper Animas, where he ended it twenty-five years later. The plant cover was consumed, but there was no remaining cultural evidence to be destroyed. Ironically, both sites had burned prehistorically. Whether that was before or sometime after being vacated is uncertain. Archaeologists generally have attributed such events to be ritualistic termination of occupancy. Even though areas surrounding the structures may have been somewhat denuded for human purposes, the current situation raises the possibility of destructive wildfires being one of many negative elements that determined the end of Puebloan stay in the northlands. ✠

# Notes

### Chapter 1

1. Lister, R. H. and F. C. Lister, 1981, 11.
2. Ibid., 6.
3. Lister, F. C., 1997a, 123.
4. Lister, R. H. and F. C. Lister, 1990, 4.
5. Lipe, 1999a, 52; Smith, D. A., 1988; Thompson, 1994, 5.
6. Lipe, 1999a, 52–53.
7. Ibid., 53.
8. Lister, R. H. and F. C. Lister, 1987, 4; 1990, 6.
9. Howe, 1947, 12.
10. Stein and McKenna, 1988, 64–65.
11. Erdman, 1970, 16–17.
12. Holmes, 1876, 17.
13. See Jackson, 1947, and Waitley, 1999, for biographical information about this man, his sketches, and his photographs of the West and its native peoples.
14. Holmes, 1876, 15; 1886, 285, 314.
15. Judd, 1968, 20
16. Morgan, 1879, 300–306. Hayes, 1985, 13, states that this Morgan was a distant relative of Lewis Morgan, a prominent ethnologist of the late nineteenth century.
17. Lister, R. H. and F. C. Lister, 1990, 5.
18. Robertson, 1990, 62.
19. McClurg, 1930, 218.
20. Letter of Jesse Nusbaum to Herbert Gregory, April 4, 1950. Mesa Verde National Park Archives.
21. McNitt, 1957, 21; Smith, D. A., 1988, 19.
22. Wetherill, 1977, 63.
23. Ibid., 96–97.
24. McNitt, 1957, 24–25; Smith, D. A., 1988, 21.
25. Wetherill, 1977, 110.
26. Nusbaum, R., 1980, 68. Jesse Nusbaum named four men, one of whom was part of a contract survey team in 1875, mapping the northern boundary of the Southern Ute Indian Reservation.
27. According to Mason's recollection, this was the route used. Watson, n.d., 6.
28. Nusbaum, J. L., unnamed, unnumbered manuscript. Mesa Verde National Park Archives. Watson, n.d., 10. Mason is cited as having found only two timbers and all roofing removed.
29. Nichols, 1965, 51–56.
30. Group C, No. 1, Hazzard-Hearst Collection, University of Pennsylvania, undated. Copy at Edge of the Cedars Museum.
31. Chapin, 1988, 156f.
32. Wetherill, 1977, 21.
33. Letter of B. K. Wetherill to superintendent, Smithsonian Institution, December 20, 1889. Tom Wetherill Archives.
34. Letter of B. K. Wetherill to superintendent, Smithsonian Institution, January 30, 1890. Mesa Verde National Park Archives.
35. Letter of B. K. Wetherill to William Holmes, February 11, 1890. Mesa Verde National Park Archives.
36. Snead, 2001, 8–9.
37. Letter of William Holmes to B. K. Wetherill, January 31, 1890. Mesa Verde National Park Archives.
38. Letter of B. K. Wetherill to William Holmes, February 11, 1890. Mesa Verde National Park Archives.
39. Letter of B. K. Wetherill to William Holmes, March 3, 1890. Mesa Verde National Park Archives.
40. Letter of S. P. Langley to B. K. Wetherill, February 20, 1890. Mesa Verde National Park Archives.

41. Nickens, 1976.

42. Gustaf Nordenskiold is often erroneously referred to as Baron, even by the Wetherills. The title was his father's exclusively. Fletcher, 1979, 345–70. Apparently young Gustaf chose not to correct his American friends but enjoyed the implied status of the title.

43. Arrhenius, o., 1984, 14–15.

44. Nordenskiold, 1979, 15–20, Fig. 5.

45. The same painted pattern is preserved in Cliff Palace and Balcony House, among others.

46. Chapin, 1988.

47. Nordenskiold called them "heliotypes," pictures obtained from sensitive gelatin film exposed to light.

48. Nordenskiold, 1979, 85–92.

49. Scott, 1973, 128–40.

50. Nordenskiold, 1979, 39–41.

51. Ibid., Plates XXIIIa, XXIV, 2.

52. Wetherill, 1977, 137–38. Gillmor and Wetherill, 1953, 42, give John credit for this discovery and the interpretation of it.

53. Nusbaum, J. L., 1981, 31. Actually, the Nordenskiold group dug into the entrance of one of the pithouses, and the Wetherill party probed along a section of roofing.

54. Ibid., 31.

55. Nordenskiold, 1979, Fig. 13.

56. Arrhenius, o., 1984, 8.

57. Letter of Charles A. Bartholomew to R. V. Belt, September 19, 1891. National Archives, copy in Mesa Verde National Park Archives.

58. Smith, D. A., 1988, 29–30.

59. Letter of R. V. Belt to Charles A. Bartholomew, October 2, 1891. National Archives, copy in Mesa Verde National Park Archives.

60. Letter of Richard Wetherill to Gustaf Nordenskiold, February 29, 1892. Mesa Verde National Park Archives.

61. According to Prudden, 1906, 173, the Utes also dug for relics.

62. Retzius, 1979, Appendix I-XI.

63. Letter of Richard Wetherill to Gustaf Nordenskiold, June 12, 1893. Mesa Verde National Park Archives.

64. Letter of B. K. Wetherill to Gustaf Nordenskiold, February 20, 1894. Mesa Verde National Park Archives.

65. Winston Hurst, personal communication.

66. Crampton, 1964.

67. Blackburn and Williamson, 1997, 26–28.

68. Charles McLoyd catalog. Special Collections, University of Colorado Library.

69. Letter of Richard Wetherill to T. M. Prudden, November 15, 1896. American Museum of Natural History Archives, copy at Edge of the Cedars Museum.

70. The description of "underground rooms" made Earl Morris think that the McLoyd-Graham party had encountered Basketmaker III pithouses rather than Basketmaker II cists. However, the lack of pottery confirms their earlier designation.

71. Letter of Richard Wetherill to T. M. Prudden, November 15, 1896. American Museum of Natural History Archives, copy at Edge of the Cedars Museum.

72. Blackburn and Williamson, 1997, 42.

73. Lister, R. H. and F. C. Lister, 1990, 6.

74. Letter of Talbot Hyde to Clark Wissler, April 16, 1930. American Museum of Natural History Archives, copy at Edge of the Cedars Museum.

75. For a detailed account of the 1893–1894 Hyde Exploring Expedition, see Blackburn and Williamson, 1997, 49–51, 54–58.

76. Letter of Richard Wetherill to B. T. Hyde, December 17, 1893. American Museum of Natural History Archives, copy at Edge of the Cedars Museum, Blanding, Utah.

77. Letter of Richard Wetherill to Gustaf Nordenskiold, December 31, 1893. Mesa Verde National Park Archives.

78. Morris, 1939, 12.

79. Letter of Richard Wetherill to Gustaf Nordenskiold, March 20, 1894. Mesa Verde National Park Archives.

80. Woodbury, 1973, 25.

81. Hurst and Turner, 1993, 167–72.

82. Gillmor and Wetherill, 1953, 41; McNitt, 1957, 74–75.

83. Smith, J. E., 1987, 79–81.

## CHAPTER 2

1. Robertson, 1990, 63–72; Smith, D. A., 1988, 40–66.

2. Nusbaum, J. L., 1978, 65; Robertson, 1990, 66.

3. Robertson, 1990, 66–67.

4. Walter, 1947, 260–61.

5. Fowler, 2000, 199; Lister, R. H. and F. C. Lister, 1968, 11; 1981, 47–48.

6. Woodbury, 1993, 35.

7. Hewett, 1904; 1905, 583–605.

8. Fowler, 2000, 263–64; Lister R. H. and F. C. Lister, 1968; 1981, 47; Walter, 1947, 260–65.

9. Smith, D. A., 1988, 69.

10. Prudden, 1927, 128.

11. Prudden, 1896, 552; 1906; 1914, 33–58; 1918, 3–52.

12. Roys and Harrison, 1949, 215–23; Woodbury, 1973, 10–16.

13. Morley and Kidder, 1917, 41–70.

14. Kidder, 1950, 92–102; Woodbury, 1973, 11.

15. Lister, R. H. and F. C. Lister, 1970.

16. Judd, 1968, 10–13.

17. Brew, 1946, 23; Lister, R. H. and F. C. Lister, 1968, 12.

18. Smith, J. E., 1987, 5–6.

19. Contrary to Walter (1947, 261), Hewett did not conduct the survey himself, although he has the reputation of taking credit for the work of others.

20. Fiero, 2002, 61; Nusbaum, R., 1980, 9–11.

21. Nusbaum, R., 1980, 69–70.

22. Smith, J. E., 1987, 8.

23. Judd, 1968, 21–25.

24. Contrary to Cassells (1997, 139–40), Fewkes never was superintendent at Mesa Verde National Park.

25. Hough, 1932, 262.

26. Fewkes, 1908, 15–30. A 2002 lightning-ignited wildfire roared over Spruce Tree Pueblo but did not damage it.

27. Recent mapping of Cliff Palace has reduced the number of rooms to about 150.

28. For a complete list of park sites recorded between 1906 and 1977, see Smith, J. E., 1987.

29. Fewkes, 1916, 3–32; 1917, 461–488; Roberts, 1999, 123.

30. Brew, 1946, 24; Lipe, 1999a, 60–64; Lister, R. H. and F. C. Lister, 1968, 11–12.

31. Woodbury, 1993, 48.

32. Fiero, 2002, 108, Fig. 6.3.

33. Ibid., 113, quoting letter of Jesse Nusbaum to Edgar Hewett, October 21, 1910.

34. Scott's son, Earl, kept three items from his father's collection which are illustrated in Lister, R. H. and F. C. Lister, 1978, Figs. 26 (top right and left), 30 (left), 40 (top left). Possibly the vessel McClurg gave to Roosevelt also came from Scott's collection.

35. Lister, R. H. and F. C. Lister, 1968, 5–6.

36. Lister, R. H. and F. C. Lister, 1978, Fig. 2.

37. Morris, E. H., 1919a, 179.

38. Lister, R. H. and F. C. Lister, 1978, 54.

39. Morris, E. H., 1919a, 167. Eagle Nest, together with Lion House, Morris 5, and Tree House now are prime exhibits in the Ute Mountain Ute Tribal Park.

40. Morris, E. H., 1919a, 164–81.

41. Morris, E. H., 1939, 19.

42. Kidder more aptly called it Slab House. Lipe 1999a, 62.

43. Morris, E. H., 1919a, 204.

44. Morris, E. H., 1939, 19.

45. Ibid., Pls. 65c, 72e.

46. Lister, R. H. and F. C. Lister, 1978, Figs. 6 (top center), 13 (top).

47. Morris, E. H., 1921b, 18–22.

48. Morris, E. H., 1939, iii.

49. Ibid., 50.

50. For full discussion of the excavation and interpretation of Aztec West, see Lister, R. H. and F. C. Lister, 1968; 1978; 1987; 1990.

51. Lister, R. H. and F. C. Lister, 1990, Fig. 3.12.

52. Lister, R. H. and F. C. Lister, 1990, Fig. 3.20; Morris, E. H., 1919b.

53. Morris, E. H., 1924a, 139–226.

54. Morris, E. H., 1939, 39.

55. Lister, R. H. and F. C. Lister, 1968, 43–46; 1990, 54.

56. Morris, E. H., 1924b, 227–58; 1928, 259–420.

57. Morris, E. H., 1939, 39–40.

58. Morris, E. H., 1919b, 93–95, 97, 100–3, Figs. 46, 71a.

59. Lister, R. H. and F. C. Lister, 1987, 80–81; 1990, 49.

60. Lister, R. H. and F. C. Lister, 1968; 1990, 50.

61. Lister, R. H. and F. C. Lister, 1990, 51–53.

62. Morris, E. H., 1921a, 109–38.

63. Lister, R. H. and F. C. Lister, 1987, 59–65; 1990, Figs. 3.23, 3.24.

64. Letter of Earl Morris to Clark Wissler, May 10, 1921. Department of Anthropology Archives, American Museum of Natural History.

65. Morris, E. H., 1939, 39.

66. Letter of Earl Morris to Clark Wissler, n.d., 1917. Department of Anthropology Archives, American Museum of Natural History.

67. Lister, R. H. and F. C. Lister, 1990, Table 13.1. Collection Accession Files, Aztec Ruins National Monument.

68. Lister, R. H. and F. C. Lister, 1978.

69. Morris, E. H., 1939, 39.

70. Lister, R. H. and F. C. Lister, 1987, 103; 1990, Fig. 4.1.

71. Lister, R. H. and F. C. Lister, 1990, 771.

72. Brown, et al., 2002.

73. Tennessen, et al., 2002, 521–27.

74. Letter of Earl Morris to Junius Henderson, September 17, 1922. University of Colorado Museum Archives; Lister, R. H. and F. C. Lister, 1968, 76–77.

75. Lister, F. C., 1997a, 12–27.

76. Ibid., 27–30.

77. Lister, R. H. and F. C. Lister, 1968, 78–79.

78. Lister, F. C., 1997a, 35–42.

79. Smith, D. A., 1988, 116–18.

80. Lister, R. H. and F. C. Lister, 1978, Fig. 40 (upper right); Smith, D. A., 1988, 9.

81. Smith, J. E., 1981, 9–23.

82. Nusbaum, J. L., 1981; Smith, J. E., 1981, 14–15.

83. Woodbury, 1993.

84. Lipe, 1999a, 63–64.

85. Kuckelman, et al., 2000, Table 1, 150; Morris, E. H., 1939, 12; White, T. D., 1992, 367–68.

86. Morris, E. H., 1939, 82.

87. Brew, 1946, 32–40; Martin, P. S., 1938, 231–34.

88. Morris, E. H., 1939, 247.

89. Ibid., 85–115.

90. Ibid., 105, 115.

91. Billman, et al., 2000, Table 8, 170; Morris, E. H., 1939, 105; White, T. D., 1992, 368–69.

92. Lister, R. H. and F. C. Lister, 1978, Fig. 25; Morris, E. H., 1939, 208, Fig. 54.

93. Morris, E. H., 1939, 143–245.

94. Shepard, 1939, 249–87.

95. Babcock and Parezo, 1988, 139.

96. Lister, F. C., 2000, 6–30; Woodbury, 1993, 70.

97. Martin, P. S., 1939, 474–80.

98. Lister, F. C., 2000, 6–18; Martin, P. S., 1936, 14.

99. Martin, P. S., 1936.

100. Martin, P. S., 1938; 1939.

101. Smith, W., n.d., 13–30.

102. Brew, 1946, 106–51.

103. Ibid., 153.

104. Lister, R. H. and F. C. Lister, 1987, 59–79; 1990, 129–34.

105. Smith, W., n.d., 794–95.

106. Lister, R. H. and F. C. Lister, 1990, 124–28, Fig. 7.7.

107. Ibid., 118.

108. Ibid., 118–20.

109. Breternitz, 1999.

110. Lister, F. C., 1997b, 26–29.

111. Ibid., 59–69.

112. Ibid., 135.

113. Seltzer, 1944.

### Chapter 3

1. Lancaster and Watson, D., 1943, 190–98; 1954, 7.

2. Reed, E. K., 1958.

3. Lancaster and Watson, D., 1954, 7; O'Bryan, 1950, 28–43; Smith, J. E., 1987, 16.

4. See Lister, R. H., 1968, for discussions of various salvage excavations conducted over several decades.

5. Lancaster and Watson, D., 1954, 1–22.

6. Lancaster, 1968, 57–58.

7. Lancaster and Pinkley, 1954, 23–86.

8. Hayes and Lancaster, 1968, 65–68.

9. Lancaster and Van Cleave, 1954, 87–113.

10. Lister, R. H., 1964; 1965; 1966.

11. Lister, R. H., 1964, 81, Fig. 12.

12. Hayes, 1964, 33–34.

13. Ibid., Map 5.

14. Cattanach, 1980.

15. Ibid., 410.

16. Ibid., 137–38.

17. Rohn, 1971.

18. Ibid., 28–29, 252.

19. Smith, D. G. and Nichols, 1967, 18.

20. Rohn, 1971, 145.

21. Smith, D. G. and Nichols, 1967, 20.

22. Hayes, 1964, 79.

23. Ibid., 89–90.

24. Hayes, 1975, 6–12.

25. Ibid., 14–63.

26. Hayes, 1975, 65–97; Smith, D. G. and Nichols, 1967, 21. In the year 2000 a wildfire raged over Wetherill Mesa, but fortunately did no major damage to the ruins.

27. Smith, D. G. and Nichols, 1967, 23.

28. Ibid., 25.

29. Rohn, 1971, 106.

30. Hargrave, 1965, 161–66.

31. Birkedal, 1976, 323–24.

32. McKusick, 2001, Fig. 5, 21, 42–49, 106–7.

33. Because of dissatisfaction with the rigidity of the Pecos Classification, the Wetherill Mesa Project staff chose to use a system of phases to express the cultural evolution of the ancestral Pueblos. For consistency, those names are not used in this text but are indicated as follows: Basketmaker III: La Plata Phase; Pueblo I: Piedra Phase; Pueblo II, Early: Ackmen Phase; Pueblo II, Late: Mancos Phase; Pueblo III, Early: McElmo Phase; Pueblo III, Late: Mesa Verde Phase

34. Smith, D. G. and Nichols, 1967, 7–9.

35. Nichols and Smith, D. G., 1965, 57–64; Smith, D. G. and Nichols, 1967, 29.

36. Fritts, et al., 1965, 101–22.

37. Arrhenius, G. and Bonatti, 1965, 91–100.

38. Erdman, 1970, Fig. 14.

39. Smith, J. E., 1987, 19.

40. Erdman, 1970, Fig. 15.

41. Miles, 1975, 36, Appendix 1.

42. Bennett, 1975, 25; Miles, 1975, 34; Reed, E. K., 1965, 38.

43. Miles, 1975, Fig. 28a, b.

44. Ibid., Fig. 29.

45. Dunmire and Tierney, 1997; Wheeler, 1994.

46. Miles, 1975, 35.

47. Breternitz, 2000, 206.

48. Lister, R. H., 1968.

49. Birkedal, 1968, 95–100.

50. Kane, 1968, 101–3.

51. Birkedal, 1976; Hallisy, n.d. (1972); Nordby and Breternitz, n.d. (1972). Mesa Verde Archaeological Research Center, field notes, Dove Creek, CO.

52. Birkedal, 1976; Smith, J. E., 1987, 22.

53. Lister, R. H., 1968.

54. Breternitz, 1999; Rohn, 1963, 450–55.

55. Lister, R. H. and Smith, J. E., 1968, 5–51; Lister, R. H., 1967.

56. Smith, J. E., 1987, 51.

57. Breternitz, 2002, 18–30; Lister, F. C., 1997b, 154.

58. Lister, R. H., et al., 1970, 57–67.

59. Breternitz, 2000, 205–7.

### CHAPTER 4

1. Crampton, 1959; 1964.

2. Lister, R. H. and F. C. Lister, 1968, 132–35.

3. Judd, 1924, 287.

4. Lister, R. H. and F. C. Lister, 1968, 133.

5. Jennings, 1966, 1–5. Because of the twists and turns of the river, the project's west bank often was the north and the east bank was south.

6. Fowler, et al., 1959.

7. Fowler, et al., 1959 (P2), 484–88; Lipe, 1960; Sharrock, 1964, 3–8.

8. Sharrock, et al., 1961, 5–9.

9. Sharrock, et al., 1961; 1963; 1964.

10. Sharrock, 1963, 34–57.

11. Judd, 1924, 294.

12. Sharrock, et al., 1963, 69–90.

13. Lipe, 1960.

14. Lister, R. H. and F. C. Lister, 1968, 134. Letter of Earl Morris to A. V. Kidder, June 23, 1929. University of Colorado Museum Archives.

15. Lister, R. H. and F. C. Lister, 1961.

16. Lipe, 1970; 1997.

17. Lister, F. C., 1997b, 143–44.

18. Dittert, et al., 1961.

19. Ibid., Fig. 1.

20. Eddy, 1961.

21. Ibid., 16–27; 1966, 268.

22. Eddy, 1961, 6–9, 27–60; 1966, 268–85.

23. Dittert, et al., 1961; Eddy, 1961; 1966. The temporal phase system for the cultural sequence used by the Navajo Reservoir Project is correlated with the Pecos Classification as follows: Basketmaker II: Los Pinos Phase; Basketmaker III: Sambrito Phase; Pueblo I, Early: Rosa Phase; Pueblo I, Late: Piedra Phase; Pueblo II, Early: Arboles Phase.

24. For distributional maps, see Dittert, et al., 1961, Figs. 60–65.

25. Eddy, 1966, 480. In 1987 this site was again exposed and reworked by Complete Archaeological Services Associates of Cortez, Colorado. Archaeomagnetic analysis obtained dates from the pits to the late sixth and early seventh centuries. Lister, F. C., 1997b, 70–73.

26. Eddy, 1966, 225–27, 230, 482–83.

27. Ibid., 232, Fig. 28.

28. Eddy, 1974.

29. Billman, et al., 2000, Table 8, 170; Eddy, 1966, 248; 1974, 81–82; White, T. D., 1992, 370–71.

30. Dittert, et al., 1961, 236–49; Hester and Shiner, 1963.

31. Schaafsma, 1963.

## CHAPTER 5

1. Gibbons, 1997, 636; Nickens, 1975, 183–293; White, T. D., 1992.

2. Akens, 1987, 14–16.

3. Lister, F. C., 1997a, 19, 35–37.

4. Eddy, 1977.

5. Eddy, 1977; Lister, F. C., 1997a, 27–98.

6. Turner, 1993.

7. Charbonneau, et al., 1999.

8. Malville, 1989, 45–56.

9. Wade, 1997, 107, Fig. 5.

10. Van West and Dean, 2000, 23.

11. Houle, 1991.

12. Lister, F. C., 2000, 18–29.

13. Hallasi, 1979, 199–425; Kane, 1986, 394–95; Thompson, 1994.

14. Reed, A. D., 1979, 110.

15. Ibid., Figs. 23–24, 54, 101.

16. Cassells, 1997, 232; Pippin, 2002.

17. Karen Adams and Rex Adams, personal communication.

18. Powers, et al., 1983, 134–38.

19. Reed, L., 2002; Reed, P., 2002.

20. Ibid., 2002.

21. Smith, J. L., 1987, Table 1.

22. Ibid., 1987.

23. Fred Blackburn, Sally Cole, personal communication.

24. Arrenhius, O. W., 1984; Mesa Verde National Park, 1991.

25. Larry Nordby, personal communication; Roberts, 1999.

26. Ibid.

27. Fred Blackburn, personal communication.

28. Rina Swentzel, personal communication.

29. Thompson, 1993; Winter, 1985, 22–28.

30. Thompson, 1993, 22.

31. Winter, 1985, 22–28.

32. Williamson, 1987, 112–32.

33. Ibid., 124–32.

34. Ibid., 124–32.

35. Matson, et al., 1985, 245–64. Cedar Mesa phases: Grand Gulch (Basketmaker II): A.D. 200–400; Mossback (Basketmaker III): A.D. 650–725; Windgate (Pueblo II-Pueblo III): A.D. 1060–1100; Clay Hills (Pueblo III): A.D. 1100–1150); Wooden Shoe (Pueblo II-Pueblo III): A.D. 1165–1210; Red House (Pueblo II-Pueblo III): A.D. 1210–1270.

36. McVickar, 2001.

37. Fuller, 1984; see Heacock, 1995, 391–410 for expanded discussion of similar trenches excavated, two in southwestern Colorado and one in southeastern Utah. One was approximately twenty-six feet in length, an unusually commodious example.

38. Ermigiotti, 1997; Fuller, 1984, Frontispiece.

39. Fuller, 1984, 53.

40. Ibid., Figs. 23–24.

41. Bernardini, 2000, 365–77.

42. Ermigiotti, 1997.

43. David Breternitz, personal communication; Robinson, et al., 1986, 28.

44. Breternitz, 1993, 118–25.

45. David Breternitz, personal communication.

46. Ibid.

47. Ibid.

48. Breternitz, 1993, 118–25.

49. David Breternitz, personal communication.

50. Brisbin, et al., 1988.

51. David Breternitz, personal communication.

52. William Lipe, personal communication.

53. Robinson, et al., 1986, Tables 1.3, 1.4, 1.5, 3–52.

54. Breternitz, 1993, 124.

55. Robinson, et al., 1986, 26.

56. Ibid., Table 1.8.

57. Kane, 1986, 355–57.

58. Breternitz, 1993, 118–25.

59. Kristin Kuckelman, personal communication.

60. Robinson, et al., 1986, 4–7.

61. Lipe, 1999a, 80.

62. Kane, 1986, 362–425. Dolores Archaeological Program phases: Cougar Springs: A.D. 1–600; Sagehen: A.D. 600–840; McPhee: A.D. 840–1000; Sundial: A.D. 1000–1200.

63. Ibid., 417, Fig. 5.22.

64. Ibid., 368. Kane suggests a population of 3,000–4,000 persons.

65. Brisbin, et al., 1988, 63–406; Kane, 1986, 38, Figs. 1.1, 2.2.

66. Kane, 1986, 4–62.

67. Smith, D. A., 1995, 11–12.

68. Lipe, et al., 1988, Figs. 18.1, 18.3.

69. Robinson, et al., 1986, 16.

70. Lipe, 1986, 439–65.

71. Kane, 1986, 398–402.

72. Smith, D. A., 1995, 4–22.

73. Breternitz, 1993, 118–25.

74. Kendrick, 1995, 23–71.

75. Fuller and Morris, J. N., 1991, 21–25.

76. Morris, J. N., 1991, Figs. 1.1, 1.2.

77. Ibid., Figs. 3.4, 3.7, 3.8.

78. Ibid., Figs. 3.14–3.26., 3. 28, 3.29.

79. Ibid., 116.

80. Ibid., 265, 270.

81. Ibid., Figs. 3.37–3.46.

82. Lister, F. C., 2000, Fig. 7.

83. Errickson, 1993, 1.

84. Ibid.

85. Dice, 1993.

86. LeBlanc, 1999, 182–86.

87. Van West and Dean, 2000, 23, 26.

88. Dice, 1993, 89.

89. Errickson, 1993, Preface.

90. Kuckelman, et al., 2002, Fig. 1.

91. Billman, et al., 2000, 145–78.

92. Billman, et al., 2000, 74–78; Marlar, 2000; Marlar, et al., 2000, 74–78.

93. Charles, 2000.

94. Martin, D. and Margolis, 2000, 8.1–8.18.

95. Lightfoot and Etzkorn, 1993.

96. Bradley, 1992, Fig. 7.1.

97. Ibid., 79.

98. Ibid., 94.

99. Ibid., 96–97.

100. Kuckelman, et al., 2002, 492.

101. Adams, 1992, 99–104; Adler, 1992, 11–24; Lipe, 1999a, 87; Van West and Lipe, 1992, 105–120; Varien, et al., 1992, 45–67. For a detailed summary of fifteen years of Crow Canyon research, see Varien and Wilshusen, 2002, 9–20.

102. Kuckelman, et al., 2000, 147–166; Kuckelman, et al, 2002, 486–513.

103. Kuckelman, et al., 2000, 158.

104. Connolly, 1992, 33–44.

105. Ancestral Pueblos grew the genus *Phaesolus vulgaris* thought to have been domesticated millennia ago in Peru. Foster and Cordell, 1992, 62.

106. Connolly, 1892, 43.

107. Lipe, 1999a, 87.

108. Ortman, et al., 2000, 127–30.

109. Ibid., 130–35.

110. Ibid., 135–41.

111. Lipe, 1999a, 89.

## Chapter 6

1. Lipe and Pitblado, 1999, 95–119; Petersen, 1987, 305.

2. Lipe and Pitblado, 1999, 120–31.

3. Tabulations now generally are of "components" because of the frequency of multiple use over time of the same location.

4. Doug Bowman, personal communication.

5. Fuller, et al., 1988; Lister, F. C., 1997b, 131; Ware, 1986, 147–94.

6. Lipe, 1999b, 132–65.

7. Smiley, 1993, 243–54.

8. Lipe, 1993, 1–12.

9. Matson, et al., 1988, 245–64.

10. Matson, 1991.

11. Eddy, 1966; Wilshusen, 1999a, 173.

12. Galinat, 1992, 52.

13. Lister, F. C., 1997b, 134–54.

14. Matson, 1991.

15. Lister, F. C., 1997b, 42, 121–22, 142.

16. Christy Turner, personal communication.

17. Wilshusen, 1999a, 166–95.

18. Great Sage Plain, 736 sites; Mesa Verde, 317 sites; Dolores Valley, 369 sites.

19. Wilshusen, 1999b, 196–241.

20. Lister, F. C., 1997b.

21. Lipe and Varien, 1999a, 242–89.

22. Nancy Hammack, personal communication.

23. Lipe and Ortman, 1999, 290–352.

24. Kohler, 2000, 191–204.

25. Duff and Wilshusen, 2000, 167–90.

26. Wilshusen and Towner, 1999, 353–69.

#### Epilogue

1. Fewkes, 1908.

# References Cited

Adams, Karen R.
    1992    The Environmental Archaeological Program. In *The Sand Canyon Archaeological Project,* edited by William D. Lipe. Crow Canyon Archaeological Center Occasional Paper, no. 2, 99–104. Cortez, CO.

Adler, Michael A.
    1992    The Upland Survey. In *The Sand Canyon Archaeological Project,* edited by William D. Lipe. Crow Canyon Archaeological Center Occasional Paper, no. 2, 11–24. Cortez, CO.

Akens, Jean
    1987    *Mountain Ute Tribal Park. The Other Mesa Verde.* Four Corners Publications, Moab, UT.

Arrhenius, Gustaf and Enrico Bonatti
    1965    The Mesa Verde Loess. Society for American Archaeology, *Memoir,* vol. 31, no. 2, pt. 2, 92–100.

Arrhenius, Olaf W.
    1984    *Stones Speak and Waters Sing. The Life and Works of Gustaf Nordenskiold,* edited and annotated by Robert H. Lister and Florence C. Lister. Mesa Verde Museum Association, Mesa Verde, CO.

Babcock, Barbara and Nancy J. Parezo
    1988    *Daughters of the Desert. Women Anthropologists and the Native American Southwest.* University of New Mexico Press, Albuquerque, NM.

Bennett, Kenneth A.
    1975    Skeletal Remains from Mesa Verde National Park, Colorado. *Archaeological Research Series* 7F. National Park Service, Washington, D.C.

Bernardini, Wesley
    2000    Kiln Firing Groups: Inter-Household Economic Collaboration and Social Organization in the Northern American Southwest. *American Antiquity,* vol. 65, no. 2, 365–77.

Billman, Brian R., Patricia M. Lambert, and Banks L. Leonard
    2000    Cannibalism, Warfare, and Drought in the Mesa Verde Region During the Twelfth Century A.D. *American Antiquity,* vol. 65, no. 1, 145–78.

Birkedal, Terje G.

1968    Site 1926, an Isolated Pueblo III Kiva near Long House, Wetherill Mesa. In *Emergency Archaeology in Mesa Verde National Park, Colorado. 1948–1966*, edited by Robert H. Lister. University of Colorado Studies, Series in Anthropology, no. 15, 95–100. Boulder, CO.

1976    Basketmaker III Residence Units; a Study of Prehistoric Social Organization in the Mesa Verde Archaeological District. Unpublished Ph.D. dissertation, Department of Anthropology, University of Colorado, Boulder, CO.

Blackburn, Fred and Ray A. Williamson

1997    *Cowboys and Cave Dwellers.* School of American Research Press, Santa Fe, NM.

Bradley, Bruce A.

1992    Excavations at Sand Canyon Pueblo. In *The Sand Canyon Archaeological Project,* edited by William D. Lipe. Crow Canyon Archaeological Center Occasional Paper, no. 2, 79–97. Cortez, CO.

Breternitz, David A.

1993    The Dolores Archaeological Program: in Memoriam. *American Antiquity,* vol. 58, no. 1, 118–25.

1999    *The 1969 Mummy Lake Excavations, Site 5MV833.* Wright Paleohydrological Institute, Boulder, CO.

2000    A Personal Perspective on Mesa Verde Archaeology. *Kiva,* vol. 66, no. 1, 205–13.

2002    Basketmaker II Site Investigations near Durango, Colorado, 1966. *Southwestern Lore,* vol. 68, no. 2, 18–30.

Brew, J.O.

1946    Archaeology of Alkali Ridge, Southeastern Utah. *Papers of the Peabody Museum of American Archaeology and Ethnology,* vol. 21. Harvard University, Cambridge, MA.

Brisbin, Joel N., Allen E. Kane, and James N. Morris

1988    Excavations at McPhee Pueblo (Site 5MT4475), a Pueblo I and early Pueblo II Multicomponent Village. In *Dolores Archaeological Program: Anasazi Communities at Dolores: McPhee Village,* compiled by A. E. Kane and C. K. Robinson. vol. 1, 63–406. Bureau of Reclamation, Engineering and Research Center, Denver, CO.

Brown, Gary M., Thomas C. Windes, and Peter J. McKenna

2002    Animas Anamnesis: Aztec Ruins, or Anasazi Capital? Paper presented at the 67th Annual Meeting of the Society for American Archaeology, Denver, CO.

Cassells, Steve

1997    *The Archaeology of Colorado.* Revision of 1983 edition. Johnson Books, Boulder, CO.

Cattanach, George S.

1980    Long House, Mesa Verde National Park, Colorado. *Publications in Archeology 7H.* National Park Service, Washington, D.C.

Chapin, Frederick H.
1988    *The Land of the Cliff Dwellers.* Foreword by Robert H. Lister. Reprint of 1892 edition. University of Arizona Press, Tucson, AZ.

Charbonneau, P., O. R. White, and T. J. Bogdan
1999    Solar Astronomy in the Prehistoric Southwest. Unpublished file copy. High Altitude Observatory, Boulder, CO.

Charles, Mona
2000    *The Emergency Excavation of Human Burials from Archaeological Site 5LP4991. The Darkmold Site, La Plata County, Colorado,* edited by Mona Charles. Colorado Historical Society, Office of Archaeological Historic Preservation, Denver, CO.

Connolly, Marjorie R.
1992    The Goodman Point Historic Land-Use Study. In *The Sand Canyon Archaeological Project,* edited by William D. Lipe. Crow Canyon Archaeological Center Occasional Paper, no. 2, 33–44. Cortez, CO.

Crampton, C. Gregory
1959    Outline History of the Glen Canyon Region, 1776–1922. *University of Utah Anthropological Papers,* no. 42. Salt Lake City, UT.
1964    The San Juan Canyon Historical Sites. *University of Utah Anthropological Papers,* no. 70. Salt Lake City, UT.

Dice, Michael
1993    Disarticulated Human Remains from Reach III of the Towaoc Canal, Ute Mountain Ute Reservation, Montezuma County, Colorado. *Four Corners Archaeological Project, Report,* no. 22. Complete Archaeological Services Associates, Cortez, CO.

Dittert, Alfred E., James J. Hester, and Frank Eddy
1961    An Archaeological Survey of the Navajo Reservoir District, Northwestern New Mexico. School of American Research and the Museum of New Mexico, *Monograph,* no. 23. Santa, Fe, NM.

Duff, Andrew and Richard H. Wilshusen
1999    Prehistoric Population Dynamics in the Northern San Juan Region. *Kiva,* vol. 66, no. 1, 167–90.

Dunmire, William W. and Gail D. Tierney
1997    *Wild Plants and Native Peoples of the Four Corners.* Museum of New Mexico Press, Santa Fe, NM.

Eddy, Frank W.
1961    Excavations at Los Pinos Phase Sites in the Navajo Reservoir District. *Papers in Anthropology,* no. 4. Museum of New Mexico Press, Santa Fe, NM.
1966    Prehistory in the Navajo Reservoir District, Northwestern New Mexico. *Papers in Anthropology,* no. 5, 2 parts. Museum of New Mexico Press, Santa Fe, NM.
1974    Population Dislocation in the Navajo Reservoir District, New Mexico and Colorado. *American Antiquity,* vol. 39, no. 1, 75–84.
1977    Archaeological Investigations at Chimney Rock Mesa, 1970–1972. *Memoirs of the Colorado Archaeological Society,* no. 1.

Erdman, James A.
    1970    Pinyon, Juniper Succession After Natural Fires on Residual Soils of Mesa Verde, Colorado. *Biological Series*, vol. 11, no. 2. Brigham Young University, Provo, UT.

Ermigiotti, Paul
    1997    The Kiln Conference at Crow Canyon: a Summary Report, 1991 to 1996. Unpublished file copy. Crow Canyon Archaeological Center, Cortez, CO.

Errickson, Mary
    1993    Archaeological Investigations on Prehistoric Sites, Reach III of the Towaoc Canal, Ute Mountain Ute Reservation, Montezuma County, Colorado. *Four Corners Archaeological Project Report*, no. 13. Complete Archaeological Services Associates, Cortez, CO.

Fewkes, Jesse Walter
    1908    Report on Excavation and Repair of the Spruce Tree House, Mesa Verde National Park, Colorado, in May and June, 1908. In *Report of the Superintendent of the Mesa Verde National Park to the Secretary of the Interior*, 15–30. Washington, D.C.
    1916    Excavation and Repair of Sun Temple, Mesa Verde National Park. *Reports of the Department of the Interior*, 3–32. Washington, D.C.
    1917    A Prehistoric Mesa Verde Pueblo and its People. *Smithsonian Institution Report for 1916*, 461–88. Washington, D.C.

Fiero, Kathy
    2002    *Balcony House: a History of a Cliff Dwelling, Mesa Verde National Park, Colorado*. With draft *Report of the 1910 Excavation and Repair of Balcony House* by Jesse L. Nusbaum. Mesa Verde Museum Association, Mesa Verde, CO.

Fletcher, Maurine S.
    1979    Nordenskiold and the Natives. *Journal of Arizona History*, vol. 20, no. 3, 345–70.

Foster, Nelson and Linda S. Cordell
    1992    *Chilies to Chocolate. Food the Americans Gave the World*. University of Arizona Press, Tucson, AZ.

Fowler, Don D.
    2000    *A Laboratory of Anthropology. Science and Romanticism in the American Southwest, 1846–1930*. University of New Mexico Press, Albuquerque, NM.

Fowler, Don D., James H. Gunnerson, Jesse D. Jennings, Robert H. Lister, Dee Ann Suhm, and Ted Weller
    1959    The Glen Canyon Survey. *University of Utah Anthropological Papers*, no. 39, part III. Salt Lake City, UT.

Fritts, Harold C., David G. Smith, and Marvin A. Stokes
    1965    The Biological Model for Paleoclimatic Interpretation of Mesa Verde Tree-Ring Series. Society for American Archaeology, *Memoir*, vol. 31, no. 2, pt. 2, 101–21.

Fuller, Steven L.
    1984    *Late Anasazi Pottery Kilns in the Yellow Jacket District, Southwestern Colorado*. Complete Archaeological Services Associates, Cortez, CO.

Fuller, Steven L. and James N. Morris

1991    Introduction. *Hovenweep Laterals*, vol. 1, 1–26. Complete Archaeological
        Services Associates, Bureau of Reclamation, Engineering and Research
        Center, Denver, CO. Galinat, Walton C.

1992    Maize: Gift from America's First Peoples. In *Chilies to Chocolate*, edited by
        Nelson Foster and Linda Cordell, 47–60. University of Arizona Press, Tucson, AZ.

Gibbons, Ann

1997    Archaeologists Rediscover Cannibals. *Science*, vol. 277, 635–37.
        Gillmor, Frances and Louisa Wade Wetherill

1953    *Traders to the Navajos*. Reprint of 1934 edition. University of New Mexico
        Press, Albuquerque, NM.

Hallasi, Judith Ann

1974    Archaeological Excavation at the Escalante Site, Dolores, Colorado, 1975 and
        1976. In *The Archaeology and Stabilization of the Dominguez and Escalante
        Ruins*, Cultural Resources Series, no. 7, part II, 199–425. Bureau of Land
        Management, Denver, CO.

Hallisy, Stephen J.

1972    An Agricultural Terrace on Wetherill Mesa at Mini-Train Route Stake 30-A.
        Unpublished file copy. Mesa Verde Archaeological Research Center, Dove
        Creek, CO.

Hargrave, Lyndon L.

1965    Turkey Bones from Wetherill Mesa. Society for American Archaeology,
        *Memoir*, vol. 31, no. 2, pt. 2, 161–66.

Hayes, Alden C.

1964    The Archaeological Survey of Wetherill Mesa, Mesa Verde National Park,
        Colorado. *Archeological Research Series*, no. 7A. National Park Service,
        Washington, D.C.

1975    Badger House Community, Mesa Verde National Park. *Publications in
        Archeology* 7E. National Park Service, Washington, D.C.

1985    Mesa Verde: a Century of Discovery. *Exploration*, 11–21. School of American
        Research, Santa Fe, NM.

Hayes, Alden C. and James A. Lancaster

1968    Site 1060, a Basketmaker III Pithouse on Chapin Mesa. In *Emergency
        Archaeology in Mesa Verde National Park, Colorado. 1948–1966*, edited by
        Robert H. Lister. University of Colorado Studies, Series in Anthropology,
        no. 15, 65–68. Boulder, CO.

Heacock, Laura A.

1995    Archaeological Investigations of Three Mesa Verde Anasazi Pit Kilns. *Kiva*,
        vol. 60, no. 3, 391–410.

Hester, James J. and Joel L. Shiner

1963    Studies at Navajo Period Sites in the Navajo Reservoir District. *Museum of
        New Mexico Papers in Anthropology*, no. 9. Museum of New Mexico Press,
        Santa Fe, NM.

Hewett, Edgar L.
    1904    *Historic and Prehistoric Ruins of the Southwest and Their Preservation,*
               Circular, Department of the Interior, General Land Office, Washington, D.C.
    1905    A General View of the Archaeology of the Pueblo Region. *Smithsonian*
               *Institution Report for 1904,* 583–605. Washington, D.C.

Holmes, William H.
    1876    A Notice of the Ancient Remains of Southwestern Colorado
               During the Summer of 1875. *Bulletin of the Geological and Geographical*
               *Survey of the Territories,* vol. 2, no. 1, 3–25. Washington, D.C.
    1878    Report on the Ancient Ruins of Southwestern Colorado Examined During
               the Summers of 1875 and 1876. U.S. Geological and Geographical Survey of
               the Territories for 1876, *Tenth Annual Report,* 381–408. Washington, D.C.
    1886    Pottery of the Ancient Pueblos. Bureau of Ethnology, *Fourth Annual Report,*
               1882–1883. Washington, D.C.

Hough, Walter
    1932    Biographical Memoir of Jesse Walter Fewkes, 1850–1930. National Academy
               of Sciences, *Biographical Memoir,* vol. 15, no. 9, 261–83. Washington, D.C.

Houle, Marcy Cottrell
    1991    *Wings for my Flight. The Peregrine Falcons of Chimney Rock.* Addison-Wesley,
               Reading, MA.

Howe, Sherman
    1947    *My Story of the Aztec Ruins.* Farmington Times Hustler Press, Farmington, NM.

Hurst, Winston B. and Christy Turner
    1993    Rediscovering the Great Discovery. Wetherill's First Cave 7 and its Record of
               Basketmaker Violence. In *Anasazi Basketmaker,* edited by Victoria Atkins.
               Cultural Resources Series no. 24, 143–92. Bureau of Land Management, Salt
               Lake City, UT.

Jackson, Clarence S.
    1947    *William Henry Jackson. Picture Maker of the Old West.* Bonanza Books,
               New York.

Jennings, Jesse D.
    1966    Glen Canyon: a Summary. *University of Utah Anthropology Papers,* no. 81.
               Salt Lake City, UT.

Judd, Neil M.
    1924    Beyond the Clay Hills. An Account of the National Geographic Society
               Reconnaissance of a Previously Unexplored Section in Utah. *National*
               *Geographic,* vol. 45, no. 3, 275–302.
    1968    *Men Met Along the Trail. Adventure in Archaeology.* University of Oklahoma
               Press, Norman, OK.

Kane, Allen E.
    1968    Site 1677, Two Stone-lined Pits and Associated Features. In *Emergency*
               *Archaeology in Mesa Verde National Park, Colorado,* edited by Robert H. Lister.
               University of Colorado Studies, Series in Anthropology, no. 15, 101–3. Boulder, CO.

1986    Prehistory of the Dolores River Valley. In *Dolores Archaeological Program: Final Synthetic Report*, 353–438. Bureau of Reclamation, Engineering and Research Center, Denver, CO.

1988    McPhee Community Cluster Introduction. In *Dolores Archaeological Program: Anasazi Communities at Dolores: McPhee Village*, vol. 1, 4–62. Bureau of Reclamation, Engineering and Research Center, Denver, CO.

Kendrick, Gregory D.

1964    *Valley of the River of Sorrow*. National Park Service, Rocky Mountain Region, Denver, CO.

Kidder, A.V.

1950    Sylvanus Griswold Morley, 1883–1948. In *Morleyana*, 93–102. Museum of New Mexico Press, Santa Fe, NM.

Kohler, Timothy A.

2000    The Final 400 Years of Prehispanic Agricultural Society in the Mesa Verde Region. *Kiva*, vol. 66, no. 1, 191–204.

Kuckelman, Kristin A., Ricky R. Lightfoot, and Debra L. Martin

2000    Changing Patterns of Violence in the Northern San Juan Region. *Kiva*, vol. 66, no. 1, 147–66.

2002    The Bioarchaeology and Taphonomy of Violence at Castle Rock and Sand Canyon Pueblos, Southwestern Colorado. *American Antiquity*, vol. 67, no. 3, 486–513.

Lancaster, James A.

1968    Salvage Excavation of Sites 353 and 354, Chapin Mesa. In *Emergency Archaeology in Mesa Verde National Park, Colorado, 1948–1966*, edited by Robert H. Lister. University of Colorado Studies, Series in Anthropology, no. 15, 57–59. Boulder, CO.

Lancaster, James A. and Jean M. Pinkley

1964    Excavation at Site 16. In *Archaeological Excavations in Mesa Verde National Park, 1950*. Archaeological Research Series, no. 2, 28–86. National Park Service, Washington, D.C.

Lancaster, James A. and Philip Van Cleave

1954    Excavation of Sun Point Pueblo. In *Archaeological Excavations in Mesa Verde National Park, 1950*. Archaeological Research Series, no. 2, 87–111. National Park Service, Washington, D.C.

Lancaster, James A. and Don Watson

1943    Excavation of Mesa Verde Pit Houses. *American Antiquity*, vol. 9, no. 2, 190–98.

1954    Excavation of Two Late Basketmaker III Pithouses. In *Archaeological Excavations in Mesa Verde National Park, 1950*. Archaeological Research Series, no. 2, 7–22. National Park Service, Washington, D.C.

LeBlanc, Steven A.

1999    *Prehistoric Warfare in the American Southwest*. University of Utah Press, Salt Lake City, UT.

Lightfoot, Ricky R. and Mary C. Etzkorn
  1993      *The Duckfoot Site.* Vol. 1: *Descriptive Archaeology.* Crow Canyon
            Archaeological Center Occasional Paper, no. 3. Cortez, CO.

Lipe, William D.
  1959      1958 Excavations, Glen Canyon Area. *University of Utah Anthropological
            Papers,* no. 44. Salt Lake City, UT.
  1959      Anasazi Communities in the Red Rock Plateau, Southeastern Utah. In
            *Reconstructing Prehistoric Pueblo Societies,* edited by William Longacre, 84–139.
            University of New Mexico Press, Albuquerque, NM.
  1986      Modeling Dolores Area Cultural Dynamics. In *Dolores Archaeological
            Program: Final Synthetic Report,* 439–68. Bureau of Reclamation,
            Engineering and Research Center, Denver, CO.
  1992      *The Sand Canyon Archaeological Project,* edited by William D. Lipe.
            Crow Canyon Archaeological Center Occasional Paper, no. 2, 1–10, 121–34.
            Cortez, CO.
  1999a     History of Archaeology. In *Colorado Prehistory: a Context for the Southern
            Colorado River Basin,* edited by William D. Lipe, Mark Varien, and Richard
            Wilshusen, 51–94. Colorado Council for Professional Archaeologists,
            Denver, CO.
  1999b     Basketmaker II. In *Colorado Prehistory: a Context for the Southern Colorado
            River Basin,* edited by William D. Lipe, Mark Varien, and Richard Wilshusen,
            132–65. Colorado Council for Professional Archaeologists, Denver, CO.

Lipe, William D., James N. Morris, and Timothy A. Kohler
  1988      *Anasazi Communities at Dolores. Grass Mesa Village.* Bureau of Reclamation,
            Engineering and Research Center, Denver, CO.

Lipe, William D. and Bonnie L. Pitblado
  1999      Paleoindian and Archaic Periods. In *Colorado Prehistory: a Context for the
            Southern Colorado River Basin,* edited by William D. Lipe, Mark Varien, and
            Richard Wilshusen, 95–131. Colorado Council for Professional Archaeologists,
            Denver, CO.

Lipe, William D. and Mark D. Varien
  1999a     Pueblo II. In *Colorado Prehistory: a Context for the Southern Colorado River
            Basin,* edited by William D. Lipe, Mark Varien, and Richard Wilshusen,
            242–89. Colorado Council for Professional Archaeologists, Denver, CO.
  1999b     Pueblo III. In *Colorado Prehistory: a Context for the Southern Colorado River
            Basin,* edited by William D. Lipe, Mark Varien, and Richard Wilshusen,
            290–352. Colorado Council for Professional Archaeologists, Denver, CO.

Lipe, William D. and Scott G. Ortman
  2000      Spatial Patterning in Northern San Juan Villages, A.D. 1050–1300. *Kiva,*
            vol. 66, no. 1, 91–122.

Lister, Florence C.
  1997a     *In the Shadow of the Rocks. Archaeology of the Chimney Rock District in
            Southern Colorado.* University Press of Colorado, Niwot, CO.
  1997b     *Prehistory in Peril. The Worst and Best of Durango Archaeology.* University
            Press of Colorado, Niwot, CO.

2000    *Behind Painted Walls. Incidents in Southwestern Archaeology.* University of New Mexico Press, Albuquerque, NM.

Lister, Robert H.
1964    *Contributions to Mesa Verde Archaeology: I. Site 499, Mesa Verde National Park, Colorado.* University of Colorado Studies, Series in Anthropology, no. 9. Boulder, CO.

1965    *Contributions to Mesa Verde Archaeology: II. Site 875, Mesa Verde National Park, Colorado.* University of Colorado Studies, Series in Anthropology, no. 11. Boulder, CO.

1966    *Contributions to Mesa Verde Archaeology: III. Site 866, and the Cultural Sequence in Four Villages in the Far View Group, Mesa Verde National Park, Colorado.* University of Colorado Studies, Series in Anthropology, no. 12. Boulder, CO.

1967    *Contributions to Mesa Verde Archaeology: IV. Site 1086, An Isolated Above Ground Kiva in Mesa Verde National Park, Colorado.* University of Colorado Studies, Series in Anthropology, no. 13. Boulder, CO.

1968    *Contributions to Mesa Verde Archaeology: V. Emergency Archaeology in Mesa Verde National Park, Colorado.* University of Colorado Studies, Series in Anthropology, no. 15. Boulder, CO.

Lister, Robert H. and Florence C. Lister
1961    The Combs Site. Part III: Summary and Conclusions. *University of Utah Anthropological Papers,* no. 41. Salt Lake City, UT.

1968    *Earl Morris and Southwestern Archaeology.* University of New Mexico Press, Albuquerque, NM.

1970    *In Search of Maya Glyphs. From the Archaeological Journals of Sylvanus G. Morley.* Museum of New Mexico Press, Santa Fe, NM.

1978    *Anasazi Pottery.* University of New Mexico Press, Albuquerque, NM.

1981    *Chaco Canyon. Archaeology and Archaeologists.* University of New Mexico Press, Albuquerque, NM.

1987    *Aztec Ruins on the Animas. Excavated, Preserved, and Interpreted.* University of New Mexico Press, Albuquerque, NM.

1990    Aztec Ruins National Monument. Administrative History of an Archaeological Preserve. Southwest Cultural Resources Center, *Professional Papers,* no. 24. National Park Service, Santa Fe, NM.

Lister, Robert H. and Jack E. Smith
1968    Salvage Excavations at Site 1089, Morefield Canyon, Mesa Verde National Park, Colorado. In *Emergency Archaeology in Mesa Verde National Park, Colorado,* edited by Robert H. Lister. University of Colorado Studies, Series in Anthropology, no. 15, 5–51. Boulder, CO.

Lister, Robert H., Stephen Hallisy, Margaret H. Kane, and George E. McLellan
1970    Site 5LP11, a Pueblo I Site near Ignacio, Colorado. *Southwestern Lore,* vol. 35, no. 4, 57–67.

Malville, J. McKim
1989    *Prehistoric Astronomy in the Southwest.* Johnson Books, Boulder, CO.

Marlar, Richard A.
  2000    A Biochemical Assay to Test for Cannibalism at a Prehistoric Puebloan Site. Paper presented at the 65th Annual Meeting of the Colorado Archaeological Society, Cortez, CO.

Marlar, Richard A., Banks L. Leonard, Brian R. Billman, and Jennifer E. Marlar
  2000    Biochemical Evidence of Cannibalism at a Prehistoric Site in Southwestern Colorado. *Nature,* vol. 407, 74–78.

Martin, Debra L. and Michael M. Margolis
  2000    Analysis of Human Remains from the Darkmold Site, 5LP4991, Durango, Colorado, from the Emergency 1998 Field Excavation 8.1–8.18. In *The Emergency Excavation of 11 Human Burials from Archaeological Site 5LP4991, the Darkmold Site, La Plata County, Colorado*, edited by Mona Charles. Colorado Historical Society, Office of Archaeology and Historic Preservation, Denver, CO.

Martin, Paul S.
  1936    Lowry Ruin in Southwestern Colorado. Field Museum of Natural History, *Anthropology Series*, vol. 23, no. 1. Chicago, IL.
  1938    Archaeological Work in the Ackman-Lowry Area, Southwestern Colorado, 1937. Field Museum of Natural History, *Anthropology Series*, vol. 23, no. 2. Chicago, IL.
  1939    Modified Basketmaker Sites, Ackman-Lowry Area, Southwestern Colorado, 1938. Field Museum of Natural History, *Anthropology Series*, vol. 23, no. 3. Chicago, IL.

Matson, R. G.
  1991    *The Origins of Southwestern Agriculture.* University of Arizona Press, Tucson, AZ.

Matson, R. G., William D. Lipe, and W. P. Haase
  1988    Adaptational Continuities and Occupational Discontinuities: the Cedar Mesa Anasazi. *Journal of Field Archaeology,* vol. 15, 245–64.

McClurg, Virginia
  1930    The Making of Mesa Verde into a National Park. *Colorado Magazine,* vol. 14, 218.

McKusick, Charmion R.
  2001    Southwestern Birds of Sacrifice. *The Arizona Archaeologist,* vol. 31.

McNitt, Frank
  1957    *Richard Wetherill: Anasazi.* University of New Mexico Press, Albuquerque, NM.

McVickar, Janet L., ed.
  2001    An Archaeological Survey of Natural Bridges National Monument, Southeastern Utah. Intermountain Cultural Resources Management, *Professional Paper*, no. 64. National Park Service, Mesa Verde National Park, CO
  1991    Gustaf Nordenskiold. Pioneer Archaeologist of Mesa Verde. Exhibit catalog. Mesa Verde National Park, CO.

Miles, James S.
  1975    Orthopedic Problems of the Wetherill Mesa Populations, Mesa Verde
          National Park, Colorado. *Publications in Archeology,* 7G. National Park
          Service, Washington, D.C.

Morgan, W. F.
  1879    Description of a Cliff-house on the Mancos River of Colorado. American
          Association for the Advancement of Science, *Proceedings,* vol. 27, 300–6.
          Washington, D.C.

Morley, Sylvanus G. and A. V. Kidder
  1917    The Archaeology of McElmo Canyon, Colorado. *El Palacio,* vol. 4, no. 4, 41–70.

Morris, Earl Haistead
  1919a   Preliminary Account of the Antiquities of the Region Between the Mancos
          and La Plata Rivers, Southwestern Colorado. Bureau of American
          Ethnology, *Thirty Third Annual Report,* 157–206. Washington, D.C.
  1919b   The Aztec Ruin. American Museum of Natural History, *Anthropological
          Papers,* vol. 26, 1–108. New York.
  1921a   The House of the Great Kiva at the Aztec Ruin. American Museum of
          Natural History, *Anthropological Papers,* vol. 26, 109–38. New York.
  1921b   Chronology of the San Juan Area. National Academy of Science, *Proceedings,*
          vol. 7, 18–22. Washington, D.C.
  1924a   Burials in the Aztec Ruin. American Museum of Natural History,
          *Anthropological Papers,* vol. 26, 139–226. New York.
  1924b   The Aztec Ruin Annex. American Museum of Natural History,
          *Anthropological Papers,* vol. 26, 227–58. New York.
  1928    Notes on Excavations in the Aztec Ruin. American Museum of Natural
          History, *Anthropological Papers,* vol. 26, 259–420. New York.
  1939    *Archaeological Studies in the La Plata District, Southwestern Colorado and
          Northwestern New Mexico.* Carnegie Institution of Washington, Washington, D.C.

Morris, James N.
  1991    *Hovenweep Laterals,* vol. 1, 90–116. Complete Archaeological Services
          Associates, Bureau of Reclamation, Engineering and Research Center,
          Denver, CO.

Nichols, Robert F.
  1965    A Large Hewn Plank from Mesa Verde, Colorado. Society for American
          Archaeology, *Memoir,* vol. 31, no. 2, pt. 2, 51–56.

Nichols, Robert F. and David G. Smith
  1964    Evidence of Prehistoric Cultivation of Douglas-Fir Trees at Mesa Verde.
          Society For American Archaeology, *Memoir,* vol. 31, no. 2, pt. 2, 57–64.

Nickens, Paul R.
  1975    Prehistoric Cannibalism in the Mancos Canyon, Southwestern Colorado.
          *Kiva,* vol. 40, no. 4, 284–93.
  1976    A Partial Account of the Activities of the Wetherill Brothers in Johnson
          Canyon During January, 1890. Unpublished file copy. Mesa Verde
          Archaeological Research Center, Dove Creek, CO.

Nordby, Larry V. and David A. Breternitz
    1972    Site MV1824–71, a Basketmaker III Pithouse and Cist on Wetherill Mesa. Unpublished file copy. Mesa Verde Archaeological Research Center, Dove Creek, CO.

Nordenskiold, Gustaf
    1979    *The Cliff Dwellers of the Mesa Verde, Southwestern Colorado*. Reprint of 1893 edition. Rio Grande Press, Glorieta, NM.

Nusbaum, Jesse L.
    1981    *The 1926 Re-excavation of Step House Cave, Mesa Verde National Park*. Mesa Verde Research Series, Paper no. 1. Mesa Verde Museum Association, Mesa Verde, CO.

Nusbaum, Rosemary
    1980    *Tierra Dulce. Reminiscences from the Jesse Nusbaum Papers*. Sunstone Press, Santa Fe, NM.

O'Bryan, Deric
    1950    Excavations in Mesa Verde National Park, 1947–1948. Gila Pueblo, *Medallion Papers*, vol. 39. Globe, AZ.

Ortman, Scott G., Donna M. Glowacki, Melissa J. Churchill, and Kristin A. Kuckelman
    2000    Pattern and Variation in Northern San Juan Village Histories. *Kiva*, vol. 66, no. 1, 123–46.

Petersen, Kenneth Lee
    1987    Geological Studies: a Review. In *Dolores Archaeological Program: Final Synthetic Report*, 303–311, Bureau of Reclamation, Engineering and Research Center, Denver, CO.

Pippin, Lonnie C.
    2002    Cynthia's Legacy. Paper Presented at the 67th Annual Meeting of the Society for American Archaeology, Denver, CO.

Powers, Robert P., William B. Gillespie, and Stephen Lekson
    1983    *The Outlier Survey, Regional View of Settlement in the San Juan Basin*. Division of Cultural Research, National Park Service, Albuquerque, NM.

Prudden, T. Mitchell
    1896    A Summer Among the Cliff Dwellers. *Harpers Magazine*, Sept., 552.
    1906    *On the Great American Plateau*. G. P. Putnam's Sons and the Knickerbocker Press, New York.
    1914    The Circular Kivas of Small Ruins in the San Juan Watershed. *American Anthropologist* (n.s.), vol. 16, no. 1, 33–58.
    1918    A Further Study of Prehistoric Small House Ruins in the San Juan Watershed. American Anthropological Association, *Memoir*, vol. 5, 3–52.
    1927    *Biographical Sketches and Letters of T. Mitchell Prudden M.D.* Yale University Press, New Haven, CT.

Reed, Alan D.
1979    The Dominguez Ruin, a McElmo Phase Pueblo in Southwestern Colorado. In *The Archaeology and Stabilization of the Dominguez and Escalante Ruins*, part I, iii–149. Cultural Resources Series, no. 7. Bureau of Land Management, Denver, CO.

Reed, Erick K.
1958    Excavations in Mancos Canyon, Colorado. *University of Utah Anthropology Papers*, no. 35. Salt Lake City, UT.

Reed, Lori
2002    Salmon Ruins: Chacoan Outlier and Big Pueblo on the San Juan. Paper presented at the 67th Annual Meeting of the Society for American Archaeology, Denver, CO.

Reed, Paul
2002    Salmon Ruins in 2002: Cynthia Irwin-Williams's Legacy and Beyond. Paper presented at the 67th Annual Meeting of the Society for American Archaeology, Denver, CO.

Retzius, G.
1979    Human Remains from the Cliff Dwellers of the Mesa Verde. In *The Cliff Dwellers of the Mesa Verde*, by Gustaf Nordenskiold. Appendix i-xi. Rio Grande Press, Glorieta, NM.

Roberts, David
1999    A Social Divide Written in Stone. *Smithsonian*, Feb., 119–128.

Robertson, Janet
1990    *The Magnificent Mountain Women. Adventures in the Colorado Rockies.* University of Nebraska Press, Lincoln, NE.

Robinson, Christine K., G. Timothy Gross, and David A. Breternitz
1988    Overview of the Dolores Archaeological Program. In *Dolores Archaeological Program: Final Synthetic Report*, 3–52. Bureau of Reclamation, Engineering and Research Center, Denver, CO.

Rohn, Arthur
1963    Prehistoric Soil and Water Conservation on Chapin Mesa, Southwestern Colorado. *American Antiquity*, vol. 28, no. 4, 441–55.
1971    Mug House, Mesa Verde National Park, Colorado. *Archeological Research Series*, 7D. National Park Service, Washington, D.C.

Roys, Ralph and Margaret W. Harrison
1949    Sylvanus Griswold Morley, 1883–1948. *American Antiquity*, vol. 41, no. 3, 215–23.

Scott, Douglas D.
1973    The Nordenskiold Camp Site. A Test in Historical Archaeology. *Kiva*, vol. 37, no. 3, 128–40.

Seltzer, Carl C.
1944    Racial Prehistory in the Southwest and the Hawikuh Zunis. *Papers of the Peabody Museum of American Archaeology and Ethnology*, vol. 23, no. 1. Cambridge, MA.

Sharrock, Floyd W.
  1964    1962 Excavations, Glen Canyon Area. *University of Utah Anthropological Papers*, no. 73. Salt Lake City, UT.

Sharrock, Floyd W., Keith Anderson, Don D. Fowler, and David S. Dibble
  1961    1960 Excavations, Glen Canyon Area. *University of Utah Anthropological Papers*, no. 14. Salt Lake City, UT.

Sharrock, Floyd W., Kent C. Day, and David S. Dibble
  1963    1961 Excavations, Glen Canyon Area. *University of Utah Anthropological Papers*, no. 18. Salt Lake City, UT.

Shepard, Anna O.
  1939    Technology of La Plata Pottery. In *Archaeological Studies in the La Plata District, Southwestern Colorado and Northwestern New Mexico*, by Earl H. Morris, 249–88. Carnegie Institution of Washington, Washington, D.C. Smiley, Francis E.
  1993    Early Farmers in the Northern Southwest: a View from Marsh Pass. In *Anasazi Basketmaker*, edited by Victoria M. Atkins, 243–54. Bureau of Land Management, Cultural Resources Series, no. 24. Salt Lake City, UT.

Smith, David G. and Robert F. Nichols
  1967    A Tree-Ring Chronology for Climatic Analysis. *Tree-Ring Bulletin*, vol. 28, no. 1–4, 7–40. Laboratory of Tree-Ring Research, University of Arizona, Tucson, AZ.

Smith, Duane A.
  1987    *Mesa Verde National Park. Shadows of the Centuries*. University Press of Kansas, Lawrence, KA.
  1995    Valley of the River of Sorrows. A Historical Over-view of the Dolores River Valley, In *The River of Sorrows: The History of the Lower Dolores River Valley*, edited by Gregory D. Kendrick, 9–22. National Park Service, Rocky Mountain Regional Office, Denver, CO.

Smith, Jack E.
  1987    Mesas, Cliffs, and Canyons. The University of Colorado Survey of Mesa Verde National Park, 1971–1977. *Mesa Verde Research Series*, no. 3. Mesa Verde Museum Association, Mesa Verde, CO.

Smith, Watson
  n.d.    one Man's Archaeology. Unpublished manuscript.

Snead, James
  2001    *Ruins and Rivals. The Making of Southwestern Archaeology*. University of Arizona Press, Tucson, AZ.

Stein, John R. and Peter J. McKenna
  1988    *An Archaeological Reconnaissance of a Late Bonito Phase Occupation Near Aztec Ruins National Monument*. Southwest Cultural Resources Center, National Park Service, Santa Fe, NM.

Tennessen, David, Robert A. Blanchette, and Thomas C. Windes
    2002    Differentiating Aspen and Cottonwood in Prehistoric Wood from Chacoan Great House Ruins. *Journal of Archaeological Science*, vol. 29, 521–27.

Thompson, Ian
    1993    *The Towers of Hovenweep*. Mesa Verde Museum Association, Mesa Verde, CO.
    1994    *The Escalante Community*. Natural and Cultural Heritage Association, Albuquerque, NM.

Turner, Christy G.
    1993    Cannibalism in Chaco Canyon. The Charnel Pit Excavated in 1926 at Small House Ruin by Frank H. H. Roberts. *American Journal of Physical Anthropology*, vol. 91, 421–39.

Van West, Carla R. and William D. Lipe
    1991    Modeling Prehistoric Climate and Agriculture in Southwestern Colorado. In *The Sand Canyon Archaeological Project*, edited by William D. Lipe. Crow Canyon Archaeological Center Occasional Paper, no. 2, 105–20. Cortez, CO.

Van West, Carla R. and Jeffrey S. Dean
    2000    Environmental Characteristics of the A.D. 900–1300 Period in the Central Mesa Verde Region. *Kiva*, vol. 66, no. 1, 9–44.

Varien, Mark D., Kristin A. Kuckelman, and James H. Kleidon
    1992    The Site Testing Program. In *The Sand Canyon Archaeological Project*, edited by William D. Lipe. Crow Canyon Archaeological Center Occasional Paper, no. 2, 45–68. Cortez CO.

Varien, Mark D. and Richard H. Wilshusen
    2002    A Partnership for Understanding the Past. In *Seeking the Center Place. Archaeology and Ancient Communities in the Mesa Verde Region*, 3–23. University of Utah Press, Salt Lake City, UT.

Wade, Cam
    1997    Total Eclipses of the Sun in the Anasazi Country, A.D. 700 to 1700. In *Layers of Time*. Archaeological Society of New Mexico, Pub. no. 23, 99–114. Albuquerque, NM.

Walter, Paul A. F.
    1947    Edgar Lee Hewett, Americanist, 1865–1946. *American Anthropologist*, vol. 49, no. 2, 260–65.

Ware, John A.
    1986    The Prehistoric Sites. In *The Cultural Resources of Ridges Basin and Upper Wildcat Canyon*, edited by Joseph C. Winter, 95–103. Office of Contract Archaeology, University of New Mexico, Albuquerque, NM.

Watson, Don
    n.d.    *Cliff Dwellings of the Mesa Verde. A Story in Pictures*. Mesa Verde Museum Association, Mesa Verde, CO.

Wetherill, Benjamin Alfred
   1977    *The Wetherills of the Mesa Verde. Autobiography of Benjamin Alfred Wetherill*,
           edited and annotated by Maurine S. Fletcher. Associated University Press,
           London.

Wheeler, Elizabeth M.
   1994    *Mother Earth's Mercantile. Plants of the Four Corners Area and Their Uses
           Through Time*. Crow Canyon Archaeological Center, Cortez, CO.

White, Tim D.
   1992    *Prehistoric Cannibalism at Mancos 5MTUMR2346*. Princeton University
           Press, Princeton, NJ

Williamson, Ray A.
   1987    *Living the Sky. The Cosmos of the American Indian*. University of Oklahoma
           Press, Norman, OK.

Wilshusen, Richard H.
   1999a   Basketmaker III. In *Colorado Prehistory: a Context for the Southern Colorado
           River Basin*, edited by William D. Lipe, Mark Varien, and Richard Wilshusen,
           166–195. Colorado Council for Professional Archaeologists, Denver, CO.
   1999b   Pueblo I. In *Colorado Prehistory: a Context for the Southern Colorado River
           Basin*, edited by William D. Lipe, Mark Varien, and Richard Wilshusen,
           196–241. Colorado Council for Professional Archaeologists, Denver, CO.

Wilshusen, Richard H. and Ronald H. Towner
   1999    Post-Puebloan Occupation. In *Colorado Prehistory: a Context for the
           Southern Colorado River Basin*, edited by William D. Lipe, Mark Varien,
           and Richard Wilshusen, 353–369. Colorado Council for Professional
           Archaeologists, Denver, CO.

Winter, Joseph C.
   1985    Hovenweep Through Time. *Exploration*, 22–28. School of American
           Research, Santa Fe, NM.

Woodbury, Richard B.
   1973    *Alfred V. Kidder*. Columbia University Press, New York.
   1993    *60 Years of Southwestern Archaeology. A History of the Pecos Conference*.
           University of New Mexico Press, Albuquerque, NM.

# Appendix A

Excerpt from Richard Wetherill diary, December 11, Sandal House, Mancos Canyon, as sent to William Holmes, Smithsonian Institution, March 3, 1890, to illustrate his observational skills and record keeping. Copy of original given by Tom Wetherill to Robert Lister, January, 1989.

Dec. 11th: After breakfast we took our picks and shovels and began to search for relics in an excavation made upon a former trip, in a pile of debris at the south end of the house, having found from experience and observation, that they were often used as places to secret many of their household utensils, seeds and frequently as places of burial. This place is composed of turkey droppings, pieces of sandstone, lumps of mortar, and sweepings from the house; making a heap thirty feet long, twenty feet wide and seven feet deep at the south end. We stationed ourselves about the pile in positions to conveniently throw the dirt over the cliff. In a short time a sandal was found in the loose dirt, made of strands of braided yucca and we continued to find them until noon, on account of which we named this house sandal house. These sandals are worn by fastening on the feet with yucca strings, over the toes and instep. The other articles found were yucca strings, grains of corn, squash seeds, beans, a small earthen pitcher full of squash seeds apparently saved for seed, as it was stopped with cedar bark, and sealed over with mud. A skeleton was found in the bottom of the pile, but being damp was somewhat decayed, a small piece of cotton cloth was still sticking to it, at the left of the head was a small pitcher, a small bowl with a piece broken from the side, and a bone needle four inches long, having the appearance of a large darning needle. A little later a wall was struck, which after digging around and clearing away the dirt we found to be a receptacle for a body. The dimensions of this grave were five feet long, four feet wide and two feet high, built of sandstone two feet long, about one foot wide and four inches thick, covered with flat stones and cemented with mortar such as was used in the buildings. This grave was filled with the same kind of debris as the pile outside; it was carefully cleaned out with shovels until some feather cloth was struck then the hands were used to be sure that nothing should be broken or destroyed; after getting out all the dirt possible it left the body undisturbed, wrapped in feather cloth, lying upon a mat of woven rushes with the head to the south, the face to the west, with the legs drawn up as if to accommodate them to the short space allowed. The head being uncovered revealed a heavy head of hair still sticking to the skull, it was about four inches in length, and straight as Indian hair, not so coarse, but black in color. At the back of the head was the bottom of a jar about five inches in diameter, a small globular unburned cup, also a string of human hair of two strands twisted together, done up as fish lines are by the manufacturer.

Getting somewhat crowded outside, John and Clayton went into a room north of the pile of debris and found about five feet of dirt, rock, etc. tumbled walls and upper flooring. The floors are made of round joists or sleepers, placed from two to two and a half feet apart, they being from six to ten inches in diameter, upon which are laid sticks close together from half to one inch in diameter which are covered with mud or mortar, four or five inches thick. All the wood work shows the work to have been done with the stone axes which must have required a long time of very laborious work; the chopping resembles the work of beavers, with the advantage in favor of the beaver.

Before the bottom of this room was reached, we found a sinew bow string one eighth of an inch in diameter and five and a half feet long, a wooden awl, bottom of a basket, made of willow and strands of yucca three fourths of an inch wide, strings, etc.

The above finished the work for the day, description of house location, etc. given day previous.

# Appendix B

*Guide to Acronyms in Relevant Technical Reports*

| | |
|---|---|
| AHC | Anasazi Heritage Center |
| AMS | Accelerator Mass Spectrometry |
| ARPA | Archaeological Resource Protection Act |
| AU | University of Arizona |
| ASU | Arizona State University |
| AZRU | Aztec Ruins National Monument |
| | |
| BAR | Bureau of Anthropological Research |
| BLM | Bureau of Land Management |
| BOR | Bureau of Reclamation |
| | |
| CASA | Complete Archaeological Services Associates |
| CAA | Center for American Archaeology |
| CCAC | Crow Canyon Archaeological Center |
| CCC | Civilian Conservation Corps |
| CCPA | Colorado Council of Professional Archaeologists |
| CHS | Colorado Historical Society |
| CRM | Cultural Resource Management |
| CU | University of Colorado |
| | |
| DAP | Dolores Archaeological Program |
| EDA | Economic Development Administration |
| FCAP | Four Corners Archaeological Program |
| FLC | Fort Lewis College |
| | |
| GIS | Geographic Information System |
| | |
| HRO | Human Remains Occurrence |
| | |
| I-SEP | Interdisciplinary Supplemental Program |
| LAS | Limited Activity Site |
| LTRR-SPP | Laboratory of Tree-Ring Research—Southwest Paleoclimate Project |
| | |
| MNA | Museum of Northern Arizona |
| MNM | Museum of New Mexico |
| MVARC | Mesa Verde Archaeological Research Center |
| MVNP | Mesa Verde National Park |
| | |
| NAGPRA | Native American Graves Protection and Repatriation Act |

| | |
|---|---|
| NHPA | National Historic Preservation Act |
| NAU | Northern Arizona Universit |
| NPS | National Park Service |
| NRHP | National Register of Historic Places |
| OHAP | Office of Historic and Archaeological Preservation |
| PDSI | Palmer Drought Severity Indices |
| SAA | Society for American Archaeology |
| SAR | School of American Research |
| SCAP | Sand Canyon Archaeological Project |
| SHPO | State Historical Preservation Office |
| SSI | Soil Systems, Inc. |
| STP | Site Testing Project |
| TCP | Technical Cultural Properties |
| UMUILAP | Ute Mountain Ute Irrigated Lands Archaeological Project |
| UNM | University of New Mexico |
| USDA | U.S. Department of Agriculture |
| USFS | U.S. Forest Service |
| VMP | Village Mapping Project |
| WSU | Washington State University |

# Index